Elegiac Fictions
The Motif of the Unlived Life

ELEGIAC FICTIONS
The Motif of the Unlived Life

Edward Engelberg

The Pennsylvania State University Press
University Park and London

Library of Congress Cataloging-in-Publication Data

Engelberg, Edward, 1929–
    Elegiac fictions : the motif of the unlived life / Edward Engelberg.

    p.   cm.
    Bibliography: p.
    Includes index.
    ISBN 0-271-00657-9
    1. Self in literature.   2. Fiction—19th century—History and
criticism.   3. Fiction—20th century—History and criticism.
4. Memory in literature.   5. Narcissism in literature.   I. Title.
PN3352.S44E5 1989
809′.9335—dc19   88–25373
                                                                CIP

IN MEMORIAM
FOR GITA KURITZKES
and for Doda, Fedor,
and Schura Kuritzkes

And say my glory was I had such friends.
—W. B. Yeats

Sighing I said to myself: What have I done in this world? I was created to live, and I am dying without having lived.
— Jean-Jacques Rousseau, Second Walk, *Reveries of the Solitary Walker*

Schick mich in deine leeren Länder
durch die die weiten Winde gehn
wie grosse Klöster wie Gewänder
um ungelebte Leben stehn.

(Send me to your empty lands
Through which the wide winds go,
Where vast monasteries stand
Like garments around unlived lives.)

—Rainer Maria Rilke, *Das Stunden-Buch (Das Buch der Armut und Vom Tode)*

Perhaps my best years are gone. When there was a chance of happiness.
— Samuel Beckett, *Krapp's Last Tape*

Destructiveness is the outcome of unlived life.
— Erich Fromm, *The Fear of Freedom*

Contents

Preface

I

This study began as an attempt to pursue part of the argument I undertook in *The Unknown Distance: From Consciousness to Conscience, Goethe to Camus.*[1] Promptings to continue on the trail did not arise from the belief that the previous study needed a second volume, but rather from a perception that certain problems raised needed analysis from a different perspective. In the conclusion to *The Unknown Distance* I wrote: ". . . perhaps in some strange way, the heroes of both James and Nietzsche, ascetics in different ways, chart the unlived life, which in Kafka and Hesse haunt the hero." As thoughts for this study began homing in on that phrase, "the unlived life," it became clear that a discrete but related work was taking shape. In addition, I had also touched upon the difference between "amour propre" (negative self-love) and "amour de soi" (positive self-love), and one of my chapter headings was "Some Versions of Consciousness and Egotism," in which I dealt with Hegel, Dostoevsky's *Underground Man,* and Ibsen's *Peer Gynt.* Although I do not deal with all these authors or works here, clearly the notion of "narcissism" and "self-love" was also on my mind—so much so that it has formed a large part of this work.

The historical separation of consciousness from conscience, which it was suggested was the result of a deliberative process in the nineteenth century, gave rise to serious consequences that were played out in the fictions from Goethe to Camus. Clearly the motif of the unlived life, though it stands independently, is not unrelated to a severance of conscience from consciousness. In the earlier work, I argued that the arbitrary division between consciousness and conscience often separated knowledge from value. This work proposes that an inauthentic consciousness, opening itself to an excess of grief, misleads us and brings us to a fixation on process that forgets the goal; a kind of perverted narcissistic "Becoming" results in eventual disappointment. Such disappointment wears many faces, especially regret for having missed the experience of life altogether; it results in manipulation of memory, and in elegizing one's life. Energy and Enervation, the terms that begin this study, also proclaim its goal: to demonstrate the various ways in which energies expended on the process of living cause exhaustion, a kind of cannibalism of the self that Shakespeare put into a powerful metaphor in one of his famous sonnets:

> In me thou see'st the glowing of such fire
> That on the ashes of his youth doth lie,
> As the death-bed whereon it must expire,
> Consumed with that which it was nourished by.

In the elegiac fictions under study here, one of the formulated phrases is "too late"—for insight, if it comes at all, is always "too late." The moment of realization is Prufrock's "Till human voices wake us, and we drown."

The trajectory of the succeeding chapters leads us from the Romantics to Beckett, and the structure of the argument is synoptic. Texts and authors are both familiar, and choices and omissions are obviously to some degree a result of personal preference and limitation of space. Still, choices had to be made. For me it seemed appropriate to begin with Goethe's *Faust* since it contains within its ample boundaries so much of the problematic in modern literature. In Beckett, with whom the study concludes, the unlived life reaches a point beyond which it cannot proceed as a "motif": we have arrived at the *unlivable* life. Much of modern literature is weighed down by the burden of Romantic optimism in conflict with and in time replaced by irony, cynicism, *ressentiment,* and nihilism. From that kind of positioning, the texts of the Classic Moderns and their nineteenth-century forbears take the shape of a single poignant Elegy, a lament for being cheated of great expectations.

II

This study is largely focused on fiction, though it contains certain dramatic works and begins with two long Romantic poems, one of them called by its author "a novel in verse." I have chosen to forego "coverage" and have instead attempted to select those texts which, in my opinion, best suited the purpose at hand.

The deeper I penetrated into the motif of the "unlived life," the more I realized how difficult it would be to separate this phenomenon from its many adjoining phenomena. Foremost there was the elegiac element and all its attendant issues; further, one could not evade solitude and boredom (different manifestations of "ennui"), nor could one avoid a passing glance at the pervasive "pessimism" of Schopenhauer and the even stronger impact of Nietzschean "optimism," or the *ressentiment* of Scheler, some aspects of the philosophy of Self in Heidegger, Freud on narcissism, mourning and melancholia, and the psychology of Self in Kohut. Hovering over all these were the various perspectives on death and dying and, preceding that, the process of existing. Since there was no effective way of paying equal attention to all of these without losing focus, I elected to bring most of these adjacent motifs of the "unlived life" and self-elegy under separate headings, giving them no exhaustive treatment but acknowledging their importance.

To that end I have divided this study into three parts: Part I: Narcissists, The Unbearable Present; Part II: Mourners and Melancholics, The Absent Past; Part III: Survivors, The Missing Future. Each part is preceded by an introduction. The Framework chapter is introductory to the total sum of the parts; the Conclusion reflects on some of the questions the study has raised. There is no attempt at establishing a strict chronology, although beginning with the Romantics and ending with Beckett provides a visible forward movement. Some authors are represented twice by different works: Turgenev, Kafka, and Mann; one chapter connects Flaubert and Hemingway.

Although I have found it very profitable to invoke Freud's introductory essay "On Narcissism" and its companion essay, "Mourning and Melancholia," this does not signal a "Freudian" reading of the texts. In surveying the cast of characters in the fictions under analysis, I became convinced that two of Freud's essays, and some of the work of Heinz Kohut and others, would serve as useful guides. I have chosen to keep the substance of these works, on the whole, within the boundaries of the Framework chapter, the three introductions to the three parts, and the Conclusion. In short, I chose not to interweave the perspective of any one "outsider" with the text; such a method would have resulted in "Freudian" or "Kohutian" readings, and I find such readings run too much danger of becoming intrusive and reductive. Moreover, no literary text as seen from the perspective of my special interest can be satisfactorily encompassed within the bounds of any single methodology. Freud and Kohut were enormously pertinent, as, too, were Nietzsche, Schopenhauer, and Scheler; and, to a lesser de-

gree, Lukács and Heidegger. The introductions to the three parts of
this work offered me ample opportunity for an unencumbered airing
of some of their ideas as they relate to the literary texts that follow
each section.

There is some overlap; and rather than avoid such overlapping I
welcome the ease with which it was accomplished. To some extent
"Narcissism" is the dominant term: Mourners and Melancholics and
Survivors follow in logical sequential order, and here again chronology of a kind asserts itself, just as "Present," "Past," and "Future" form
(it is hoped) a structural triad intended to help advance the argument.
It seems fairly easy to demonstrate that the earliest signs of the motif
of the unlived life, articulated (and embodied) in self-elegiac expressions, are the *positive* manifestations of the "autonomous Self," and
this has been dated (with some confidence) in Rousseau. Although the
debate between "positive" and "negative" narcissism continues, it is
some time before the tide really turns, and in the fifties and sixties of
our century many currents and merging parallels managed to make
"self-love" not only respectable but placed it at the head of the line.
The spirit of how such self-love was manifested was quite different
from what Pope had meant in *The Essay on Man* when he wrote that
"Self-love and social are the same"; however, that is exactly what the
modern argument was based on—a narcissism that would lead to
universal love—at least among the members of the rebelling generation. Perhaps not until Christopher Lasch published *The Culture of
Narcissism* in 1978 did we experience a reaction, so that the accusing
finger now points to the earlier decades as the prelude to the "me-
ism," detected as having been transformed today into "yuppi-ism." A
variety of views of narcissism have been applied to literary texts in a
volume entitled *Narcissism and the Text* (the results are generally of very
high quality), and the case for such analysis is well stated in the Introduction to this volume:

> Critics of twentieth century texts have long focused on the frag-
> mentation of modern form, on the "nothingness" at the center
> of . . . a text by Robbe-Grillet or Beckett. Theories of narcis-
> sism . . . can help critics to interpret and demystify that nothing-
> ness and fragmentation.[2]

The same is true for Freud's "Mourning and Melancholia" or some of
Heidegger's ideas on Being/*Dasein* that I have introduced into the
introductions to Parts II and III, respectively. "The Idea of the Modern," to use Irving Howe's phrase, has perhaps been overindulged by

the same catchwords, so that the terminology has been devalued—the void, neurosis, Angst, fragmentation. Perhaps the major terms of this study will be fresher and will be more enabling, even when related to well-known texts. Those texts were chosen with an eye toward unfolding the development and complex nature of a critically important motif. While narcissism is, as stated, the common link, there is progression toward the inevitable disappointment of the narcissist, ending first in the "rage" of "mourning" and "melancholia," and finding its ultimate state in some form of the "existential" imperative to survive.[3]

There are many debts I have incurred over the years, and I will do my best to acknowledge them all. My colleagues at Brandeis have been generous and supportive, especially those who have read all or part of the manuscript. To these I should like to express my gratitude: Robert Szulkin, who read the whole of the first draft and gave me invaluable impressions and suggestions, often with a loan of books from his wonderful library (and who helped me to deal with the Russian authors); Robin Miller, who was so generous with her time and who read all of a later draft and provided me with innumerable comments, most of which I took to heart, all of which were valuable—sharp, instructive, corrective; Rudy Binion, James Clay, Jane Hale, and Alice Kalikian, each of whom read a chapter and made valuable comments. For the loan of books and the gift of insights I thank as well Richard Lansing and Danielle Marx-Scouras. To Harry Zohn, seldom a borrower, always a lender, many thanks for books and essays.

My thanks also to Haskell Block for his careful reading and his challenging remarks. While I did not always agree fully, he has kept me honest and made me clarify and sharpen my positions; and to Ralph Freedman, who is on my wavelength and who, once again, spotted some important matters I would not otherwise have been aware of as clearly.

At Penn State Press my sincerest thanks to its Senior Editor, Philip Winsor, who believed in the manuscript and acted on it speedily and courteously; to Cherene Holland, who let me off easy but read and copy-edited with a keen eye. Thanks, too, to Janet Dietz for many kindnesses.

To the Mazer Committee and Brandeis University for a grant that helped me to prepare the manuscript for publication, and to Gregory Shesko, facilitator of funds: I am very appreciative for their help. I am in debt to Evan Harriman for typing two drafts. Thanks to Timothy J. Baehr, who prepared the index.

My appreciation is extended to numerous graduate students in the Joint Program of Literary Studies at Brandeis who helped me to work out many of the ideas that have finally come to some kind of fruition in this book.

Last but never least, I acknowledge with love my wife, Elaine, who stood by when I most needed it, who read everything, and who, a student of Habermas herself, introduced me to more of his work than I knew and provided me with valuable linkages. And a bow toward my children, Stephen Paul, Michael Joseph, and Elizabeth Joyce, who saw to it that my life would never be "unlived."

For permission to reprint, I thank the editors of *Comparative Literature Studies*, where, in different form, I first published an essay on Flaubert and Hemingway, now chapter 7. To the editor of *arcadia*, my thanks for allowing me to reprint a few pages on *The Ambassadors* published in the context of an essay in that journal.

A Note on Documentation

I have used, for the most part, the most accessible texts and translations. For plays I have indicated line numbers (when available) or Act number. For secondary materials and other more special texts, I have cited page numbers. With the exception of Beckett's trilogy, which contains three separate novels, I have omitted page numbers so as not to clutter the text. I am confident that the context is always clearly identified and the edition, of course, is listed.

Acknowledgments

The lines from *Faust* by Johann Wolfgang von Goethe, translated by Walter Arndt, A Norton Critical Edition, edited by Cyrus Hamlin, are used with the permission of W. W. Norton & Company, Inc. Copyright © 1976 by W. W. Norton & Company, Inc.

Excerpts from Alexander Pushkin, *Eugene Onegin,* translated with a commentary by Vladimir Nabokov, Bollingen Series LXXII (Copyright © 1964, rev. ed. © 1975 by Princeton University Press), reprinted by permission of Princeton University Press.

Excerpts from *Anton Chekhov: Four Plays* by Anton Chekhov, translated by David Magarshack. Copyright © 1969 by David Magarshack. Reprinted by permission of Hill and Wang, a division of Farrar, Straus and Giroux, Inc.

Excerpts from *The Oxford Chekhov,* translated by Ronald Hingley, © Ronald Hingley, 1971, are reprinted by permission of Oxford University Press.

Excerpts from *The Magic Mountain* by Thomas Mann, translated by H. T. Lowe-Porter, Copyright 1927 by Alfred A. Knopf, Inc., Copyright 1952 by Thomas Mann, reproduced by permission of Alfred A. Knopf, Inc.

Excerpts from *Death in Venice* by Thomas Mann, translated by Kenneth Burke, Copyright © 1970 by Random House, Inc., and Alfred A. Knopf, Inc., reprinted by permission of Alfred A. Knopf, Inc.

Excerpts from *The Metamorphosis* by Franz Kafka, translated and edited by Stanley Corngold, © 1972 by Stanley Corngold, reprinted by permission of Bantam Books.

Excerpts from Franz Kafka's *Letter to His Father/Brief and den Vater,* translated by Ernst Kaiser and Eithne Wilkins, Copyright © 1953, 1954, 1966 by Schocken Books, Inc., published by Pantheon Books, a Division of Random House, Inc.

Excerpts from *The Complete Major Prose Plays of Ibsen*, translated by Rolf Fjelde, Copyright © 1964 by Rolf Fjelde, reprinted with arrangement by NAL Penguin Inc., New York, NY.

Excerpts from *Ibsen: Peer Gynt*, translated by Peter Watts (Penguin Classics, 1966), copyright © Peter Watts, 1966, reprinted by permission of Penguin Books Ltd.

Excerpts from *The Sound and the Fury* by William Faulkner reprinted by permission of Random House, Inc. Copyright 1929, by William Faulkner. Copyright renewed 1956, by William Faulkner. Copyright, 1946, by Random House.

Excerpts from *Mrs. Dalloway* by Virginia Woolf, copyright 1925 by Harcourt Brace Jovanovich, Inc., renewed 1953 by Leonard Woolf, reprinted by permission of Harcourt Brace Jovanovich, Inc.

Excerpts from *A Farewell to Arms* by Ernest Hemingway reprinted by permission of Charles Scribner's Sons. Copyright 1929 by Charles Scribner's Sons. Renewal Copyright © 1957 by Ernest Hemingway. Copyright 1949 by Charles Scribner's Sons.

Excerpts from material in the Hemingway collection in the John F. Kennedy Library is published by permission of and is copyright 1989 by The Ernest Hemingway Foundation [d.b.a. The Hemingway Society].

Excerpts from Samuel Beckett's works reprinted by permission of Grove Press, Inc.: *Endgame, A Play in Four Acts,* Copyright © 1958, by Grove Press, Inc.; *Krapp's Last Tape and Other Dramatic Pieces,* Copyright © 1957 by Samuel Beckett, Copyright © 1958 by Grove Press, Inc.; *Waiting For Godot, A Tragi-Comedy in Two Acts,* Copyright © 1954 by Grove Press, Inc.; and *Three Novels by Samuel Beckett: Molloy, Malone Dies, The Unnamable,* Copyright © 1955, 1956, 1957, 1958 by Grove Press, Inc.

Excerpts from *Collected Poems* by W. B. Yeats reprinted with permission of Macmillan Publishing Company. Copyright 1940 by Georgie Yeats, renewed 1968 by Bertha Georgie Yeats, Michael Butler Yeats, and Anne Yeats.

Excerpts from *Collected Plays* by W. B. Yeats reprinted with permission of Macmillan Publishing Company. Copyright 1934, 1952 by Macmillan Publishing Company. Copyrights renewed 1962 by Bertha Georgie Yeats, and 1980 by Anne Butler Yeats.

Excerpt from "The Waste Land" in *Collected Poems 1909–1962* by T. S. Eliot, copyright 1936 by Harcourt Brace Jovanovich, Inc., copyright © 1963, 1964 by T. S. Eliot, reprinted by permission of the publisher.

Excerpts from "The Dry Salvages" and "Burnt Norton" in *Four Quartets,* copyright 1943 by T. S. Eliot, renewed 1971 by Esme Valerie Eliot, reprinted by permission of Harcourt Brace Jovanovich, Inc.

Excerpt from *The Family Reunion,* copyright 1939 by T. S. Eliot, renewed 1967 by Esme Valerie Eliot, reprinted by permission of Harcourt Brace Jovanovich, Inc.

Excerpt from *The Cocktail Party,* copyright 1950 by T. S. Eliot, renewed 1978 by Esme Valerie Eliot, reprinted by permission of Harcourt Brace Jovanovich, Inc.

Excerpts from Ezra Pound, *Personae,* © 1926 by Ezra Pound, reprinted by permission of New Directions Publishing Corporation.

Excerpt from *Naive & Sentimental Poetry* by Friedrich von Schiller, translated by Julius A. Elias. English translation © 1966 by the Frederick Ungar Publishing Company. Reprinted by permission of the publisher.

Excerpt from *Wuthering Heights* by Emily Brontë from Riverside Edition, ed. V. S. Prichett, copyright © 1956 by V. S. Prichett. Reprinted by permission of Houghton Mifflin Company.

Introduction: Toward a Framework

Every man has his paradise, his golden age, which he recalls.
—*Schiller,* Naive and Sentimental Poetry

I

Because heroes from ancient times onward have without interruption established themselves in our literary consciousness as those who meet and overcome—even in death—all manner of adversity, one does not associate them with the plaintive note; it is not their proper demeanor. At times heroes may mope, as Achilles does in his tent, but the condition is almost always temporary. As Yeats wrote:

> All perform their tragic play
> There struts Hamlet, there is Lear,
> That's Ophelia, that Cordelia;
> Yet they, should the last scene be there,
> The great stage curtain about to drop,
> If worthy their prominent part in the play,
> Do not break up their lines to weep.
> "Lapis Lazuli"

Even so controversially interpreted a hero as Hamlet ("How all occasions do inform against me") is no mere complainer: the rage he articulates with his sword (and by other means) leaves six of his adversaries dead. In contrast to such efficiency, heroes of many nineteenth-century texts (inclusive dates would add the late 1700s and the early decades of the twentieth century) do not use the gun with such efficacious results. They are likely to turn the weapon on themselves (Goethe's *Werther*), to miss the mark (Stendhal's Julien Sorel), to forget the firing-cap (Dostoevsky's Ippolit in *The Idiot*), to shoot themselves accidentally (Ibsen's Lovbørg), to make fools of themselves (Chekhov's Vanya), to help their felled victim (Turgenev's Bazarov), or to shoot in the air and thus precipitate the enemy's suicide (Mann's Settembrini). In addition, many protagonists allow themselves more self-pity than we expect. Often they are figures of scorn, trapped in their own inertia, victims of such self-consuming emotions as envy and *ressentiment*, symptoms recognized and analyzed, as we shall see, in such diverse texts as Robert Burton's *Anatomy of Melancholy* (1621) and Freud's "Mourning and Melancholia" (1917), nearly three centuries later.

"Anti-hero" is a limited designation for those numerous personae who generally fail to meet adversity with the panache we associate with heroes and heroism. One needs to tease out several variations of the type. The prototype in elegiac fictions (the term "fictions" is used broadly, like the German *Dichtung*) on whom this study focuses may be briefly defined. He (or she) savages himself or others, pines for what is not, is full of regret for actions not taken, or feels that to take them now is "too late"; in addition, this character type views his own life as wasted, indeed as unlived.

The term "elegiac," however, needs to be situated within the particular context of this study. Here, then, "elegiac" shall be used to invoke a particular manifestation of the modern sense of personal loss and dispossession, and of a special kind of sadness that validates the belief that one's life has been a series of missed opportunities. Freud described this state with his usual accuracy when he defined the difference between "mourning" and "melancholia": "In mourning it is the world which has become poor and empty; in melancholia it is the ego itself."[1]

Traditionally, "elegiac" has been associated with poetry, most often lyrical poetry that expresses the poet's mourning for a lost friend or a lost age, if not golden at least better than the present. From classical times elegies have on the whole been lamentations about death. In the Renaissance, elegies were also written for other occasions, especially those celebrating various states of love; some elegies were mere expressions of nostalgia. But it is in the nineteenth century that a "still more diffuse elegiac tradition spread," one of many "elegiac transformations"—the "elegiac strain in many novels" and, it should be added, in many plays.[2]

In the course of the succeeding chapters, it will become clear that this modern elegiac mood pervades more texts than can be accommodated in any single study. What was once almost exclusively a convention of poetry turns into a pervasive means of conveying, in narrative and drama, the essence of an almost ubiquitous motif: the unlived life. Why the elegiac impulse is so dominant from the Romantics onward yields no simple answers. What is apparent is that the acknowledged shift to introspection develops a concomitant sense of personal guilt. Despite their narcissism our heroes often lacerate themselves: if life disappoints, the fault lies in them, not the stars. Surely part of the price of modern melancholy is the enormous sense of self-indictment that springs it loose. After all, Kafka did not invent the haunting sense of guilt and punishment without a clearly correlative crime; Josef K. in *The Trial* has his roots from Sophocles' *Oedipus* to Coleridge's *Ancient Mariner*. Regret and personal musings about deprivation are thrust from personal (and often unpublished) memoirs, diaries, or correspondence to the fictions themselves. The private more than becomes public: it displaces the silent conventions that the fable *is* fable and destroys—in many instances—any clear boundary between subject and object. One part of the ego detaches itself and judges the other, and as Freud said, "takes it as its object."[3]

Of all human experiences, that of loss is perhaps the most common and the most repeated, since from the moment of birth one experiences it. While time moves forward it also leaves behind time irrecoverable. We do not always feel this as loss, else we could not exist. Yet at some point during one's life there is a moment of reckoning, a turning back to survey what has been left behind, a synchronic confrontation with one's memory-chamber—with the past. Sometimes this encounter brings forth the image of a graveyard filled with actions either not taken or, when taken, embarked on in the wrong direction. Some objectives that once seemed legitimate might now lack the investiture of meaning. Such discoveries trigger a double vision: a grieving for the past accompanied by an increased anxiety about the future; or, if no future remains, a grieving for what *might* have been. Once we experience loss as loss we are permanently altered: neither forward motion nor backward remembrance retain their previous shapes.

This is one way to describe the elegiac mood which, in a manner peculiarly its own, so dominated the literature of the nineteenth and early twentieth centuries.

"Shades of the prison house begin to close / Upon the growing boy," observed Wordsworth in the "Immortality" ode. And the acknowledgment that the passage from innocence to experience involves a breaking through the enclosures and encumbrances of life had by, say,

1800, become almost a cliché. Throughout the nineteenth century, and into the twentieth, prisons, literal and metaphoric, play prominent roles.[4] Society, family, class—all exercise a constrictive function that both underlines and punctuates a sense of overdetermined fatality. In Beckett's trilogy (*Molloy, Malone Dies*, and *The Unnamable*) inert bodies (or parts of bodies) are confined to deathbeds, no longer screaming for three days like Tolstoy's Ivan Ilyich but merely in attendance at their own wake, waiting in a vacuum of time for the end. Such progression from one sort of awareness—the suffering that leads to clarity of vision—to quite the opposite—the awareness that clarity is elusive, that there is no "end"—constitutes a progression in the tracing of our motif.

Our works tend to be centered on metaphors (or actual means) of confinement, especially the bed—not the lovebed or the sickbed but the deathbed. Turgenev's Chulkaturin composes his diary on his deathbed; Bazarov perceives with horror his own superfluousness on his. Midway through *Wuthering Heights* Cathy gives birth and dies, less of childbirth than of inconsolable grieving; at the close of the novel Heathcliff betakes himself to her coffin-bed and, in all but name, commits suicide: he starves himself. Gregor Samsa wakes from one nightmare into another on his bed, from which vantage he hears his future unravel on the other side of his locked door. In Mann's *Magic Mountain* the beds and mummy-like lounge chairs keep patients enclosed at various stages of illness; and Ivan Ilyich's passion is enacted on his deathbed. Joyce's Gabriel Conroy concludes "The Dead" on a bed he shares with a sleeping wife now more distant, and something in him has died; Mrs. Dalloway refers repeatedly to her "narrow" bed in her narrow room. Beckett's beds are virtual graves for the barely living.

In addition to beds there is much emphasis in most of these texts on constricting interiors: doors and windows in *Wuthering Heights;* Bazarov's remark that life is a "box"; the carefully blueprinted interior geography of rooms in Kafka's "The Judgment" and *The Metamorphosis;* Aschenbach's gondola-coffin and the pestilent-ridden air of Venice; Chekhov's houses where people talk to bookcases and dream of Moscow. The view is from within, where the spectrum of feeling from regret to horror is articulated: "So once it would have been—'tis so no more" (Wordsworth, "Elegiac Stanzas").

Indeed one may conceive of the elegiac mood as a kind of disease, just as melancholy was in earlier times. We can then list certain symptoms of the disorder. A few examples suffice. There are the young, whose origins lie in the conflation of Werther, the Byronic misanthrope, and the superfluous man in Russian literature from Pushkin to Chekhov. These literally experience a loss of life at an early age, and most of them embrace death with fatalism and passive regret—or both. Some, like Lermontov's Pechorin, Turgenev's Bazarov, and Brontë's Heathcliff, are in some fashion "rebels," but their rebellions are ultimately engendered not by or in the name of some external cause but rather by an increasingly self-conscious recognition of their impotence and thwarted will. Accompanying this etiology is a rage quite without external object, a floating rage (an element of misanthropy) that Nietzsche and later Max Scheler called *ressentiment* and Heinz Kohut identified as "narcissistic rage" (see the introduction to Part I).

Other manifestations of the unlived life are the middle-aged or older man (or woman). One type (as Nietzsche was to characterize it) has no capacity to forget; memory serves as a continual reminder of the past which, in turn, is littered with unrealized potential: roads not taken, risks not engaged. James, Chekhov, and Woolf provide the best exemplars. Here the overwhelming insight is that insight itself has come "too late." Many of Chekhov's characters and James's, Mrs. Dalloway and her former would-be lover, Gustav Aschenbach, and a host of Ibsen's dramatis personae experience this sense of temporal deprivation, having arrived at a point where the possibilities that have been missed are still tantalizingly in view but out of reach. Another version of the disorder is the middle-aged or old man (or woman) whose proximity to death generates quiet panic (Chekhov's "Dreary Story," Mann's *Death in Venice*) or an attempt to change life in the face of the impossibility to do so ("The Death of Ivan Ilyich"). Not only does this type fail to overcome impending disaster; he experiences a sudden and sometimes terrible vision that what he had smugly considered a good life had, in fact, been nothing but a delusion and self-deception—in some instances self-denial. Versions of this type appear in Kafka, James, Chekhov, and Mann.

The unlived life may, then, be literally unlived because the protagonist dies too young to have had a chance to live. Or, the opportunity of fulfillment has either been missing, headed in the wrong direction, or is too late now to undertake. These are merely sample variations; no rigid framework will work, nor should it. What unites all these figures is a sense of personal dispossession, loss, enervation, resentfulness, and a yearning for experiences encapsulated in a past—but a past that has shut its doors and is therefore elegized.

To say that these laments issue forth from persons devoured by self-pity would be too simplistic, for their self-pity is so fronted by rage it often masks and distorts the true experience altogether. One conviction marks them all, the moment of realization that Leopardi lamented in "The Solitary Life" ("La Vita Solitaria")—irrevocable time ("irrevocabil tempo") endured silently and alone ("solingo e muto"). This lack of commonality and communality raises profound and fundamental questions of social and psychological origins, and most of these are simply beyond the scope of this study. Yet one cannot ignore the terrifying loneliness of these protagonists, the inevitable egotism and narcissism that such isolation often breeds, and what damage is left in its wake, especially for those who survive. The affect spent and wasted necessarily involves a classic case of dis-ease, a lack of focus, purpose, or value: to turn to Leopardi again, a sense of being possessed of a "stony heart" ("Questo mio cor di sasso"). Exiled from society at large, these plaintive selves suffer a greater exile still: an inner exile, or *Entfremdung*, so total that it obliterates all considerations outside the self while accentuating the acknowledgment of sorrow that so much has had to be sacrificed. All this creates certain paradoxes, the most obvious perhaps being the creation of a self which, while regretting its own waste, in the process of that regret mobilizes energies that might well have delayed, if not staved off, the waste it decries.

Lamentation is, of course, no new phenomenon, but beginning sometime in the late eighteenth century (perhaps Goethe's *Werther* [1774] is as good a date as any) it is *how* one views the articulation of excessive grief that changes. In the Renaissance, for example, and for several centuries thereafter, the melancholic, the morose misanthrope, the plaintive voice were often considered with scorn and ridicule, even with comic derision when they appeared outside the formal Elegy of verse. One thinks of Shakespeare's Jaques in *As You Like It* or of Malvolio in *Twelfth Night*, Marston's *Malcontent* or Molière's *Misanthrope*, or some of the fops on the English Restoration stage. Their comic effect may sometimes be "dark" and ambivalent (perhaps even hovering on the edge of a certain kind of tragedy), but, like the "delusions" of Don Quixote and especially his heirs, their melancholy was a sign of imbalanced "humours," sometimes to be reckoned with seriously but as aberrations often viewed with undisguised contempt or, at best, pity.

A Schopenhauerian pessimism takes root wherever one looks; life seems voided of obstacles to conquer. Of what use is it to play hero when the inevitable outcome is to be victim? Better to renounce or to rebel, and much of nineteenth-century literature divides itself almost too neatly along those two paths. Often the refusal to travel the one path strengthens the resolve for choosing the other. For Flaubert's Emma Bovary renunciation is so repugnant—so life-denying and denying of her nature as she perceives it—that she chooses to rebel. That rebellion consists of hopelessly embracing foolish fictions she believes will release her from immolation within her stifling, confined existence. Yet in the end the rebellious Emma is no less an unfulfilled victim than Stendhal's "schöne Seele," the repentant Madame de Rênal.

By introducing Schopenhauer one does more than drop a name, whose far-reaching impact in England and the Continent has yet to be fully assessed. Schopenhauer's postulation of the relentless Will, which robs us of "free will" by becoming an overdetermined force, was the first of several sledgehammers that descended on nineteenth-century stability and early twentieth-century smugness. After Darwin, Freud, and Einstein, it became increasingly difficult to sustain even microcosmic hopes amidst what seemed to be such macrocosmic determinism. No simple cause/effect pattern will serve; nevertheless, the motif of the unlived life would scarcely be imaginable without the considerable erosion of the feeling that we control the outcome of our lives. For such a faith to be maintained, there must be some sense of futurity; it is this sense that falls victim to various forms of determinism. A concept of future implies at least a partial faith in self-mastery. Once the future is gone we look to the past; but the past as Cornelius, Thomas Mann's Professor of History in "Disorder and Early Sorrow," maintains is always "dead."

Quite another form of elegy exists as well in post-Romantic fictions, and it is not always possible to disengage it: the elegy in which the grieving is not primarily for personal loss but for the passing of a whole civilization. Tennyson's *Idylls of the King* or Proust's opus; Mann's *Buddenbrooks* or his *Doktor Faustus;* Faulkner's family chronicles; Pound's *Cantos* and T. S. Eliot's *The Waste Land:* all are fictions in which anguish is expressed for a shattered world. In such works individuals play out their private confrontations with time or death or loss, but always the foreground of the single self is swallowed up by the background of larger historical and social forces. It is the special genius of, say, Chekhov's plays (and stories), Kafka's parabolic tales, or Woolf's *Mrs. Dalloway* that manages to keep the foreground and the background sufficiently placed in hierarchical order, so that in the end the lone human voice—however dense the context—resonates the loudest and, therefore, remains embedded in our consciousness. Both kinds of elegy share certain conventional elements: regret, melancholy, mourning over loss. The idea of a Golden Age possessed but now lost is deeply rooted in many traditions;[5] but the expression of a most intimately suffered anguish for a lost self shaped a wholly new kind of art.

Romantic elegies, often autobiographical plaints, set in motion a kind of literature of self-mourning that occasionally penetrates the territory of tragedy. The motto of the modern elegy is not "too bad," but "too late!"—not wise affirmation of sorrow but despairing denial and anger. "Too late!" conveys a fugitive sense of time quite different from the traditional acceptance of (if lamentation about) the powerful destructiveness of inevitable Time. Shakespeare's obsessive concern with mutability (it was after all a Renaissance *trope*) is always a cosmic statement: against the ravages of time we are all defenseless. The individual protest against time in our texts is more like an urgent cry of one trapped in what might have been, the elusive and the eluded. For their very despair in this cry implies its opposite: a hope, now vanished, that indeed—except for this or that event, which either occurred or did *not* occur—matters *might have been* different; an expectation, now unfulfilled, that one *might have* taken a different road.[6] It may be argued that a hallowed poetic convention has thus been diminished, even trivialized, becoming merely a subjective effusion of self-regret, self-pity, and unwarranted despair. Yet as with all changes, it may also be argued that in time this private note of elegy assumes its own stature as a convention. Indeed, the regret of one's personal missed opportunity, and the pain that accompanies it, is as deeply felt as (if not more so than), say, the sense of grief in Milton's "Lycidas" or the historicized sense of rupture and dissolution in Donne's *Anniverary* poems.[7]

When we speak of "poetry" in the narrow English sense, such terms of Elegy, Pastoral, Idyll, and Eclogue live in uncomfortable proximity. There is no better work from which we seek help than Schiller's *Naive and Sentimental Poetry* (1795), in which Schiller includes elegy and idyll, along with satire, under the general heading of "sentimental," or modern, poetry. Furthermore, Schiller does not feel constrained by genres and is willing to subsume all genres under the various perceptions.

Schiller labeled that elegiac in which the opposition between nature and art favored nature, or the ideal. In this he was following tradition. But his distinction between elegy and idyll is useful:

> Either nature and the ideal are an object of sadness if the first is treated as lost and the second as unattained. Or both are an object of joy represented as actual. The first yields the *elegy* in

the narrower sense, and the second the idyll in the broader sense.[8]

Moreover, a merely sensuous expression unennobled by genuine conviction was a false elegy:

> Sadness at lost joys, at the golden age now disappeared from the world, at happiness departed with youth, with love, and so forth, can only become the material of an elegiac poem if those states of sensuous satisfaction can also be construed as matters of moral harmony. (126–27)

Also "external object(s)" are never suitable for "poetic lamentation"; the poet must always transform such objects into "inner" ideals. Even an actual loss deserving to be grieved over must be "transformed into an ideal loss." The "particular loss" is "broadened into the idea of universal evanescence . . ." (127–28).

So elegy must mourn what is *not* there, not so much something possessed and lost as something never had at all. Though Schiller does not use the phrase, *ubi sunt* implies something possessed in an ideal state. Too much focus on loss, observes Schiller, tends to dwell too much on our "limitations" and not enough on our "capacities." This disturbed Schiller, who preferred a forward look at Elysium to a backward glance at Arcady. His whole endorsement of modern "sentimental" poetry rested on its inherent capacity to visualize the infinite possibilities of the future rather than the cancelled moments of the past. And he complains of the poet who writes idylls that are elegiac by nature, "they imbue us only with a sad feeling of loss, not with joyous feelings of hope" (149). What Schiller feared was a calm that would be stasis, not the classical calm of grandeur but the paralysis of such modern works he did not live to see, the "calm of . . . inertia" (153). Instead, he hoped for a full "reconciliation" between the ideal and the actual, producing a "calm of perfection." Satire exposed the "*contradiction* with actual conditions"; the idyll "*correspondence* with the ideal"; but elegy featured the conflict that "*alternates* with harmony, [a] calm [that] alternates with motion" (146, note).

As it turned out, Schiller's fears, not his hopes, would be realized. For much of modern literature, if one begins to date it from Schiller's own lifetime, tended to become more a series of disharmonious episodes, ending eventually in stasis where only absence is painfully present, where only the sense of loss and sadness and an all-pervasive impotence govern.

Here we will be concerned with the phenomenon of elegiac fictions that eventually turn the lament for a lost world into a lament for a lost self. This "ego-ization" is paramount; it defines the motif of the unlived life, and it represents one of the truly profound changes in perception that contributes to an explanation of the emergence of a large portion of modern literature that we identify with pessimism, despair, and nihilism. These are words that begin to resonate at the very moment that Schiller hoped for something very different.

II

Before all else one is bound, yet once more, to raise some of the issues attendant on the "autonomous self": subjectivity as a reaction not merely against reason but against other broad social contexts; or the capacious conception of "post-modernism" that identifies itself temporally with the "counter-Enlightenment" stage. In this context two names figure prominently, a Viennese-born American and a German: Heinz Kohut and Jürgen Habermas. Kohut has developed some radical theories of self and narcissism (see the introduction to Part I), and Habermas is a social philosopher who has taken on the mantle of the "Frankfurt School," though altering it extensively to suit himself. My aim is to suggest how certain of their leading ideas will help us to understand the roots of the motif under scrutiny, and how, in turn, that motif can illuminate the fictional texts.

Habermas's concern with the "authentic self" confronts head-on Kohut's revisionist conception of narcissism. Clearly some rapprochement is necessary to achieve the breakthrough each is seeking. Joel Whitebook recognizes the problem and examines it in an important essay:

> . . . one point of Kohut's remains valid: . . . narcissistic pathology is to our time as hysterical pathology was to Freud's. . . . This is why the moralistic critique of "me-ism" . . . misses the important point. The spread of narcissistic phenomena in the society at large and the increase of narcissistic psychopathology . . . both result from the fact that as the individuation process approaches the pole of isolation, the content of subjectivity concomitantly approaches the zero point. . . . The paradox concerning narcissism is that the narcis-

sistic preoccupation with the self, which ostensibly aims at its enrichment, is in fact a symptom of the poverty of the self, and results in even further improverishment.[9]

Habermas is clearly aware of the importance of narcissism and its relation to his own social concerns. Narcissists are not especially useful in the reification of culture or in the reclaiming of "The Project" of the Enlightenment. One commentator suggests:

> The recent emergence of a new type of patient in psychoanalysis, one who suffers from a precarious sense of self . . . reflects the ambiguity of the achievement of a modern differentiated domain of subjectivity. . . . [There is] an increased possibility of human autonomy and responsibility, but . . . also . . . [it] brought into being massive narcissistic defenses against the powerlessness and insignificance of the individual.[10]

Self-realization may be a noble aim, but if it is achieved at the price of ultimate aloneness it threatens not only the self (increasingly imprisoned within itself) but the social realm necessary for a healthy self. This is surely among the most problematic of modern dilemmas. Ibsen used the metaphor in *Peer Gynt:* one may peel away the onion layers to get at the core; but in the process there is the danger that you peel away the onion altogether.

In dealing with modernism/post-modernism, Whitebook needs first to clear the ground, to state the issues and positions that formulate the often-invoked "crisis of modernity." He posits three responses: "anti-humanism," "counter-Enlightenment," and the Habermas compromise. The first two have in common a fixed view that "modernity is irredeemably aporetic"; Habermas is unwilling to discard the modern cause and recommends that its "intentions"—however defective—be rescued and that the goals of the Enlightenment, properly refocused, be reinstated to complete the modern "Project." In short, Habermas intends to "rehabilitate . . . practical reason." In that context he comes to grips with the "problem of individuation" so central to the Western tradition from the Renaissance onward. Instead of Schopenhauerian pessimism, which insists that individuation is hopelessly outmatched by the overdetermined Will, and therefore a futile weapon for self-survival, Habermas maps out a strategy designed to enable individual and social order to coexist and strengthen each other. Obviously there is a trade-off: social order always inhibits personal development. (It was the major argument of Freud's *Civilization and Its Discontents.*) Anything that impinges on personal potential, one's "life possibilities" and expectations, is bound to be troublesome for those who argue for limitless self-actualizing as the prime goal of the autonomous self. Practically such a position was, of course, impossible for both the extreme Left and the extreme Right, since both demand individual subservience to a greater good, whether the State or some other abstraction.

Many post-modernists have rejected the "project" of modernism initiated with the Enlightenment because of what they feel was the excessive "focus on the thinking subject," which in turn was one cause of malaise and a perspective that foresaw "the 'end' or 'death of man' [as] immiment. . . ." Such were the fears of the so-called anti-humanists who argued for " 'overarching structures' . . . that . . . [would] exclude the subject," at least as much as possible. So philosophical concepts from the Enlightenment through the nineteenth century filtered into the general consciousness: we were liberated from "self-development unencumbered by the restrictions of tradition or status," although clearly this would set up an inevitable tension.

It is sometimes forgotten that one link—and it is not an inconsequential one—from the Renaissance was this conception of human potential freed from its subservient position it had held, whether relative to State, to Church, or to Bourgeois Culture. The means (reasons versus feeling and empiricism versus subjective perception) much more clearly divided epochs than the actual ends, or needless to say, the results of the means as such. The increasingly "atomized" individual, free from so many social and theological constraints, nevertheless found himself filled with Pascalian anxiety. Indeed, the more the individual became "autonomous," the more he found himself inhabiting a prison. It is an old dilemma: freedom *from* involves bondage *to,* whether to the self or its mirror image, a course of development linking the process eventually to narcissism.

Whitebook quotes Habermas: " 'By remembering in melancholy what was unsuccessful and invoking moments of happiness that are in the process of being obliterated the historical sense of secular progress threatens to be stunted.' "[11] This sounds very much like Nietzsche's warning against incorporating the epigoni syndrome. There is little volition to move on if the distant past seems lost, the recent past failed, and the future devoured by a failing present. No one can doubt the enormous price we have had to pay for our "autonomy." Understandably, the early voices that bravely fought for such autonomy (convinced that we would thereby be liberated forever) could not foresee how deeply abandoned and how painfully conscious we were to be in reaching for what Keats called that "sole self." But we would learn the paradox all too quickly, experiencing both the triumph of autonomy and the dread of isolation.

III

There are a number of contiguous coordinates that may help shape the framework of a study of the unlived life, and I take most of them from philosophy: Schopenhauer's "pessimism," Nietzsche's warning about the dangers of human memory that lead to the abuses of history, and Max Scheler's adumbration of Nietzsche's "*ressentiment.*" In addition, nearly all lamentations are inherently narcissistic if the object being lamented over is one's Self, an idea elaborated in the introduction to Part I.

"Unlived life" unleashes a chain reaction: renunciation, death (suicide, homocide, illness), ennui, superfluousness, the void. A review of literary suicides in the last century and a half would be worth a separate study; so would an analysis of the various kinds of literary renunciation. But Death, Negation, Ennui, "The Superfluous Man," the void—all have been subjected to detailed attention.[12] The "unlived life" in some way subsumes them all. As a motif it appears to have become almost obligatory, and the reasons are as complex as they are various. From the despair of Goethe's Werther to the *ressentiment* of Dostoevsky's Underground Man and the malaise of *fin de siècle* we encounter everywhere, it seems, meaningless, wasted lives. Such meaninglessness takes many forms, from cosmic anguish, of which there are many manifestations, to the discovery that daily life, in its repetitious banality, leaves us little to embrace. Generally speaking, that curve operates on a time-scale: cosmic anguish tends more to initiate the early stages of a general malaise; the horror of banality gains momentum with Flaubert, circa mid-century, and finds its most empathetic voices in the stories and plays of Chekhov and the stories and novels of Henry James. With cosmic despair we shall deal very little, except in chapter 1.

As the chief spokesman for German Idealism, Fichte is reputed to have said to his students at the University of Jena, where he taught philosophy: "Think of yourself. Now think of yourself thinking of yourself. If you cannot do that do not remain in this room." One suspects a high dropout rate. In addition, it is a commonplace, but therefore no less true, that a consciousness of historical consciousness paralleled this emphasis on self-consciousness, making the latter that much more acute. To think of oneself is one thing; to think of

oneself placed as a nineteenth-century dramatic persona (it is difficult to find any instance of persons identifying themselves as members of a particular century before the nineteenth) is indeed thinking
of yourself thinking of yourself. Such historical placing initiated a
heády adventure in cultural identity that ended in an acute sense of
inferiority, a feeling of the epigone come too late in the history of
the world and obliged to look to the past for grandeur and glory.
Often enough, it forced a looking even beyond history itself to an
Arcadian past which one had little chance of experiencing, let alone
repeating, except in what today we would call "altered states":
dreamworlds and myth-worlds, and sometimes madness.[13] That the
nineteenth century moved from profound idealism to profound despair is too facile a claim, but some such change did take place, and it
played its role in the progressive unfolding of the unlived-life motif.
Still it will help to keep in mind the close proximity of the two
feelings: the personal unlived life, with a sense of having exhausted
historical time; or, as the Russians were to call it, superfluousness in
a socio-historical void. The parallelism of historical and personal
waste will eventually merge and produce the profoundest sense of
regret and despair. Late in the century (too late to prevent it) in his
On the Advantage and Disadvantage of History for Life, Nietzsche was to
caution us against this dangerous historical illness that only worsened
and spilled over well into our own century. Nietzsche's primary target was Hegel, but he needed also to overcome his earlier infatuation
with Schopenhauer.

Schopenhauer's "pessimism" was, to some extent, not unlike Freud's
rationalism: a hard-nosed admonition that we accept as a state of happiness an absence of unhappiness. It is folly, Schopenhauer argued, to
cling to life-goals when—in his scheme of the world—such goals are
chimerical, at best only momentary triumphs. In addition, however, to
this avowed dim view of life, Schopenhauer was a shrewd and practical
observer, and, like all of his tribe, cynical: "Our constant discontent is
for the most part rooted in the impulse to self-preservation. This passes
into a kind of selfishness, and makes a duty out of the maxim that we
should always fix our minds upon what we lack, so that we may endeav-
our to procure it."[14] The attempt to occupy the allegedly vacated space
of fulfillment is merely a futile exercise. It also produces envy and
hatred. Hayden White calls Schopenhauer's philosophy "both the starting point and the barrier to be overcome" by the likes of Nietzsche,
Wagner, Freud, Mann among others; and he seizes on Schopenhauer's
discovery that *streben* was "both the fundamental fact and the fundamental burden of human existence." Most salient, however, was Scho-

penhauer's consequential conclusion that "There is only present. Past and future are merely the modes of organizing an anticipation of change in one's own mind"; therefore, White concludes, "Schopenhauer's philosophy ends by being perfectly narcissistic."[15]

It is no contradiction, only an extension, to call the elegiac (as used here) "narcissistic," even though the elegiac involves the past. All elegy evokes (and invokes) the past for the sole purpose of illuminating its absence in the present. Although White's use of the word "narcissistic" is aimed at the worship of the past in the mode/mood of *carpe diem* (seize enjoyment at the moment of its occurrence), the elegiac as it is used here is not any different. Modern elegy must in some way end up as "ironic," both in White's sense and in the common meaning. Irony is always, among other things, potentially self-deprecating and reflexive: the ironist is struck back by what he renders, a victim, that is, of his own irony. This is the sort of "modern" irony Nietzsche feared so much, and this fear led in part at least to a repudiation of Schopenhauer after an initial embrace. Irony is self-emasculating, cancelling any possibility of forward progress (and eternal recurrence); it is a shoulder shrug at history potentially as destructive as the Hegelian bondage to the "world-process."

As we consider the protagonists of the elegiac fictions we gloss, we might keep in mind some of Schopenhauer's darkest pronouncements, for they became guideposts for the nineteenth century and, despite Nietzsche's repudiation, beyond that century into ours. For example:

> Awakened to life out of the night of unconsciousness, the will finds itself an individual . . . among innumerable individuals, all striving, suffering, erring. . . . No possible satisfaction in the world could suffice to still [the will's] longings, set a goal to [the will's] infinite cravings, and fill the bottomless abyss of [its] heart. . . . Earthly happiness is destined to be frustrated or recognized as an illusion. . . . Happiness accordingly always lies in the future, or else in the past, and the present may be compared to a small dark cloud. . . . The present is therefore always insufficient; but the future is uncertain, and the past irrevocable.[16]

In place of cheerful expectations of fulfillment, Schopenhauer warned that we had best get used to "continual illusion and disillusion," that we must learn to cope with the fact that "nothing at all is worth our striving," since we do not control our destiny—and even

when we think we do, attainment never matches expectations. Schopenhauer would have thought Keats wise to withdraw from his over-
hasty wish to *become* the nightingale: it would merely have cancelled
forever even the desire itself, a desire he admitted saints and artists
might indulge even if only in "spots of time," moments given to the
rare. Schopenhauer's language is always blunt: ". . . the longer you
live the more clearly you will feel that, on the whole, life is *a disappointment, nay, a cheat.*" As "Time is constantly pressing upon us," there
really cannot be a present: "That which *has been* exists no more; it
exists as little as that which has *never* been. But of everything that
exists you must say, in the next moment, that it has been." Of course it
is precisely this flux that makes our "whole life *the present,* and the
present alone, that we actually possess": when young, we survey a long
future; when old, a long past.[17]

Nietzsche's major concern in *On the Advantage and Disadvantage of
History* was "a surfeit of history" that inculcates in us "the belief of
being a latecomer and epigone," and renders us weak, bringing on the
condition that the "Romans call *impotentia.*" The case is clear: when we
cease to believe that we are creators of history, and consider ourselves
merely the flotsam on a polluted temporal river, we become slothfully
inert like Dante's Belasqua. We shrug our shoulders. Nietzsche finds
his culture suffused with a destructive *"ironical self-consciousness"*; *memento mori,* he observes, still dominates over the "timid" presence of
memento vivere, and all this is eventually debilitating, nurturing in us
"the instinctive belief in the *old age of mankind:* it is now fitting for old
age, however, to engage in the activity of old men, that is, to look
back . . . to seek consolation in the past through memories . . . [for] a
deep feeling of hopelessness has remained. . . ."[18] Although the burden of Nietszche's attack is on the course of Christian belief, solidifying in the Middle Ages, he knew as well as anyone that the Romantics
themselves, whatever their faith, helped to reinvigorate this excessive
sense of historical burden that indeed did in time turn so many of
them into self-conscious ironists and prepared the path for the remainder of the century and the beginning of the next.

Whether we like it or not, Nietzsche concluded, we can be trapped
in our memories to be always in the past—a *"fixed past,"* as Hayden
White observes.[19] Hence we are challenged to learn how sometimes to
"forget" (not to deny) the past, especially on those occasions when
such forgetting allows the creative process of living in the present and
for a future unmolested by the burdens of memory and pastness.

Historical self-consciousness is synonymous with Hegel and his concept of the "world process," the contemplation of which, according to

White, "yield[s] the apprehension of it as a sequence of Tragedies."[20] What the "world process" was designed to accomplish was to make us aware that Becoming (process) was a dynamic configuration of time, encompassing past, present, and future. Since "consciousness" remains the password into Hegel, it is two small steps into self-consciousness and historical self-consciousness. The latter tended to produce a worship of the past, and with such worship it endowed the moment with value beyond itself: that is, the present was in the process of being continually historicized. In this respect, as Nietzsche recognized, Hegel's philosophy was as pessimistic as Schopenhauer's: it forced one to assess the departure of this present as loss as it slid through time until it could be sanctified "historically." The moment of spatial synapse between such a passage had its lurking abysses. Hegel's *Selbstbewusstsein* (self-consciousness), in its initial meaning, indicated literally an awareness of self that has a doubling effect so that one self becomes aware of its other—one self observing its double, an underlying structural pattern in *Doppelgänger* stories throughout the nineteenth century.

To be always reminded of the past, especially such a past as yields unfavorable comparison with the present, is one cause of *ressentiment*. The difference between envying the abstract past or envying a particular present in the shape of live beings is merely one of scope. In his *Ressentiment (Über Ressentiment und moralisches Werturteil*, 1912, 1913), Max Scheler went beyond Nietzsche's general definition. As applied to human behavior he defined it clearly:

> *Ressentiment* is a self-poisoning of the mind which . . . is a lasting mental attitude, caused by the systematic repression of certain emotions and affects. . . . The emotions and affects primarily concerned are revenge, hatred, malice, envy, the impulse to detract, and spite.
>
> The thirst for revenge is the most important source of *ressentiment*.[21]

While this sweeping catalogue does not apply to all those whom we survey as victims of the unlived life, we shall see that *ressentiment,* and Scheler's symptoms, fit the cast of characters more often than not. Hatred, spite, and envy mobilize many of the self-destructive actions of figures ranging from Byron's misanthropic archetype to Beckett's nearly lifeless torsos. Some form of *ressentiment* is almost by definition a consequence of having seen a life either taken too early or, if taken late, seen as wasted. Even in some benign sufferers like James's

Strether, one finds that if *ressentiment* is not played out, it remains close to the surface and is suppressed only by a stronger feeling (which may indeed be self-punitive): renunciation. And it is always suspect.

IV

If history was a mansion in the nineteenth century, it was an orphanage in the twentieth, or worse, a false cause, a pretext for slaughter that would masquerade as a commitment to keep the faith with "the past." So at least according to Pound:

> There died a myriad
> And of the best, among them,
> For an old bitch gone in the teeth,
> For a botched civilization . . .
>
> . . . .
>
> For two gross of broken statues
> For a few thousand battered books.
> "Hugh Selwyn Mauberley"

While Pound perceives history as an "old bitch," Yeats, through the persona of the Old Man who introduces his last play, *The Death of Cuchulain* (1939), calls history "that old maid." History has not, he suggests, begotton anything (at least of late), certainly not anything legitimate. "I am old, I belong to mythology": and the distinction between "mythology" and "history" carves out most clearly the sense of separation Yeats and others felt, the need to reject not merely history but historicizing.

Once we had a passion for genealogies: family, social, and cosmic; we thrilled at the prospect of pursuing beginnings, and "history" was a means of finding identity within flux, meaning and linkage to traditions—whether we became followers of or rebels against them. There was delight in assuming that the collective wisdom of the past had made us superior to it. All that changed: the past was disowned, denied, or, worst of all, ignored. True enough, in the last several decades we have shown much enthusiasm for oral history, statistical social history, and "roots," but none of these resembles anything like the reverential connectedness to the past that so possessed so many in the nineteenth century. It is not a decline of interest in the discipline of history which is at issue, but rather a radical shift in our perception of the past. Although numerous voices in the nineteenth century were

raised against the tyrannous reign of the past over the present—
Nietzsche's was one of the loudest—there was nevertheless general
agreement that *some* past, however distant, was necessary to our survival, and in addition agreement that we were in mortal danger of
losing our pastness forever under the onslaught of an urgently powerful present with visions of an even more urgently powerful future.

In 1854, when Nietzsche was still a child, Flaubert vented his rage
against the "anarchy" around him, the cause of which he saw in the
"historicizing tendency of our epoch." With anger and regret he concluded that "the Nineteenth Century seems to be taking a survey
course in history"—playing the scales of "vogues" (Roman, Gothic,
Pompadour, and Renaissance) as if everything were some kind of
game. And this feeling of outrage against a "historicizing" epoch was
expressed just as he was finishing *Madame Bovary*, eagerly so that he
might return to his own "vogue": the *Saint Antoine*.[22] Perhaps there is a
clue to the mysteries of Flaubert when we consider that *Madame Bovary* and *Saint Antoine* were appearing simultaneously in serialization
in two different publications in 1856–57. The first was a book surely
"historicizing" the writer's own epoch, so much so it has earned a
definitive place as a mirror of Flaubert's society; the second (like
Salammbô) was an excursus into the remote past, one which was to
remain Flaubert's near obsession to the end of his life. Whatever the
meaning of this rather curious double vision, it is in *Madame Bovary*
that Flaubert writes his ironic elegy of a life unlived because its foundations were constructed on those ubiquitous "chimeras" that Baudelaire said we all carry on our backs.

The provenance of modern disconnectedness has been much scruti-
nized, and in the main ascribed either to boredom or nihilism, to two
cataclysmic world wars, to the rise of a depersonalized industrial tech-
nocracy and the ensuing anonymity of the individual. All these are
reasonable explanations, but they ignore the acute sense of dispossession, of loss, of mourning which lies behind whatever manifestation of
disconnectedness one chooses to underscore. To say that the elegists
we consider here eventually felt themselves to be orphaned by history
is not to deny their "anxiety of influence," which turned their
parricidal impulses against all parentage and hence, in time, against
all history. They suffered even more from the influence of anxiety.

As for the ubiquitous "void," it has been much chronicled, and we
will do well to remain close to the shoreline of the topic—the unlived
life. Once again there is cosmic void and personal void, and the eventual merger of the two. We deal here less with those who exploit the
void with deliberateness and self-awareness and, instead, are inter-

ested in those for whom the void more often comes *unawares*. For the
most part our fictions present those in whom the discovery of void is a
sudden severance and a sense of deepest isolation, a deprivation of
energy and life-goals that they may once have had in abundance;
those who lose the enabling creativity which permits completion, leaving them incomplete and without closure. Absence and emptiness are
the symptoms of the unlived life; the process of their (often belated)
discovery becomes the disease itself. The void one sees in the unlived
life is not the elected void but the received void. One observes a sense
of ebbing vitality, and the terrifying realization that waiting itself (a
form of energy) becomes the only remaining meaningful activity.

As already suggested, any conception of an unlived life assumes a
position about the value of the experiential which, at a certain point,
ceases to be valid. The idea of an experiential value must underline
the conception of a *lived* life in order to assess an assumed failure
which is subsequently judged to be the *unlived* life. Conceptions of
growth, especially in the various forms of the *Bildungsroman,* are central to identifying and measuring achieved experience. Even the isolation of intensity, the focus on epiphany, the shift from chronological
time to duration abandoned the duality of lived and unlived life.
Clearly the emphasis on the momentary experience, sharp and passing, as against the accumulated experience of time was a transitional
moment, a final attempt to see wasted lives as individual history, as
individual responsibility, perhaps even as a matter of choice. What
followed the abandonment of any conceptions of "lived" and
"unlived" is not part of our analysis. When the view of life becomes so
dark that the distinction between "lived" and "unlived" is abandoned,
when life is not seen as offering either a chance to experience it or to
miss its experience, we have arrived at a radical disjunctive rupture. It
is a point where nothing experiential matters, neither the achieved
accumulation that may finally bring us order and clarity nor the sudden vision which, if we are sensitive to its occurrence, enriches our
affect. The end of the conception of an *un*lived life signals a major
shift, not merely in a view of life but in the art that reflects it; and that
shift occurs considerably later than is often assumed.

The change in perception that takes root in nineteenth-century
fictions reflects both the pessimism with which Schopenhauer began
the century and the sometimes overreaching faith in human achievement with which Nietzsche closed it. If there was a sense in which it
was felt that setting for oneself specific goals as repositories of happiness and achievement was efficacious, that sense already began to
diminish in Goethe's *Faust.* Faust's wager that no goal would ever

seduce him sufficiently to a state of complacency announces that shift clearly. For Goethe understood that Schopenhauer's assertion of our hopeless state as hostages to the Will was correct; but he attempted to counter the pessimism of the conclusion with a more acceptable proposition. The progress and the process toward a goal (and beyond that goal to still others), must, he felt, provide us with the meaning. Many readers have been disappointed and puzzled that at the conclusion of *Wilhelm Meister's Apprenticeship* the hero has not reached any particular goal, has still years of wandering remaining before he attains any sense of certitude. Indeed, at the end of one apprenticeship begins another; the fool has merely been purged of foolishness, but wisdom has yet to be earned. Pater's "Not the fruit of experience but experience itself is the end" is not so much proof of Pater's debt to Goethe (which is obvious) but of Goethe's anticipation of a central modern concept: if time becomes a space in which we merely wait, we will miss entirely what supposedly we wait for in the first place, like the hapless figure in Kafka's parable "Before the Law" (*The Trial*) who waits a lifetime until the door is finally shut. *Waiting for Godot* is the culminating work of that proposition—is, indeed, the ultimate modern anti-*Faust*.

V

T. S. Eliot writes:

> What might have been is an abstraction
> Remaining a perpetual possibility
> Only in a world of speculation.
> (Burnt Norton)

Yet even "a world of speculation" is enough to make the "perpetual possibility" live powerfully. All the more, one might argue, does the absence and emptiness of unfulfillment flood us with an ache of loss. Such despair is always the other side of the seesaw, hope; and dispossession that reminds us of the possibility of *possession* is sufficient to the sense of longing so necessary to all elegiac literature. When loss no longer exists, and possession neither, then, as already suggested, we have come into a territory barren of all experiential value. In most of the texts that dominate in the chapters to follow that point has not yet been reached, and the abyss we encounter is always felt deeply because the view from its depths is still beyond and above it, highlighted by an awareness of what has been lost, what has been missed, what is too late to recover and out of reach. It is still, in a mythic sense, a tantalizing abyss. The man *under*ground longs, so to speak, to come *above* ground.

As the nineteenth century progressed one observes a variety of intensely felt stress points. I have already mentioned self-consciousness and historical self-consciousness, and the discomfiture of the void, from which one contemplated loss. There were, as well, the urbanization of life, the bureaucratization of existence, with its deadly ritual of repetition so fatal to mind and spirit. Still other pressures intruded: the challenge to faith, the emergence of skepticism about our control of the universe, and the disillusionment with political and social utopias. Infinite reaches were made inaccessible by intrusively finite realities. Many broke under such strain, in life and in art, and many became converts to pessimism. The proposition that had once extolled labor, good works, a clean life, or merely the exertion of one's will to achieve ends (honorable or megalomaniacal) was being discredited. Will no longer sufficed; holding on at all costs merely led to total collapse. The old standby wisdom, which supported the notion that Will was self-controlled, collided with an increasingly pervasive malaise questioning the efficacy of a restrained and disciplined life. (Thomas Mann would chronicle this dilemma in *Death in Venice*.) As a consequence of such doubts one began to question nothing less than the meaning of existence. The radical quest became the radical question, and with it came all forms of defiance, rebellion, and resentment—in short, a new kind of misanthropy which at times was more pathological than philosophical. Such was the *Zeitgeist*, a word of which even the English became so fond they adopted it—"Time-spirit," Matthew Arnold called it.[23]

In his chapter "Dante 'Poco Tempo Silvano,' " in *The Oaten Flute*, Renato Poggioli writes:

> The two great divisions of bucolic poetry are the pastoral of innocence and the pastoral of happiness. . . . Those two kinds of pastoral differ in emphasis and outlook. . . . Dante must choose. . . . It is evident that throughout this section of *Purgatorio* he intends to convey an idyllic vision of man's happiness in the present of individual life, rather than an elegiac evocation of the lost innocence of the human race.[24]

The elegiac fictions I am about to discuss could no longer deal with either of these—the "pastoral of innocence" or the "pastoral of happiness." Their lament—if that is the proper word—is consumed with the personal sense of vacuity, "meditation[s] about death and personal loss, transience, and unfortunate love."[25] But in the place of the "lyric of regret" we begin to see in fiction and drama an unmediated expression of personal grief. To return to Schiller: "All peoples who possess a history have a paradise, a state of innocence, a golden age; indeed every man has his paradise, his golden age. . ." (148).

That absence creates presence is a logical, if paradoxical, sequence. Once we bring that loss to consciousness, what we have lost is found; only, of course, we find the memory (or the wish for an experience that might have made a memory) not the lost object itself. Proust perhaps was the master of shaping the dilemma: the pain of pleasurable recall. But it is also everywhere in the elegiac fictions I am about to examine. A few examples suffice. The torture of Brontë's Heathcliff is the absence of his beloved Cathy; the more keenly he feels that void, the more relentlessly does her presence haunt him. Chekhov's characters call to mind expectations that have turned sour and hopes never fulfilled; their desire to consummate any act in the present is constantly inhibited by the nagging spirit of the past. (That is true as well in much of Ibsen.) Virginia Woolf's characters in *Mrs. Dalloway* are under siege by the relentless memories of the might-have-been; their most poignant moments crystallize when they recognize the distance between where they are now (aging, accommodated to life but joyless) and where they fancy they would be if another choice had been made. Flaubert's Frédéric of *L'Education Sentimentale* is attached to the sacred memory of his ideal until her absence is punctuated by her sudden and unprepared-for material presence, at which point he turns away from her with something close to revulsion. Mann's Castorp, seven years absent from the flatland, is awakened from his spell not merely by the cataclysm of war but by the strains of a simple Schubert *Lied*, stirring within him memory and desire for a commitment he cannot live without. And Ivan Ilyich does not appreciate the presence of good health until he notices its absence.

Such a pattern is consistent with rudimentary mourning: we may exorcise the past as Freud suggested; but loss does not replace memory, it enhances it. The grieving we engage in is not only for what we have lost but also for our inability to retrieve that of which we have been dispossessed. This distinction is not without a difference, for our impotence both to forget and to recover places us at an enormous disadvantage. When, in *The Cherry Orchard*, Lyubov Ranevskaya returns to her childhood room and to the inanimate objects which were once her world, there is only one consolable strategy: making that presence progressively more absent from thought. Hence her alleged indifference, her frivolity, her irresponsible posturing in the face of her crises—all of these are propitiatory. Her departure for Paris at the conclusion of the play is, like the departure from a burial, a blending of pain and relief, insight and accommodation. That, too, may be a way of defining the modern elegiac fictions in which the motif of the unlived life is centrally located.

Georges Poulet has commented suggestively on the issue of presence and absence. If one feels that "one's existence is an abyss," then clearly one feels "the infinite deficiency of the present moment." The Romantics sought to possess "within the moment . . . all that our soul desires to regain of itself." Such a desperate concentration of the "moment" was one antidote to "deficiency." Yet this "momentary possession ends in becoming a dispossession; it ends in the feeling of a loss renewed, in a consummate separation." That such separation furthers the elegiac perceptions of the past is clear; soon an "infinite distance separates afresh the present from the past." Between past and present one confronts a "negative time . . . destruction and absence, an existence finished." Such perceptions in turn further "sorrow" and "sadness of the past, to which is added the anguish of the future" (and recall the "deficiency" of the present). This impasse can have but one outcome: "the romantic feels at once the presence and the absence of his future being." With such a formulation there seems little alternative but to agree with Chateaubriand's René, whom Poulet quotes: " 'Something was lacking to fill up the abyss of my existence.' " And that turns on its head what had up to the time of the Romantic been standard wisdom: the perception of an integrated self that needs to reach awareness first in order to fill the abyss (emptiness) around it with experiential time, rather than an empty self whose imprisonment barred it from relationships to what existed beyond its boundaries: "Incarcerated in the instant, the romantic escapes into thought all the rest of his life." So escaping into "thought" he misses "being"—in short, he does not really "live."[26]

Part I

Narcissists: The Unbearable Present

Introduction

*[People] sometimes would rather die than live with
narcissistic injury.*
— *Kohut, "The Self in History"*

To mourn for oneself (for whatever reason) obviously requires a considerable mobilization of one's attachment to self—in other words,
some form of narcissism. It would be a mistake to identify all narcissism with negative connotations (the French differentiate positive and
negative narcissism by calling the one "amour de soi" and the other
"amour-propre"). Equally wrong, however, is the tendency, observed
by some current critics, to heighten self-lavishment into some kind of
holistic cure for all human ills. "Self-realization" has become cheap-
ened in the last several decades, so that it has given rise to all sorts of
counter-positions. In any case the word "narcissism" has a long history, originating with the myth of Narcissus and up to and beyond
Freud.[1]

The idea that narcissism is a psychological disorder, and the first
attempts to define it, came from Freud. A challenging version of
narcissism emerges in the work of Heinz Kohut. And in 1978 Christopher Lasch's *The Culture of Narcissism*—quite to the surprise of author
and publisher—became a national best-seller. What this suggests is
clear: in this century narcissism has generated a great deal of interest,
has become a perspective from which modern cultural behavior is
being evaluated, and even when presented on a more popular, less
clinical level as in Lasch's book has attracted millions of readers
whether they see self-love as a palliative to our modern anxieties or as
a destructive element to an ever-increasing cultural worship-ritual of
the self.

We need think only a moment to realize that it is not necessarily a contradiction for narcissism to coexist with self-hate, insecurity, despair, and rage. In addition, narcissism takes energy to activate, and again such energy may be activated in a seemingly exhausted person. The common denominator in what Kohut calls "narcissistic rage" is a familiar litany: "The need for revenge, for righting a wrong, for undoing a hurt by whatever means, and a deeply anchored, unrelenting compulsion in the pursuit of all these aims. . . ." Kohut (perhaps even better read in serious literature than Freud) alludes to Kleist's *Michael Koolhas* and *Moby-Dick,* fine examples of megalomania. But Brontë's Heathcliff embodies "narcissistic rage" in all its facets, and it manifests itself, in various ways, in all the major figures of the works discussed in the chapters following Part I, which I have called "Narcissists": "aggression, anger, and destructiveness," or sometimes "heightened sadism" or "preventive attack."[2] One of Kohut's seminal terms is "Tragic Man," who "expends his energy in keeping intact and protected what little sense of self he has," until such time as "disintegration anxiety" proves to be his undoing, plunging him into "despair, shame, boredom . . . feeling empty, depressed. . . ."[3] The pattern of Kohut's "narcissistic rage" follows a familiar course: injury (real or perceived), lack of empathy (real or perceived), and the reaction. Sometimes—and we can see it in figures like Heathcliff, Pechorin, Bazarov, and Gregor Samsa—the reaction features a "boundless *exhibitionism* of the grandiose self" with "its insistence of the exercise of total control" and "omnipotence."[4] Clearly when such figures either will themselves to fall, or fall unwittingly, unexpectedly, the crash and clamor are proportionately more "grandiose": Chekhov's aging doctor in "A Dreary Story," or Kafka's Samsa in *The Metamorphosis,* or if we concentrate on the term "exhibitionism" (that borders on the dark comic), Mann's Aschenbach in *Death in Venice.*

Narcissism is inevitably linked to regret. Its overarching aspect is that one pays attention to one's self beyond "normal" bounds. After all, even suicides, the mentally distressed, the clinically depressed are—whatever else they may be—also narcissists. In a recent study "shame" has been called "the veiled companion of narcissism," and since this notion fits the particular works that follow in this part of this study, an explanation of this relationship between shame and narcissism is helpful.

In *The Masks of Shame,* Léon Wurmser links "contempt" to "the form of aggression intrinsic to shame affects." At the same time he also links shame and aggression to "Narcissistic conflicts"—to questions of "self-esteem" and "self-worth . . . power and self-love." Such conflicts conclude in an all-too-familiar fashion, recognizable in the personae of the next three chapters, "[involving] wishes for massive over-evaluation of the self and the pertinent other, leading to inevitable disillusionment and its consequent overwhelming affects, mostly in forms of rage, shame, envy, loneliness."[5] Another analysis of narcissism asserts that it was in the nineteenth century that, "for the first time, attention was paid to a different kind of narcissism—that of the psychotic who withdraws from society and the world." Childe Harold, Onegin, Heathcliff, Pechorin—all belong to a range beyond "normal" behavior, though we would not call it "psychotic." In the same study we are offered the narcissism of the "common man," again a nineteenth-century phenomenon which "today we call . . . the sense of identity, or self-image."[6]

The question of "identity" (what Hegel meant by "self-consciousness") has so dominated the critical discussion of literary texts that it would serve no purpose to restate it here. However, one point particularly relevant to the narcissists I discuss is worth detailing. Wurmser cites Leo Rangell's " 'three horsemen' "—"Ambition, power, and opportunism" as growing " 'wild and proliferate,' " a condition of "narcissism . . . out of control."[7] When does narcissism become uncontrollable? When Self (or identity) is submerged. Many commentators on narcissism caution us not to misinterpret the original Narcissus myth. Narcissus, they point out, did not fall in love with himself: he fell in love with a *reflection* of himself, an imaged self. The distinction is important, for it stresses that Ego, Self, Identity (whatever name we give to the "I") projects a desirable image, and is therefore in danger of self-cancellation. And the consequent attention lavished on the *image* robs the person of a stable ego. This is why Narcissus dies, pining away, starving himself (a familiar motif in many texts of the nineteenth century). That his death is in some measure a suicide is indisputable. He dies because he cannot possess what he loves, that is, his imaged self; and in this respect his dilemma is repeated in Childe Harold and Onegin, Pechorin, Bazarov and Heathcliff—even in Ivan Ilyich. What destroys all of them is not death or illness leading to death: these are consequences, not causes of their collapse. From a fresh perspective it will emerge clearly that it is an insidious case of narcissism that becomes the common denominator—the real cause—of the rapid (sometimes slow) disintegration of these protagonists.[8]

Alexander Lowen calls narcissism "an exaggerated investment in one's image *at the expense of the self*" (italics mine), and sees narcissists as "manipulative" people "striving for power and control . . . egotists." "Alienation" is a logical consequence when the ego divides itself from its image: "Without a solid sense of Self, [narcissists] experience life as

empty and meaningless. It is a desolate state." Most important, Lowen
suggests, is the moment "when the narcissistic facade of superiority
and specialness breaks down, allowing the sense of loss and sadness to
become conscious [and when] it is often too late." This is true of nearly
all of our self-elegists, especially Onegin, Pechorin, and Bazarov—
even Heathcliff and Ivan Ilyich. That such people's actions are "self-
destructive" is *prima facie:* "narcissists love their image, not their real
self." An "outburst of narcissistic rage" is akin to frustration, to "feeling powerless"—in short, to feeling the impotence detailed in the
protagonists of many of the fictions in this study. "An exaggerated
investment in one's image at the expense of the self": this is not really
introspection; it is, like Narcissus, looking outward (and downward).[9]

In Childe Harold and Eugene Onegin, Byron and Pushkin present
us with a kind of evolutionary narcissism. Like his author, Childe
Harold is, by and large, an alienated and arrogant egotist whose
search for "meaning" and "self" becomes serious only when Byron
drops the fictive persona, and the poem turns into versified autobiography.

Even then it is clear that, in the spirit of the century, he places
himself into a state of war with society ("mankind"). Surely he fits
several of the characteristics we have described in delineating
"narcissism"—anger, sadness, loss. Pushkin's Onegin is a mutation of
Childe Harold who has no real consciousness of the true self until his
losses are clearly irrecoverable. Possessing the gift of self-irony and
the burden of self-consciousness, Onegin is far more complex than
Childe Harold. While Byron's traveler muses about the state of the
past, his reveries on history are a deflection from the more painful
present, a displacement of his less-than-enviable state as outcast, wan-
derer, a man full of "strife." Onegin's conscious rejection of a social
niche also places him into the spotlight of the isolated, but Onegin's
musings are almost always practical, distant, ironic. Instant gratifica-
tion is not an invention of our time; Onegin *expects* to have his way.
When he rebuffs, he does so with haughtiness, pride, a patronizing
tone; when in turn he is rebuffed, he cannot understand, or believe,
that this could occur, and the self observes the reflection's humiliation
with disbelief.

Pechorin, Bazarov, and Heathcliff are men in a rage. For each the
realization of their impotence to act comes as a shock; each uses his
cruelty to manipulate others and themselves; all surrender, sooner or
later, to the realization that they have expended their will, that the
course of their lives has, in a sense, been devoured by their own self-
absorption with it. The great enemy is neither the past, which they

have rejected, nor the future, in which they can find no role for themselves, but rather the present, which ceases to have meaning and purpose. All "feel entitled to have what they want when they want it just because they want it."[10]

Why should one feel superfluous, assuming we can accept a working definition of superfluity as one in which the sufferer (for superfluity itself becomes an "illness") believes that life has no more use for him or her—not vice versa? The rebelliousness disappears, and in its place comes a sense of uselessness. The self submerges itself even more, but the displaced symptomology is a feeling of complete worthlessness. Like Bazarov's ultimate perception, such a feeling asserts (rather than assumes) that not only is one no longer needed, but also that the act of isolation is an act of abandonment. So Turgenev's diarist believes his death is an event important only to himself—as, of course, he equally thought was his life; Tolstoy's Ivan Ilyich recognizes with bitterness that what creates a physical and spiritual crisis for him is to wife and daughter merely an annoying prolongation, just as Gregor Samsa's insecthood is a profound embarrassment to his family. Both Ilyich and Samsa are anxious, ultimately, for death to come. A life of narcissistic self-perception moves at the end into its final two stages: "narcissistic rage" followed by loss of will to live.

Chekhov's dying scientist in "A Dreary Story," older than either Ilyich or Samsa, becomes the observer who can, in some uncanny way, dissect the process of his dying virtually without affect. His "diary" reads like an instrumentality of science itself—detached, almost neutral, but devastating. "Observation" remains *just* this side of judgment; he measures his slow disintegration, manifested mostly in disinterest and disappointment. (It is not yet the death-soliloquy of Beckett, but it is a close ancestor.) Once again the dying man sees the world around him in a state of controlled separation; the anxiety, if one can call it that, is also controlled: wife, daughter, colleagues, students—all are entities no longer incorporated but excommunicated. In Chekhov's story there is an additional narcissistic element which afflicts those who "live in terror of losing their sense of perfection. . . ."[11]

Thomas Mann's Aschenbach is a case of implosion, a strangely perverted episode of the Narcissus myth.[12] For all his life Aschenbach has denied love, even to himself, although such denial, as Freud noted, has its own aspects of narcissism. When he sits in a Venetian barbershop, facing the mirror, attempting to rejuvenate himself to come closer, he hopes, to the young boy with whom he has fallen hopelessly in love, what the *reader* sees is a grotesque reflection. Dark hair, rouge, a touch of lip color make him a pitiful object, at the close of the novella, abandoned alone on the beach in focus, one might say, for the abandoned camera left on the beach. His contemplation of the ocean—yet another Narcissus pool—brings uneasy visions, nightmarish dreams, and salacious, deadly thoughts. Having previously resisted love for the sake of art only heightens the irony of his dilemma; and his abandon for the youthful Adonis is perhaps less homoerotic than autoerotic, and Freud stressed the latter as an important function of narcissistic "disease."

Gregor Samsa also acts out a form of "suicide": he starves himself to death. He too pines away, becomes wasted and shrinks, as he perceives more of the "good" things about himself—his sacrifices for his family, his caring for his sister's future, his fastidiousness toward his work—are not enough to save him.[13] Is there in all of literature a more explicit case of precipitous diminution, the disappearance of self (even from the initial metamorphosis) than Gregor Samsa's twofold decline? First Gregor becomes a self without human body; then he becomes an insect-self severed (if not entirely) from human consciousness. In effect, the daring of Kafka's story is that Gregor really *becomes* his reflection. More and more, his daydreaming becomes abstracted from the human domain, and he begins to feel and behave as alienated from all shapes of human selfhood, just as Gulliver did when he retreated from the human in disgust to spend his life in the stable with the horses in that terrible indictment of humanness, the fourth book of *Gulliver's Travels*.

In *The Heresy of Self-Love*, Paul Zweig expresses a "liberal" disclaimer, defending narcissism in the spirit of the 1960s, when the book was published. He traces the path of "self-love," a part of our cultural tradition, and he notes that it is "always condemned and yet central to our most familiar values." He also notes that nineteenth-century social critics, nurtured on the concept of "alienation" from Rousseau to Hegel to Marx, everywhere "discovered isolation: men broken apart from each other. . . ." And he concludes by positing a "defense" of the "heresy" of self-love, diagnosing it as almost exclusively a reaction to rejection:

> The "modern" world had, in the eyes of many, become a veritable anti-society; instead of forming the individual, it oppressed him. The problem then became either to change the society . . . or to teach the individual how he might resist a society whose inhumanity threatened to overwhelm him.

That narcissism is merely a kind of "subversive individualism" is an interesting conception, but it fails to take account of what such subversion is made and what generates its *ressentiment*. The loneliness of the "aesthetic" choice (Kierkegaard, Baudelaire, Nietzsche, Dostoevsky) is a refusal to acknowledge personal "failure"—indeed turning such "failure" into a "transforming mirror," thereby making "the danger worse, in order to make it better." Yet Zweig concludes that we have come to be trapped in a conflict between the uncritical acceptance of spurious values ("destructive conformities") and being "wary of the old poetry of alienation . . . self-punishment and isolation."[14] Zweig's book was published in 1968—the critical moment of the unrest of that decade—and in one sense it marks a particular point of that decade, exposing what he calls the "moral dilemma" between the equally strong urges of self-realization and social involvement: it was, for many who partook of the Sixties seriously, an ubiquitous paradox. The Underground Man had come out of his hole, so to speak, but was blinded by the sun. He is still *against* the world and *for* himself (or the reflected image of what he would like to be), but he has had enough of hiding and self-loathing—even of loathing others. The explosive phenomenon of self-love in the last twenty or thirty years has taken its energy not from isolation but from aggression. The libido virtually bursts with energy, but again in the very process of creating such powerful resonances it is, however unwittingly, preparing itself for another bout with exhaustion. If those who cared and wanted change have now spawned those who look mostly after their own well-being, then it is possible that history will repeat itself and we are in for a period of an even more pervasive narcissism than before. And its nature may become both more self-destructive and other-neglecting than the earlier manifestation.

Certainly Christopher Lasch's work suggests that this appears already to be happening; if he is right, one might argue that such a turn is not the consequence of the so-called "me generation": the seeds for such narcissism were probably sown in the last quarter of the eighteenth century, and though progress has been uneven, many complex manifestations emerging along the way, the end result appears to have been inevitable from the start. Indeed the current "me-ism" (not incidentally confined to the young) is a classic example of what Kohut describes as "narcissistic rage," for the excess of self-love cannot help being prompted and accompanied by rage. Fulfillment necessarily is intertwined with aggression, against others and, more often than not, finally against oneself.

Narcissism has become a far-reaching concept, and its applicability to modern literary texts is obvious. Indeed, the whole of Western culture since the Enlightenment has moved inevitably toward a conception of a strong Self, which in turn has spawned various kinds of narcissistic behavior. As I have noted, there are positive and negative, normal and pathological "interpretations" of narcissism as a general manifestation of an increasingly strident focus on the "autonomous self" (see the introduction to Part III).[16]

In nearly all the work analyzed in this study narcissism has had a devastating effect. It is in fact the very dashing of high expectations that causes so many of these protagonists to crash:

> The concept of narcissistic love . . . functions as accusation and punishment. Similar to fascination, the concept it replaces, narcissism presented a situation in which society has isolated an individual. . . . Isolated and surrounded simultaneously, the individual finds himself alone against society and unable to escape its condemnations.[17]

As Freud—who deserves the last word—rather inclusively outlined the matter in his "On Narcissism: An Introduction":

> A person may love:—
> (1) According to the narcissistic type
>   (a) what he himself is (i.e. himself),
>   (b) what he himself was,
>   (c) what he himself would like to be,
>   (d) someone who was once part of himself.[18]

Although these characteristics subsumed under narcissism do in some measure fit a characterization of virtually all the figures in the works I analyze, they best suit those in the chapters that follow.

1 Romantic Ancestry: Energy and Enervation

. . . sadness, sorrow, acedia, despair, and other troubled, dejected states.
—*Stanley W. Jackson*, Melancholia and Depression

I

To define Romanticism has become an uncomfortable task because to place it accurately, either in time or in place, is probably a futile exercise. Nevertheless, commencing in the 1770s one may identify changes in taste, perception, and articulation; and among these the emergence of the motif of the unlived life and its elegiac overtones is paramount. From *Werther* (1774) onward heroes and heroines in great numbers recognize that the lives they have embarked on suddenly founder; that the journey toward maturity, wisdom, and contented adjustment—the ideals of eighteenth-century life—is being interrupted by various impediments, both from within and without. Rousseau certainly felt haunted by a sense not merely of persecution but of unfulfillment. *The Confessions* sometimes reads like a propitiatory gesture against the recognition that his life has been one huge vain gesture of waste. *Sic transit gloria mundi, ubi sunt,* and *carpe diem* are not nineteenth-century phrases: they inform the literature of Europe from the late Middle Ages onward. Yet it is precisely the "translations" of such stock phrases from their conventional usage that ultimately change their meaning. The glories of the world not only pass, they seem irrevocably gone; the mourning for what no longer was is no ritualistic exercise with regenerative promise but a funeral oration punctuated with finality; and to seize the day was to enjoy the moment not for the sake of salvaging one's life but, eventually, for the sake of salvaging the moment. After Rousseau came many other "confessions"; indeed they were to become a vogue and, not coincidentally, a method of delivering oneself of one's mortality into what one hoped were the unaging monuments of print. Some confessions, like DeQuincey's, were accompanied by a *Suspira de Profundis,* the sighs of abandoned seafarers—from Baudelaire to Eliot's *Four Quartets.*

A catalog of Romantic unlived lives would be tedious and not helpful; it would be a list vaster than any single study could contain; the disillusioned and the surfeited, the victimized and the deranged, the superfluous and the bored. One could not clearly demarcate where such a list would end, and soon enough one would need to advance along the decades in the nineteenth century right through it to the end—and beyond. Clearly one needs to be selective, and to linger longer than necessary among the Romantics, however tempting, would be unwise. In any event it has been argued for some time now (and correctly so) that the continuity of the nineteenth century is best defined as a resonating Romanticism, which assumes a series of mutations rather than a death of the "movement," and that unlike other such "movements" what seems like a reaction was more critique than rejection. The point is of some significance, for one cannot understand later texts without appreciating how deeply the powerful optics of Romanticism affected their vision.

If the Romantics did not invent the motif of the unlived life, they certainly defined it. Their often elegiac posture, gloomy and despairing, reaching toward *unreachable* objectives, rather than *unreached* ones, made them likely candidates for dashed hopes. In addition, overly ambitious goals set the stage for disappointment. Sometimes suicidal and often acting on impulse, many Romantics explored with a kind of fascinated horror the emptiness of their lives, real or fictional, anticipating confirmation of their deprivation not the hope of redemption. In some ways, they became as obsessive about the unfulfilled as they were about the anticipated. Small wonder then that completion so often eluded them, for the energies spent on anticipation simply led to exhaustion.[1] The case of Novalis's *Heinrich von Ofterdingen* is a classic example: the two parts of the novel follow Novalis's own life. Part I, "Expectations" (*Die Erwartung*) was completed; Part II, "Fulfillment" (*Die Erfüllung*) is a fragment, uncompleted when Novalis died in 1801 at the age of twenty-nine.

Unrequited or distressed love brought many a youth to grief, from Werther to René, from Adolphe to Julien Sorel. Madness and illness cut short lives of high promise, and the "imp of the perverse" undid untold numbers, not merely in Poe, who coined the phrase, but in Hoffmann and Kleist, Byron and Hugo. One common thread in the variety of unfulfillment is the innocence of the victims and often the brevity of their lives. Few of the categories mentioned, for instance, featured those whose realization of loss, of missed opportunity, surfaced later in life, for there seldom was a "later life." This marks them off, by and large, from their successors; and there is, of course, a great difference between the innocent youth who is disillusioned and is cut from life before he can even test his instincts and the more experienced, often much older hero who can look back over the "Ridiculous, the waste sad time / Stretching before and after" (T. S. Eliot, *Burnt Norton*). The latter feelings need not in every case belong to the chronologically middle-aged: Childe Harold and Onegin, Pechorin and Bazarov, are still very young men; but in suffering, and therefore in experiential time, they perceive themselves as aged. Their insights are sometimes deep and searing, final; there is little of the impulsive in their various hardened manifestations of discouragement and disengagement.

Poulet comments: "Romantic nostalgia appears thus as the forlorn desire of a life that the mind can never give itself fully in any moment and that, notwithstanding, it sees from afar, there, beyond both ends of the moment, in the elusive realm of duration. . . ." As Poulet recognizes, this describes not only the Romantics but the whole nineteenth century—up to and beyond the *symbolistes*, Bergson, Pater, and Proust. Implicit in "continuous duration" is suspension (not stasis), a condition that leads to a number of virtually irreconcilable tensions. For example: "The romantic effort to form itself a being out of presentiment and memory"—the burden of the past *and* the future—"ends in the experience of a double tearing of the self." Is not this *one* meaning of Faust's famous declaration that he is being torn apart by "two souls"? The process of "becoming" in the nineteenth century, according to Poulet, is "always future." Instead of bringing past and future to the "center," the conscious "I" of the present, could one not work outward from the "I" ("mobile and migratory") in order to achieve "continuity"?[2] The difference of direction signals major and disturbing changes. If the conscious "I" assimilates and consolidates past and future, its emphasis is on a temporal but forward-moving present. If, however, the "I" itself traverses spatially, migrating and acting as a mediating consciousness *between* past and future in order to achieve continuity, then certainly it runs many risks. Not merely is the voiding of the present a real danger, but the lure of remaining either in the past or in the future is menacingly tempting. Throughout the century many could not sustain the goal of "continuity" and instead fell victim to immersion in pastness or prophecy. Keats, no less than the young Yeats, saw the dangers clearly, at the beginning and at the end of the century.

II

Goethe's *Faust* raises virtually every issue which we have come to identify as "modern," including, not surprisingly, the problem of the unlived life. This serves not only as testimony of the author's breadth but of the duration of the act of writing *Faust* itself, from the 1770s to the year of his death in 1832. This chronology includes that crucial turn between two centuries, for Goethe's hero (and the work) features most prominently the double bind of the emerging Romantic-Modern dilemma: the expenditure of limitless energy to transcend and overcome limitless despair. Early on in the Romantic configuration there develop concepts of two infinites: the infinite ascent and transcendence toward some spiritual awakening and consummation and the infinite descent into abysses. At first despair was primarily a consequence of the failed attempt at transcendence. Unparalleled energies were mobilized in the pursuit of the ideal, the infinite, the unattainable. But the price of failure was an equally gloomy disillusionment that eventually led to various manifestations of enervation: suicide, nervous exhaustion, hysteria, despair, ennui, and a general *taedium vitae* which, by the end of the nineteenth century, had become endemic. True, many Romantic heroes were deliberate and self-conscious poseurs; but even this does not diminish the *effect* they often sought to achieve by means of their posturing. And while their energies were often spent on achieving such an effect—activity followed by passivity—too often they discovered that posturing can itself become a dangerous game, a self-fulfilling mode of behavior which sometimes trapped one in the reality of the supposed make-believe. This becomes clear in several of the works I examine.

To the last it can be argued that Faust alternates between what Goethe elsewhere called the manic-depressive condition of being "himmelhoch jauchzend, zum Tode betrübt" (deliriously joyous, grieved to death). This swing of moods, this seesaw between ecstasy and despair, governed much of European Romanticism. Eventually despair rather than ecstasy tipped the scales, but that despair, in its main forms, objectified itself in the obsessive motif of the unlived life, especially in the sense that the Ego (or Self) experienced an awareness of its own diminution.

Faust begins with the lamentation over an unfulfilled life, or at the very least a sense of intellectual finitude, intellectual claustrophobia, the "cramp[ing]" of "every vital urge" (Part I, 410–13).[3] This sense of being hemmed in helps both to assemble Faust's energies and to find a way beyond limits; it also plunges him into the despair of ever achieving transcendence of the quotidian and encloses him in a gloomy mood that results in near paralysis. Jubilant when he beholds the symbol of the macrocosm, he is quickly daunted by the "boundless Nature" which he cannot hope to embrace: "You brim, you quench, yet I must thirst in vain?" Hopeful that the image of a lesser spirit— that of the earth—is approachable, he is rebuffed even by that spirit and warned not to think himself peer to what his fantasy can image:

> *You resemble the spirit you imagine,*
> *Not me!*
>
> (Part I, 454–515)

The "uncertain human fate" into which Faust is once more placed creates a better prelude to the near suicide which consummates in the negative submission to the pact with hell. Worm, not god: the shock is so severe that fantasy is momentarily subdued ("now it contents itself with little scope"), but he is joyless and welcomes the poison that will deliver him from all further expectations, though it involves the danger of flowing into "nothingness" (Part I, 629–719).

The ambiguity and irony of Faust's wager lie at the heart of the work. Faust vows never to cease striving, never to lie down in contentment sufficiently long to wish the moment to remain. The usual interpretation of this stipulation emphasizes a form of lust to unleash the energy of striving; but, equally, the terms of the wager represent Faust's dread of the lure of inaction, the terror of *acedia*—of stagnation, sloth, inactivity—all of which he, like any mortal, is heir to and must resist. It is precisely the seizure of the "moment" that becomes a fixation for later generations taking their cue from the desire of so many Romantics to encapsulate the Keatsian moment of release from the travail of the world, an opposition around which Schopenhauer built a sizable part of his philosophy of the Will. Flaubert, Mallarmé, Pater, Joyce, Proust, Woolf—all will seek to expand the moment precisely to hold it fast for intense experience: time is spatialized. Faust himself is not unaware of the positive potential of staying the moment, even if it momentarily interrupts the onward progress of striving. The

insubstantial sojourn with the shade of Helen is one such experience
and, before that, there are others, even the ephemeral fantasy (however impractical) of a contented union with the innocent Gretchen.

Especially in Part I, and again in Act III of Part II, Faust alternates
between moods of striving and gloomy reflection, that is, between
energy and enervation. Within him rages a struggle far more persis-
tent than he ever admits: "Ah, nothing perfect is vouchsafed to man, /
I sense it now" (Part I, 3240–41). These lines are spoken after the
pact, after the seduction of Gretchen, after realizing that he cannot
strive and be content but must choose between these states, and that
contentment, his earlier hope to the contrary, will not reside in mere
striving. (In his near-parody of *Faust, Peer Gynt,* Ibsen demonstrated
the absurdity of striving for its own sake.) In language that could well
serve as the epigraph for many nineteenth-century texts, Faust laments his having been trapped, feeling neither at peace nor exhila-
rated, but as his progeny will be wont to say, disowned:

> Am I not fugitive, the homeless rover [*der Unbehauste*],
> The man-beast void of goal or bliss,
> Who roars in cataracts from cliff to boulder
> In avid frenzy for the precipice?
>
> (Part I, 3348–51)

Or, on a "Dreary Day," Faust learns of Gretchen's fate:

> In misery! Despairing! Long roaming the earth . . .
> and now imprisoned!
>
> (Part I, 110)

For a brief moment he identifies with her fate: both are now "homeless."

Faust's journey into the world of the Mothers, where he will meet
Helena, is certainly from one point of view a metaphor for striving
and ultimate defeat, both of which he must experience. While the
experience does not exactly humble, it enlightens; and the episode
serves a paradigmatic function. Faust is told that there is no road into
the realm of Helena: "No road! Into the unacceded / The inaccessible . . . ," only the promise of "wastes of solitude" (Part II, 6223–27).
But Faust remains jaunty, not put off by Mephisto's ominous road
map. "Within your Naught to find the All I hope" (Part II, 6256) is
certainly an immodest goal; and though the sound of the mysterious
realm of the Mothers—the very words make him shudder—he goes

forward with great expectations. Faust's epiphanous moment is his dream of Leda, and it is a moment he easily would wish to prolong.

By Act II Faust has transcended all temporal and spatial zones and has penetrated into the mythopoeic; we find him in the historical-mythic realm where Helena, self-conscious of her role, comes alive as a vision. Faust realizes his dream in the person of Helena's daughter, Leda:

> Breathless I seem, my tongue is faltering, chained;
> This is a dream, and place and day have waned.
> (Part II, 9413–14)

After the death of their son, Euphorion, Helena must once more return to her historical time, and Faust to his "real" time. Her disappearance, signified by leaving only a robe and a veil in Faust's arms, is appropriately ephemeral. The garments serve to lift Faust out of this descent back into the "present," and Goethe's instinct, always so unerring, leaves Faust in a state of swooning speechlessness throughout this episode.

There is ample room for interpreting Faust's final insights, but on one matter he states unequivocally that he now knows more, that we are bound to live a Kantian "as if" existence when we touch the realms of the beyond:

> [I] stormed through my life . . .
> But now at pace more prudent, more sedate.
> (Part II, 11440–441)

Faust's admission that there are limits to human attainment (though he is careful not to eliminate the *desire* toward such overreaching) is part, of course, of Goethe's corrective to what he considered the "sick" part of Romanticism, the rejection of Werther's progeny. It was a utilitarian decision and made for long life; certainly neither Faust nor his octogenarian creator could possibly feel they had not lived. Yet Faust's dilemma raises all the questions, poses all the dangers, and proposes, if not solutions, possible resolutions. Faust has attempted to balance the energies of striving and the enervation of disillusionment. Goethe's interventionist ending may indeed distort Faust's disillusionment, but is does not deny the fact that total collapse after a fruitlessly expended energy is highly probable for *ordinary* mortals—which Faust, of course, is not.

III

That the Romantic response to life—even if one considers it on the highest level of abstraction—was ambiguous is not in dispute. One need step back only a little to survey the major European literatures between, say, the latter half of the eighteenth century to the midpoint of the nineteenth in order to recognize the double reaction. There was, on the one hand, optimism, revolutionary fervor, a feeling of bursting energies directed toward an infinity of potential; and, on the other hand, a bleak and disillusioned, even suicidal vision, a brush with the abyss. Romantic disappointment emanated from many sources, ranging from political disenchantment with the French Revolution and its violent resonance to a personal feeling of failure (and guilt) at not achieving the idealist's goals that had once seemed within reach. In any case the gaps between expectation and fulfillment shaped the post-Romantic abysses of the mid-nineteenth century and beyond and led directly to the exhaustion of will and the epigoni syndrome that characterized the second half of the nineteenth century and survived well into the twentieth.

In the course of the nineteenth century several attempts were made to account for these dualistic responses. The world was divided into Aristotelians and Platonists, Hebraists and Hellenists, Dionysian and Apollonian, the Naive and the Sentimental—to cite but a few. No doubt all of these pairings would help us to understand the overall problems better, but one pairing which has received less attention and yet is particularly insightful is Turgenev's analysis of Hamlet and Don Quixote as outlined in a speech he delivered in 1860. In our original division between energy and enervation the Don would, of course, represent energy; Hamlet would embody enervation. Turgenev's analysis may please neither the Hamlet scholars nor those of Quixote, but his accuracy is of less importance than his perception.

For Turgenev, Don Quixote, though portrayed as "hideous," is a genuine "archetype of self-sacrifice"—a man willing to give up everything in pursuit of an ideal *outside* his ego; Hamlet is precisely the opposite, an internalized man. These two are, for Turgenev, the "two poles of the human axis about which they revolve," and all men are either of one camp or the other.[4] Quixote stands for the eternal, for faith, for the ideal: "The continuous striving toward one and the same goal has fixed the unvarying tenor of his thoughts. . . ." Knowledge is "superfluous." Quixote is an "enthusiast, radiant with his devotion to an idea"—certainly a familiar description of some Romantic types. Hamlet, on the other hand, "lives wholly for himself," an egoist, a "skeptic," "forever agitated," a doubter—and yet one who clings tenaciously to life. Like Coleridge's, Turgenev's Hamlet torments himself on the "double-edged sword of analysis."

Quixote is a figure of benign laughter, but it is the "persistence of the conviction[s]" which earns for him our high regard. The Hamlets, who are snobs, "invent nothing" and leave an impress only of their personality. Yet Turgenev acknowledges a "positive element" in the Hamlet type, and he is not being ironic when he calls it the "creed of negation" (and compares it to Goethe's Mephisto), a negation not touched with Will but with genuine suffering. Further, Hamlet's negation is arrayed against real evil ("falsehood and lying"). So we have the Hamlets, "meditative, scrupulous . . . ineffective and condemned to inaction," and the Quixotes, "half-frantic . . . who aid and urge forward the human race solely because they behold and know only one thing. . . ." Egotism is altruism, motion and immobility two "perpetually contending forces, two unremitting opposites." In life these extremes are never pure: Hamlet steers toward tragedy, Quixote toward comedy. Had Turgenev been alive to read Chekhov, especially the plays, he might have found here and there a momentary perfect union of the two elements. In any case the inertia of a brooding introspective skeptic as against the abandon of a pursuer of the truth shape an important duality of the Romantics and their heritage. *Faust* remains an attempt to embody, very early, both qualities in one figure: the high ideals and aspirations of Quixote and the skeptical self-analysis of Hamlet. The burden Goethe placed upon Faust's admittedly ample shoulders was already recognized by Rousseau (whom Goethe read with care), especially in the Fifth Promenade of *Reveries of the Solitary Walker (Les Reveries du Promeneur Solitaire)*:

> Everything is in constant flux on this earth. [Everything] recall[s] a past which is gone or anticipate[s] a future which may never come into being; there is nothing solid there for the heart to attach itself to. Thus our earthly joys are almost without exception the creatures of a moment. . . . Even in our keenest pleasures there is scarcely a single moment of which the heart could truthfully say: "Would that this moment could last for ever!" And how can we give the name of happiness to a fleeting state which leaves our hearts still empty and anxious, either regretting something that is past or desiring something that is yet to come?[5]

Rousseau has here inaugurated the modern elegiac posture. That Goethe turned the question upside down by having Faust declare it essential *never* to bid the moment stay is clear, but salvation, however arguable, is not tantamount to happiness, and in the end Faust is perhaps no happier than Rousseau.

If, then, ennui and languor are more than merely fashionable moods inspired by fictional models like Werther, René, Adolphe, or the Byronic hero, one must search out more legitimate origins. History, and the individual's awareness of and relationship to it, certainly played a contributing role.

IV
Byron's *Childe Harold's Pilgrimage* and Pushkin's *Eugene Onegin:* Byronic Hero and Byronic Epigone

Byron's persona, Childe Harold, who in time becomes the poet himself, begins as a self-exiled young rake who nurses his grievances and wears his bitterness upon his sleeve with such self-pity that he often verges on the absurd. Yet for all that he is also on increasingly serious terms with history writ large, the remote as well as the recent past. To see him merely as another version of the gloomy egoist or the Byronic hero is not sufficient, not even for the flawed Cantos I and II. By now every close reader has noted the significant metamorphosis which Childe Harold undergoes in the course of the poem, from the almost archaic beginnings, where he is presented to us as a knight errant out of some medieval epic, to the end, when Byron has dropped any pretenses and has supplanted his persona with, if not quite his own person, the poetic persona of the man Byron wished us to see as himself. This shedding of external identifications eventually freed Byron sufficiently to exercise the privileges open only to the autobiographer. This does not imply complete candor or factual accuracy any more than *The Prelude* is a precise account of Wordsworth's "real" life. Yet in both instances—and the comparison is not entirely idle—the final voice is that of the man-poet; and the final authority bares a perspective with artistic honesty which the poet could validate only by use of his own persona. Byron understood this; it accounts in large part for his decision to disentangle the poem from all other personae. This mixture of personae helps to defeat the poem but gives it at least some authenticity.

The more Byron becomes himself, the more he appears to recognize that all the frenetic activity of his hero—the whirlwind travels from country to country—merely masks an emptiness. The initial stanzas of the poem introduce us to a typical good-for-nothing, a rake who has committed mysterious sins, and "felt the fullness of satiety," has left home with pangs on his Cain-cursed brow, unloved, without even an adieu. In short, Harold is launched as a gloomy hero, partly out of the Gothic novel, partly kin to *Werther;* a precursor of Stephen Dedalus who goes into "silence, exile and cunning" without a good-bye to his mother—like Harold, who "parting from [his] mother . . . did shun" (I,X). Cantos I and II have been called travelogues, and not without cause; but they prepare the way for subsequent cantos, though in truth without conscious plan. Although the narrator speaks solemnly of the waste of war or the vanity of nations, these pious sentiments are as yet without genuine conviction. However, the sights of ruined lands are not entirely lost upon the poet, as he feels doomed to wander and observe, possessed of a "life-abhorring gloom / Wrote on his faded brow curst Cain's unresting doom," viewing life with "misanthropic hate" (I, 83–84). Harold's *ressentiment* exposes a sense of waste, guilt, and self-hatred, all of which are made manifest in an essentially "homeless" framework.

In Canto II Childe Harold travels to Italy, where he senses "her gentle glories gone." From Italy he descends still further into the past, to Greece, "where sad Penelope o'erlookd the wave" (II, 39), a journey that touches, like Faust's, the mythic, not merely the historic. He sails past the great battle sites: Actium, Lepanto, Trafalgar; and to distant places of the Grecian isles, "sad relic of departed worth! / Immortal, though no more; though fallen, great!" (II, 73). The tone fits precisely that of Nietzsche's world-weary epigone whom he thought so danger-ous, the only salvation being Byron's increasing interest in contempo-rary Greek politics and his allegiance to a war of liberation. Yet this journey through ruins (a word vital later in the poem) confronts him with perished monuments and pushes him to the simplistic conclusion that Nature alone survives the punishment of Time. As the Canto concludes, Byron, already speaking very much in his own voice, con-siders the "worse of woes that wait on age," to "be alone on earth as I am now," sated not by reckless youth but by waste:

> Roll on, vain days! full reckless may ye flow,
> Since Time hath reft what'er my soul enjoy'd,
> And with the ills of Eld mine earlier years alloy'd.
> (II, 98)

So History and Time now converge. The hero is burdened by both, and the great attraction of these forces creates a personal void which, in the last two cantos, becomes a true abyss.

Isolated, then, by History and Time, Byron broods, feeling aged by "woe, / In deeds, not years piercing the depths of life":

> What am I? Nothing. . . .
> (III, 5–6)

His "springs of life" have been "poison'd," and " 'Tis too late!' " for recovery, for a future. The almost indistinguishable Harold reappears, disillusioned, empty: "life's enchanted cup but sparkles to the brim," and "His had been quaff'd too quickly, and he found / The dregs were wormwood . . ." (III, 7–9). Repeatedly Harold is caught in the "vortex," the "giddy circle," "chasing Time" (III, 11), but now with a "nobler aim" than the dillentante years of a misspent youth. The posturing of Harold is often sophomoric, yet

> The very knowledge that he lived in vain,
> That all was over on this side the tomb,
> Had made Despair a smilingness assume . . .
> (III, 16)

is authentically felt. Byron continues to prop up his ever more shadowy Harold persona, commenting on historical places of interest like a travel book in rhyme with occasional flashes of genuine poetry and personal insight. Napoleon's wasted life shadows Harold's—and Byron's. "There is a very life in our despair, / Vitality of poison" (III, 34): these lines, famous for a number of reasons, also suggest the paradox of energy-enervation, for even despair, passive as it often is, requires energy to sustain it, an egoistic, Hamlet-like energy of self-appraisal, inward and therefore only seemingly passive. Napoleon, a Faustian figure who would so fascinate artists of all kinds in the nineteenth century, strove beyond his limits. He was one of those in whom

> . . . there is a fire
> And motion of the soul which will not dwell
> In its own narrow being, but aspire
> Beyond . . .
> (III, 42)

The traveler reflects on his exile, on his separation from social intercourse, his loneliness, and slowly a note of conciliation begins to color his words. To seek separateness from Mankind must not be equated with hatred. Indeed, he concedes, the fault may lie in him, not the world; and in a mood of reflective stock-taking, he seeks (once more) to find a Wordsworthian solution vis-à-vis Nature: "I live not in myself . . . ," but rather he is part of the natural world which envelops him. But after several stanzas he admits that "this is not my theme," as indeed it is not. And, he promises to "return / To that which is immediate" (III, 72, 76), not the cosmic, an important signal for the reader; for the immediate, rather than the cosmic, draws the poem away from any of the possibilities that permit Wordsworth his "spots of time," his philosophic reveries, his apocalyptic conclusion to *The Prelude*. Byron's desires are frustrated by the limits of his nature: he may desire a Wordsworthian symphony in which time past, present, and future counterpoint into a melodious strain that culminates in triumphant crescendo, but he cannot find a way to "unbosom . . . / That which is most within [him]"; could he do so, could he find a single word to articulate the epiphany, it would be "Lightning." But he must remain "voiceless"—his thought imprisoned (III, 97). It is astonishing that in a poem as verbose as this Byron should seriously feel hampered by an inability to express in language the feelings closest to him. For a moment he appears to admit that the poem and all its language have been only a screen; that words which are equivalents of feelings are either unavailable altogether or at least unavailable to him. "Lightning"—the word is melodramatic, but its Zeus-like swagger suggests an enormous desire on the part of the poet to break through the haze and webs of verbiage. Further,

> Thus far have I proceeded in a theme
> Renew'd with no kind auspices:—to feel
> We are not what we have been, and to deem
> We are not what we should be . . .
> (III, 111)

This betokens both a realization of lost opportunity as well as the moral insight into guilt and consequences. So he remains resigned to a mutual standoff with the world: they have not loved each other. Unlike the more hardened disciples he will foster, Byron still feels that though he has failed to find them there are indeed "Words which are things," hopes, virtue, goodness, even happiness (III, 114). Reconciled that he will not find such words, that for him it is "too late," Byron finally drops the mask and, in an unmediated fourth canto, brings the poem to a conclusion that manages to obscure some of the major insights won in the third canto.

For the last canto, though it has its moments, is weak in the shape of the whole because Byron is incapable of handling his personal voice. (It is the recognition of that limitation which fortunately led him to write *Don Juan.*) "Existence may be borne . . . / In bare and desolated bosoms" (IV, 21); and "All suffering doth destroy, or is destory'd / Even by the sufferer" (IV, 22). Within the context of such rueful homilies Byron demands his soul

> To mediate amongst decay, and stand
> A ruin amidst ruins.
>
> (IV, 25)

This is elegiac with a vengeance. Byron has now shored his fragments against his ruins and beholds, as his sole comfort, the disembodied universe whose meaning he can no longer link to his own existence. The travels in Italy become forays; the commentary becomes a gloss on a kind of buried subtext: it seems as if the poet, coming too near the nerves, has withdrawn to safer ground. In this case safer ground is remote history, the long view backwards, "The double night of ages":

> The Goth, the Christian, Time, War, Flood, and Fire . . .
> . . . .
> Chaos of ruins! who shall trace the void,
> O'er the dim fragments. . . .
>
> (IV, 80, 81)

France and the Reign of Terror are linked to a common fixation on Freedom, an indictment of mankind's folly, a judgment on "History" which "hath but *one* page," the triumph of Tyranny over Freedom (IV, 108). And so "Alas! our young affections run to waste"; "Our life is a false nature"; Time is an "avenger!" Yet he "has not lived in vain"—something internalized perseveres. This reassurance is not especially convincing, but it leaves the poet with a certain resilience necessary for observation, and in addition permits the elimination of the Pilgrim forever, "his visions ebbing fast, / And he himself as nothing," a mere phantom (IV, 120, 126, 130, 137, 164). However attenuated, Byron's life is partially redeemed, and the "unlived life" belongs to the fading Harold. The grand eloquence of language and imagery which concludes the poem is symphonic after all. Byron seeks a desert where he might feel "exalted"; he reconciles himself partially to Man, and sings once more to Nature, bidding the ocean to roll on in its archetypal, rhythmic, synchronic patterns. All things pass, even the greatest empires: "Assyria, Greece, Rome, Carthage, what are they?" (IV, 177, 182). Once more he seeks linkage with "the image of Eternity" (more Shelleyan than Wordsworthian), "the Invisible" (IV, 183). His "theme" dies into an "echo," and the whole pilgrimage has been but a "protracted dream"; if there is any suffering it rests with the pilgrim (or the poet); for the reader has only the gift, or the responsibility, of the "moral of his strain" (IV, 185, 186).

Written—from all the evidence we have—without a master plan, and certainly without any attempt to mend unevenness when changes of direction took the poem here or there, *Childe Harold's Pilgrimage* is almost an accidental, and therefore flawed, attempt at Romantic autobiography. Yet, like many failures, the attempt is interesting; it introduces a treatment of the wasted, unlived life beyond what had clearly been the initial intention: the story of the neer-do-well prodigal who wastes his life in dissoluteness. In the process of change Byron touched on several serious aspects of the theme of unfulfillment: waste, the struggle with historical identity, the confrontation with the faded glories of the past (an "ubi sunt" far more personal than philosophical), the consideration of Time itself as a devourer as well as something to be devoured; the loneliness of exile; and, not least, the exhaustion of a defeated and disillusioned idealism, a striving for infinitude which is decisively limited by the contingencies of the actual. These provide the groundwork for much of what is yet to come in the subsequent analyses of the unlived life.

Finally, *Childe Harold's Pilgrimage* is more attempt than achievement because Byron was unable and unwilling to identify himself with any of the personae of the poem, not even his projected self. The "meaning" of Harold's life lies not in Harold but in his creator; the meaning of the creator of the poem lies not in Byron but in the poem. Still, the issue has been tested. The triple figure in the poem has in substance no palpable life to bring to account. History and Time both dwarf him and, paradoxically, drive him to the isolation which engenders egotistic introspection. Nevertheless, Byron sees his hero(es) placed in a historical continuum and within a temporal frame that urges on us the necessary linkages between individual and society.

In Pushkin's *Eugene Onegin*, his "novel in verse," certainly related to Byron's poem, there is no longer such urgency. Onegin is loosed upon us, free of the moorings of his author—or perhaps more accurately, controlled by Pushkin with unerring skill. And, though the author permits himself both observation and judgment, the drama plays itself out consistently within a given frame. If Onegin experiences the regrets of an unlived life, it is no longer wholly in relation to the massive contexts of abstractions, like Time and History. Pushkin's hero is in part a victim of vanity, boredom, spleen—all deepening symptoms of the *maladie du siècle* which bring to view, as Yeats said of a certain kind of tragedy, "character isolated by the deed"—or, as in this case, by the lack of one?

Pushkin's relationship to his hero is deliberately ambiguous: a "scapegrace," Onegin is nevertheless "a good pal of mine."[6] But the author spares us little in his description of a dissolute dilettante who learned so early how to "dissemble," a poseur who has studied the moods of indifference and moroseness, and has perfected the art of seduction. Onegin is introduced to us as a totally irresponsible, but charming, gay blade, a womanizer, a man with a reputation for wit, good times, and loyalty to no one and nothing but himself. Quite unlike the gloomy Childe Harold, Onegin lives to the limit: he is the busybody of social life (so long as it does not bore him); goes to balls, seduces the young, and cuts a figure around town. The Onegin of the first half of the novel in verse is a self-satisfied, egotistical, manipulative young man who behaves much older than his chronological years, as if there were truly nothing more to learn.

But Onegin's gaiety is forced; inside him slumbers a restive soul, disillusioned with friendship and sincerity. A victim of the English "malady," "spleen," he is hardly suicidal, but finds life devoid of meaning, finds it in fact "quite cold":

> He like Childe Harold, gloomy, languid,
> appeared in drawing rooms . . .
>
> . . . .
>
> nothing touched him;
> he noticed nothing.
>
> (I, 38)

But this is misleading if it is read as an affinity with Byron's hero. Pushkin's creation is a *reader* of *Childe Harold's Pilgrimage,* and as a reader he is also a distanced persona, emulating only the surface while being a creature very much himself. Onegin is one of the early European heroes who is an avid reader of significant books; it would take an extended discussion to assess all the implications of this breed (it may well have begun with Werther's reading of Homer, Lessing, and *Ossian*), but it is not an insignificant subject. A reader of Byron, as we shall see, is far different from being the Byronic hero.[7] For Onegin, Byron's heroes are not models, nor parallels, but precisely what they are literally made to be in the poems: fictional personae about whom one reads and who lend a remote and oblique validation of themselves to the reader's perception. Onegin's story is both personal and detailed, and, indeed, the relationship to Byron becomes a source of Onegin's failure when he leaves his Byron on his library shelves and goes off to travels in search of life's meaning. Onegin's irony (at times even cynicism) is the polished urbanity of a city-dweller. Nature merely becomes an urbanite's escape of which he tires very quickly, in the space of two days (I, 54). Pushkin makes a point of this by arguing that *he*, unlike Onegin, loves the countryside, for

> I'm always glad to mark the difference
> between Onegin and myself. . . .
>
> (I, 56)

To an extent this caution is necessary and deliberate, for Pushkin, from the start, wishes to establish the separation and remain consistent. Moreover, he takes the opportunity to attack Byron's personal intrusion, the abortive autobiographical aspect of *Childe Harold's Pilgrimage:*

> lest a sarcastic reader . . .
> repeat thereafter shamelessly
> that I have scrawled my portrait
> like Byron, the poet of prides
> —as if we were no longer able
> to write long poems
> on any other subject than ourselves!
>
> (I, 56)

The force of this is not misplaced. Although Pushkin's poem clearly reflects some autobiography, the creation of a hero who reads Byron—and, as we later discover, even annotates him!—puts a proper distance between creator and creation. In Harold Bloom's phrase, it anticipates "the anxiety of influence."

Onegin's unlived life takes a very different turn, of course, from Childe Harold's. For Onegin, the missed opportunity—as it will be for some of Henry James's heroes—consists of an inability of recognize it,

until it is, proverbially, "too late." Lensky, the young student infatu-
ated with German idealism, is Onegin's alter ego—albeit a younger
one; a self of Onegin which has been overcome, and hence external-
ized. Although superficially friends, Pushkin makes clear that the two
men were also very different:

> They got together; wave and stone,
> verse and prose, ice and flame,
> were not so different from one another.
>
> (II, 13)

One knows the story: innocent Tatyana, herself a reader of novels
she takes quite seriously, throws herself upon a bored, cruel, arrogant
Onegin. Tatyana's declaration of love is met by a sermon of homilies
and a frank admission that he, Onegin, is incapable of a serious commitment. What he fails utterly to see is the possibility of genuine fulfillment, and this he shall, of course, rue: "this was the way he killed eight
years, having lost life's best bloom" (IV, 9). Country living bores
Onegin, and this boredom, turning to spleen, sets the stage for the
foolish duel with Lensky with its tragic outcome for the younger man.
The cynic kills the idealist: "Onegin like a regular Childe Harold lapsed
into pensive indolence . . ." (IV, 44). In Onegin's case this indolence
turns once more into "the imp of the perverse," and the resultant sport
which Onegin makes of the feelings of others becomes a patented
quality in self-and-other-torturing figures that will inhabit some of the
most famous of Russian fictions. Indolence or idleness may give one the
time to map strategies for such emotional wars, but one needs in addition to be possessed either of an overbearing arrogance or of a very
vulnerable ego. It may be that both come to play their part in Onegin,
but what we see mostly before the duel is the former.

Onegin still regrets his fits of spleen, his insensitivity, his having
hurt others—qualities missing in his later reincarnations. However,
his youthful opponent prepares himself by reading Schiller and com-
posing verses:

> Thus did he write, "obscurely
> and limply" (what we call romanticism—
> though no romanticism at all
> do I see here . . .)
> his weary head,
> upon the fashionable word
> "ideal," Lenski dozed off gently;
>
> (VI, 23)

Falling asleep on one's ideal will cost him his life. Not so Onegin, who, fast asleep, must hurry to be on time. The "ideal" eluded Onegin long ago; and whether on the night preceding the duel he had read any of his Byron, or anything at all, we are not told: we must doubt it. Onegin is contemptuous of all the sham which the duel forces upon him; his only wish is to be done with the affair. Lensky is a predictable victim, a foolhardy Euphorion, a mute inglorious poet indeed. But Pushkin will not let matters lie there; with grave irony he offers us the "other" Lensky, the man who, had he lived, might have been a husband, happy at first, then cuckolded, and at forty suffering from gout, turning eventually dull until death. Implicit is the question: Should one mourn the possibility of *such* a life not being realized?

Onegin, too, becomes a victim of scandal and remorse, and like Byron embarks on a journey, a self-exile. Tatyana's visit to Onegin's abandoned library tells us more about this Byronic epigone than any previous biography by Pushkin. In that library Tatyana, and we, really gets to know our absent hero. On the wall hangs a portrait of Byron, and on a "small column" stands a statuette of Napoleon. We are told that, with a few exceptions, Onegin has ceased to read fiction or anything serious. Byron and "two or three" novels he had spared—

> novels in which the epoch is reflected
> and modern man
> rather correctly represented
> with his immoral soul,
> selfish and dry,
> to dreaming measurelessly given,
> with his embittered mind
> boiling in empty action.
>
>   (VII, 22)

No Schiller this. Here is a reader of works that depict Turgenev's egotistical Hamlet-type: the Heathcliffs and the Underground men of the future, assorted heroes of *ressentiment*. Yet as Tatyana leafs through the volumes she finds no idle man seduced by fictions but a serious and critical reader, one who annotates assent and disapproval—in short, an inquiring spirit. What emerges from these glosses is the true Onegin, not the dashing man she succumbed to so ineptly in her youthful moment of infatuation but

> A sad and dangerous eccentric,
> creature of hell or heaven,
> this angel, this proud fiend, what, then, is he?
>
> (VII, 24)

Is he "a Muscovite in Harold's mantle," a fake: "Might he not be, in fact, a parody?" (VII, 24). Pushkin lays a snare here; the temptation, of course, is to assent to the idea of a parody, for it is very enticing. Yet Onegin, at least once removed from the heroes he judges, is no parody; for as a fictional annotator of another's fiction he has become that other fiction's epigone.

Onegin travels, but Pushkin offers no running commentary on his hero's trips. Instead we get the famous digression on the nature of Russian roads. Onegin's travels are off-stage; he will interest us again only when he returns, and when he does, the gossip about him is not complimentary:

> Is he the same, or grown more peaceful?
> Or does he still play the eccentric?
>
> . . . .
>
> a Harold? A Quaker? a bigot?
> Or will he sport some other mask?
>
> (VIII, 8)

The repeated accusation that Onegin is a poseur, a man of many masks but no real self, is meant, one is certain, in part to make us ask the question ourselves. For in fact Onegin is a complex man, no mere poseur; yet true enough he leaves himself open to the charge of shallowness because he will not permit a stable self to take the measure of the social context. He is as we will learn a weaker man than we ever suspected. Twenty-six now, "without a goal," without employment, unmarried, Onegin is restless and bored: "But it is sad to think that youth / was given us in vain," blown away "like leaves in putrid autumn" (VIII, 11).

On his return Onegin makes his way to a ball where, of course, he rediscovers Tatyana, married, grown into a lovely woman—his missed opportunity. Onegin falls in love and owns up to it; it may be argued that he now simply desires that which he cannot have, but this is not convincing. Smitten, he is described as hopelessly enveloped by feelings as genuine as any he has experienced. Moreover, he is humbled, and such humbling humanizes him. To gain solace in his state of having been rejected—for Tatyana has not responded to his notes—

he reads not Byron now but, among others, Manzoni, Herder, Rousseau, impassioned spirits all. From an egotistical Hamlet Onegin has turned into a Quixote in pursuit of the elusive: he, too, must experience the "ideal." In a scene which reminds one of many Henry James would write, Tatyana concedes that she still loves Onegin, dislikes her society life, and would prefer to live in the country. But for all that she will not renounce her loyalty to her husband. Onegin, struck dumb by such a rebuke, is pictured like a figure in suspended motion; but Pushkin tells us that in his heart there was an ocean of revolt. The sounds of spurs signal the entry of Tatyana's husband, unexpected, and in this compromising moment Pushkin decides to leave Onegin—"forever." Onegin will make no scenes; he will withdraw from the battle, a loser. What his life will be like from now on we are not privileged to know, but enough of it has been rendered for us to call it unfulfilled, not because he loses the love of his life, but because he has permitted himself to be in the position of losing what he could have had. A man's pride and arrogance, cynicism and moroseness, have caused three events which are certainly prominent and serious. He has killed his own youth, his "ideal," when he shot the young poet; he has rejected the redemptive innocence of offered love and knowledge when he lectured Tatyana; and he has now lost forever the opportunity to satisfy what may be the first genuine feelings to rise within him in a very long time. His life is far more void now than it was before, because for the only time in the poem *his* feelings are displaced and deflected, and one may only wonder what books in his library remain to be read, and whether he will again be given to editorializing in their margins? In a sense, of course, it will be others to follow, like Lermontov's Pechorin, who will "read" Onegin, and in that act define themselves, just as Onegin's reading of Byron had defined him.

V

The energy-enervation opposition highlights one of the central dilemmas which the Romantics first encountered and then struggled with mightily. Expenditure of great energies became increasingly deflected, wasted; and such energies so exhausted its participants that the final outcome eventually dissolved into emptiness. It is, of course, no contradiction, only a paradox, to suggest that the very transaction of energy was a depleting process; and, further, that in time the only energy expended would occur at the moment when depletion, or its threat, became as clear to the protagonist as a death sentence.

Even the architecture of the literature reflects the uneasy tension between movement and pressure on the one hand and immobility on the other. That Keats's great "Ode on a Grecian Urn" is an example is, of course, obvious; but the same tension characterizes other works beyond the lyric, where such internal combat is most common. The long and often seamless structure of Byron's *Pilgrimage* is interrupted by the counter-movements of occasional lyric intensity which push vertically against the horizontal line of the poem's seemingly endless journey. Within the very energies of sustaining such a pilgrimage, the pilgrim is reduced to exhaustion. Onegin's case is almost a reverse, since the protagonist's indifference and ennui push against the inevitability of the story's forward progress. If he could, Onegin would contain what cannot be contained; events, however, have their own energy, and ultimately he is swept along in their tide. The result is the same as in Byron: a tension between motion and arrest. While Childe Harold exhausts the narrative, the narrative exhausts Onegin. Writes Albert Cook: "Byron's 'pride' . . . unites elegy and irony in . . . [an] overpersonalized mix of self-pity and contempt for the world."[8]

In Lermontov, Turgenev, and Brontë—the subjects of the next chapter—this process is objectified in differing manifestations, but in each work there is a continuing linkage between restless striving and a desire for rest—indeed for death. In these three works there is a palpable sense of almost physical assertiveness deflated in the end by an equally palpable sense of mental fatigue. The rebels are without cause not because they lack goals, but because they lack the resolve, at the critical moment, that bears the imprimatur of meaning that would otherwise invest their actions with an accompanying purpose.

2 Rebels Without Cause:
Lermontov, Turgenev, Brontë

Wherever the social critics of the nineteenth century looked they discovered isolation: men broken apart from each other.
                    —*Paul Zweig,* The Heresy of Self-Love

The three works examined in this chapter were published between 1840 and 1861. Two are Russian and the third is from the pen of a writer certainly unknown at the time she published *Wuthering Heights,* and probably, one who neither knew of nor was known to the other two. Yet the three works share certain common post-Romantic preoccupations, so to discuss them in relation to one another is not as curious as might appear. Lermontov and Turgenev are sequentially related, of course; and each created characters who have earned the label "superfluous man." It seems Turgenev coined that phrase when, in mid-century (1850), he published his *Diary of a Superfluous Man.* Yet the *Diary* is quite different from Lermontov's *Hero of Our Time* (1840) and Turgenev's own *Fathers and Sons* (1861), and a discussion of it appears in chapter 3.

"Rebels without cause" is not intended to convey in each instance the same thing. Lermontov's Pechorin, Turgenev's Bazarov, and Brontë's Heathcliff do not form a natural circle. Pechorin is a shrug-of-the-shoulder fatalist, whose interest in life is to play it like a game; Bazarov is a serious, if somewhat putative, rebel whose convictions appear to be simply overcome both by his own emotional reservoir (which he resists) and the absurdity of the life he is obliged (or so it appears to him) to live. Heathcliff, whatever his motives—and he has several very good ones—succumbs at the precise moment of his triumph to a weariness and a loss of will which effectively foreclose his

activity and even fail to keep him alive. All three characters are possessed of an enormous energy, however differently it manifests itself;
and all three display a destructive and self-destructive power which
has serious consequences for those who are in the way; each arrives at
a state of lassitude leading to early death; all three are variations of the
ressentiment type. Pechorin dies off-stage in what is clearly a senseless
duel; Bazarov commits what is tantamount to suicide when he fails to
treat an infected wound, a neglect which, as a would-be physician, he
knows will be fatal. Healthcliff simply lies down on his coffin-bed and
starves himself to death. None of the three is able to sustain his rebellious posture beyond a certain point, when it collapses. Heathcliff
remains defiant to the end, as do the others, but defiance is not synonymous with rebelliousness. It becomes evident that in the final stage
of each life the hero does not and cannot muster sufficient conviction
for *any* cause—even the cause of nihilism itself—to sustain life. Without such a cause their deaths become as superfluous as their lives.
Although Heathcliff is by far the oldest of the three[1] (Pechorin and
Bazarov are barely in their early twenties when they die), his death,
like theirs, is testimony to a common failure. Whatever their age at
death, none of the three has lived a teleological life in his own view;
and all three leave behind them an emphatic sense of waste, unrealized potential, and a recognition, however true or false, that they had
seen enough of life, that its vicissitudes were, in the final analysis, not
worth the effort to survive them. All three are convincingly governed
by a will outside themselves, whether that will becomes inimical to
continuing the struggle or simply inimical to further existence.

I
Pechorin: The Shoulder Shrug

Pechorin is most often seen as a Byronic prototype, a "strong individual at odds with the world . . . [and] embittered, cynical and bored."[2]
There is seemingly little to quarrel with such judgments, but to understand the fate of Pechorin it might be best to understand too that he
was, primarily, a weak individual at odds with himself. His weakness
was not, of course, inherent: it emanated from a sense of impotence, a
resentment against life, a failure to integrate, within his identity, his
good and his bad angel. It is true that he tells Princess Mary (in the
story by that name), whom he torments to the threshold of a nervous
breakdown, that he was once an idealist, but, finding himself superior,

or others inferior and insincere, he has renounced his good instincts for the kind of improvised and careless life he now leads. Such an explanation is misleading; in fact, Pechorin's own explanations of his behavior read like double texts: the outer obvious text belies the second truer text, carefully screened out. Like Raskolnikov's reasons for his double murder, Pechorin's explanations are insufficiently cohesive to explain his actions. Psychological and environmental factors may both contribute a share to his behavior, but there remains something else. It is a contest within Pechorin, not between idealism and cynicism but between the meaningful potential in rebellion (existentially speaking) and the potential meaninglessness when rebellion suddenly finds no objective worthy of its energy—in the opinion at least of those generating that rebellion.[3]

"Princess Mary" is the longest and most developed story in *A Hero of Our Time:* the second in a sequence, the last in Pechorin's Journal, and the penultimate story as arranged in the book. The story opens with an ode to a romantic landscape—storm clouds, flower scent, cherry blossoms—and these are being ironically prepared for the dark and even despairing course the story will take. Pechorin is one of those anti-Romantic Romantics, more in the spirit of Heine than Byron. Even more so than Onegin, Pechorin has *read* Byron, not aped him. The misanthropy, the *weltschmerz,* the moodiness—these are superficial poses mobilized in the playing out of various roles, especially when Pechorin ranges himself against the absurdist Romantic, Grushnitsky, an older, more foppish Lenksy. This latter peacock, who voices all the excessively Romantic clichés, which by 1840 (the date of Heine's *Romantische Schule*) were already being scorned, even in Russia, serves as the antithesis to Pechorin: it is Grushnitsky, not Pechorin, whose flaw is being at odds with a world that cannot, and will not, take him seriously. This sense of being slighted, of being made the butt of others' derision, generates a deep hatred in a man whose life is dependent on the size of his epaulettes.

Pechorin's friend and confidante, Dr. Werner, is still another version in this triad of Romantic variants: the total cynic whose sense of "play" is tempered by a certain prudence which makes him stop short of realizing action for fear of the consequences. Up to a point he is a cynical gymnast playing at life for his own amusement, but that point stopped at a boundary line Pechorin was prepared to—and did—cross. Werner's drawing-room witticisms are not equivalent to Pechorin's actions: the duel and its consequences, and the price he exacts from an incipient neurasthenic girl.

Pechorin's leitmotif is the shrug of the shoulder; and since it is so insistently used (it occurs on five occasions), its meaning in each instance serves to delineate his character from yet another perspective. Clearly a shrug of the shoulders can mean several things, ranging from indifference to exasperation, from cynicism to genuine puzzlement. Although Pechorin seems to feel all of those at one time or another, each act is engendered by a slightly different motive. Seeing the act of shoulder shrugging in context becomes not merely important as a means of understanding Pechorin but serves also as a chronological biography which Lermontov, with his placement of stories, builds with great structural care. He is, as Werner tells him, like the hero in some modern novel for the young princess, much as Stendhal's Julien Sorel was for Mme de Rênal and Mathilde de la Mole or Rodolphe and Léon were for Emma Bovary. It remains one of the more constant and intriguing themes in nineteenth-century literature: the fictions which characters have read often distort their expectations, which, when they clash with realities, undo them. The Princess of this story fancies a Prince, but the story is not a fairy tale; if anything "Princess Mary" is an anti-Märchen, and as such it intrudes not only on the Princess's expectations but also on ours. Every element of the Romantic Märchen, even the enchanting drinking well, turns out to be merely a prop in an all-too-real world.

Pechorin's one genuine commitment appears to be a love he feels for Vera, a woman with whom he has had a previous affair. She now turns up married, gravely ill, loyal to her older and infirm husband— but, like Tatyana, still in love with Pechorin, whose code of honor, however, requires that he treat the husband with respect, even with affection. Meanwhile he has also witnessed Princess Mary flirting with Grushnitsky, and he has determined that for such an assault on his pride he shall punish her (and, eventually, Grushnitsky as well). The exultant Grushnitsky, thinking Princess Mary is really smitten with him, asks Pechorin's opinion. Resisting an urge to speak, to call him an idiot, Pechorin merely shrugs his shoulders. But the context is clear. This shrug is not primarily a reply to Grushnitsky's question but to Pechorin's own, a sentence earlier: "What does [Vera] love me for so much—I really don't know; particularly since she is the only woman who has completely understood me. . . . Can evil possibly be so attractive?" This question and shoulder shrug are followed five days later with an attempt at self-analysis under the diary entry 3 June. Why, asks Pechorin, does he bother to play these games with Grushnitsky? Is it an "imp" of perversity, a desire to destroy someone else's illusions? He is possessed, be believes, with a craving to see both suffering and joy in others only as they relate to him, like "food sustaining the strength of [his] soul." What, after all, is happiness but to be "the cause of sufferings and joys"—"the sweetest possible nourishment for our pride?" He recognizes his own emptiness, his state of anomie, and within that loneliness he recognizes also that his resentment takes the form of sadism and revenge: "the first ache gives us an idea of the pleasure of tormenting another." In the remainder of this, the first of two self-analyses, Pechorin asserts that tranquillity may be a sign, albeit not always visible, of "great, though concealed strength," and that outbursts of passion are merely that, antithetical to "plenitude and depth of feelings." What he may really be justifying is a husbanding of energy which, lying dormant, uses itself up in the act of being contained with the predictable result of exhaustion.

Unlike the "mysterious" Byronic hero, whose past is both unexplained and fraught with hints and guesses, Pechorin's account of his own past is reasonably detailed and serves as an attempted explanation (and justification) of his behavior. He tells Vera:

> I was modest . . . I became secretive. I felt deeply good and evil; . . . I became rancorous. I was gloomy. . . . I felt myself superior to [others] . . . I became envious. I was ready to love the whole world—none understood me: and I learned to hate. My colorless youth was spent in a struggle with myself and with the world. . . . I became a moral cripple. One half of my soul did not exist. . . .

Yet the fact that this is told to Vera and, moreover, that it is followed by an analysis of what effect it has and will have on Vera sends suspicion on, and undermines, the whole passage. Vera "was sorry for me!"—that seems to be what he is after. Of course that he is a "moral cripple" may indeed be true; the accuracy of the sequence of events as Pechorin tells it, however, is questionable. Pechorin is nearly always on stage; and whenever he seems to step outside his diary, we must be cautious.

Only a few pages later Pechorin gives us a more honest accounting. He wonders whether he was destined to function as the agent of ruin in "other people's hopes," to be the precipitating agent, "the indispensable persona in the fifth act" (as Ibsen's Gregers in *The Wild Duck* is fated to think of himself as the thirteenth at the table). Perhaps he was fated to be no more than the writer of "bourgeios tragedies" and "family novels." Pechorin squarely faces the folly of delusions of grandeur, and like later Chekhovian characters he realizes the absurdity of vaunting pride. "How many people," he writes, "in the beginning of life, think they will finish it as Alexander the Great or Lord Byron, and instead, retain for the whole of their existence, the rank of titulary counsellor?" Such insight is on the mark: Pechorin's realization that he, too, has become a reader of Byron, hardly an emulator (or, like Grushnitsky, a grotesque Byronic manqué), reads more true than the account of his misanthropy. Life is a drama; the resolution requires a negative agent, and Pechorin sees himself as the intrusive and destructive force, "the denouement of other people's dramas." Such a self-appraisal as intruder, interloper, *homo ex machina* in the drama of life suits Pechorin's role in this story to perfection. An outsider who swoops in at the kill but remains himself uninvolved: he almost succeeds in playing that role to the end.

The next shrug of Pechorin's shoulders comes during his horse trot with Princess Mary. He has overstimulated her sexuality, already vulnerable; the poor woman prostrates herself out of sheer desperation. " 'Perhaps you wish me to be the first to say that I love you.' " After a silence, a second question: " 'Do you wish it?' " He merely answers, " 'What for?' "—and shrugs his shoulders. Again the shrug seems clear: he is pulling the Princess's nerves tauter still, so that she whips her horse and flees in a state of near hysteria. Still, once again, the shrug is not meant entirely for the person to whom it is given; it is not unreasonable to assume that both " 'What for?' " and the shrug are also intended for Pechorin himself. Truly *he* does not know "What for?"

In his penultimate interview with the Princess, Pechorin once again shrugs his shoulders:

> "I shall tell you the whole truth," I replied
> to the Princess, "I shall neither justify
> myself, nor explain my actions. I
> do not love you."
> Her lips paled slightly.
> "Leave me," she said almost inaudibly.
> I shrugged my shoulders, turned, and walked
> away.

It is not without reason that the very next sentences, opening a new diary entry two days later, should articulate what might well have inspired the opening sentences of Dostoevsky's *Notes from the Underground:* "I sometimes despise myself. . . . Is this not why I despise others? . . . I have become incapable of noble impulses." The shoulder shrug coupled with this self-hatred relate: they cut a figure whose habit of shrugging has moved close—both physically and psychologically—to shuddering. No reasonable reader can dismiss the physical gesture of shrugging as mere boredom and indifference; the interrogative complicity of a shrug is a disabling rather than an enabling gesture, and it removes, always with more force, any chance for Pechorin's regeneration: he really has become an enervated "moral cripple."

After reading in Scott's *Old Morality* (reading seems to be a habit among literary duellists and suicides), the restless Pechorin asks himself the most fundamental questions. Well, what if he is to die? He will not be missed. Why did he live—so far as he *has* lived—"and for what purpose was [he] born?" It would seem a purpose existed, and that it even may have been "lofty," for in his soul he feels "boundless strength," energy. But, not knowing his purpose, he has become fate's axe, "an executioner's tool," enamored of self only. Life is both "Absurd" and "vexatious," and yet even in the face of this one lives on, perhaps out of "curiosity," perhaps out of sheer habit.

Any attempt to force Grushnitsky into reconciliation fails. All offers for a peaceful resolution are rejected.

> "We shall fight."
> I shrugged my shoulders.

And this shrug seems to say: I cannot prevent it; I am once more the agent come to intrude in the fifth act, the axe of fate: there is no *will* in this. It is ordained. After the duel has resulted in Grushnitsky's death, the *"Finita la Commedia"* is followed by Dr. Werner's "horror" and Pechorin's shrug of the shoulder, this time conveying more than a mere "Well, that's life!" or "So it goes!" but, also, "I could not prevent it: it was beyond my doing. You saw me try to prevent it." Literary body language conveys here, as in later writers, like Hemingway, a tone of voice which is not spelled out. Gesture for language is rich as a device; Mann and Proust will use both to create a wholly new way of solidifying character(istics). Pechorin's last shrug of the shoulders invites speculations, and the story provides sufficient materials to make them plausible. Pechorin's dilemma is his impotence, not his world-weariness: he cannot control events; they control him. That perception must be validated on his terms. For to make his shrug a mere gesture of callousness is belied by the response a few lines later when he involuntarily shuts his eyes to avert seeing Grushnitsky's bloody corpse. Still more to the point, when he reads Vera's letter ("We part forever . . ."), he pursues her hopelessly on horseback until he kills the animal and, falling beside it on the wet grass, "began crying like a child" for "a long time." Pechorin weeps and sobs, shedding himself of all feelings he has succeeded in imprisoning in himself and others. Only alone, in the dark, concealed from others, does he abandon the pursuit of "perished happiness"; only then does he cease to elegize over the vanished ideals of his youth. But the expended energy of this cathartic outburst has left him totally depleted, emptied of the desire to continue playing the game of life. With redemptive honor as a last refuge of his own code, he visits Princess Mary. On the way he meets Dr. Werner, but he feels "as cold as stone." His audience with the Princess, in which he tries to persuade her that she must despise him, is no longer merely the fifth act, though it still has something of that in it. He accepts her "I hate you" with a thank you, a bow, and a departure. This time, there is no shoulder shrug; the bow is assent, not query: it is indeed so, it says; and your contempt, your hate, however well deserved, can have no further effect on me.

The closing story (in Lermontov's arrangement, not chronologically), is "The Fatalist," and it follows "Princess Mary." (Chronologically it is the third story.) It is far less rich and detailed, but it nevertheless succeeds in being a most appropriate ending to the known career of this hero. For in "The Fatalist" Pechorin deliberately tempts fate, having given himself over to the shrug of the shoulders which leaves few ambiguities: life is fate; fate is life. A man called Vulich decides to test his own fate, and, when he survives a game of Russian roulette, he is shortly thereafter killed by a drunken cossack run amuck. Pechorin's "fatalism"—after he decides to test his own fate by successfully capturing the homicidal cossack—is certainly couched in empirical language. After all, what has this taught me, he muses, but that individual exertions on behalf of anything are quite useless: "I like to have doubts about everything: this inclination of the mind does not impinge upon resoluteness of character. . . . For nothing worse than death can ever occur; and from death there is no escape!" In Turgenev's terms, Pechorin has become an incipient "Hamlet": he will doubt; he will be melodramatic; he will play with life with the abandon bred not of ennui or depression but of the conviction that control over life is illusory and useless. Pechorin's conviction of his impotence in the face of fate is not, however, the resignation we associate with the *moira* of Greek tragedy, and the distinction between the two is essential. The helplessness in the face of fate, which was the heart of Greek tragedy, was the consequence of an acceptance (albeit one which came in the wake of the shock of recognition) that the gods ruled our future whatever our individual destiny in the space that life allotted to us from birth to death. Clearly the matter of personal comportment in this interval became the central issue. Although Oedipus's fate was sealed, his behavior was not, and this makes for the tension of the play. In Pechorin the acceptance of fate is neither gracious nor compliant, and deportment becomes irrelevant. Pechorin accepts the dominance of fate and the impotence of will with something already approaching the naturalistic hiss of later decades: we are overdetermined and victimized. There remains only a sense of defiance in the helplessness to avert the source of events, and in addition a sense of justification for one's deportment, not of dignity but of rebelliousness and resentment. Such a state of mind is quite different from the heroic concept of the Greek tragic hero. The latter's unlived life was indeed to steer us into tragedy; the modern unlived life, before it ends in a kind of nihilism, was first to travel, as we shall see, the routes toward comedy.

It is Hegel not surprisingly who offers us the most lucidly stated distinction between the ancient and the modern conception of Fate. For the Greek Necessity is a form of *freedom:* it enables him to choose his manner of accommodation. "The Greek . . . calms his soul with that. *It is so;* there is nothing to be done against it; with this I must content myself; just in this feeling that I must be content with it . . . [;] we have the freedom which is implied in the fact that it is mine." In adopting this attitude, the Greek freed himself from the vexatiousness of particular ends and particular disappointments. Disharmony comes only when the "*It is so*" is accompanied by "That ought to be." "Misfortune, discontent, is nothing but the contradiction implied in the fact that something is contrary to my will." Moderns speak of Fate quite differently from the Greeks: "We speak of just, unjust, merited fate. We use the word fate by way of explanation . . . as suggesting the reason of any condition in which individuals are . . . fate implies that there exists some sort of reason," and we conceive of fate as "that which befalls [one] as something unmerited." As Hegel recognizes, such a view of fate is "the direct opposite" of "the reverent regard for necessity," and it engenders directly the opposite of serenity: turmoil, vexation, rage. Hegel's distinctions serve to explain much in the modern perceptions of life, and they are applicable to other works I deal with in succeeding chapters.[4]

II
Bazarov: Life in a Box

To join Turgenev's and Brontë's heroes in a parallel discussion may seem perverse, for aside from some rather general typological similarities their association is by no means natural or obvious. Both, it is true, are rebels; both develop a dour personality; each pursues living with little joy; and in the end each gives up the struggle. But these are not superficial similarities; they describe a growing family of characters in the fictions of the nineteenth century both in Britain and on the Continent. However, one can achieve still more in pairing these heroes, not so much by "comparing" them but by identifying rather closely certain traits of character which bring each to his final surrender, for it is the end, more than the means, which, in this instance, compels our attention.

Remembering the essential cultural differences between Bazarov and Heathcliff is essential, of course. For example, there is a significant political element in the former which is altogether missing in the latter. How serious Bazarov is about his professed "nihilism" remains in dispute: one guesses that his nihilism as a cause for his political actions—such as they are—is over and done with by the time Turgenev introduces him to us in the novel. Still he has been politically conscious. Now Heathcliff is no neophyte about the ethics of property, class, and contempt for the ruling authority, but to suggest that such a concern is as primary or as articulated as in Bazarov does not conform with the facts of the book.[5] So whereas Bazarov is at least a proto-political creature, Heathcliff is something less; while the former's agenda of ideological antagonisms is spelled out in detail, the latter's is more limited and more personal, more intensely individual. Hence Heathcliff draws fire more as a cosmic aberration than an antisocial good-for-nothing, which is often Bazarov's fate. And yet, as we may come to see, the two are ultimately not so far apart as may appear, even in this arena. *Fathers and Sons* is certainly full of oral history, and Bazarov's conception of his eventual uselessness is closely tied to his disillusionment with the utopian visions of negativity—a paradox he is clever enough to recognize. Heathcliff, on the other hand, self-educated (off-stage) on the laws of genealogy and property, comes on the scene to right the wrong which a snobbish and debilitated society has heaped upon him. At the end of his pursuit, as megalomaniacal as Ahab's of the White Whale, he suddenly experiences a collapse of will, serene enough, it appears, in the recognition that the fruits of revenge are not worth having, that energy expended—while it served to feed revenge—was viable only to the point of achievement.[6] Bazarov may have more in common with Onegin; Heathcliff perhaps more resembles Pechorin. All four, one thinks, would have understood one another.

Although Heathcliff precedes Bazarov chronologically by fourteen

years, we do better to reverse chronology and deal first with
Turgenev's hero, for Bazarov may illuminate certain aspects of
Heathcliff to which we would otherwise not be alert. Surely at a point
which may antedate his appearance in the novel, Bazarov was a rebel
with a cause: whether that cause be called "nihilism" or simply a protest against fathers, a generational division.[7] But we are likely to be too
much taken in by Bazarov's verbal (and later physical) duels with
Arkady's uncle, Pavel, who deliberately removes himself not only
from the historical process (he is, it will be recalled, an Anglophile).
Pavel is, in one sense, an epigone; so, too, in another sense is Bazarov.
Neither believes he is needed, and each ultimately believes himself
excluded, not merely in ordinary cultural terms but in a time-sense as
well. Pavel sees himself excluded from the present as much as
Bazarov, though, of course, from different ends of the time-line.
Pavel clings tenaciously to a vanished past, and his whole life becomes
a dirge, an elegiac interlude; Bazarov, rejecting his genuine potential,
abjures the present for a future in which he sees only surcease: that is,
death. Their eventual duel is not between idealism and nihilism, past
and present, reaction and revolution, the old and the new. In structural terms, it is a duel between impotence and impotence, for the
impotence in the face of realities bedevils Pavel as much as it does
Bazarov. Each would assert the energy to effect an altered state more
fitting to his temperament; but neither finds it possible to mobilize
that energy, and both are exhausted by the effort. Although literally
speaking Pavel survives Bazarov, Turgenev makes it clear that, after
the last exertion, the duel, Pavel, too, is "dead," and his "ruined life"—
a series of unlived possibilities—has come effectively to an end. Urging his more accommodating brother to marry the woman bearing his
child, peasant though she is, and so overcoming his strong sense of
class pride on that crucial point (he has himself more than felt a
twinge of affection for the same woman), Pavel puts behind him his
life in Russia, that is to say the struggle itself. "I will go away as soon as
he is married, somewhere a long way off—to Dresden or Florence,
and will live there till I drop." And so "Pavel Petrovich moistened his
forehead with eau de cologne, and closed his eyes. His handsome,
emaciated head, the glaring daylight shining full upon it, lay on the
white pillow like the head of a dead man. . . . And indeed he was a
dead man."[8]

Bazarov has proved to be a problem from the start, and it is not
necessary to detail the various contemporary reactions to him and to
Turgenev's novel. However, it is useful to keep in mind that Bazarov is
not merely a "problem" because political factions have quarreled about

what they perceive him to represent. Bazarov's problem is also personal; a young, bright, talented prospect for a productive life, he not only fails to fulfill that promise but also deliberately permits himself to become useless—or convinces himself that he is and so hastens his death, with self-malice aforethought.

At the beginning of the story, Bazarov's so-called nihilism is already a negative, self-destructive defensive cloth which Bazarov uses to cover his authentic emotions. Clearly his belief is no longer attached to an active principle (which is why his more naive friend, Arkady, is so puzzled), but it shapes for him the only available countermeasure against a general state of insipid hypocrisy and romantic nostalgia for which he has the highest contempt. His verbal jousts with the aristocratic pretender, Pavel, are more amusements than impassioned articulations of political convictions: they relieve his boredom and also provide his contempt with an appropriate target. Bazarov's rudeness, his uncouth demeanor, his ungratefulness even to his indulgent parents are all far more the result of a deep-seated self-hatred and a sense of unworthiness than they are arbitrary expressions of arrogance. Why does Bazarov have such a damning vision of himself? Perhaps because he finds himself in a middle position between beliefs he has already forsaken and a society he cannot embrace. Rebelliousness, having no genuine creed on which it rests, finds itself merely sparring with easily vanquished opponents, like Pavel or young Arkady and his father. That being insufficient, rebelliousness returns with some vengeance back upon itself, where it destroys the rebel himself.

Pavel's unlived life is a romantic version of Bazarov's. Both men, it turns out, fall madly in love, pursue, and lose. For Pavel the loss is crushing: "a lonely bachelor, [he] was entering upon that indefinite twilight period of regrets that are akin to hopes, and hopes that are akin to regrets, when youth is over, while old age has not yet come"— that state so familiar in, say, Chekhov and Henry James. Bazarov's love affair is quite different (it is not ever really an "affair"); and yet there is some irony in his response to Pavel's grand passion which he hears about before he meets Odinstova, to whom he eventually succumbs. About Pavel he says, ". . . I must say that a man who stakes his whole life on one card—a woman's love—and when that card fails, turns sour, and lets himself go till he's fit for nothing, is not a man, but a male." Little did Bazarov suspect that soon he, too, would be embarking on a grand passion of his own, and at a much younger age, though it is true that Bazarov comes to *his* love-crisis with a ripe history for disillusionment.

For what, after all, is Bazarov's nihilism except the inability to place himself either personally or historically. If, as he says, he feels even Arkady's father to be "behind the times; his day is done," then he, Bazarov, is *outside* the times, rather than abreast of them. The facile politicization of "nihilism" is not for Bazarov, who sees through a charade quickly. He may regale everybody's "romanticism"—these are almost the 1860s—but his own version of romanticism, like Onegin's and Pechorin's, is itself out of fashion. These are no longer the days for Promethean individualism or Faustian self-aggrandizement. Nor is there any room for self-pity, which Onegin and Pechorin were wont to indulge in at critical points in their stories. Bazarov will not shed a tear in the course of the book, not because he is without feelings—of tenderness or rage—but precisely because he cannot give them expression. Such a conflict often produces what Freud defined as "melancholia."

Bazarov's desire to believe in nothing is naturally an affirmation, and the nothing he believes in becomes pointedly suffused with a sense of aggression, so that often in the course of his story we see him as if he were trapped, clawing in vain at emptiness. There is no doubt that the novel thrusts at us a generational motif: fathers and children, Romantics and Nihilists, the 1840s and the 1860s. But to see only the clash of generations limits the work. Or, to put it another way: to see the story as confined to a particular generational struggle isolates the problem historically. What Turgenev recognizes is the inevitable repetition of the dilemma: the young rebel, become older, beget their own young who in turn rebel against the sobered parents once themselves children. The dates are not incidental, to be sure; but their chief end is to locate a time-span which was readily recognizable to Turgenev's readers. Arkady's father, more pliable and flexible, and less of an ideologue than either Bazarov or his brother Pavel, recognizes the repetitiveness of conflict to his benefit; to their detriment neither Bazarov nor Pavel does. Both are so rooted in their historicity, their present and recent past, that they fail to see the archetypal quality of their problem.

Nicolai, like his son, Arkady, is able and even eager to accommodate; Pavel and Bazarov cannot. Early in the book, one evening, Nicolai has an attack of sadness which has him "shedding tears, causeless tears" as he ponders the loss of his former life and the possible gain of a future one. Not so, however, Pavel:

> Pavel Petrovich went to the end of the garden, and he too grew thoughtful, and he too raised his eyes towards the heavens. But nothing was reflected in his beautiful dark eyes except the light

> of the stars. He was not born a romantic, and his fastidiously
> dry and sensuous soul, with its French tinge of misanthropy,
> was not capable of dreaming. . . .

The distinction is critical and informs the whole novel, for Bazarov
bears a striking resemblance to such a description; in the duel scene
they quarrel as admirers more than as enemies. An inability to dream
implies that one is fixated on a past and a present. The past is seen as
lost, whether one mourns it (Pavel) or welcomes its passing (Bazarov);
the present is seen as empty with the loss it has sustained. And since
the dreams we dream are in part an attempt to leapfrog between past
memory and future fantasy over the dangerous present, the inability
to dream deprives one of the sustaining elements which define continuity. Hence the unlived life of the nondreamer is truncated existence
rooted to a moment in time and advancing only as time moves, incre-
mentally. One is never either behind or ahead of time, never in the
past nor the future. For Pavel this means "death" and a retreat, not to
a fantasy world in the future but to a contrived world of a past in
which he is just as unmoving as he was in the clutches of the present.
Bazarov literally dies feeling equally useless. Both have wasted their
lives since neither has the ability to be in touch, affectively, with a
before and after. Ironically Pavel considers Bazarov's "nihilism" a
"void, a vacuum," but though he might not recognize it by that name,
Pavel, too, is a "nihilist."

For each man there are moments when, unawares, they are thrust
into a future. For Pavel it is his hidden affection for his brother's mis-
tress, Fenichka; for Bazarov it is the shattering experience with the
stylish older widow, Odinstova, which is not hidden but, on the contrary, much too fully expressed. The lady herself is highly repressed,
compulsively orderly; and the disturbance of feelings which the arrival
of Bazarov initiates makes her uneasy and stiffens her resolve to remain
unattached. This occasions the famous "misunderstanding" scene.
Bazarov's anti-Romanticism is sabotaged by his infatuation: "he expressed more strongly than his calm contempt for everything romantic; but when he was alone, with indignation, he recognized the romantic in himself." She, on the other hand, is less susceptible, though she
admits to her unhappiness " 'because . . . I have no desires, no passion
for life.' " Indeed what is true of Pavel and Bazarov with respect to their
inability to dream is true also of Odinstova: " 'So many memories, and
nothing to remember, and before me, before me—a long, long road,
and no goal. . . . I have no wish to go on.' " She is, as she says, not
disillusioned but dissatisfied, in search of a compelling interest. Love?

asks Bazarov, and then renders judgment: "and you can't love; and that's where your unhappiness lies." To some extent he is right—for both of them. When he finally confesses his love for her, he finds a stronger person than himself. He rushes at her with passion, with lust, and with love, but she stands cowering in a corner of the room: " 'You have misunderstood me.' " Bazarov is checked; his pride and his prejudice will not permit him to remain. She feels remorse for having had her peace disturbed, her tranquillity in the static present; she is forced to ponder "the sense of life passing by . . . she had forced herself to go up to a certain point, forced herself to glance behind it, and had seen behind it not even an abyss, but a void . . . or something hideous." Her final thought about Bazarov during this episode is fear, but she deceives herself (" 'I'm afraid of this man' "): she is afraid not of him but of her own feelings, which have begun to stir memory with desire. " 'You can't bring back the past,' " Bazarov warns her; but Odinstova is trapped in its misleading and seductive emptiness, which she mistakes for reassurance.

Bazarov's misanthropy is psychologically validated by Odinstova's rejection. Inevitably the hatred he professes mirrors a hatred of self, exposed, vulnerable, and now humiliated, maintaining a "negative attitude, by virtue of [his] sensations." After the near fight with Arkady in the haystack, interrupted by the appearance of his father, Bazarov is on his way toward total indifference. He reminds us then of Pechorin: " 'Wouldn't you like some currant tea, Enyusha?' inquired Arina Vlasyevna. Bazarov merely shrugged his shoulders." He leaves home, returns to Arkady's house, where he throws himself into work, and ignores Pavel until the latter discovers him flirting with Fenichka and subsequently challenges him to that fated duel. The duel over, it is now Bazarov's turn to snub Odinstova. From melancholy and wounded love to misanthropy, and now to despair! Bazarov has now reached the last of his phases in a journey that has permitted him little motion. " 'Ah, my dear friend,' " he tells Arkady, " '. . . You see what I'm doing; there seems to be an empty space in the box, and I'm putting hay in; that's how it is in the box of our life; we would stuff it up with anything rather than have a void.' "

"The box of our life": it is a telling metaphor, for it explains not only the central meaning of the novel's major characters but also perhaps helps us as well to appreciate what has sometimes been called the novel's lack of plot. For it is true that the novel seems static; Bazarov and Arkady move back and forth like so many pieces on a chess board: departure and return from and to Arkady's home, Bazarov's home, Odinstova's estate.[9] In a sense the novel is a "box."

Bazarov feels trapped in it as if he were indeed the captive of one of life's experiments. With few exceptions Turgenev generates a claustrophobic feeling; the peripatetic nature of Bazarov's life is hemmed in by the walls of his "box of life," and at the end he suffocates. In the haystack scene Bazarov rationalizes away the meaning of the present by indulging in cosmic wool-gathering: " '. . . the period of time in which it is my lot to live is so petty beside the eternity in which I have not been, and shall not be. . . . Isn't it hideous?' " Such self-diminution is the last refuge of the defeated misanthrope. The young Bazarov, already foreseeing his death, real or in spirit, begins to banter with the peasants about the future. " 'Come,' he would say, 'expound your views of life to me, friend; you see they say all the strength and future of Russia lies in your hands, a new epoch in history. . . .' " But the peasants are not interested in new epochs of history, only in continuing the status quo which indeed makes them subservient: " 'the stricter the master's role, the better for the peasant.' " Bazarov, hearing such talk, "shrugged his shoulders contemptuously. . . ." He stands on an island; there are no followers, neither the Arkadys headed for middle-class life, nor the peasants desiring no change, nor certainly the gentry who live frozen in a precarious *tableau vivant* not to be disturbed by passion.

What is left but to shrug one's shoulders at a cut about to be infected by typhus? Is this suicide? Well, not in a literal, but in an unconscious sense, the failure to apply the caustic to the wound is like a final shoulder shrug. Life, said Mann, is an infection, and we die of it. As he lies down knowing he will not get up again, Bazarov knows there remain inevitable sequences: Odinstova will visit, he is no longer a threat; his father will urge upon him the rites of religion; and he will himself, in his semidelirium, tell us what he truly feels, and appropriately he tells it to Odinstova:

> " 'Well, good-bye! live long, that's the best of all, and make the most of it while there is time. . . . And, you see, I thought too: I'd break down so many things, I wouldn't die, why should I, there were problems to solve, and I was a giant! . . . My father will tell you what a man Russia is losing. . . . That's nonsense. . . . I am needed by Russia. . . . No, it's clear, I am not needed. And who is needed? The shoemaker's needed, the tailor's needed. . . .' "

What an irony that, at Bazarov's death, it is the mild, otherwise stoical father who, in his grief, finds the cause to vent his rebelliousness that ought to have been his son's—a rebelliousness against the meaning and wanton ways of life. " 'I said I should rebel,' he shrieked hoarsely, 'and I rebel, I rebel!' "

Turgenev's final pages are suffused with gentle irony. Odinstova marries one of the "future leaders of Russia, a very clever man, a lawyer, with vigorous practical sense, a strong will, and remarkable eloquence . . . cold as ice"—each a quality Bazarov did *not* possess, for even Bazarov's cleverness was not slick. Nicolai and his son live happily on the farm, the father busily involved in the ongoing process of emancipation. Once Fenichka's voice has intruded upon the sacred reveries over his dead wife and had "brought back to him his grey hairs, his age, the present," an unwelcome jolt. But Nicolai can survive. In Dresden, meanwhile, living the life of a dilettante, is the self-exiled Pavel, forever the man without country and without history and without a future. Bazarov's parents hover over the tranquil grave of their dead son, praying in silence, wiping dust from the gravestone. Can all this prayer be for nought? asks Turgenev. "Oh, no! However passionate, sinning, and rebellious the heart hidden in the tomb," the flowers on the grave site "tell us . . . of eternal reconciliation and of life without end." Life without end from the life ended without really having been lived. Rebelliousness has been subdued, for it had no object on which to chafe, no cause either to challenge or to uphold. Pavel and Odinstova live, but it is clear Turgenev does not believe their lives to be authentic expressions of a purposeful existence. Perhaps Arkady, his father, their wives and children live—decently, unimpassioned, uninspired. Only Bazarov's parents, in feeling their love as deeply as they feel their prayers, are true survivors who possess a passion, albeit that passion is clothed in the grief of dispossession and, with gentle irony, restricted by a simplicity and naiveté that could not have understood the dead son for whom they grieve.

III
Heathcliff: Doors and Windows

If Bazarov's life is enclosed in a box—or, as he says, he perceives life to be a box, necessary to fill in order to escape the void, since nature cannot tolerate a vacuum—then *Wuthering Heights* is a story of doors and windows, of delineation, enclosure, and struggle, either of being out and getting in or of being in and getting out. The prisons in this novel depend on one's perspective: they may be either inside or outside. Except for a brief absence from the book, during which he educates himself off-stage, Heathcliff's location in the book (as is nearly everyone else's) is highly confined and circumscribed. Wuthering Heights and Thrushcross Grange are the two geographical sites between which lie the moors, beyond which lies the town. Heathcliff is seldom absent from these three coordinates.

That *Wuthering Heights* is a book of enclosures is not meant to be a fresh insight. Dorothy van Ghent's essay on the use of the window in the novel is brilliant in opening up to us a range of thematic material directly related to the inside(r)/outside(r) dialectic which structures the book's motif and its leading characters.[10] In addition to the window, however, which with its transparency has its defined functions, Brontë also used, in even more abundance, the image of the door (or the gate). Indeed the door dominates the novel from beginning to end, and it literally forms its architectural structure. Throughout, persons struggle at doors and doorways; their entries and exits are seldom, if ever, idle, but most always signal some significant, if repetitious, act of trying to penetrate to the inner world, however dangerous, behind the door; or to the outer world, however uncertain, beyond the door. No door, no gate, is secure enough to keep anyone in or out indefinitely. Hence the struggle always succeeds; people always do get in or out. It is only when Healthcliff ceases to struggle that doors and gates are no longer locked or bolted, and intercourse from one place to another is achieved with tranquillity and with ease. Ultimately it is Heathcliff who holds all keys—literally and figuratively; so his cessation of will equals his surrender of all keys.

The energy Heathcliff expends in pursuit of domination has been called in the novel—and by some critics—otherworldly. It is certainly an awesome display of willpower, aggression, and rebellious defiance. No one in the world that surrounds Heathcliff is spared his outbursts of violence and cruelty, vengeance and passion. That at some point he would exhaust himself by such an expenditure seems in itself neither surprising nor unexpected. Yet Heathcliff's sudden collapse is not merely a breakdown of will: it is a vision which, like Pechorin's and Bazarov's, reveals the void of *his* life, its uselessness, its negativity, its triviality. These, then, are the matters that shake him and will concern us, for that rather sudden glimpse into the uselessness of one's life, even the uselessness of all that preceded, is as powerful as the motives that originally propelled him on his twenty-year-long rampage.

And what, after all is said, is the cause of Heathcliff's towering rage? No sensible reason can be entirely ruled out: he is certainly an outcast, a classless waif, a rejected man who finds no home either with the fading aristocrats, like the Lintons, or the dissipated gentry, like the Earnshaws. To make himself complete master of both by appropriating the deeds of their respective properties is an eminently sensible plan which succeeds. On the level of his immediate life, the lack of social and economic status leads to his being rejected by his sister-like lover, Cathy; and the resentment of the spurning is reinforced by the baseness of its reasons. Doubly checked, Heathcliff's revenge is perfectly understandable, and it is only by understanding the justness of his resentment that we can come to understand the renunciation of its effort at the end. This does not call for approval of individual acts of cruelty; approval is in any case irrelevant. Sufficient (and efficient) cause exists for Heathcliff's feelings, and one need not, as some have, remake Heathcliff into some supernatural creature, no matter how often he is compared to the devil or called once by Nellie Dean, by way of question, a "ghoul" or a "vampire."

Heathcliff differs from his predecessors precisely because he has, initially, a better cause for his embittered views of life than they. The cause in which he has enlisted his energies is at least rooted in actual events that describe a humiliation worthy of being redeemed. In the end, the cause may be in Heathcliff's eyes *un*worthy, as indeed it seems to be, at least on his terms. For Heathcliff's collapse of will is calculated to assuage, as he says, not the turmoil in others but in himself. The cause he had once thought so just, so worthy of his efforts, now seems small and petty, achieved, and hence only idle to continue pursuing. In retrospect all the hard-won battles have really been useless since they have not really restored loss, have not altered dispossession. He has wasted his life, and its waste stretches before him—futile activity without meaning:

> "It is a poor conclusion, is it not. . . . An absurd termination to my violent exertions? I get levers and mattocks to demolish the two houses . . . and, when everything is ready, and in my power, I find the will to lift a slate off either roof has vanished! My old enemies have not beaten me—now would be the precise time to revenge myself on their representatives—I could do it; and none could hinder me—But where is the use? I don't care for striking, I can't take the trouble to raise my hand! . . . I have lost the faculty of enjoying their destruction, and I am too idle to destroy for nothing."

So Heathcliff's rebellion, too, ends without cause. Once Heathcliff's "self-love would endure no further torment," but now that narcissism has turned against him. His renunciation of further struggle is no idle gesture: he means it; his only wish now is to die and lie down next to his beloved Cathy, whose casket he has already prepared so that he may join her under the sod: " 'It is a long fight, I wish it were over!' " And even to die becomes in Heathcliff's case an effort; even the act of starving himself takes all the mental and physical energies which a strong and healthy man needs to deploy. Not to sustain himself becomes a willed decision, so that even in the act of giving up his will he must, paradoxically, use it. This exertion of will to subdue it very much enriches the book; Tolstoy will summon up a similar struggle in "The Death of Ivan Ilyich."

To return to the image of the door and its function: beyond the more obvious levels on which the door functions, there is a more complex purpose the door fulfills. It is this purpose which throughout the novel announces the motif of Heathcliff's essential futility, for in some of its most prominent appearances, the door acts out the reminder of just how fragile an instrument of enclosure it is. Though he uses cunning and expertly manages to secure the two properties, Heathcliff accomplishes his more immediate goals almost exclusively by violent means. And most of the incidents of violence which involve not only him but others occur at the threshold where a door bars entry or exit. Heathcliff does win most of these battles; in a few he might be considered temporarily stalled or impeded. But for the most part he keeps in and he keeps out. The door serves as his device, really, which controls and manipulates his strategies. Despite his successes with the door, however, his activities are from the very beginning futile, for doors, like windows, are artificial barriers. The unlocked and unbolted gates and doors at the end of the novel, after his death, not only signal the breaking of his siege; they announce, passively, the uselessness of them having been shut and bolted, guarded. What transcends doors is not some supernatural power but the sheer force of events. What is kept by force—in or out—is only a temporary distraction to Heathcliff's master plan: life itself operates on an open plain. Cathy will die, and he cannot bring her back to life. That alone is a certainty, and no amount of locked doors and gates can change this. Even for Heathcliff the door is an unfriendly guardian: it separates him as much as those whom he separates by its continual use as a weapon.

At the start of the novel, the narrator, Lockwood (the name itself, of course, being fully suggestive), is almost locked out of Wuthering Heights, and this, we remember, occurs close to the end of events in the novel, chronologically speaking. Wuthering Heights has become not just inhospitable but impenetrable from the outside and a danger to leave once inside. Heathcliff is a jailer; but he is also the jailed. That is what he learns at the end when he makes his decision, at last, to lie down and die. For the remainder of this discussion several key door scenes will be sufficient to illustrate the rich and complex meaning Brontë has managed to endow upon her highly symbolic use of a most natural object, and how this object illuminates Heathcliff's helplessness.

In one scene the three principals—Heathcliff, Cathy, and her husband, Linton—confront one another. Heathcliff has returned from his off-stage journeys, and he has easily overwhelmed Cathy, whose marriage to the anemic Linton has been an undernourished, unhappy affair. But Heathcliff first vents his husbanded resentment at Cathy (" 'I want you to be aware that I *know* you have treated me infernally—infernally!' "). His pursuit is now of Isabella, Linton's sister, and Cathy attempts to stop him: " 'Hush,' said Catherine, shutting the inner door." Behind the closed door, Edgar Linton listens. The two men exchange threats; Linton signals for his men; Cathy, sensing danger to Heathcliff, "slammed the door to and locked it." Like the characters in Sartre's *No Exit,* these three are momentarily trapped with one another. Linton attempts to retrieve the key, but Cathy throws it into the fire; Heathcliff taunts him with accusations of cowardice and receives in turn a desperation blow to the throat. Gaining a moment's time, Linton walks out "the back door" to the "front entrance" for pistols and reinforcements. Against such odds Cathy urges Heathcliff to escape, and for all his anger he considers this the better part of valor: "he seized the poker, smashed the lock from the inner door, and made his escape as they tramped in."[11]

The scene is revealing in several ways: both men escape through doors, but Heathcliff, not Linton, is forced to resort to force; Heathcliff is trapped; Heathcliff is the pursued, not the pursuer. That pattern, here literal, remains consistent. He, too, lives in what Cathy calls a "shattered prison."

In the scene when Hindley attempts to murder Heathcliff at Wuthering Heights, the details are different, but the essential texture of the confrontation is similar. When Isabella first arrives at Wuthering Heights and meets Hindley, he vows: " 'If once I find [his door] open he's done for!' " Eventually the opportunity comes about in a different way. Once at Wuthering Heights, Isabella is held virtual prisoner. There are at least two entrances (or exits) to that prison. Hindley, emboldened with drink, tells Isabella that he will lie in wait for Heathcliff and when he returns kill him. This sets up a door conflict. When Heathcliff tries to enter through the kitchen door, the latch is closed, and the "entrance was fastened." Outside a storm rages, to which Heathcliff is now hostage. Hindley closes the front-door bolts and attempts to recruit Isabella for his plot. She, however, refuses to be part of "treachery and violence"; Hindley is on his own, and Isabella counsels passive resistance: "Let the door remain shut," she reasons, and he is the prisoner, not we. Meanwhile Heathcliff orders the door opened, is warned by Isabella of Hindley's impending treachery, and while his adversary waits by the door, enters through a window he breaks. Once in the house he overwhelms his enemy. Yet Isabella speaks more accurately perhaps than she realizes when she recognizes Heathcliff's enslavement: " 'Heathcliff, if I were you, I'd go stretch myself over her grave, and die like a faithful dog. . . . The world is surely not worth living in now, is it?' " In time, Heathcliff will in fact do just as she advises; and the rage he releases against Hindley just after these words are spoken is already no longer a rage against a provocative object but a rage against his own impotence. For in the end Hindley, though surely ruined by Heathcliff's designs, excludes his tormentor and chooses the time and place of his death in a measure declaring his freedom: " 'he [Hindley] fastened the two doors of the house against me, and he has spent the night drinking himself to death deliberately!' " Before Hindley's death, Isabella escapes Wuthering Heights by springing to a door and beyond it leaving behind her the view of a helpless Heathcliff "checked by the embrace of his host . . . locked together on the hearth."

Heathcliff is an inefficient jailer, not because he lacks intelligence and foresight but because, being himself jailed to the memory of Cathy and her grave, he cannot attend as vigilantly as he must to his prisoners. So when he takes Ellen and young Cathy hostage, plans go awry. " 'Our first thought on [Heathcliff's] departure,' says Nelly Dean, 'was to force an exit somewhere. We tried the kitchen door, but that was fastened outside.' " They were clearly "regularly imprisoned" and Cathy the younger, tenacious like her mother, vows: " 'I'll burn that door down, but I'll get out.' " Ellen is indeed locked up, reduced to rattling latches; "And there I remained enclosed, the whole day, and the whole of the next night; and another, and another." Elsewhere young Linton and Cathy are also imprisoned. After five days Ellen is at last released to carry a message to Thrushcross Grange, where Cathy's father is dying. She leaves Wuthering Heights—"the door stood wide open"—but first tries to free Cathy by cajoling her husband, the sickly, child-like Linton, son of Heathcliff and Isabella. She decides to leave and return to Wuthering Heights with a rescue party, but it is not necessary: Cathy has come back, not through doors but through the window of her mother's bedchamber, appropriately enough, and with the help of her pathetic husband, who facilitated her escape. When Heathcliff returns to fetch her, this time not forcibly, Brontë attempts to underscore the continuity of events. Heathcliff's mellowness, relatively speaking, presages the collapse of his will and the conviction that he has a cause worthy of pursuit: "It was the *same* room into which he had been ushered, as a guest, eighteen years before: the *same* moon shone through the window; and the *same* autumn landscape lay outside. . . . Time has little altered his person either. There was the *same* man . . ." (italics mine). This insistence on *sameness,* this attempt to recreate the past, to imply that what has transpired in eighteen years has really changed nothing—that may be Nelly Dean's observation, but it is Brontë's insight.

A melancholic Heathcliff relates how only the night before he had removed the one "door" which had literally blocked his final entrance: the panel of Cathy's coffin. Now they will be joined in the next world, and the next world is where Heathcliff's focus now is and will remain. He relates how once before, the day she was buried, he had tried to open her coffin door to join her; he had clawed the earth with bare hands like a maddened animal. But at the last moment Cathy's "ghost" came to resist him. Suffused with the happiness of having seen her again, he had rushed home: ". . . I rushed eagerly to the door. It was fastened; and, I remember, that accursed Earnshaw and my wife opposed my entrance." The incident, of course, refers back to the one I have already described, but it now gains a new dimension, for truly Heathcliff, that night, barred from entry into Cathy's domain, came back to a house now his and yet barred again. Once more Heathcliff is locked out; once more the jailer is himself jailed. He knows this now; perhaps he had always suspected it.

Once Heathcliff dies, the need for bolting is gone. When the narrator happens to chance by and is curious to visit the house which so affected his life, he comes upon a very different Wuthering Heights: "I had neither to climb the gate, nor to knock—it yielded to my hand. . . . Both doors and lattices were open. . . . There was unobstructed admittance on [the other] side also; and, at the door, sat my old friend, Nelly Dean, sewing and singing a song. . . ." It is then that we learn of Heathcliff's death. The man had enacted the only action he really believed: to wander the moors, to visit Cathy's grave, simply to die by ceasing to eat to sustain himself. He does so by locking his door and lying down in the "famous panelled bed—its window . . . wide enough for anybody to get through"—indeed a window as large as a door. With only the window-door of the paneled bed open to the elements, Heathcliff dies, locked out of the world, but leaving for the release of his spirit the open window panels, the only open door remaining for him, the door to death.

Like the metaphor of the "box" in *Fathers and Sons*, the repeated use of doors and gates (as well as windows) in *Wuthering Heights* signals the recognition by each author that the world they have undertaken to describe is contained and confined. For all the expanse of the moors that separates Wuthering Heights from Thrushcross Grange, the novel is, as its images and metaphors indicate, a series of enclosures that imprison not merely the body but the spirit. This existential sense of "no exit" pervades both halves of the story: Cathy and Heathcliff before her death; Heathcliff and the survivors after her death. And for all the violence in the novel, people rarely connect on any communicable level. Such disjunction underscores the terrible deprivation to which nearly everyone is exposed, for who in this novel can be said to have lived his or her life? Heathcliff's final capitulation bears witness to his unconsummated life, and one need hardly keep this to a purely sexual meaning. Of all the characters, he begins and ends as the most dispossessed; and it is indeed his mission to dispossess others, not merely out of a sense of revenge but as the only way he knows how to bring others to a level of his own sense of perception, defined by the deep and forlorn experience of deprivation. The doors that open and shut throughout the novel are almost like carnivorous jaws preying on life itself, consuming time and opportunity that would allow for living as process. If Heathcliff is the chief manipulator of those doors, he is nevertheless, as already suggested, hoisted on his own petard. As if afflicted by repetition-compulsion, even his final tampering with the caskets is an attempt to keep open the one "door" in death that in life, being shut, always barred him at its other side.

The end of *Wuthering Heights,* like that of *Fathers and Sons,* has been regarded as too sentimental when perhaps it is only ironic. Both novels conclude with our attention drawn to the contemplation of the dead: a graveyard. In each case, the living, the survivors, have not fully understood the dead, for not only is this always the case but here especially, since the dead were such willing travelers and held such an unwilling sojourn in this life. Like Bazarov's, Heathcliff's case is a study in impotence, rage at impotence, and an exertion of will and energy so titanic that collapse seems both inevitable and desirable. True, Heathcliff's great effort, of longer duration and greater intensity than Bazarov's, is almost cosmic, but the course of the three lives I have examined has been recognizably similar. Pechorin has little of Bazarov's intellectual conflicts; he had the least cause to live, for there seemed nothing worth living for. Bazarov might have lived had he been able to find some parallel between his self and the space of world it occupied, but he could not, and so he, too, sought death. Heathcliff, of course, had only Cathy; she made life worth his living, but he was doomed never to possess her. And so, too, he was doomed merely to rage until he realized even the futility of that. He does not so much surrender life as embrace death. Pursuing the absent consumes his present. So these were three lives which were surely "lived," but just as certainly unfulfilled, each of them—as Yeats said—before they could even comb gray hair.

IV

Some of Freud's remarks about melancholia help us to understand the manifest actions of Pechorin, Bazarov, and Heathcliff. Mourning, of course, is a "normal" condition stilled by time; as I have noted, melancholia corresponds almost precisely with mourning with the exception of a single additional symptom: the "disturbance of self-regard." Freud also suggests that the melancholic loses some things of which he is unconscious, which he cannot identify. Pechorin tries to explain his losses to Vera, and later on his loss *of* her; but nothing that he articulates quite seems to measure correlatively with all his behavior. Bazarov's love extended to Odinstova is lost; so are his disciples, his *raison d'être* for his nihilistic beliefs. But again there appears to be an internal loss which he does not perceive: the loss of his future, life itself. The "box of life" has had its lid put on it, and Bazarov is essentially incarcerated within its darkness. That is why Freud suggested that the world, not the ego, is "empty"—represented to us as "worthless, incapable of any achievement and morally despicable." Pechorin does call himself a "moral cripple"; Bazarov on his deathbed feels unneeded, unworthy, and most certainly morally betrayed; Heathcliff may be beyond good and evil, but his own self holds no value anymore, and its destruction, therefore, is welcomed. All three certainly succeed in "overcoming . . . the instinct which compels every living thing to cling to life." Self-hatred is in part the fruit of anger turned inward and results in "obsessional states of depression": "If the love for the object—a love which cannot be given up though the object itself is given up—takes refuge in narcissistic identification, then the hate comes into operation on this substitutive object, abusing it, debasing it, making it suffer and deriving sadistic satisfaction from its suffering."[12] That the elegiac mood of loss can turn into hatred not merely of the depriving world but of the deprived mourner should not come as any great surprise. In the figures I have dealt with here that double hatred seems clearly set before us. In the works to come it will be more subtly shaped, more cautiously imaged forth—but it will be there, if we are alert to it.

3 Life from the Perspective of Death: Turgenev, Tolstoy, Kafka, Chekhov, and Mann

A strong egoism is a protection against falling ill, but in the last resort we must begin to love in order not to fall ill if, in consequence of frustration, we are unable to love.
— *Freud, "On Narcissism: An Introduction"*

I
Turgenev: "Narcissistic Rage"

The Diary of a Superfluous Man, which gave superfluity its name and currency in Russian literature, is a deceptive work. It negotiates a tightrope between pathos and irony. Appearing in 1850, a decade after Lermontov's *A Hero of Our Time* and a little more than a decade before Turgenev's own *Fathers and Sons,* it deviates significantly from both. On the one hand it is far more self-consciously critical than Lermontov and on the other far less serious about its hero than *Fathers and Sons.* Its tone is not merely frivolously mocking, but Chulkaturin, the diarist, is a self-destructive man whose denigration of himself is suspiciously overdone. It is the imminent approach of death that has moved him to undertake this diary, purportedly to be an analysis of his life. In fact, however, the diary records a single humiliating experience in that brief life (he is only thirty); the sense of superfluity it conveys is a direct consequence of inadequacy. The diary is a means of soliciting our sympathy for a life the diarist sees as having been misspent and now so prematurely to be cut off before it has had a chance to run a reasonable course that might have allowed time for redemption. The frequent references to nature are a deliberate attempt to juxtapose the diarist's wounded pride and the vagaries of the natural world, which represents his deep sense of loss. Were it not for its tone, the *Diary* could easily be read as an elegy; but its tone makes it almost a mock elegy (much like the final paragraph of *Fathers and Sons,* but far less subtle).[1]

It is difficult to know how much of the diary is the story of a poseur, how much a genuinely felt experience of a lonely man's dying. Of his illness he tells us almost nothing; of death he speaks very little; and the burden of his confession is a fixation on the episode in his life that most injured his pride, confirming—so he asserts—his superfluity, but also asking the reader to take sides and acknowledge the injustice of the injury to his ego. The episode in question is the pursuit of a young lady who in turn prefers a young Prince; the Prince, a more sophisticated Pechorin, dallies, and when he is ready to leave departs without fanfare, having taken advantage of the young girl. A third man, a friend of the young lady, is then found to comfort her, and the hero, despised by the young Liza, is left to ponder how of three men he has come last—or worse still, not acceptable at all—indeed, "superfluous."

In the opening pages we are given a sketch of an unhappy single child, an unhappy childhood and youth. He has not lacked for parental love, but a weak father placed great strain on the family. His mother, he admits, loved him, but he did not return the love to this "virtuous" and strong woman; rather, it went to the weak "sinful" father. Almost as if to evade these early memories, the diarist interrupts his flow of thought with observations on the weather (spring is coming; it is March) and on nature. His rhapsodic invocations of spring and nature are at times out of place for a dying man, but it signals, it would seem, a certain falseness in the voice, a distraction, a momentary longing perhaps, but no more than those overt observations of the moody Pechorin. And what is more, Chulkaturin is aware of everything:

> Spring, spring's coming! I sit by the window and look across the river at the fields. O Nature, Nature! I love you so, yet I came from your womb incapable of living. There, the male sparrow is hopping around with outspread wings; he's shouting, and every sound of his voice, every ruffled feather on his little body breathes health and strength. . . .
>
> What follows from this? Nothing. He's healthy . . . and I'm

sick and have to die—and that's it. . . . And lachrymose apostrophes to Nature are really ludicrous.[2]

Following his father's death, mother and son move to Moscow. In this new urban estrangement the diarist feels keenly the loss of the gardens of his youth, where his happiest memories were generated:

> O my gardens, O overgrown paths beside the little pond! O little sandy spot under the decrepit dam. . . . And you, tall birches with the long, hanging branches. . . . I send you my last good-bye! . . . Parting with life, I reach my arms out to you alone—I would like once more to breathe in the pungent freshness of wormwood . . . to hear in the distance the unassuming jangle of the cracked bell . . . to lie once more in the cool shade. . . .
>
> Ah, what's all this for? But I can't go on today. Until tomorrow.

This elegiac note is, however, only deepened by the contrast of "tomorrow"—a late March day, "cold and bleak"; the memories serve only as a painful counterpoint, childhood lost. Once more he resolves: "I'll simply and quietly tell the story of my life." Yet, he admits, the thought does keep coming back: Is it a life "worth telling?" And, in a reflective moment, Chulkaturin abandons his plans at autobiography; instead "I better try to give myself an analysis of my own character. What kind of man am I?" This shift from (by his own admission) ludicrous apostrophes to Nature and idyllic evocations of lost childhood to weighty metaphysical questions of existence once again verges on the ironic, for Chulkaturin's metaphysical ponderings do not go much further than his panegyrics on Nature or his reveries of the past. Still, he pleads, it is not unwarranted to find out who he really is before he dies. And it is then that he makes the sweeping self-judgment: "I was a completely superfluous man in this world. . . ." Full of self-consciousness and anxiety, this tortured soul analyzes himself "down to the last thread," realizing he was not one of the crowd, mocking himself for thinking so, short on courage and steeped in melancholy. His life was circular and aimless, "sterile" and without purpose.

With superfluity as his subject the diarist changes course once more: he ceases self-analysis (as he had abandoned autobiography) and now decides simply to prove to us the justness of the label,

"superfluousness." To accomplish this he selects the incident of the
young lady, Liza, and his humiliation in suffering her rebuff. The
details of the story very much resemble Lermontov and Pushkin
and look ahead to Dostoevsky's account given to his paradoxalist
from the underground. In a certain way the diarist has proven his
self-analysis as a superfluous man, a "fifth wheel." That is, the act
of analysis itself proves to be itself without use with death near and
with no hope of reprieve. But when death is at last imminent, and
he reflects on the story he has told, the diarist is dissatisfied:

> I wanted to keep a diary, and instead of that what have I done?
> Told the story of one incident in my life. I got carried away
> talking; . . . I wrote leisurely . . . as if I still had years ahead of
> me; and now there's no time left to go on. Death, death's com-
> ing. . . . I feel I'm going; I'm getting simpler, clearer. I've got-
> ten some sense, but *too late*. (Italics mine)

The psychological structure of the diary is now completed. From autobiography to metaphysical self-analysis, to the purgation of relating a
painful episode: each has served the overall purpose, and each, in
sequence, has established with subtle irony that, in fact, superfluity
may not exist but is perhaps merely a perception, a figure of speech, a
denial, a pose, a perspective of life from the certainty of death. "Too
late": for Chulkaturin, too, the refrain is that insight, if that is what it
is, has come too late; that life is over for him very early. His admonition to us is no less intense than Bazarov's was or Lambert Strether's
will be: "I am dying. . . . Live, you who are alive."

The Diary of a Superfluous Man sets the stage for succeeding works
discussed in this chapter: Tolstoy's "Death of Ivan Ilyich," Chekhov's
"Dreary Story," Kafka's *Metamorphosis,* and Thomas Mann's *Death in
Venice.* In each of these works life is reflectively seen by the protagonist from the perspective of death; though their ages range from
young, to middle-aged, to old ("bodily decrepitude"), the intensity of
viewing life from the imminence of certain death shapes the visions of
each. There is regret, self-reproach, disenchantment, fear and loathing, and in all of them a somber recognition of not having lived at all,
of having been cheated—by time, by circumstance, by betrayal of self
or world. Chulkaturin's lament at the end of the *Diary* is genuine
enough, and its elegiac rage is a fit gloss for his literary progeny: "O
my Lord, my Lord! Now I'm dying . . . without ever having known
happiness. . . . If only . . . before death . . . some sweet, sad friendly
voice were to sing a farewell song to me . . . about my own sorrow . . . I

might, perhaps, be reconciled to it. But dying is stupid, stupid." The final paradoxical realization that disintegration makes judgment necessary, that death releases one after all, places everything, even regret of the past, into a different light: "Becoming nothing, I'm ceasing to be superfluous." That is Chulkaturin's most cunning insight in his so-called Diary.

II
Tolstoy's "The Death of Ivan Ilyich":
The Dying Life
Chekhov's "A Dreary Story": The Living Death

Tolstoy's "The Death of Ivan Ilyich" preceded in date of publication Chekhov's less well-known "A Dreary Story" by three years: 1886 and 1889. Chekhov's tale has been called a response to the challenge laid down by Tolstoy's. Certainly both stories are sufficiently similar and dissimilar to be discussed together (as they have been), for each author explored a common problem from a somewhat different aperture.[3] It is worth knowing that, like Chekhov's story, Tolstoy's was originally planned as a first-person-narrative memoir, that is, Ivan telling his own story by means of a diary which Ivan's widow hands over to the narrator. This narrator states: "It is impossible, absolutely impossible, to live as I have lived, as I live, and as we all live. I realized that as a result of the death of an acquaintance of mine, Ivan Ilyich, and of the diary he had left behind." The ur-version of the story dealt only with Ivan's life and the onset of his illness; later the diary was added. Clearly Tolstoy's final version was possible only by eliminating the diary, just as Chekhov's story gains its strength precisely by having it. The stories are by no means the same, but in each a character is viewed from the inside and found wanting. Tolstoy's story allows him to reveal Ivan Ilyich's dissatisfaction with his life, and with himself, and the illness serves as the metaphor for the revelation. Chekhov, always intent on objectivity, irony, and inconclusiveness, permits the reader to judge his protagonist precisely by *not* giving him insight into his own failings, but instead having him measure his failings almost exclusively against a failing world that surrounds him or, even more specifically, against the natural organic decay that accompanies old age and death. Chekhov commented on his hero, one of whose "chief characteristics" is that he is "too off-hand in his attitude to the inner life of his associates. While those around him shed their tears, make their mistakes and tell their lies, he's laying down the law about literature and the theater with sublime imperturbability."[4]

Of course the dying Professor Nicholas Stepanovich is sixty-two years old; Ivan Ilyich is forty-five when he dies, and certainly never thinks of himself as "old." Furthermore, though both men are in a sense egotists, Ivan has some glimmer of recognition; the professor's almost clinical preoccupation with his death gets in the way of genuine self-analysis. The professor is full of "decisiveness towards himself"; so, too, is Ivan Ilyich. The essential similarity between the two is clear: both are dying; both regret their lives; both are suffused with intro-spection, almost to the point where an excess of *amour-propre* over-whelms their lives. Yet they are also very different: in age, in what insight is permitted each, in the nature of their disaffection. Most of all whereas Tolstoy's hero looks back with regret and wished he had the chance to live his life over, Chekhov's clinically-minded professor of medicine merely accepts, sometimes passively, the fate of aging, death, dissociation, observing his symptoms, occasionally almost as if he were outside himself looking at a patient. Any regrets he may have are based on a life passed with too little joy, but not one that is really a candidate for repeating. Perhaps the greatest irony of Chekhov's story is that his hero fails to see the opportunities before him, even at the last, and in dismissing those chances for meaning he not merely de-prives another but, most of all, himself—and without ever being aware of it. In this he resembles Henry James's John Marcher more than Ivan Ilyich.

Ivan Ilyich's sudden illness, rapid decline, and unexpected death provide him with an enforced opportunity of self-examination and reappraisal. Himself a judge, now being judged, the highly intelligent Ivan Ilyich does not miss any opportunities to see the irony of his position. A carefree but ambitious young man he had married and—so he thought—set himself on a course for a rapid rise to the top and a satisfying family life. But children and domestic obligations soon tire him, and the marriage deteriorates rapidly. He and his wife embark on a life of mutual nagging and petty quarrels with a determined effort by Ivan to regain his independence. Of five children, three die, as if to augur defeat; only a son and daughter live to grow beyond childhood. For a time Ivan Ilyich does not advance in his profession either. He retires to the country, develops "*ennui* for the first time in his life," and is beset by fits of depression.[5] One day the awaited call materializes: a new post, a promotion, a move, a new house.

But Ivan Ilyich's climb to the exalted heights he envisions goes no further than a stepladder onto which he climbs to show his decorator how he wants to have his curtains hung. Slipping, he falls and hits his side against the knob of the windowpane. A domestic tragedy, a deliberately trivialized punishment for his hubris, is now set earnestly in motion, for this innocent fall from the stepladder is the catalyst which brings to the surface Ivan Ilyich's "incurable illness." This sequence embodies an experience meant to generalize an unextraordinary experience so devastatingly expressed in the justly famous opening sentence of the second section of the story: "Ivan Ilyich's life had been most simple and most ordinary and therefore most terrible." The sentence spears us with its oxymoronic counterpoint: precisely the absence of life neither simple nor ordinary has made it so terrible. We are prepared very early for Ivan Ilyich's ultimate, relentless self-doubt: " 'Maybe I did not live as I ought to have done. . . .' "

All the parrying with the doctors, the false diagnoses, the tests, the coverups, the lying, the verbal duels that accompany his steady decline—these serve only to sharpen his self-consciousness and to develop in him a hatred which spreads from those around him eventually to himself. The illness itself becomes his executioner: " 'Here he is, the judge. But I am not guilty!' " Yet can he be certain? He must deny it: "whenever the thought occurred to him, as it often did, that it all resulted from his not having lived as he ought to have done [rather than the fall off the stepladder] he at once recalled the correctness of his whole life and dismissed so strange an idea." Ivan Ilyich faces a common dilemma: the search for an explanation of suffering and, what his suspicions soon confirm, explanations for impending death. The whole story now hinges on his ability to reverse the question, What have I done? to What have I *not* done? His initial attempt to justify the correctness of his life finally gives way to a stark glimpse into a void. In a dialogue with himself he asks, "What do I want? . . . To live? How? . . . Why, to live as I used to—well and pleasantly!" But when he begins to recall just how and when his life had been pleasant, the "best moments . . . now seemed [not] at all what they had then seemed. . . ." Only childhood moments glimmered. Eventually the imaging is put more abstractly, more ominously, more forbiddingly: " 'There is one bright spot there at the back, at the beginning of life, and afterwards all becomes blacker and blacker and proceeds more and more rapidly—in inverse ratio to the square of the distance from death. . . .' " At last, one night, awake with pain and fearful of that void of death, as he watches his servant Gerasim, natural and healthy in a sleep, the question reveals itself to Ivan Ilyich in unalloyed and unmitigated nakedness: "What if my whole life has really been wrong? It occurred to him that what appeared perfectly impossible before, namely that he had not spent his life as he should have done, might after all be true."

The title notwithstanding, Tolstoy's story, written at a time when its author was beginning to suffer his own spiritual crises, is concerned more with the *life* of Ivan Ilyich than with his death—at best a death in life. We are, it is true, drawn into Ivan Ilyich's dying because his own preoccupation is with that process for most of the story, shielding and masking those painful questions about his life. Tolstoy makes it clear that even the excruciating pain, which takes on an almost preternatural personality of its own and becomes an enemy, an "It" (in Russian, "it" is "she") subsides once Ivan Ilyich attains to levels of self-perception. Tolstoy's own crisis of faith perhaps gives the ending a measure of hope and illumination which, if not precisely Christian, is redemptive. Just before he dies Ivan Ilyich glimpses a light, however much this, too, *may* be a delusion: "At that very moment Ivan Ilyich fell through and caught sight of the light, and it was revealed to him that though his life had not been what it should have been, this could still be rectified."

But all the light in the world cannot erase Ivan Ilyich's bitter recognition that his life had not been fulfilling, neither to others nor to himself. One is apt to shudder at the callousness and hypocrisy of the doctors, the wife, and the daughter who look upon Ivan Ilyich's illness as a nuisance, an interference, even an imposition: by the third month of his illness all became aware that "the whole interest he had for other people was whether he would soon vacate his place and at last release the living from the discomfort caused by his presence. . . ." These are not loving and giving people, but then Ivan Ilyich has done little to earn the pity he so much craves. Arrogant, selfish, ambitious, stern, this judge has long ignored penitence, and what he now reaps he has sown. Tolstoy does not permit his hero to delude himself on that score: his life has been what he had made of it—and had failed to make of it. For the longest time his suffering is simply a form of denial: "He was hindered from getting into [the black hole of death] by his conviction that his life had been a good one. That very justification of his life held him fast and prevented his moving forward, and it caused him the most torment of all."

Chekhov's "A Dreary Story" allows no such redemptive glimpse. While Tolstoy examines the meaning of an unlived life as a dying man faces its emptiness, Chekhov's story, dealing with an older man, chronicles the emotional obtuseness of a brilliant scientist whose disappointment with life is fully and openly acknowledged. There is no denial of the void his life has become, and there is little solace in memories of the past. What Chekhov dissects is the old professor's realization that time has ravaged those around him (his wife in particular) as well as himself. His lectures have lost meaning for him—they are boring; his health is gone; his patience short. But unlike the raging Ivan Ilyich, Nicholas Stepanovich takes an almost morbid clinical interest in his own disintegration. Like Ivan Ilyich, he, too, begins to dread the void of death. All around him colleagues are dying; he feels keenly the superannuated status of his daily life, which he lives mechanically. He thinks of himself as the "superfluous parentheses" which he notices in his writing, and "If anyone should ask me what constitutes the essential core of my life . . . I should answer insomnia." Being "perfectly well aware" that he has "less than six months to live," he keeps his extraordinary diary not as a record of metaphysical speculation but as a kind of self-interested and even disinterested hobby. There are three women in his life now: his wife; his daughter; and his ward, Katya, a rebel, a would-be actress, a mother of an illegitimate child, now dead. Katya alone understands him and in her way loves him, but he is too numbed to respond—even to understand. Nicholas Stepanovich describes his being as a state of feeling dissociation as if indeed he were already dead. One entry: "only now at lunch does it dawn on me that their inner life has long since vanished from my field of vision. . . . I feel . . . [that] I'm just the lunch guest of a spurious wife, looking at a spurious [daughter]." Perhaps most revealing is what follows, his recognition that his separateness is not recent: "A great change has taken place in them both, but I have missed the long process by which it occurred. . . ." What else can this mean but that he has missed life itself? In late afternoons he finds himself weeping without cause, burying his head in his pillow, and feeling himself dispossessed: "Some force . . . is thrusting me roughly out of my home, and I'll leap up, quickly dress and slip into the street, heedful to elude the attention of my family. Where shall I go?"[6]

Katya tells him, " 'Throw everything up and leave—go abroad, and the sooner the better.' " But he dismisses such thoughts, as well he might, speaking from the perspective of practicality, for Katya's advice is twenty years too late, at the least. With increasing frequency, however, he visits her; they talk and he confesses, "another senile weakness—reminiscences. I tell Katya about my past. . . ." Yet reliving it with her brings no pleasure, though it passes the time. The professor's relationship with Katya, the only one who understands him, eclipses his instincts even more; "Tugging my door-bell and walking upstairs, I feel I've lost my family and don't want it back." His daughter's elopement with a man he dislikes leaves him unmoved. His wife's nagging ignites anger: " 'Leave me alone,' I shout! . . . ," and falling into a swoon he remains for a time prisoner, homebound, visited each day by only one sustaining human being: Katya.

Inevitably, like Ivan Ilyich, Nicholas Stepanovich also experiences his *saison en enfer,* his night of despair: "terror clutches at my heart, as if I'd seen the huge glow of some sinister conflagration." He is panic-stricken; he does not know whether his fear is prompted by "an urge to live" or by the prospects of more suffering. Momentarily he is called away to visit his daughter's bedroom, where the young woman is in the midst of an attack of hysteria. Occupied with calming her, he regains his own composure. Presently Katya comes to the darkened window, and she, too, is depressed, offering him money to spend on a rest cure. Of course he must refuse: " 'your money's no good to me now.' "

"These last months of my life, this waiting for death, seem to last far longer than the rest of my life put together." Nicholas Stepanovich finds himself tracing down his daughter's questionable suitor in Kharkov when a telegram in the middle of the night informs him of their elopement. His own "dispassionateness" frightens him—it is like "spiritual atrophy and premature death."

At last he asks what Ivan Ilyich had asked: "What do I want?" The reply is different only in degree, not in kind:

> I want our wives, friends, children and pupils to love us as ordinary people—not for our reputation, not for how we're branded and labelled. . . . I'd like to wake up a hundred years from now and cast at least a cursory glance at what's happening in science. I'd like to have lived another ten years or so.

Beyond that he cannot think of anything more, for all these feelings fail to combine for him, to make a unity, a "general conception," or what he calls simply "the God of a live human being." No light of any kind appears to this lonely man; what might have occurred while crossing the bar Chekhov does not give him, or us, an opportunity to know. "And if one lacks [a general conception], one has nothing."

The last scene is the most painful. Without warning, a distraught Katya appears in Kharkov and begs this worldly man for advice: " 'Help me! . . . you're my father, aren't you?' " Yet not even this accusatory truth can move the professor, for he simply does not know what to say or do, except " 'I shall soon be dead, Katya,' " or he is tempted to ask, " 'So you won't be at my funeral?' " To the end Nicho-

las Stepanovich can think first only of himself and his approaching
death, and of his life and its seemingly vacuous course. He has
achieved renown and success equal to (or perhaps surpassing) Ivan
Ilyich's; he is a famous personality, a name known to the public. And
yet he laments that "these things won't save me from dying a miserable death on a strange bed in utter loneliness."

Chekhov's story, which has none of the immediate urgency of pain
which marks Tolstoy's, which does not match the wounded anguish of
Ivan Ilyich, is nevertheless, for all its quiet despair, a far more grim
parable of how, from the proximity to imminent death, two men view
their lives. What the two men have in common, in addition to glimps-
ing life from the closeness to death, is their dissociation from their
families to which both had once been bound. In this respect both
stories presage Kafka's *Metamorphosis,* that unmatchable articulation
of waste. Neither sixty-two nor forty-five, Kafka's hero is a young man
whose life is twice wasted: once, before the metamorphosis, in isolation from it, and the second time in a literal wasting away as the insect
shrinks, grows weak, and is at last starved, a dry skeleton light enough
to be swept away with a charwoman's broom.

III
Kafka and Tolstoy: Rooms with a View

Kafka's diary entry for 27 December 1921 is very brief: "Again sat
over *Nás Skantik* [a Czech scout magazine], Ivan Ilyich." Max Brod's
footnote simply states: " 'The Death of Ivan Ilyich' by Tolstoy. This
and his *Folk Tales* ('The Three Old Men' particularly), were great
favourites of Kafka." But so many elements in Tolstoy's story must
have struck a chord: the glimpse of a voided life; the loneliness; the
sense of despair and disappointment; estrangement from the family;
physical pain and illness; the dread of dying; the desperate search
for meaning and especially the specter of meaninglessness. The diary entry for 12 January 1914: "Youth's meaninglessness. Fear of
youth, fear of meaninglessness, of the meaningless rise of an inhuman life." *The Metamorphosis* had been written a year earlier.[7]

Philip Rahv's essay, "The Death of Ivan Ilyich and Joseph K.,"
brings the two authors together from a slightly different point of
view: the common alienation of two urban men, both suffering all the
deleterious consequences of subsequent isolation, dehumanization,
death. "Standardized urban man, K. and Ivan Ilyich are typical prod-

ucts of a quantitative civilization." In a sense, like K., Ivan Ilyich, Rahv remarks, "understands at last that his life has been trivial and disgusting."[8] Gregor Samsa's insight in *The Metamorphosis* goes much further, for it is actualized by the metamorphosis itself. So unbearable is his routinized existence that his only escape from it is to convert into a dung beetle.

What *The Metamorphosis* "means" has led one critic to compile a book he calls *The Commentators' Despair;*[9] yet among many important significations, one surely centers on Gregor's profoundly painful survey of a life that so far has been only a waste of his strength and a future life which holds out little if any change except continued drudgery. On that point most commentators can agree. Whether Gregor has himself created his dilemma or is victimized by his family, whether he is truly unfeeling before the metamorphosis and becomes sensitized to life only after it—these are among the questions that have divided readers since the story has been subjected to analytical reading. It is likely that there is some truth in both positions: that is, Gregor's metamorphosis can hardly help placing him into a perspective from which, through the beingness of an insect, he can experience for the first time acute human feelings of which he was hitherto incapable. That is part of Kafka's achievement, to make this paradox inevitable. On the other hand, even if, as some have suggested, the metamorphosis is self-willed, it is a last-chance endeavor to abandon the bleak and hopeless existence he has been leading as a traveling salesman, provider for the family, dutiful son. That Gregor's relationship to his family becomes almost reversed is, of course, a natural development of the metamorphosis. Before it he was the respected if not loved son and brother. His own feelings appeared to have been fueled less by love and devotion and more by guilt, a sense of duty, and a perception that fate had provided no other way. As for the family, it somewhat took him for granted, and there surely was no love communicated: not given, not returned. Gregor's metamorphosis, however, provides an opportunity, one suspects his first, to reflect, to ponder, to analyze. That opportunity proves to be fatal—literally.

Like Ivan Ilyich, Gregor's reflections take him to states of doubt and self-questioning: "If I didn't hold back for my parents' sake, I would have quit long ago. . . ."[10] Once he is imprisoned in his room, Gregor is able to review his past life by analogously viewing his present life, for the latter appears as a metaphorical reconstruction of the former. Had he not, in a way, been a dung beetle all these many years? Had he not been subjected to humiliation, unstructured eating time, bad food, uncomfortable lodgings, loneliness, isolation, and discomfort? His life had really been as wasted, as empty, as *useless* as the metamorphosis has made his existence in his present prison-room. Like Ivan Ilyich, Gregor will now begin the lonely, self-conscious, and self-observant vigil over his own death. And like Ivan Ilyich, it involves an increasingly alienating process from family, from life itself, from all normal surroundings. But Kafka takes matters to extremes far beyond Tolstoy, the metamorphosis giving K. the opening to show the utter dispossession he has experienced. What Ivan Ilyich, in a "realistic" story, experiences mentally and spiritually, Gregor Samsa undergoes, primarily, physically: "Had he really wanted to have his warm room, comfortably fitted with furniture . . . changed into a cave, in which, of course, he would be able to crawl around unhampered in all directions but at the cost of simultaneously, rapidly, and totally forgetting his human past?" But Gregor's sister thinks otherwise, and her efficiently ruthless handling of his "case" ensures Gregor's total separateness not only from family but also from anything human. What this forces on Gregor is a continual counter-attack, a rebelliousness, the strain of which ultimately exhausts him and costs him his life. Ivan Ilyich "saw that he was dying, and he was in continual despair." Gregor, too, knows he will never again be a normal "human," neither in shape nor in spirit, and he too dies in—if not of—despair. Like Ivan Ilyich's, Gregor Samsa's life has also been "senseless and horrible," and "simple" and "ordinary." Partly because he was of a higher social and economic class, Ivan Ilyich's life had more elasticity for fulfillment: he "might" or "could" or "should" have done things which, even in the best of circumstances, Gregor was excluded from achieving, and that is why Gregor's feelings of being trapped without choices is as strong before the metamorphosis as after. It may be a fateful error for Gregor to feel such a fated life, for it colors his thinking. Whereas Tolstoy was still able to make his hero regret what could have been a different life, Kafka permits no alternatives: it would appear that Gregor's life is ordained by forces larger than himself, and Kafka often thought this about his own unhappy existence. Ivan Ilyich asks and searches; Samsa asks and accepts. Nor does Gregor have a peasant servant to give him succor, only a servant who comes to sweep away his dead and dried-up corpse. Nor does Gregor have a priest, however perfunctory a service might be offered. His death, after pain in *his* side, a lingering pain inflicted by his father's apple throwing, is somewhat quieter than Ivan's, though he has experienced anguish for a long time. Like Ivan Ilyich, Gregor is given a glimpse of light: "He still saw that outside the window everything was beginning to grow light." This is the penultimate sentence before, from his nostrils, "streamed his last weak breath." Ivan Ilyich's act of dying can still be seen as a rebellion, not merely against death itself but against the *process* that life turns out to be, the process that brings one to the inevitable closure. As some readers have pointed out, the uncanny aspect of Kafka's story is that this "process" (the metamorphosis) begins the story; and everything that occurs after that (which, of course, comprises the entire story) transpires in a special temporal and spatial vacuum.

Kafka's admiration for "The Death of Ivan Ilyich" is not difficult to appreciate, for Tolstoy had provided him in this story a matching tale for much of his own work, especially *The Metamorphosis*. We do not know for certain when he first read the story—before or after writing *The Metamorphosis*—and "influence" is not a question that concerns us here. Confirmation rather, an affinity of intent, is what Kafka must have discovered in Tolstoy's story: humanity, slowly dehumanized, slowly dying from a great pain; a life of waste, severance, and dispossession; even a hatred of family, in Kafka less overtly stated, which in time forms the symptomology of the "incurable" disease. Even like Gregor, Ivan Ilyich is moved to a separate room to die alone; like Gregor, Ivan Ilyich knows that he has become a burden on others, and like Gregor he realizes that they only wait for the deliverance of his death. Kafka's final pages deal with the liberated feelings of the family after Gregor's death; Tolstoy, beginning his story with the end, also shows us through the insincere tears of Ivan Ilyich's wife a relieved family: "After many details of the really dreadful physical sufferings Ivan Ilyich had endured . . . the widow apparently found it necessary to get to business. . . . She knew how much could be got out of the government in consequence of her husband's death. . . ." So Kafka found a kindred story, one he took much further, making of what Tolstoy had done with Ivan Ilyich a literalization that concentrated less on the *unlived* life than on the *unlivable* life, a change that was both subtle and significant for the motif's future treatment. Kafka's story still mediates between reality and the suprareal. In spite of its grotesque metaphor, it is more like in spirit to Chekhov and Tolstoy than, say, to Dostoevsky's underground man, who leads a somewhat different path to the holed-in/-up protagonsists of Beckett.

IV
Death in Venice: Narcissus by the Seaside

Death in the fiction of Thomas Mann is so exclusive a motif it tends almost to push aside most of the others.[11] From an early unpublished story, "Death," to *Death in Venice, The Magic Mountain, Doktor Faustus,* and *The Black Swan (Die Betrogene)*, Mann is preoccupied with death: with its many guises, its clinical causes (that is, illness itself), and its ambivalent feelings, ranging from revulsion to reverence and release. If ever one was half in love with easeful (or perhaps not so easeful) death, it was Thomas Mann. That needs no emphasis, but about the various ways in which Mann approaches the perplexities of death there is some room for comment. In a subsequent chapter I will deal with that compendious commentary on death, *The Magic Mountain.* Here *Death in Venice* is my focus, keeping in mind that Mann had already written one large novel *(Buddenbrooks)* and many stories which treated the various forms of exhaustion, regret, and the release from life by the intervention of death.

Gustav von Aschenbach is as good as dead from the moment we meet him. The sojourn in Venice, though it opens for the hero a heightened sense of being, is no healing sojourn but an unmitigated disaster, a nightmare that can end only in death. A distinguished writer, a man perhaps in his mid-fifties, literally falls apart, disintegrates before our eyes, from an exalted position in which he prided himself for his discipline to a decadence that barely disguises a lurid dissipation. Aschenbach's motto had been "Hold fast!"; by the time this novella ends there is nothing to hold onto anymore. There is certainly something elegiac in Aschenbach's discovery of Eros in the young Polish boy, Tadzio, something elegiac as well in the dawning realization, prompted by the discovery of Eros, that he has not really been wooed to live, to indulge his senses, to "let go" rather than to "hold fast." Predictably when the holding fast is so rigid, the letting go will be a floodgate that will destroy. Aschenbach cannot control his Dionysian nightmare, nor can he control the darker and specifically identified "obscene" qualities which make of him, in his waning days, a caricature of the international figure commanding respect and awe, dignified and acutely civilized, which once he was. He jealousy of youth, and of missing out on life, turns to rage, not the articulatable remorse which James was still able to give his characters, not even Ivan Ilyich's cries in the night, not even Nicholas Stepanovich's dour, if perceptive, record of slow death and impotence. "Knowledge *is* the abyss" *(Phaedrus)*; and since avoidance of knowledge for a man like Aschenbach is impossible, the abyss is equally inevitable. So Aschenbach becomes a brook of ashes,· for that is what his name literally means—with the allusion to Bacchus implicit.

Thomas Mann had already thoroughly explored both the breaking of will, the destructive and insinuating nature of art, and the wasted life in his first novel, *Buddenbrooks*.[12] Aschenbach is an advanced, more developed Buddenbrook, a man who, unlike his predecessor, would have understood and completed his reading of Schopenhauer—in short, an intellectual, an artist. But in the end, the curve of Aschenbach's experience, albeit on a higher orbit, is very similar: *durchhalten*, holding fast, a contempt for flabbiness and weakness, a sense of rigor and self-punishing discipline. All that is followed by crisis, glimmerings, and death. Even Thomas Buddenbrook's desires to keep himself looking young with doses of eau de cologne, and a mustache carefully held in place with brilliantine, fastidious gestures of the morning toilette, foreshadow the grotesque metamorphosis of Aschenbach, the would-be rejuvenated, passion-hungry lover of young Tadzio.

For most readers the climactic moments of this novella come in the final pages when the dying author sits at the beach in a reverie, a half-dream, recalling the words of Plato, especially from the *Phaedrus*, on love, death, form, spirit. Nevertheless, the opening pages, too, have solicited their proper share of interest and attention: Aschenbach, on his lonesome walk past the cemetery, the snub-nosed stranger, the dream vision of the jungles and the tiger—a whole mythopoeic tapestry is woven here. Indeed density is a primary feature of this novella, especially of its opening and closing pages. It seems as if Mann is desperate to fill in sufficient material to make the actions that follow logical and sensible.

Aschenbach, "overwrought," unable to sleep, ventures out in the sultry spring air. Inside he feels restlessness, a "roving unrest" and indeed a "youthful longing after far-off places"—an urge to travel.[13] Despite the portentous vision of the jungle and the tiger, his longing remains, for this "European" soul is so suffused with "the onus of production," he is untrained for the role of dilettante. Life for Aschenbach is itself a profession; and having given that profession his every ounce of energy, in addition to his calling as artist, Aschenbach is now thoroughly exhausted, a man still under sixty. Aschenbach embodies much of the late nineteenth-century conflict: the desperate attempt to steer clear of dangerous abysses often culminating in total enervation from the effort itself. To some extent this is the nature of Aschenbach's "European" spirit, for we are told that his life "was slowly on the decline," and the artist in him suffers from the "fear of not having finished—this uneasiness lest the clock run down before he had done. . . ." So it is that this sharply self-conscious and honest man knows how his "yearning," "this appetite for freedom . . . for forgetfulness" was an impulse for flight from what is clearly described as the "steady drudgery of a coldly passionate service." Flight, we know, is the alternative response to fear, to stand and fight being the other. Aschenbach—it is not to be lost on us—has stood and fought all his life; but not now, and he admits it. To remind ourselves of his name, he is indeed the ashes of a burnt-out case. It seemed "to him that his work lacked those marks of fiery, sportive emotionalism which [are] the fruits of joy" Alone now, he dreads thoughts of a Gerontian life, alone except for his maid and the familiar mountain peaks: "he must attempt something out of his usual orbit."

Aschenbach's literary biography, as is by now common knowledge, somewhat resembles Mann's; only Aschenbach completed the works Mann left abandoned so that *Death in Venice* becomes a compelling nightmare in which the author forgives himself for his own failures by projecting potential successes on a fictional author who lives a lonely life and dies a barren death, cheated even of the one real passion he can still muster. It must have been an exorcistic experience for Mann; in his autobiographical sketch, he uncharacteristically reveals with relish that nothing in *Death in Venice* needed invention, everything was at hand in real-life experience.[14] The *Diaries,* however, show only relief; they conceal, one suspects, the inner satisfaction with which Mann, the artist of the unfinished works, took his revenge on the successful Aschenbach, joyless, exhausted, and soon dead. Critics have taken note of the ironic disdain Mann uses with Aschenbach, and have attributed this to an opportunity for Mann to put more distance between his own occasional homoerotic urgings and those of his creation. This may be so in part, but the artist's scorn may be equally at work; after all, the author, a mere thirty-seven in 1912, was writing of a man nearly a generation older. And was this, then, the harvest of *durchhalten,* a successful completion of art but a lonely, barren life which, when touched by love, succumbs to the barbarities of a barber's touch-up, rouge, delusion, and a Dionysian nightmare and philosophical dispute that ends in death? That indeed is a plague.

Widowed early in life, Aschenbach has a married daughter of whom we hear nothing: clearly she is no longer—if she ever was—close to her father. And: "He had never had a son." A quickly given piece of information, to which Mann never returns: Aschenbach is alone, except, of course, for his status as a *public* figure. Yet the lack of a son must be noticed, for is that lack entirely irrelevant to Aschenbach's love for young Tadzio? Is not the whole affair, whatever the homoerotic sideshow, whatever the intellectual debates about Beauty, Spirituality, and Carnality, also a more simple search of the father for the son? What a price Aschenbach has paid for his sternness, his somewhat Nietzschean denial of pity and compassion. In his novel *The Wretch* he first put on notice an age he felt was mired in psychology and relativism that this sort of flabbiness won't do. No, Aschenbach will have no "sympathy with the abyss," nor with the sentimental notion that to understand all is to pardon all, a relativistic "moral skepticism" unworthy of the author's classical rigor. Well, Aschenbach's life has not been trifled away; he has been dutifully the helmsman of his destiny, exercising a strong will against all the easy enticements of a trivialized age in which compassion, forgiveness, and sentimentality are pretexts for moral and physical lassitudes. Yet *Death in Venice* is, ultimately, a book about waste, loss, dispossession, regret, the reluctance of aging and death. What had seemed so fulfilling—the rigorous life of art—turned out to be barren; what had felt so productive left Aschenbach an emotional cripple, unable once overwhelmed to sort out and acclimatize himself to the emotions of love. For love he permits himself to become deluded, to stay time by the crude, grotesque methods of the barbershop transformation: In short, repression begets uncontrollable frenzy. In the end the putative father and the putative son must part without more than a hint of recognition. The pestilence will victimize him who has so scrupulously sought to avoid it all his life.

No longer can Aschenbach evade the abyss. Sitting by the ocean he has yearnings, "a forbidden hankering," and he is lured to the opposite: "the inarticulate, the boundless, the eternal, sheer nothing." He dreams deep into "the void" just at the moment when the embodiment of the salvation he cannot have—Tadzio and his own youth—pass for the first time across his line of vision.

At first the sight of such perfect beauty impels Aschenbach to write: he feels the craving of creative energy. But soon "he felt exhausted, or even deranged; . . . his conscience was rebuking him, as if after a debauch." The next morning he resolves to catch up with this beauty, to lay a hand on his shoulder or head, to speak to him. Agitation and hesitation conspire to thwart him: " 'Too late!' he thought immediately. 'Too late. Yet was it too late?' " Had he done as he had planned it might have normalized his relationship—a friendly adult striking up a casual acquaintance with a young boy—but "the fact was that Aschenbach did not want soberness: his intoxication was too precious." The "too late" has a rich context at this point: it is "too late" for Aschenbach to turn back from his love-seizure; it is the wrong age, the wrong sex, the wrong city, the wrong time: "He had never had a son."

Once he discovers the truth about the plague, he faces a moral dilemma: inform Tadzio's family, allow them to leave, and depart himself. He decides against all these choices, and instead reflects on his life, a life so devoted to art it has left him a solitary, "der Einsame":

> He too had served, he too had been a soldier . . . for art was a war, a destructive battle. . . . A life of self-conquest and of in-spite-of's, a rigid, sober, and unyielding life which he had formed into a symbol of a delicate and timely heroism, . . . and it almost seemed as though the Eros that had got hold of him were somehow peculiarly appropriate to such a life.

The answer is in ironic indifference. What this life of resignation has done is to despise, to inhibit, to deny Aschenbach of all those essential impulses of which human existence is compounded. Then his art? Well, that, too, has been touched. Its excellence lay in its classic rigor and form, but like life, his art was dry and stiff, emptied of feeling. He had overcorrected the course from an excessive dread of succumbing to easy feelings. Now it was his destiny to pursue those feelings unto death itself. The poignancy of Aschenbach's regret suffuses his reveries and justifies—to him—his silence about the pestilence. Selfishness consumed him now: after a life of deprivation he will not surrender a few moments of bliss, and this even at the risk of not only his own life but of young Tadzio's as well. If they fall to the pestilence, let them fall together.

This "solitary" becomes the "stubborn one" ("*der Starrsinninge*'), a man whose tenacity on the one hand belies the overt lassitude of his behavior on the other. Mann, ever delighted to describe illness and disease in great detail, tells us that pestilence strikes one in several ways, the luckier ones—like Aschenbach—destined to fall merely into unconsciousness. Yet before such release Aschenbach must still suffer the nightmare which his emotionally frugal life has now unleashed. It is a bestial dream, a dream of disease, lust, obscene symbols; of rites, of Pan, demons, orgies, promiscuous embraces, of enemies to his dignity and his self-control. It is only after being touched by this anarchic nightmare that Aschenbach, in an act of desperation, sub-mits to cosmetic rejuvenation, only to sit like his own "Elender," facing the sea and the image of a Tadzio who is about to leave him, wretched and solitary. Life has taken its revenge, paid back in spades the fierce denials which Aschenbach had so insisted on as essential to "moral" decisiveness. The final pages of *Death in Venice* are not, however, painful; quite the contrary, they strike an elegiac note. The victim has exhausted his choices and is himself an exhausted creature; and the last glimpse of Tadzio after a scuffle with an older boy is the image of a lovely youth "tracing figures in the wet sand with one toe," before turning to look, it seemed, at the curious old man in the reclining chair. Aschenbach, when he first saw Tadzio, pronounced him ill and prophesied a short life. That this is a case of wish-fulfillment is clear, for Tadzio leaves Venice and survives. (Indeed it is an irony that a man purporting to be the model for Tadzio surfaced in the 1960s at the age of sixty-eight.)[15] *Death in Venice* is a very compressed work, and its discussions of Beauty and Form, its homoerotic suggestions, have perhaps obscured its strong elegiac overtones, for it is a work about the unlived life—with a twist. Aschenbach's attempt to live ends in death and disillusionment, and for him the cry of "too late" rings with more ominous soundings than even he had suspected. However fraught with nightmare, the visions of Pan also suggest the counterpoint of an elusive Arcadia from which the self-conscious are, in any case, barred.

At the close of *Death in Venice* Mann, who sometimes exploits symbols for their obvious resonances, achieves a masterful effect. Aschenbach, exhausted and defeated, has taken to his beach chair; the Dionysian nightmare behind him, he sinks back to observe his love-object, young Tadzio, roughhousing with another youngster on the beach. Feeling all the protective instinct of a lover, he nevertheless resists the temptation to interfere; his strength is beyond any act of intrusion. The air is filled with the chill of season's end, and Mann plants in Aschenbach's line of vision a "camera, seemingly without owner, [which] stood on its tripod at the edge of the sea . . . a black cloth thrown over it . . . flapping noisily in the wind." This abandoned camera, with its funereal drapery, is powerful testimony to Aschenbach's total isolation. The camera's instrumentality has been made impotent, its magic useless without an owner, since the camera can capture no further memories, nor has it any of the past to offer up. Unused, it serves as a staring parallel to the man who now sits facing it in death, equally abandoned, equally incapable of further imaging—equally useless.

What, then, is the final achievement of *durchalten*, when in the end fame and wisdom remain unharvested? *Death in Venice* is yet another version of life from the perspective of death, of "The Death of Ivan Ilyich" or "A Dreary Story," of a man who, looking backwards, finds the vast expanse of the ocean of the past as empty ("*oed' und leer*") as the expanse of ocean he now faces falling into the sleep of death. Yet there is a difference, and it is that Mann's irony digs deeper than Tolstoy's or Chekhov's. Aschenbach is granted not only success, like Ivan Ilyich and Nicolai Stepanovich, but at the end of the novella two visions: the Dionysian nightmare and the final sight of his love-object.

That latter vision is concrete, not vague and ambiguous, like Ivan Ilyich's "light," and, of course, it exceeds anything proffered Chekhov's dying doctor, who sees nothing as he nears death except desolation. Still, Mann's gift of vision to Aschenbach approaches an ironic hoax. It accompanies his death, but at the same time is so devastating it may almost be said to occasion that death. What it reveals is the terrible waste of a man's life, without son, that is, future. Neither literary fame nor notoriety have bestowed upon him the happiness of fulfillment, however painfully any such fulfillment is earned. Happiness becomes possible only by passing through the grim and unrewarded detours of self-perversion (I do not here mean homoeroticism): the love that has been withheld too long for the son finally found can neither be given nor received. For Aschenbach the final vision of young Tadzio embraces the Tantalusian absurdity of the unreachable; to be released into death is now deliverance from anguish. Gustav von Aschenbach is a victim of the unlived life; his energies to live it with discipline and dignity are ultimately dissolved in collapse of nerves and a falsification of self.

Mann always feared the price, in human terms, of being the artist, and he fought the implications of this duality from *Buddenbrooks* to *Doktor Faustus*. In a way the dilemma of choosing between art and life was perhaps a cover for a broader problem: that of achieving life through a process of living "through it" without the need of abjuring life by observing its process as a nonparticipant. That such a nonparticipant was an artist was for Mann probably a fortuitous accident at a time when he personally faced this self-division most seriously. The artist's rewards *are* his fictions, and the writing of *Death in Venice* did apparently exorcise some of Mann's own demons. The anomie of spirit had to be fought through to survive it; the thirty-seven-year-old Mann had created the late middle-aged Aschenbach in part as a warning to himself. There was life to be lived, even as an artist: "holding fast" was no better than "letting go." The northwest passage lay between the Apollonian and the Dionysian in the processes of productivity as writer, husband, and father—three roles which, as the *Diaries* and the letters show, he took on with nearly equal determination, if not with equal success.

Part II

Mourners and Melancholics:
The Absent Past

Introduction

Melancholia, therefore, borrows some of its features from mourning.
—Freud, "Mourning and Melancholia"

Anyone familiar with Robert Burton's *Anatomy of Melancholy* (1621) realizes at once how complex the subject really is, and that even Burton's exhaustive treatment is not—and could not be—the final word on this ancient malady about which the Greeks and Romans wrote long before Burton. From ancient times to Freud (and, of course, beyond him), the subject of melancholy has been a compelling and mysterious aberration in human behavior. It has always been considered to be some form of abnormality, indeed a disease, an incapacitating one at that, something that set the sufferer apart, but Burton was melancholia's first clinician.

In addition, the malady of melancholy has a host of adjacent maladies, all of them in some way expressions of disaffection, either with the world or with the self. It was, of course, fashionable by the end of the 1700s to cultivate melancholy or one of its related manifestations. Death itself became a palliative, not the medieval comfort afforded by faith at the end of one's life that would bring eternal salvation, but rather the stylized affect of peace, the desire eventually, in many Romantic writers, to descend into the dark either as a reprieve from unbearable realities or from a desire to participate in the seemingly benign provinces of silence and even beauty. Such longings for death were not without conflict—an awareness (as in Keats, for example) that death was not only final but that salvation was dubious and, worse still, that death would prevent one from enjoying its anticipation, which frankly was often the single most relished emotion.

Burton's *Anatomy* was a very serious work, and its major premise was clear: it was the melancholic misanthrope and his unending disaffection that were out of joint, not the society against which he railed. Burton's undertaking was to diagnose and to propose some cures. He does not mince words: "we commonly complain . . . want of encouragement, want of means, when the true defect is in our own want of worth, our insufficiency."[1] Among the myriad causes of melancholy Burton did not forget "Shame," "Disgrace," "Envy," "Malice," "Hatred," "Anger," all in addition to the scores of physiological causes ranging from "Diseases of the Head" to "Bad Diet." Nor did "Idleness" and "Solitariness" escape his sweeping view of this disease, nor "Self-Love" and "Worldly Losses." In general Burton covered the territory so extensively there seems little to add; what he does offer, as our authors do not, are a series of "cures." Not even Freud would call his treatment a "cure": for modern melancholics there are no cures, only an acceptance of and thereby a surcease to suffering. Until the mid-1800s melancholy was the result, not the cause, of justifiable discontent. Even Dr. Johnson, himself a melancholic, could but label discontent the "vanity of human wishes."

Slowly, however, such views were superseded. An increasingly benign view of death was a harbinger. Thomas Gray mused about the many "mute inglorious Miltons" who might lie under the sod, and by the time we reach the Romantics, discontent became not merely a respectable but a necessary function of the artist's anguish. Some of this discontent was, of course, social and political—full of energy and fervor. The larger portion of it, however, resembled more Coleridge's real and imagined dissipation of creative powers:

> A grief without a pang, void, dark, and drear,
> A stifled, drowsy, unimpassioned grief,
> Which finds no natural outlet, no relief,
>   In word, or sigh, or tear—
>
> . . . .
> There was a time . . .
>
> ("Dejection: An Ode")

In his recent overview study of melancholia and depression, Stanley W. Jackson concludes that since Freud the separating lines between mourning and melancholia have been far less clearly drawn.[2] As Freud acknowledged, both states show a remarkably similar profile, and even some of Freud's clearest demarcations do not hold up as much as he had first thought in his pioneering study. For instance, the mourner, like the melancholic, may also suffer from loss of self-esteem, and the melancholic often turns out to have something to mourn about—in short, he or she is not always sad without cause. Clinical depression aside, the two states, mourning and melancholia, often merge, and the one may lead easily into the other (and vice versa). Both, of course, deal with loss, and "loss is a continuous process."

Freud first wrote "Mourning and Melancholia" in 1915, a year after publishing his study on narcissism. The distinction between mourning and melancholia lay as we recall in this: mourning (unlike melancholia) had an "objective correlative," being a response to a real loss for which the emotion elicited was entirely appropriate. I have already cited Freud's critical observation: "In mourning it is the world which has become poor and empty, not the ego." But even Freud's line is somewhat thinner than appears and easy to cross; and the relationship of both emotions to narcissism is stated.

The dramatis personae in Chekhov's four tragicomedies is full of mourners, but their realization of an empty world also turns some of them into melancholics. The loss of a cherry orchard, or a loved one, or the mythic "Moscow" in *Three Sisters*—real as such losses are—makes the mourner despair, turn inward, take on "symptoms" of melancholia, and, in the search for a framed self, approach and sometimes reach the realms of narcissism. Freud clearly states the intertwining nature of the mourner and the melancholic who approaches narcissism: "Melancholia . . . borrows some of its features from mourning, and the others from the process of regression from . . . narcissism."[3] So-called normal mourning gets beyond loss after a reasonable time-span; melancholia does not. Chekhov's characters, and James's, as well as those in the works of Ibsen, Kafka, and Faulkner (see the chapters that follow), appear to cross over and back again between mourning and melancholia. Surely there are moments when Chekhov's characters appear to come to grips with the reality of loss; indeed at times they already appear to be "over" the concrete loss when the play begins. Yet a fragmented memory keeps intruding elusively, and it turns out to be the absent past, the past that has devoured the possibilities and offers, in some cases, not even proper mournable memories but instead an expanse of waste.

True, we hear much about the cherry orchard's better, more productive time or about Vanya's youth and his aspirations, but in the end such backward glances are rather melancholic evocations of ephemeral dreams than the memories that offer solace and joy in the act of remembrance (as they so often do in Proust). Again Freud helps:

> Each single one of the memories and situations of expectancy
> which demonstrate the libido's attachment to the lost object is
> met by the verdict of reality that the object no longer exists; and
> the ego, confronted as it were with the question whether it shall
> share this fate, is persuaded by the sum of the narcissistic satis-
> factions it derives from being alive to sever its attachment to the
> object that has been abolished. . . . [S]everance is so slow and
> gradual that by the time it has been finished the expenditure of
> energy necessary for it is also dissipated. (p. 255)

A good example: Lambert Strether's deliberate renunciation of Paris,
Maria Gostrey, and Mme de Vionnet. In Ibsen and Kafka, it turns out,
the past is an empty past; and in Faulkner the past is incorporated into
the figure of a father who, when he cannot be slain, becomes himself
the slayer of the son. For Kafka's Georg Bendemann the past is splint-
ered into fragmentations of the present, persons and events: the
friend in Russia, the dead mother, the abandoned father, the absent
fiancée. And for Quentin Compson in *The Sound and the Fury* the past
is lost in the words of the father that push away, and push down, the
pain, especially the incestuous fantasy relationship with a sister made
impossible by her marriage. When we have a past stable enough to
stay put, it can sometimes sustain us; it acts like a tree limb, a branch,
anything we can grab as we are swept down the rapids. When such
support is missing, we drown, literally as do Georg Bendemann and
Quentin Compson, or metaphorically as do so many of Ibsen's failed
men and women.

To speak of a "wasted" life is not always objective, for in some sense
no life is ever "wasted": the economics of psychic trade are merely
tilted one way or another. That is to say a person's energies are in
intercourse with the allotted time, and it is what that intercourse provides for the person that determines what we call it. One person's
"sacrifice" is another's "waste." Sonia's life in *Uncle Vanya* is as
"wasted" as Vanya's, but her faith and her benign nature (she is in the
tradition of "the beautiful soul") make her renunciation of any personal gain a beatific gesture (only gently ironic) rather than a bitter
loss. Unlike Mme Ranevskaya, she never attacks life, she permits it to
float over her like a beneficent baptismal wave. Vanya, on the other
hand, had expectations: his ego was subjected to the bruising experience of self-conscious disillusion. It is, finally, not only his futile devotion to the old professor that creates his bitterness, but rather his own
inability to realize an image of himself that would not be subjugated to

anyone, not even a successful idol. Vanya is bitter at his own failure, not really the professor's, just as all the major figures in *The Cherry Orchard, Uncle Vanya,* and *The Three Sisters* take psychological revenge on themselves. Ostensibly their disappointments are articulated in despairing speeches about "life," but they are, most of them, victims of Kohut's "narcissistic rage" (see the introduction to Part I); against their inability to realize whatever potential they imagine they have a "right" to form their perspective, whether it is a person, a place, or professional success (author, actress, a Schopenhauer). What they mourn, therefore, is not really a loss but the failure to attain (which, of course, is the worst of all losses). Actual loss activates grief for the object lost; loss of a possibility mobilizes a languishing sense of deprivation: 'Tis better to have had and lost than never to have had at all.

James's characters suffer a similar fate. What they lose—and therefore "mourn"—is not nearly so much something possessed and lost but something not ever possessed and now irretrievable. From the early story, "Diary of a Man of Fifty," to its mature version in *The Ambassadors,* the major note we hear is plaintive wistfulness. A certain note of anger and resentfulness is also incorporated into these plaints, and in this respect it resembles the features of the affect of actual object-loss. Of course, it can be argued that the loss of "nothing" is always a greater loss than the loss of object. Repeatedly the bitterness we discern in "waste" is characteristic not of "normal" mourning but of something else: the sense of memory is missing (increasingly, so that in Beckett it is scrambled or nonexistent), and what stirs is at bottom the *ressentiment* against an unrealized life, wasted potential. Contemplation of waste (which always signifies that something was there to be wasted) generates the twofold sadness of being spectator to the emptiness both personal and general. Hence the significance of the opening lines of T. S. Eliot's *The Waste Land:*

> April is the cruellest month, breeding
> Lilacs out of the dead land, mixing
> *Memory and desire* . . . (italics added)

The mixture of memory and desire perfectly describes the emotional stress of the observer of waste: what memory there is will be disjunctive; what desire there is will be frustrated.[4]

> I sat upon the shore
> Fishing, with the arid plain *behind* me . . . (italics added)

These lines may be read in two ways. Literally we can imagine a man sitting by the shore fishing with the land—the "arid plain"—behind him, at his back. Not so literally we have the fisherman (whose fishing may yield nothing) who has the arid plain (his life) "behind" him. It is this that prompts him to shore the "fragments" against his "ruins": he (like Childe Harold) is himself a "ruin," and the fragments are the parts of a potential unity that has never coalesced. Like a magnet, the ruin is able to draw to itself only the disjunctive, the nonwhole: in short, waste. Finally waste can be something or nothing, and in this context it is the latter. The "nothing" of waste is the absent past, and though this description can suit some of the works in Part III, it seems most appropriate when highlighting the works discussed in this part.

"Man," Nietzsche wrote, "resists the great and ever greater weight of the past."[5] We collectively try to "forget" because we mourn at the thought of what we have fallen from—some form of Paradise. So some kind of "forgetfulness" is essential just to survive (of this more will be said in the Introduction to Part III). Meanwhile Nietzsche warns us not to be defeated by the past, not to permit its passing to isolate us. For "only the builder of the future has a right to judge the past." By "looking forward and setting a great [goal] for yourselves you will also curb that rank impulse to analysis which now lays waste your present and almost makes impossible . . . [the process of] "ripening." Indeed, Nietzsche advises us to project "an image" of future achievement and discard the pessimism that such an idea is impossible because the past cannot be surpassed. Clearly our mourners and melancholics do not heed such advice, for not only do they see themselves as historically inferior (epigoni) but as familial epigoni. Nietzsche laments that "modern man suffers from a weakened personality."[5] Overly susceptible to inferiority and at risk of being drawn into the abyss (*Abgrund*), our future does not look bright unless we reassert our will—that same will which Schopenhauer had robbed us of in fashioning his hopeless future for humanity. This became an intractable problem. If we built our expectations unreasonably high, then we would surely see our egos crash; if we negated expectations, we would just as surely end up being rendered helpless. Either way lay the path of deprivation, and with it inevitable mourning.

To return to Freud: "Mourning is regularly the reaction to the loss of a loved person," (243), and we have already alluded to the overlaps of mourning, melancholia, and narcissism. In the works discussed in the next three chapters it is obvious that mourners can—and do— become melancholics. Further, mourners and melancholics have common roots in narcissism, for in the context of "Narcissists," the "loss of a loved person" is clearly primarily the loss of *one's self*. Moreover, it is the self which, when contemplated as a loss, serves to push the mourner over the line into melancholia. The world has indeed become "poor and empty" precisely because self-image has been "lost": the self searching in effect for *itself* has been deprived of its narcissistic mirror, and it is at that point that mourning turns into melancholia. Freud stressed that melancholia precipitated a "lowering of the self-regarding feelings" (244). Chekhov's characters, and those of Kafka and Faulkner, are almost clinical examples of such a metamorphosis from mourning to melancholia; and Woolf, Mann, and Ibsen all offer variations of the type. We need only glance at a few obvious cases in point.

Whereas the stricken person laments "the loss of a loved one," the melancholic insists on his own "limitations and inadequacies." Take, for instance, Chekhov's Uncle Vanya. What he mourns is, of course, the loss of himself (and the self must be one's "loved one"—up to a point), but his "limitations and inadequacies" (though seen through the optics of rage and helplessness) are clearly stressed. When he insists that he *might* have been someone of stature ("a Schopenhauer, a Dostoevsky"), he compares his nullity to an unrealized potential, and however far-fetched this particular might-have-been may be, the issue remains true to itself. Indeed, exaggeration is natural to its expression. While he hates the old professor and blames him for having inflicted this wound, Vanya really hates himself for having allowed himself to become the victim: "You've ruined my life!"

Everyone is agreed that "loss" need not be of a person:

> A loss, a deprivation, or a disappointment to be reconciled does not necessarily involve a relation to another person. The same process . . . takes place when the loss refers to a satisfying image of oneself that is forgone. Daily losses from the vicissitudes of life, contrary to conventional belief, are probably not simply accepted.[6]

James's characters sometimes do indeed suffer losses of others: Strether in *The Ambassadors,* for example, has lost a wife and a son. But the "daily losses" of his empty life in Woolett, Massachusetts, are far more damaging and contribute (daily it would seem) to his loss of self-esteem. Therefore the only way for Strether to deal with what is clearly a state bordering on melancholia is to reject personal gain and accept the condition of loss—loss of everything that had made his stay in Europe such a fulfilling, but temporary, interlude. Like Vanya,

Strether must hang on without rewards, not because he is a masochist, but because the nurturing of mourning that hovers on melancholia requires (and maintains) the memory of possibilities.

Although the world of the modernists continued to appear "empty," the possibilities of fulfillment were an ongoing source of solace. However, were the possibilities themselves realized (in Strether's case, for instance, marriage to Maria Gostrey), even the poignancy of loss would be gone, and while it may seem paradoxical, it is the poignancy of loss which alone is strong enough to palliate, to ameliorate, to substitute for the feeling of *having* succeeded. Mrs. Dalloway can survive only the *memories* of Peter Walsh; possessing him now would truly kill her. And Gregor Samsa needs to *feel* the daily losses and deprivations, for they are the only way he can experience himself, albeit to the point of ultimate death.

Narcissists, mourners and melancholics are close relations, and all three can (and do) coalesce in a single human experience. Add to this the need and the struggle for survival, exemplified, of course, in Beckett, and we have closed the circle.

4 The Tragicomedy of Wasted Lives: Chekhov and James

Self esteem . . . is perishable. It is easily lost and difficult to recapture.
— *Gregory Rochlin*, Griefs and Discontents

Haven't they waited . . . too long—till something else has happened?. . . the wasting of life [which] is the implication of death.
— *Henry James*, Notebooks (*On the "Beast in the Jungle"*)

The terror of too late!
—*D. H. Lawrence*, St. Mawr

There is now a consensus that Chekhov composed tragicomedies: *The Seagull, Uncle Vanya, Three Sisters*, and *The Cherry Orchard*. Theoretical discussion of tragicomedy does not abound,[1] but there is general agreement that the admixture explicit in the label sufficiently defines the genre, for tragicomedy, in order to earn that label, must embody certain elements from each of the two pure forms. Perhaps few writers, especially dramatists, have been such natural candidates for the tragicomic designation as Chekhov. Any working definition should probably allow this much: tragicomedy ought to be not necessarily an evenly balanced work between tragedy and comedy but rather an almost imperceptible fusion of the two. Modern tragicomedy is not tragedy with what used to be called "comic relief." It could be argued that tragicomedy is in fact a peculiarly modern phenomenon, using irony, existential acceptance of human absurdity, and a measure of metaphysical despair tempered by a recognition that such despair itself can be comic in its manifestations. How these various elements are articulated can differ enormously, and Chekhov and James are very sharply contrasted masters of the art. In Chekhov especially we deal with plays that with a tip of the finger could become either melodramatically tragic or farcically comic. It is the equipoise Chekhov keeps that saves the plays from either of these diminutions. Tragicomedy has all the ingredients necessary for tragedy but, failing to achieve certain characteristics essential to tragedy, these ingredients somehow do not mix properly, and the result is often comic, more properly "absurd," so long as that word does not trigger immediate associations with its more recent use in terms of drama or of literature and philosophy in general.

"Waste"—as noun, adjective (wasted) or verb—encompasses many meanings. Surely the "waste" in Chekhov and James is not the same as the "waste" in Beckett. Some characters may even claim "victories": say, Nina in *The Seagull,* or Strether in *The Ambassadors,* but such triumphs are often undercut by irony, or they are so attenuated they almost seem phyrric. In general the term "waste" is used here to denote something lost, missed, or experienced "too late." Here are some definitions of "waste" from *The Oxford English Dictionary:* "to consume one's strength or faculties"; "To employ, put forth (energy, effort, qualities, talents) uselessly or without adequate return"; "To lose strength, health or vitality"; to be "devastated, ravaged, ruined": for different characters there is something in each of these descriptive definitions that fits. Subtle differences exist, and I hope that the context will make these clear. But in the end, even where there is understanding of waste by an awareness of it— gathered in the process of "recognition"—the final result is still grim enough to earn the term.

I
Chekhov: Fetishes: Bookcases and Orchards, Seagulls and Moscow

Perhaps no other play so articulates the unlived life as a major motif in Chekhov than *Uncle Vanya.* It is clear from start to finish that the hero of the play is Vanya himself; at forty-seven, he is the chief character of the play who bitterly bemoans his wasted life, his energies attached to false causes and failed gods. In Act III, just before he shoots, unsuccessfully, at the fallen idol, the aging professor, his brother-in-law, Vanya says:

My life's ruined! I'm gifted, I'm intelligent, I have courage. . . . If I had lived a normal life, I might have been a Schopenhauer, a Dostoyevsky—but I'm talking nonsense! I'm going mad. Mother, I'm in despair! Mother![2]

Vanya is not alone in his despair. Here is Astrov, the doctor and environmentalist who wants to save the Russian forests for posterity but who has become disillusioned and drinks too much:

My time is over, it's too late for me. . . . I've grown old, I've worked too hard, I've become vulgar, all my feelings have become blunted. . . . (Act II)

And Yelena, the professor's young wife:

As for me, I'm just a tiresome character—an episodic character. . . . In my music, in my husband's house, in all my love affairs—everywhere in fact—I was only an episodic character. Come to think of it. . . . I'm very, very unhappy. (Act II)

Even the old professor feels superfluous, despite his arrogance ("My life's over" [Act III]); and Sonia, for a time, loses her faith and sees herself as the eternal spinster she is. In all, the play is a forum for several characters' dirge on wasted lives, though none, it is true, more so than Vanya's. Moreover, Vanya's sense of waste does not originate in a sense of causeless lethargy but, rather, in the acrid realization of betrayal: what he believed in has turned out to be false; the man he revered is really an ignorant fool. "We looked upon you as being of a higher order," he tells the professor: "You've ruined my life! I haven't lived! I haven't lived at all! Thanks to you I've wasted, destroyed, the best years of my life!" (Act III). Uselessness is the overriding feeling in the play, and even stage props are designed to be non-sequiturs. Vanya's bedroom at the start of Act IV is described as having on its wall "a map of Africa, apparently of no use to anyone," except that it might be a kind of fantasy symbol or a reflection of Astrov's attenuated ideals. As Baudelaire said in titling one of his prose poems in a note of despair: "Anywhere out of the world!"

Astrov is a blend of idealism and cynicism, or impulsiveness and exhaustion. His actions are not always consistent with either mood, and his infatuation with Yelena is doomed from the start. "Well, go, *Finita la commedia!*" he tells her. "*Finita!*" he repeats a few lines later, and it is, in fact, finished: nothing has come of any of these crossed relationships; and Sonia submits that "It can't be helped, we must go on living however unhappy we are!" She does indeed believe it, but who else does? She promises "rest" after an unfulfilled life, but such solace is renunciation only. It is solace only Sonia can believe, and for how long we cannot know. For Vanya—and the rest—such solace is not enough. The major dilemma in *Uncle Vanya* is the realization, especially on the part of Vanya, that the wasted life he has discovered is unredeemable. His own infatuation with the deposed professor's wife is a fantasy, a projection, and an avenging emotion more than it is love. Its hopelessness, even its ridiculousness, is made clear to him by the circumstances themselves. Yelena treats his advances with disdain and annoyance. Sonia, scolding him for drinking with Astrov, gets a poignant reply: "When there's no real life, one has to live on illusions. It's better than nothing, anyway" (Act II). Astrov, when asked by Sonia, "Are *you* dissatisfied with life?" receives an equally acerbic response: "I love life in general, but I simply can't stand our Russian provincial, philistine life. . . . And as for my own personal life, I wish to goodness I could say there was something good in it. But there's absolutely nothing" (Act II). And when Sonia asks Yelena, "Tell me honestly, as a friend—are you happy?" the reply is quick and brief: "No, I'm not" (Act II).

Vanya's case is acutest because he is most bereft. Not only does he lack activity and the prospects of a future (Astrov loses himself in vodka, doctoring, and environmental plans for forests); worse still, he has no personal history:

> Day and night the thought that my life has been hopelessly wasted weighs upon me like a nightmare. I have no past. It has been stupidly wasted on trifles. And the present frightens me by its senselessness. . . . My whole inner life is being wasted to no purpose . . . and I'm running to waste, too. (Act II)

Not only has he wasted his life, but also he has done so on what turns out to be a sham: his reverence for the professor: " '. . . I have been cheated,' Vanya laments, ' . . . Stupidly cheated' " (Act II). Chekhovian irony does not spare us the professor's self-diagnosis, no more cheerful than that of others. Just as Vanya had felt imprisoned—"For twenty-five years I sat like a mole within these four walls" (Act III)— so, too, the Professor finds himself "buried alive in this tomb. I want to live! . . . Every minute to be grieving for the past, watching others making a name for themselves, being afraid of death . . ." (Act II).

Each of the persons in the play, then, is in a state of advanced lamentation, for a life not lived, an opportunity missed, an achievement fantasized but unrealized. In some ways the play encompasses Chekhov's widest spectrum: the youthful Yelena, the still-vigorous Astrov, the middle-aged Vanya, the old professor. Only Sonia has recourse to any hope, and although her piety is surely sincere and her renunciation reminiscent of "die schöne Seele" complex, which the Russians blended together with German and French infusions, the general conviction remains that Sonia, as much as the others, has not had, and will never really have, a lived life that will be self-satisfying. Of all the figures she is the most sympathetic because her wants are relatively modest: love and affection. Yet she is also most pathetic because Chekhov does not permit her the insight which converts frustration into Yelena's guile, Astrov's cynicism, Vanya's rage, or the professor's streak of meanness and self-hate. All these qualities sufficiently compensate, however briefly, the sense of loss. But Sonia has only her hope of the future beyond life and that may make her a martyr, but it also somewhat dehumanizes her. It is a classic case where self-delusion becomes converted not into the sublime saintly renunciation but into a fearful, starved withdrawal convincing only perhaps to the victim herself (as is the case with Ottilie in Goethe's *Elective Affinities*). The play has often been viewed, not without cause, as a quadrangular mismatch, typical of Chekhov, in which everyone is in love with someone who in turn does not reciprocate but bends affections elsewhere. No evidence can be cited, but some of Shakespeare's comedies might have left their mark on Chekhov.

On the other hand, *Hamlet* clearly hovers over *The Seagull*. The opening dialogue, though comically melodramatic, sets the tone of the play:

MEDVEDENKO: Why do you always wear black?
MASHA: Because I'm in mourning for my life. I'm unhappy.

Masha's unhappiness turns out to pale besides those miseries of other characters, but in truth *The Seagull* is full of people mourning for their lives. Irina Arkadina is mourning for her faded youth, fearing the young and jealous of competition in her role as actress. Her son, Konstantin, is a *Sturm und Drang* personality, a manic depressive whose mourning is often metaphorical as well as quite real: he thinks himself a Hamlet, and he ends his life in a fit of perceived failure. As the would-be actress and the has-been novelist, Nina and Trigorin are both mourners. Nina's case is more complex at the end of the play, but Trigorin's problem is clear enough: he is a man whose peculiar honesty allows him to recognize the truth about himself, namely that while he may be popular he is mediocre. After a disillusioning long speech about the monotony of his craft ("I feel I am consuming my own life"), Nina asks: "But, surely, inspiration and the very act of creation must give you moments of ecstasy and happiness." Trigorin replies, both with candor and frustration, that people will always say of his books: "Yes, yes, very charming . . . but it's a long way from Tolstoy!" (Act II). What Trigorin admits, quite freely, is that while he has talent he is shallow: "I'm false, false, false to the marrow of my bones" (Act II). The seagull metaphor, which he is about to apply to a story (and which is, of course, associated throughout with Nina), also applies to himself, for he, too, is a victim of unachieved dreams.

Masha finally succumbs to disappointment. At the start of Act III she tells Trigorin that she will no longer wait for a love that cannot be realized: she will marry the dull schoolmaster: "To love without hope, to wait for years and years for something to happen—no, thank you." She has also become cynical; she drinks; her hopes and dreams are abandoned. And she turns her cynicism into sentimental self-pity. During the intense verbal battle between mother and son, Arkadina accuses Konstantin of jealousy, calls him a mediocrity, a decadent, a parasite, a tramp, and, finally, a "Nonentity." Her own jealousy of Nina's youth finds a lightning rod, for Trigorin is now captivated not so much by Nina as by the dream of a lost youth, and a lost love, both of which she represents. He uses her, not merely as a source for his fiction (which is sometimes seen as his only motive) but as a vision he wants desperately to materialize, a kind of love fantasy—"As a young man, I never had time . . ." (Act III). When Arkadina calls him the greatest Russian writer of his time, and pleads with him to stay with her, he submits at once: "I have no will of my own. I never had" (Act III). Of course, as we learn, he will succumb to Nina as well—which proves only that he has indeed no will of his own.

Konstantin's uncle, Sorin, sympathetic and lonely, falls ill. At sixty-two he looks back at *his* missed opportunities:

> I've thought of a damned good idea for a short story for Konstantin. It will be called "The Man Who Wanted To." *L'homme qui a voulu.* When I was young, I wanted to become a writer—and I didn't. I wanted to speak well—and I spoke abominably. . . . I wanted to marry—and I didn't. I always wanted to live in town, and here I am ending my days in the country. And so on. (Act IV)

When he is chided for complaining at his age, he cries out: "I don't want to die."

The emptiness of the lives in *The Seagull* is finally expressed in the bird's symbolic devaluation, for when Trigorin is reminded of his desire to have the seagull stuffed—which has been accomplished—he does not even recall having asked for this: "I don't remember." Nina, returning a chastened woman, hardened by the loss of a child, a lover, and perhaps a career, tells Konstantin, "I'm a seagull—no, that's not what I was going to say." Her penultimate speech, like other close-to-the-end speeches in Chekhov, is ambiguous. Her confusion verges on hysteria. Her identification with the seagull is almost pathological. She more than recalls some of Ophelia's last ramblings, which, in a play acknowledged as echoing some of *Hamlet,* is not surprising:

> I'm a seagull. No, that's not it. I'm an actress. Yes! . . . I'm a seagull. No, that's not it. Remember you shot a seagull? A man came along, saw it, and just for fun destroyed it. . . . No. I don't mean that. [*Rubs her forehead*] What was I saying? (Act IV)

Her assertion that she has learned how to endure—in her final words—sounds more like an attempt to cheer herself up than a resolved achievement. And her dreams of still becoming a "famous actress" are equally unconvincing. What does sound real at the end is the shot that ends Konstantin's life, for it shatters the illusions and confusions that have lingered over the play. This is admittedly a bleaker reading of Nina's words than other have offered. But if she has broadened her awareness in learning to "endure"—and that much one cannot deny her—it is nevertheless a very small victory compared to the enormous losses she has had to suffer. If Nina is, as it were, "saved," she has surely been more sinned against than sinning.

As for the seagull, its symbolic value is deliberately jeopardized by repeated thrusts of irony. The very character who really initiates the seagull identification with Nina—Trigorin, who wants to write a story about it—does not, in the end, recall very much, not even (as mentioned) that he wanted to have the seagull preserved. Throughout he trivalizes the potential of the symbol to which Nina clings so tenaciously. Nina, the object on whom the symbol is, so to speak, hung, persists in identifying with the seagull to the very end, though she, too, is not certain of its validity. Ironically she never sees the stuffed object to which her "symbol" has been reduced. The play is characteristic Chekhov: no one is happy; nearly every character regrets a wasted life or, at the very least, a life that did not yield to its expectations. Even Arkadina, the most obviously successful person, is a mere provincial actress; she is frustrated, disappointed, frightened; resents her uncouth husband and the product of their marriage, their son; and would, one feels, much rather have had neither.

The Cherry Orchard and *Three Sisters* are both plays suffused with disaffection. In the first the characters are forced into roles they do not wish to play; in the second they are victimized by their own folly. The feeling of regret, which clings to both plays, goes far beyond a sense of loss. In *The Cherry Orchard* it is manifested almost as a pain of irritation at being reminded that dispossession has been the source of their individual and collective misery. The orchard has outlived its use, overtaken by time, and speeded along by absentee ownership and poor management; and its value, as also the value of the estate in general, lies in memory, in the "what was" and the "what might still be"—"if only." Gayev, the faithful if ineffectual toiler in this orchard, admires the century-old bookcase. To it he addresses, with an irony Chekhov does not entirely hide even from the speaker, a tearful apostrophe: "Dear, highly esteemed bookcase, I salute you. For over a hundred years you have devoted yourself to the glorious ideals of goodness and justice" (Act I). This Keatsian mock-apostrophe to a bookcase lacks the sense of urgent bliss which we associate with a Grecian urn or a nightingale; but the poignancy and the sense of loss are no less sharp. Gayev's sister, Lyuba, mourns a less tangible loss: "Oh, my childhood, oh, my innocence!" (Act I). And together they mourn the loss of their Edenic orchard, though as the play makes clear at the end, for Lyuba that loss occurred earlier than its lament. Her life has long since been away from the estate where she has lost what is much more treasured than the orchard: her child, drowned in one of the estate's ponds. Her return and her departure frame the play, but the interval is not a convincing display of loyalty to a connectedness with the cherry orchard, now a memory at most and, to boot, a burden.

Chekhov found it a major problem to depict Lyuba without inviting a fatal misreading. To create an attitude wholly, or consciously, insincere would have undermined the play: she may at times behave like a hysteric or a simpleton, but she is neither. Truly Lyuba is, however temporarily, recaptured by the visionary reflections of the orchard past; about the orchard future she does not care; and much of the orchard's present during the course of the play is poised between past and future. It is, of course, this present which most troubles her—and the play. Yet it is also precisely this present which Chekhov in a sense must keep alive for four acts. He invokes the past of the orchard, with all its usefulness and its memories; and its future, signaling the changing conditions of people and the economy of progress. Neither past nor future, however, make any impression on the affected owners. Forced, nevertheless, to ponder the crisis of the imminent sale of the orchard, they withstand the pressure by acting out some rather eccentric behavior, and the fate of the orchard remains something far-off and obscured. This creates the many non-sequiturs in the play, people talking to themselves or past each other:

> GAYEV: A long time ago, Lyuba, you and I slept in this room. Now I'm fifty-one. . . . Funny, isn't it!
> LOPAKHIN: Aye, time flies.
> GAYEV: I beg your pardon.
> LOPAKHIN: "Time flies," I said.
> GAYEV: The place reeks of patchouli.
>
> (Act I)

For Gayev ("a man of the eighties") to contemplate the actual passing of time is more painful than to wallow in memories of the past, for both he and his sister can play a game with the past, sever it and create a discontinuous realm, something truly dissociated, a secret they can share. Hence the smell of patchouli is more tolerable by far than the thought of the orchard's plight; and the cliché that "time flies" is, like most clichés, too true to be borne. Nor must we forget that when Lyuba last left the orchard she had sustained two losses: a child and, shortly thereafter, a husband. And for most of the play—certainly from the start of Act II, when she receives the telegram from Paris— her thoughts are divided between the wake for the orchard over which she must preside and the urgency to return to her profligate lover. Her life abroad has been difficult, but it has provided her with more identity and meaning than the orchard now can. She has become, in every sense, an exile. Trofimov's lectures may be tedious, but they contain more than a grain of truth: "Here in Russia only a few people are working so far. The vast majority of the educated people I know, do nothing" (Act II). The clarion call for useful work is a familiar one in Chekhov, but it is only partly serious, partly ironic, for of all the people in the play, Trofimov, "the eternal student," is the least likely candidate to cast stones. He spends all his time evoking visions, and twenty years hence he will be, perhaps, no better than Gayev, a man with a wasted life which he always held out for some future. "And yet, always, every moment of the day and night, my heart was full of ineffable visions of the future. I feel, I'm quite sure, that happiness is *coming*" (Act II, italics added).

If Lyuba's anxiety during the play is centered more on the life she left in Paris than on the orchard, her feelings nevertheless are not always insincere. When she tells Trofimov in Act III that "Life has no meaning" for her without the orchard, she conveys several layers of meaning. In the immediate sense she is exaggerating: Life has meaning, but not here. In a deeper sense she reviews life as a whole—a life in which the dispossession of the orchard merely completes the losses of child and husband. In that sense she is right: her life has been truncated, or she has been severed from it, and what she returns to in Paris is more the life of exile than the fusion she once had living on the estate. The loss of the orchard is therefore the final loss, the loss more of a symbol than a useful and productive property. Her brother has a similar problem. When Gayev returns from the auction, he cannot talk about it to Lyuba. With tears in his eyes he speaks of anchovies and Kerch herring. Lyuba's throwing the keys at Lopakhin's feet is neither defiance nor anger but an admission of helplessness: they are keys that no longer belong to her.

Much as Act I was preoccupied with arrival, so much of Act IV is preoccupied with departure. Yasha and Anya reveal their impatience with the estate, their desire to go to Paris to seek a "new life," a new beginning. And Lyuba's "nerves are better": the great test was not the suspense of what *would* happen but the process of its inevitable happening. That being over, Lyuba can leave, assured that there is truly nothing left for her now. As Lopakhin correctly says: "Life's come to an end in this house." Varya searches for something in her luggage, but we are never told what, or whether, she finds it. It is a symbolic search; after all, no one can take all of one's life in a piece of luggage—something is always left behind. "Yes, life's come to an end in this house. It will never come back." And Anya bids farewell: "Good-bye, old house! Good-bye, old life!" (Act IV).

So *The Cherry Orchard* is not merely a play about the squandering of time, the loss of an era, the individual events of dispossession and death: it is also about people caught at precisely the moment when their old lives no longer suffice and their new lives seem as yet unrealizable or, certainly in the case of Lyuba and Gayev, diminished. That moment happens to coincide with the change from one social order to another, but Chekhov's major focus does not appear to have been merely in exploring that change but, rather, in viewing peoples' lives as they cope with a parallelism of change, their own personalities being inextricably bound to the environment in which they function.

Lyuba and Gayev might have been different if, say, cherry orchards were still viable places on which to live and from which to make good and profitable use. However, one doubts it. That they are caught for us at the moment of change does not *create* their dilemma, but it does make both poignant and effective their responses to what is clearly felt as waste. For the situation confuses them into a mode of behavior which by turns is evasive, hysterical, silly, sentimental, impractical. This is what helps to create the play's tragicomic power.

One may have doubts as to the fervor with which Chekhov really felt "work" to be the antidote to the useless lives he so often described. But of one thing we may be certain: the lack of activity he always considered a serious symptom. Chebutykin, in *Three Sisters*, keeps telling us: ". . . I have never done a stroke of work in my life." Tusenbach says: "I've never done a stroke of work in my life." The former with some cheerful admission offers his own self-analysis: "I shall soon be sixty. I'm an old man, a lonely, worthless old man." Vershinin complains, "I shall soon be forty-three. . . ." And, like Vanya and Gayev, he has many regrets:

> I often wonder what it would have been like if we were to start our life all over again. Consciously, I mean. If our first life had been . . . only a rough copy of our second, a fair one. In that case, I believe, every one of us would first of all do his utmost not to repeat himself. At least he would create a different environment for himself. (Act I)

"Not to repeat himself": so much of the Chekhovian fear is that special form of boredom to which he felt we are often doomed, the failed life that might have been altered by choices—not different choices, merely *choices*. Sometimes this desire for a second chance at life is kindled by love. Tusenbach admits: I've such a passionate yearning for life, for work, to strive for a better life. This yearning has, somehow, become mingled with my love for you . . ." (Act I). For Vereshinin time and its passing is panic: ". . . the longer I live, the more I want to know. My hair's turning gray, I'm almost an old man, but I know little—oh, how little! . . . All we must do is work, work, and work" (Act II). Tusenbach consoles himself with the conviction that, after all, life does not change so very much: "Life will be the same, not only in two or three hundred years, but in a million years. It never changes, it remains constant." Masha feels that man must have or seek religion to find meaning, otherwise "life is empty, empty." She quotes Gogol, " 'It's a boring world, my friends' " (Act II).

Moscow, that distant symbol of release for the three sisters, is evoked and invoked, sometimes in a spirit of hope, sometimes de-spair: "I'm forgetting everything," says Irina, "every day I'm forget-ting, and life's passing and will never return, never! We'll never go to Moscow" (Act III). Andrey says plaintively:

> Oh, where's my past? Where's it gone to? Where's the time when I was young, gay, clever, when my dreams and thoughts were so exquisite? When the present and the future were so bright with hope? Why is it that before we even begin to live, we become dull, drab, uninteresting, lazy, indifferent, useless, un-happy? (Act IV)

Masha exclaims, "My life's a failure," and Irina and Olga end the play with pleas for "work" and hopeful prophecies about the future. "Let us live!" says Olga, ". . . it almost seems that in a little while we shall know why we live and why we suffer" (Act IV).

In Chekhov waste and regret are like a dialectic, the one engender-ing the other. In addition to a sense of loss, Chekhov also recognized a certain folly in crying about what, when all is said and done, is inevita-ble anyway. Perhaps, he felt, we always sense our losses, our waste, our missed opportunities as obligatory propitiation, as a gesture of guilt at having experienced essentially meaninglessness. That fact is certainly tragic; the effort to ameliorate it can often be comic.

II
James: Varieties of Renunciation Experience

James's characters were once considered to be the idle rich who wasted their lives on the trivialities and niceties commensurate with the leisure upper classes who never had to work for a living. Happily, this view has become tempered; in fact, of course, money is very often a central motif in James's fiction, and there are countless characters in his tales and novels who do not have it and whose chief aim is to get it. Even so late and major a work as *The Wings of the Dove* builds precisely on the foundations of avarice and cupidity; it is by no means true that James's dramatis personae are all indolent and frivolous, though with an exception or two James did not concern himself with the proletariat.

The real nature of waste in James's characters, which one notices in the earliest and latest works, is not caused by dilettantism: it is, rather, the realization, often sudden, that one's life has been wasted by timid-

ity, denseness, blindness to opportunity, and sometimes an ambigu-
ously judged self-sacrifice. The discovery of what has been missed—if
it comes at all—comes "too late." *The Ambassadors* comes to mind at
once, and so it should, and James's interest in this motif was consistent. One story, which may in some sense be read as the *ur-
Ambassadors,* is "The Diary of a Man of Fifty" (1879), which James
never included in his New York edition.

The diary reveals ultimately the doubts of the diarist: doubts about
choices and the failure to have risked making them. As has commonly been noted, it is James's men, not his women, who suffer
from the weakness of hesitation, obtuseness, minimal risk-taking:
They are, many of them, Hamlets, or more accurately Prufrocks. In
the *Diary* a British Indian army officer returns to Florence after a
twenty-seven-year absence. He is actually fifty-two, and when last in
Florence he had courted a widow whom he decided not to marry for
he thought her a flirt, a coquette. In Florence he meets a young
American who is courting this late love's daughter, and the story is
taken up mostly with the older man trying to persuade the younger
that he take the same course: abandon the woman, for surely like
mother, like daughter. The young man, however, is not dissuaded;
he marries the young lady, and sometime later when they meet again
in London, the marriage appears to be a very successful one indeed.
The young man then puts it to the older: Perhaps *he* has after all
made a mistake about the mother as well?

The story begins with a deliberate tone of smugness: "When a man
has reached his fifty-second year without being, materially, the worse
for wear ... I suppose he is bound, in delicacy, to write himself
happy."[3] Yet he quickly admits that even this he cannot say for himself: "positive happiness" he has obviously not achieved, else he would
be married, have heirs, and not be recounting this tale from the past.
Though he is certain his decision was correct, he concedes that whatever such decision one makes at twenty-five, it must leave one with "a
certain element of regret; a certain sense of loss lurking in the sense of
gain; a tendency to wonder, rather wishfully, what *might* have been."
As the diary entries show, the older man identifies with the younger,
indeed relives his experience: "He continues to represent to me, in the
most extraordinary manner, my own young identity. . . ." Intimations
that he may have judged the mother unfairly come from the daughter, who makes it quite clear that his departure had been a very painful episode for her mother. But the diarist stands firm: the woman
was a dangerous coquette; he had done the right thing. The first sign
of doubt comes in an entry brief and simple: "Ah, but did my *denoue-*

ment then prove such a happy one?" But he continues to argue against the match of the young couple, feeling even a sense of frustration that he is so little effective, for the young man is "an obstinate little wretch; it irritates me to see him sticking to it." More than that the young man counterattacks: How could the diarist have deserted "the most charming woman in the world?" And the diarist is eventually put on the defensive: "Has it ever occurred to you," says the young man, "that *you* may have made a great mistake?" The diarist replies casually that "everything occurs to one sooner or later," but then comments candidly: "That's what I said to him; but I didn't say that the question . . . had, for the moment, a greater force than it had ever had before." When the young man finally marries he sends a note: *"Things that involve a risk are like the Christian faith; they must be seen from the inside."* From the inside is where the diarist has not seen things, and the final encounter with the young happily married couple has its effect:

> *Was* I wrong—*was* it a mistake: Was I too cautious—too suspicious—too logical? Was it really a protector she needed—a man who ought to have helped her? . . . God forgive me, how the questions come crowding in! If I marred her happiness, I certainly didn't make my own. And I might have made it—eh? That's a charming discovery for a man of my age!

This tale, in addition to prefiguring *The Ambassadors,* is a characteristic example of James's treatment of the "too late" motif. James's decision to omit it from his canon was correct: the story is no artistic masterpiece; its value lies elsewhere. Two stories which he did include, and which precede the *Diary,* approach the question of waste from different perspectives. "A Passionate Pilgrim" (1871)[4] and "The Madonna of the Future." Each story has as its protagonist a pathetic figure whose waste is not a result of having made mistakes but of being fated from the start to make them. The passionate pilgrim, destitute and in search of his roots, is incurably ill when the narrator meets him, a man who has lost his health, property, and ambition. By no means unintelligent or uneducated, the pilgrim is beset with a malaise of missed opportunity both openly acknowledged and deeply felt: " '. . . I'm a failure, a failure, as hopeless and helpless, sir, as any that ever swallowed up the slender investments of the widow and the orphan. . . . What I might have been—once!—there's nothing left to show. I was rotten before I was ripe.' " In his search for family he meets a woman, forty-four, with whom he falls hopelessly in love, as she with him. But they are both "too late." " 'If I had only come here ten years ago!' "

The woman, too, wonders: " 'To think of these ten years that we might have been enjoying you!' "

"The Madonna of the Future" is one of many James stories about inhibited, paralyzed artists who, on the whole, deny failure. The painter of this story "didn't know the very alphabet of drawing." Yet there are two stories here: the painter's vision of the beautiful Madonna, whom he never painted, and the reality of the model's aging, which he can neither perceive nor admit. In time the narrator understands: "The immensity of his illusion; how, one by one, the noiseless years had ebbed away and left him brooding in charmed inaction, for ever preparing for a work for ever deferred." And, in time, too, the painter has premonitions of his illusions: "The poor fellow's sense of wasted time, of vanished opportunity, surged in upon his soul in waves of darkness." By the end of the tale the poor painter understands it all. When the narrator uncovers the easel to find an empty canvas, "cracked and discoloured by time," the painter is defeated by self-knowledge:

> "You were right! . . . I'm a failure! I shall do nothing more in this world. You opened my eyes, and though the truth is bitter I bear you no grudge. . . . I've been sitting here for a week face to face with it . . . with the past, with my weakness and poverty and nullity. . . . I never began! I waited and waited. . . . I wasted my life in preparation."

By the time James wrote "The Beast in the Jungle" (1903) he had reached his so-called major phase, and the story, though a little too melodramatic for some tastes, is a powerful statement about waste, opaque vision, and the "too late" motif. John Marcher, the ultimate narcissist, with an ancestry reaching back to the diarist in "The Diary of a Man of Fifty," misses his life and his chance for love with an irony built into his dilemma that few if any preceding stories were able to sustain. Marcher's ultimate fate, to be "the man in the world to whom nothing whatever was to happen," is predicated on the very opposite, to be *the* man awaiting something great to happen. In the process of waiting Marcher fails to see that what he awaits is happening before his eyes: May Bartram's love. Until the end, that love, which is in him as well, remains locked from view, stubbornly secreted by an overriding ego.

James's Preface to "The Beast in the Jungle" (completed just after *The Ambassadors*) is explicit, as are the entries into *The Notebooks*, dated 1895: "What is there in the idea of *Too Late*. . . . I mean too late in life altogether. . . . [And] the wasting of life is the implication of death. . . . It's *the woman's sense of what might have been in him* that arrives at the intensity."[5] By 1901 James had developed the idea in detail: her death, his initial inability to understand what has passed him by, "it's too late." The title of the story, which supplies Marcher with the metaphor for his experience, is a link to the violent emotions which this story and "The Jolly Corner," ironically titled as if to mislead, explore. That James was capable of dealing with such violent explorations has now been conceded. John Marcher's story is more than the experiences he misses, whether it be May Bartram's love of him or his of her; on the deepest level, the "beast" is Marcher's peculiarly agitated perception of *experience,* a perception which James was at great pains to describe—and to reject—in this story and subsequently. For as James says in the Preface, "the conviction, lodged in his brain . . . [was] that experience would be marked for him, and whether for good or for ill, by some rare distinction, some incalculable violence or unprecedented stroke." It turns out that the waiting itself, however, *really* constitutes the violence; the violence of discovery, though actual, is anticlimactic and perhaps constitutes a flaw in the story. Marcher, says James, waits and regrets because he has come under the spell, the "sterilising habit" of finding anything good enough: "He perforce lets everything go. . . ." The intensity of waiting fills his life; the expectation substitutes for the experience, the anticipation for the fulfillment. When he finally recognizes how blinded he has been and, through such new sight, surveys the waste that lies behind in arid years, the recognition itself is triggered by the sight of a grieving face at the cemetery where May Bartram now lies buried.

Now it is not merely "too late" but "too much." What has happened cannot be appropriately absorbed, cannot truly be made use of as in the case of, say, Lambert Strether in *The Ambassadors.* "The Beast in the Jungle," then, which is not one of James's most accomplished stories, is nevertheless the most nakedly self-conscious analysis of the "too late" motif. Its hero possesses none of the pathos of some of the earlier stories, none of the grace of a Strether, nor is he the villain some have made of him. He is an obsessed character (obsession itself is a Jamesian motif), whose brutality lies not merely in his blurred vision, his egotism, his failure to be perceptive, but in his bruising pursuit of a spatially conceived Time. Marcher veritably prowls the years, clawing at them with what James explains in the Preface is the same kind of excitement and frustration, like "the blinded seeker in the old-fashioned game," at times coming close—he " 'burns' on occasion," he is hot—only to be thwarted.

Marcher's poor memory when he meets May Bartram—his inaccurate memory about their first meeting—is often cited as proof of his self-absorption, his inability to integrate with anyone else. It is this partly, but more to the point his poor memory serves as a metaphor for James's treatment of Time in the story. Marcher is caught in a kind of paralyzed Time, self-created, a kind of "eternal fixity" within which he waits. In that posture of waiting most memories of the past are not clearly sequential: "he had got most things rather wrong. It hadn't been at Rome—it had been at Naples; and it hadn't been eight years before—it had been nearly ten. She hadn't been, either, with her uncle and aunt," and so on. Nor does the story begin when they reencounter each other, for on the first occasion of meeting her he had already confided his dream of the "beast," told her he had "the sense of being kept for something rare and strange, possibly prodigious and terrible, that was sooner or later to happen." Is it something he will be made to suffer, asks his companion—more right then she can yet know—but he replies, "Well, say to wait for . . ."

Indeed, far from being a self-possessed indulging man, Marcher is haunted, exhausted by the "apprehension that haunts me—that I live with day by day." For this vigil he enlists May Bartram's willing aid—after asking for it three times. The manner of the vigil is, by and large, silence, under her watchful eye, and so as in some parable (the story has a parabolic form), "they grew older together": "He had been struck one day . . . with her suddenly looking much older to him than he had ever thought of her being; then he recognised that the suddenness was all on his side—he had just simply and suddenly noticed. . . ; inevitably, after so many years, she *was* old, or almost; which was of course true in still greater measure of her companion. If she was old . . . John Marcher assuredly was. . . ." Her illness does indeed make him afraid, not primarily out of concern for *her* health but for *his*—that is, what if she, his partner in waiting, dies and leaves him in the lurch? "What did everything mean . . . unless that . . . it was simply, it was overwhelmingly too late?" There is a final opportunity—missed. " 'It's never too late.' " And May Bartram tells an uncomprehending Marcher that, indeed, what was to have happened *has* happened.

When she dies, Marcher's "torment" is no longer to wait; he accepts her insistence that the beast has indeed sprung. But what *was* it? This becomes the new torment—"his unidentified past," his unnamed experience. For a year Marcher travels, "to the depths of Asia," where he might search out real beasts but spends his time instead "on scenes of romantic interest" and in a state of psychic bewilderment. Something, he senses, is missing, something has been left incomplete: what, he does not know. He fails to feel an "identity," and the void of it brings him home, "the sounded void of his life," back to May Bartram's grave. There at last he encounters his experience, the "image of scarred passion" in a fellow mourner in the cemetery. Then the beast springs: "No passion," he realizes, "had ever touched him . . . ; he had survived . . . but where had been *his* deep ravage?" The answer lay in love: "*then* he would have lived. *She* had lived," and now he shudders at the "chill of his egotism and the light of her use." The horror of realization is its terrible awakening; "*this* was knowledge," and after such knowledge what forgiveness? What springs finally is the beast of the past, leaping like a "hallucination" with its vengeful, reproachful visage: "He saw the Jungle of his life and saw the lurking Beast . . . rise, huge and hideous, for the leap that was to settle him." His only way to avoid its sight is to bury his face on the tomb. What he had always sought in the future was all this time in the past, and the past having happened is alone possible of real torment, for the future, not yet having come, can only create speculative anxiety. James titled his story brilliantly. What was love could be no beast, if it were acknowledged; unacknowledged, it is no longer love. What the beast is for Marcher is like the specter of Christmas Future for Scrooge: a wasted life. John Marcher, however, gets no second chance. "He had seen *outside* of his life, not learned it within. . . ."

Of "The Jolly Corner" (1908) James said very little, but readers have tended to link it to "The Beast in the Jungle." In one sense this is correct, since both stories deal with a "might have been" situation. Yet "The Jolly Corner" is, as James called it, "a finished fantasy," and it has a happy ending. Indeed the alter-ego Spencer Brydon pursues in the old house is a "might have been" he did well to avoid, though both pursuit and discovery were perhaps necessary rituals in his desire to come to terms with himself, his choices in the past, and his future.

Scores of James's other tales and novels could be enlisted for this motif of waste and the unlived life, for it appears in many guises: "The Jolly Corner," "The Aspern Papers," "The Pupil," *Roderick Hudson, Washington Square, Portrait of a Lady, The Wings of the Dove, The Spoils of Poynton, The Princess Casamassima, The Sacred Fount, The Golden Bowl*—the list is long and various, for in all these fictions men and women come away, as James might well have said it, empty-handed, regretting, renouncing, missing out on their lives. Yet *The Ambassadors* ranks chief among such works: James himself indicated this when in the Preface he places such special emphasis on the episode which is recounted in the famous scene of the novel as the hero admonishes a younger man to "Live all you can; it's a mistake not to."

Wilde's *The Picture of Dorian Gray*, once thought to be notorious, is of the English *fin de siècle,* but its unabashed hedonism also places great emphasis on draining life's experiences to the fullest. Like Pater, Wilde urged upon us the strategy of opportunism with respect to time: nothing so much shocked Wilde, nothing seemed more criminal to him, than the wasting of a single moment. This he found in Pater's *The Renaissance,* in which, in the also-once-notorious "Conclusion," Pater had summoned us to experience the sensations of life freely. "Not to discriminate every moment," he insisted, "some passionate attitude in those about us . . . is, on this short day of frost and sun, to sleep before evening." The "awful brevity" of life commands us to take it in to the last drop, "gathering all we are into one desperate effort" of total immersion. Our only chance lies in "expanding that [brief] interval" we know as life, "in getting as many pulsations as possible into the given time."[6] Of course, Pater recommended that we seek such an expended interval in art, not as others (and sometimes Wilde) sought to interpret it in experimentation of vices and in what was then called the pursuit of "unnatural" urges. Pater's admonition was in fact bent from its purely aesthetic focus into what he was himself dismayed with—the arena of reality.

James, not unaware of either Pater or Wilde, attempted in *The Ambassadors* to strike a balance between aesthetics and life. For Lambert Strether the ambassadorship to Paris is, as everyone has agreed, the opportunity to experience a brief, intense revival of deadened feelings. Acutely aware that for him so many things are "too late," he begins early on in the novel to experience through others: through Chad, the young man he has been charged to bring home; through Mme de Vionnet and her daughter, the two women who are thought to be leading Chad astray; and most of all through the atmosphere of Europe itself, Paris in particular, which stirs within him feelings either long dormant or in fact never tapped at all.

One may argue that Strether's awakened sensibility is recompense enough; that the enrichment of his consciousness is powerful and fulfilling. Yet in the end, Strether's victories are attenuated, and his renunciations—though they serve as a liberating act—bring him back to an emptiness, a future that will rely on memories. He is a wiser man for having served his ambassadorship, but wisdom is also painful. To be conscious of what one has *not* had—and can, in effect, never have in future—is both rewarding and poignant. In effect Strether has, indeed, lengthened the interval of time—his stay in Paris and France—but, in the end, as in fairy tales, the moment comes when enchantment ends and the rest is a dreamt memory.

James himself quotes the "gist" of Strether's importunate speech near the beginning of his Preface:

> "Live all you can; it's a mistake not to. It doesn't so much matter what you do in particular so long as you have your life. If you haven't had that what *have* you had? I'm too old—too old at any rate for what I see. What one loses one loses, make no mistake about that. Still, we have the illusion of freedom; therefore don't, like me today, be without the memory of that illusion. I was either, at the right time, too stupid or too intelligent to have it, and now I'm a case of reaction against the mistake. Do what you like so long as you don't make it. For it *was* a mistake. Live, live!"

The actual speech to little Bilham, the young painter, spoken in Gloriani's garden, is much longer and it is reproduced here with some omissions:

> "It's not too late for *you*. . . . All the same don't forget that you're young—blessedly young; . . . Live all you can; it's a mistake not to. It doesn't so much matter what you do in particular so long as you have your life. If you haven't had that what *have* you had? This place and these impressions—mild as you may find them to wind a man up so; all my impressions . . . well, have had their abundant message for me, have just dropped *that* into my mind. I see it now . . . and now I'm old; too old at any rate for what I see. Oh I *do* see, at least. . . . It's too late. And it's as if the train had fairly waited at the station for me without my having had the gumption to know it was there. . . . What one loses one loses; make no mistake about that. . . . The affair of . . . life—couldn't, no doubt, have been different for me; for it's at the best a tin mould, either fluted or embossed, with ornamental excrescences . . . into which, a helpless jelly, one's consciousness is poured—so that one 'takes' the form . . . and is more or less compactly held by it. . . . Still, one has the illusion of freedom; therefore don't be, like me, without the memory of that illusion. I was either, at the right time, too stupid or too intelligent to have it; . . . at present I'm a case of reaction against the mistake. . . . You've plenty [of time]; that's the great thing; you're as I say, damn you, so happily and hatefully young. Don't at any rate miss things out of stupid-

ity. . . . Do what you like so long as you don't make *my* mistake. For it was a mistake. Live!"[7]

There are several obvious motifs that leap out from this long and even uncharacteristically polemical Jamesian speech. The "too late" idea of course; the "too old" idea; the notion that loss is loss, really irretrievable, "make no mistake about it." In addition, however, there is the question of freedom and the illusion of having it; the question of one's consciousness being poured into a mold deterministically; and the search for a state between too much intelligence or too much stupidity—a state in which the illusion of freedom (of choice) permits the illusion of living. The speech is complex; it is not a simple admission of having missed the train but of having missed the *illusion* of being on one: there *is* a difference. In short, James's novel, like Chekhov's plays, is not merely about the *real* loss of life, the *real* waste, but about the illusion of a might-have-been ("I might have been a Schopenhauer, a Dostoevsky!"). That shifts the whole perspective on the novel, and in doing so it opens up possible answers to questions that have so vexed readers. Why is Strether so innocent? Why, at the end, does he renounce marriage and exile himself?

Strether's speech, set beside that of Lord Henry to Dorian Gray, shows both similarities and differences. Lord Henry, the cynical hedonist, warns the young and innocent Dorian Gray:

> "Ah! realize your youth while you have it. Don't squander the gold of your days, listening to the tedious, trying to improve the hopeless failure, or giving away your life to the ignorant, the common, and the vulgar. . . . Live! Live the wonderful life that is in you! Let nothing be lost upon you. Be always searching for new sensations. Be afraid of nothing. . . . The world belongs to you for a season."

Youth, the dread of losing it and wasting it, the admonition to live— these are much the same in both speeches; but the "illusion" for Dorian Gray lies in the portrait not in his life, which Wilde turns into a work of art sustained by the subterranean "vices" of reality. Although James saw the ritual of life as aesthetically as anyone, he stopped short of conversion to Wilde's unremitting division between art and life. For James the human, the all too human, remains an unalterable fact.

Strether's life has been squandered because he has failed to have the courage necessary to face loss—wife and son—and to break new ground. Not lack of sensibility or ignorance or lack of opportunity are responsible for the poverty of his experience of life. Rather, it is a kind of pride, a conviction that abstinence was not only good for one but the better part of valor. In short, too much, not too little, intelligence proved to be Strether's undoing. He did not allow himself the luxury of illusion, of knowing that, though bound, we may nevertheless attempt to live the illusion of freedom and that this, too, can be a salutary and beneficent way out of an overly deterministic life pattern. Like Mann's Aschenbach, Strether has also lived by the motto "Hold fast!" But to what? Not only his New England conscience—as Austin Warren has shown—but his American pragmatism conspire to thwart his potential pleasures. We know that James minimized Strether's loss of his wife and son,[8] that he devoted to both losses far less space than the original draft of the novel indicated. It is possible that he did so for reasons purely technical: to achieve unity, to keep the narrative flowing, and not to risk the indictment of a character for whom we were to develop forbearance and understanding. Still it is also possible that too much emphasis on those losses would have made too explicit what James wished to leave somewhat ambiguous: Strether's bitterness at himself, at life, and at his own too-keen perception that perhaps illusion was, after all, not worth the experience. Only in the speech to Little Bilham does he bare his soul, if not completely certainly more so than anywhere else.

In the *Notebooks,* in the entry dated October 31, 1895, James thrashes out his conceptions of Strether. Here Strether is, indeed, seen as a man whose experiences in Paris have awakened in him a sense of regret and loss, as truly feeling that life has passed him by: "he perceives that—ever so sadly, so bitterly, now."[9] The bitterness which James here foresaw as necessary almost totally disappears in the final rendition; with the exception of the outburst at Little Bilham there is little overt bitterness (though occasional sadness) in Strether's demeanor. In fact it may be argued that he is almost unnaturally calm, bearing himself with great equanimity and patience; that he remains self-possessed at times to a point incommensurate with his experience. Some of this could be accounted for by the New England restraint and the need for self-control; some of it not. The elegiac note in Lambert Strether has none of the despair, bitterness, forlornness, fear, frustration, and rage that mark the haunted characters of Tolstoy or Chekhov. In his way Strether is complete; his incompleteness, if such it be, is less the failure to have fulfilled a preordained destiny than the realization that he has not permitted himself the luxury of the illusion of such fulfillment. This is not to deny that he seems genuinely softened by Paris and its stimulants; that he sincerely feels, at fifty-five, old, tired, and "too late" to take the full measure of life. Yet his outburst—and it is that—in Gloriani's garden is almost inappropriate for the man we see before and after it. Did James err in leaving it as it is, rather more bitter and harsh than the man he conceived for the novel as a whole and more like the one he had projected in his notes and in the long outline he wrote for his publisher? Even in the "Project" for the novel he wrote: "[Strether] has had a life by no means wasted, but not happily concentrated; and rather makes on himself the impression of having come in for many of the drawbacks, even perhaps for a little of the discredit, of an incoherent existence, without, unfortunately, any of the accompanying entertainment or 'fun.' " He is tired without having exerted himself; "disenchanted" without having been tempted; "*vaguely haunted* by the feeling of what he has missed, though this is a quantity, and a quality, *that he would be rather at a loss to name*" (italics mine).[10] In the novel James makes it clear that Strether thinks "that he has failed . . . in everything. . . . ."

In the notes James felt that he needed someone close to Strether of whom he could be dispossessed: "The young man is dead: it's all over. Was he a son, was he a ward, a younger brother—or an elder one? Points to settle: though I'm not quite sure I like the *son*."[11] Without engaging in psychobiography we do note that it is in the end a son, despite James's hesitations, who was taken from Strether. First he loses a wife to whom he was very devoted. For the boy's death, Strether blames himself indirectly: "He had again and again made out for himself that he might have kept his little boy . . . who had died at school of rapid diphtheria, if he had not . . . so insanely given himself to merely missing the mother. It was the soreness of his remorse . . . because the father had been unwittingly selfish." So is not Chad a surrogate son and is not Mme de Vionnet a surrogate wife and is not Paris a surrogate experience of what *might have been* the quality of his life? Is that one reason he seeks occasional refuge, alone, in the dimness of Notre Dame? His "acceptance of fate was all he had to show at fifty-five." It is perhaps this passivity against which he rebels, for to assert himself need not mean, say, marriage to either of two available women, nor need it mean an exodus from Woolett, Massachusetts, to Paris. Ironically, self-assertion is attained, for Strether, by what appears to be yet another act of self-dispossession and renunciation. But there is another way of viewing this, namely as an act of asserting the *freedom,* the illusion of which he had not permitted himself before. And that brings us back to his polemical speech.

The first point in Strether's encomium is that living, the process itself, is more important than any specific goal: "It doesn't so much

matter what you do in particular, so long as you have your life."
Strether does not, then, miss some special accomplishment as much as
the sheer pulse of life itself. "I see it now. I haven't done so enough
before—and now I'm old; too old . . . for what I see." Not to *see,* and
hence to act on, this failure has been his most obvious omission. Now he
does see, the train has left. What he lacked was not opportunity but
courage (most Jamesian males lack it while females have it in abundance). Strether himself blames his lack of "gumption," but he is not
certain: a loss is a loss. Therefore the notion that Strether is spending
his time in Paris to recover some of what he has lost is inconsistent with
his own view of irrecoverability. What his continental sojourn achieves
is to provide him with the bittersweet moments of realizing his loss, for
heretofore even that he was not privileged to see. In short, Strether
revels not in recovery but in elegiac musings of the might-have-been,
and there is ultimately a pleasure principle in such indulgence in loss.

Now the "affair of life" is at best a mere "mould" into which the
"helpless jelly" of one's consciousness is "poured." Once poured, the
jelly takes permanent shape; one is "held" by the form. True, we do
indeed have an "illusion of freedom," and the worst of it for Strether is
to be "without the memory of that illusion." Even though we recognize
that we are prisoners of our jelly-forms, the illusion of freedom permits
a certain indulgence Strether now, belatedly, sets out to exercise. Too
much stupidity or too much intelligence (one is certain it is the latter)
had prevented that; the only problem, of course, is that now Strether is
fully conscious, and to a certain extent such awareness must militate
against the full enjoyment he might once have experienced. The "bless-
edly young," which a few lines later becomes "hatefully young," must at
all costs avoid *that* mistake—especially the possibility of being too stupid. What may seem at first to be a merely rueful and elegiac lament
about having missed out on life turns out to be a carefully contained but
bitter regret at having been *too* conscious of life's ultimate futility.
Robbed of illusion, he has been robbed of life as well. Nor is it impossible, he seems to be saying, to have the illusion and to know it as one, for
we need such illusion disguised in order to participate in the "affair of
life"; unawareness permits a rich participation in the process of living.
So astride his New England conscience there is also a pragmatic consciousness, a sense of reality which James felt was of ambiguous help.
One who spends life refuting its ultimate possibility of fulfillment fore-
closes fantasy, dream, and sheer enjoyment, none of which may achieve
for one a particular goal but all of which make the ultimate failure to
arrive there—to use Strether's metaphor—a more pleasant journey.[12]

Viewed this way Strether's seduction and his final decision not to "have got anything for myself" make better sense. He had all along decided, it seems, that what he wished to experience just once was the freedom lost, the freedom to indulge consciously in illusion, no goals, no rewards. This, too, accounts for the calm and sober manner with which he accepts the disruption of that illusion when he discovers that Mme de Vionnet and Chad have not enjoyed an innocent relationship but have been deeply enmeshed in an affair. His generosity and forgiveness for having been deceived are not merely the result of his affection for Mme de Vionnet or the kindly compassion one might expect from a middle-aged man of breeding. Rather, his forgiveness and his acceptance of being deceived are gestures of gratitude for having been given the opportunity of the experience, for while it lasted it bestowed upon him a dim if brief vision of what the process of living *could* be like. That he also feels some vague guilt for engaging in a kind of self-indulgent voyeurism is apparent in the determination not to reap any gain from his experience. One scene especially demonstrates the illusory sense of lavish freedom and submission, the meeting, by accident, with Mme de Vionnet in the dark chapel of Notre Dame.

The cathedral scene in *The Ambassadors* occurs almost precisely in the center of the novel, at the beginning of book VII. Strether, in the autumn of his life, and full of regret for not having sufficiently appreciated its spring and summer, still has the capacity to take in—and be taken in—by the stimulants of charm and beauty which Paris has to offer. The first time he meets Mme de Vionnet he falls under her spell: this woman cannot be bad for the young man; she seems in fact to have changed him much for the better. Strether is misled, almost to the end, as to the true nature of the intimacy between Mme de Vionnet and the young man, needing for himself, one suspects, more than for others, to believe in its platonic essence. It is the cathedral scene which serves to seduce him and to unravel his ambassadorial resolves. After this episode he will struggle not to take the young man from Paris but to keep him there.

Strether, we are told, has more than once visited Notre Dame: "It wasn't the first time Strether had sat alone in the great dim church"— it soothed his nerves. Capable, still, of "good moments," James's hero makes his "pilgrimage" as something less than a celebrant and something more than a tourist. The church becomes his place of consolation and he has just purchased a seventy-volume edition of Victor Hugo, which supplies him with imaginings and reveries as well. Notre Dame literally becomes an island where he realizes his fictions severed from reality. James is quite blunt: Strether was in a mood "it being at present just from himself he was trying to escape." In this Catholic chapel, this New England Puritan finds a "sense of safety, of simplification." In the "afternoon of [his] life," Strether is truly stricken by this great church: "the mighty monument laid upon him its spell." Under this spell he will experience an "encounter that deeply stirred his imagination." Strether habitually observes "a fellow visitant" whose back he sees and who he guesses as being young. She, too, is not in prayer but, rather like him, is sitting in immobile stillness. His curiosity impels him to wander down the nave of the church when the lady in question turns and he beholds Mme de Vionnet: "She was the lurking figure of the dim chapel, she had occupied him more than she guessed. . . ." Like him (it turns out), she comes often, even though she is "terrible, in general, for churches," and in that nonreligious (if not irreligious) commonality they find in each other an instant sense of ease and conspiratorial understanding.

The male, not the female, fantasizes: "She was romantic for him, far beyond what she could have guessed. . . ." Indeed, attempting to reassure himself of the lady's innocence, Strether argues that the haunting of churches was proof for it rather than against it, for "she would never have come to flaunt an insolence of guilt" in such a sacred place. Poor Strether, as James calls him. She haunted churches, he reasons, for "continued help, for strength, for peace." So seduced, Strether resolves to give the lady a "sign"—a sign of trust, of bond, of mutual understanding: "The sign would be that . . . he understood; . . . [that] she was free to clutch."

When they leave Notre Dame, they are bound to each other; they lunch at a lovely café on the Left Bank where their "understanding" is sealed with *omelette aux tomates* and a bottle of "straw-coloured Chablis" at a table covered with white linen. Strether now feels the gentle pleasure of sweet surrender, and James's evocation of this mellow eroticism is characteristically rendered in a language overtly innocent, eschewing not only the suggestion of vulgarity but, in his usual adroit manner, intimating the willingly sacrificial nature of this adoring admirer as he permits himself to be transported: "he could only give himself up. . . . their walk, their déjeuner, their omelette, the Chablis, the place, the view. . . . To this tune . . . was his surrender made good. . . . It *was* clearly better to suffer as a sheep than as a lamb." Mme de Vionnet gratefully accepts Strether's "sign": " 'A man in trouble *must* be possessed somehow of a woman,' " and though this is said half in jest, its meaning later on in the novel is more to the point than either can realize at the time. For Strether asks why he is in trouble— he is appalled at himself, for he "hated to pass for anything so idiotic

as woundable." Yet by the end of the chapter he has gone further than
had seemed possible. "Strange and beautiful to him was her quiet soft
acuteness." Voluntarily he had now sacrificed himself to her cause,
feeling at last the experience of having been enchanted. In the outline
sketch of *The Ambassadors* James sent his publisher he had described
Strether as being tired, "disenchanted without having known any
great enchantments, enchanters, or, above all, enchantresses. . . ."[13]
The cathedral scene has changed all that. However slyly James may
try to disguise the meaning of that scene, it is and has all the consequences of a seduction with overtones of a pleasurably erotic willing-
ness on the part of the seduced: "The golden nail she had then driven
in pierced a good deep inch deeper."

Strether's "illuminations" in the course of the novel are several, but
the most important remains that which leads to the reversal of his
mission: to keep the young man in Europe, not to retrieve him. James
is clear about this reversal: it is a change in Strether's perception, in
how he sees, and for the good of all three—himself, the young man,
and the lady. Strether's decision to accept Mme de Vionnet's influence
as both innocent and beneficent awakens in himself an enlarged sympathy for life, a bittersweet recognition that his narrowness both of
thought and of deed has robbed him of the pulsations of life, and a
resolve that, however briefly, he will appropriate, even vicariously,
and with a new sense of freedom, the symbolic gifts of Europe. When,
very close to the end of the novel, he discovers that his trust in the
innocence of the relationship has been misplaced, Strether does not
change his course. Embarrassed, hurt, and astonished he may be, but
he refuses to become vindictive toward the source of his deception.
Quite the contrary, his compassion enlarges still more, his understanding is sharpened: "Women were thus endlessly absorbent, and to deal
with them was to walk on water."

No, the discovery that the relationship between the young man and
Mme de Vionnet was an intimate affair moves Strether closer than
ever as an ally to the woman—he is truly absorbed. Mme de Vionnet,
in tears, laments her having led him astray; she mourns what she
believes was a friendship missed. " 'You see how' " she says to him
" ' . . . I want everything. I've wanted you too.' " Strether replies: " 'Ah
but you've *had* me!' he declared . . . with an emphasis that made an
end." Since the cathedral scene Strether has indeed been had—in all
the several connotations that expression carries.

It must be said that Strether—though he explicitly says that he
should not "have got anything for [himself]" out of "the whole affair"—
cannot be taken literally. Indeed he does not "get" Mme de Vionnet,

who, in a sense, offers herself somewhat less clearly than Maria Gostrey, whom, of course, he also does not "get." Strether's sojourn has deepened and widened his consciousness; he has had his adventure, and this has provided him at least the freedom *not* "to get." To minimize that would be to distort, though there is ample irony in gaining the freedom *not* to choose "to get." For it is the very capaciousness of his imagination, gained by this continental adventure, that has given him both the means and the rationale for renunciation. If, at the end of the novel, Strether were to meet Little Bilham again, would his "Live all you can!" speech be any different? One must doubt it. For we remember that the original speech came in the midst of the glorious garden so filled with the exquisite beauty Strether feels has passed him by. Strong feelings also prompt strong regrets: the pain of having missed out hits hardest at the moment of realizing that it has been missed. And surely that pain is even sharper at the end of the novel—more understood but more painful, too, than it had been in Gloriani's garden—and this because of (rather than despite) Strether's enlarged consciousness. As I have argued elsewhere, the rewards of an enlarged consciousness are always double-edged, and quite clearly a sharpening of insight brings both the positive gift of knowledge and the negative effect of the heightened sense of whatever it is that this knowledge reveals. Strether's life in Europe has given him much to see and feel, and much personal enlargement of "spirit"; but to have experienced those feelings for the first time, in the "autumn" of his life, has strengthened his resolve to renounce further gain. And this is cause for poignant sorrow. In the final reckoning there is only so much that, in James's time, a man of over fifty can be expected to "make up"; and whatever it is, Strether (through his creator) feels that his consciousness of just how much there *is* (or *might* have been) is enough.

In any case, the ending of *The Ambassadors* and the fate of its hero have been debated by serious critics almost from the start. The argument continues. Consider this excerpt from a recent study:

> As much as F. O. Matthiessen admired James and this novel, he felt compelled to write: "The burden of *The Ambassadors* is that Strether has awakened to a wholly new sense of life. Yet he does nothing at all to fulfill that sense. Therefore . . . we cannot help feel his relative emptiness." Here Matthiessen is wrong. It is a mistake to be disappointed by the ending of *The Ambassadors* or to read it pessimistically. Although all is not for the best in the best of all worlds, Strether is not empty: he is full of possibility. And although he will not always be right or successful, when he

returns to America he will continue to do what he can—for others and for himself.[14]

No, Matthiessen is not wrong: to imagine the fate of a character beyond the final word of the fiction is to take over the creative function. James leaves him and so must the reader. There can be no argument about Strether's enlarged consciousness; and this may well make the past easier to understand and the present more sensible. But the future is an unknown. Strether is a different man at the end of the novel; surely no one can say he is not. But such change does not oblige us to read the ending as some sort of redemptive apotheosis for a fruitful life *to be*. The last period of the book is the last. Or, as Strether himself said: "What one loses one loses; make no mistake about that."

For those who wish to allow Strether his "vision," there are these comments from a recent study dealing explicitly with "equivocal endings." Calling *The Ambassadors* an "elegiac novel, whose theme [is] the unlived life," this critic allows Strether "the integrity of a private vision" and a "version of manhood." Yet Strether's "vision" is not seen as benign salvation: he has learned more about "reality," his "loss" has been "terrible," and the experience, in sum, highlights his "impotence." Moreover, what Strether will take back home is "not a new recognition of himself and his limitations, but quite the reverse: a more absolute vision of the ideal possibility and a deeper disgust with the world as it is." In short, according to this reading, Strether has been betrayed by his own idealizing. Such a view approximates my own, except perhaps that mine places more emphasis on the paradoxical nature of Strether's "end": the "vision" (if we accept so strong a word) given to Strether is truly one of loss and dispossession at the same time that gaining such insight is in itself a "gain" within "loss." Indeed, in some ways it is not improper to compare (not parallel) Strether's "vision" to that of Gustav Aschenbach just as he slips into the sleep of death or to Ivan Ilyich and his "vision" of light just as he crosses over into his death. Like most of Chekhov's characters, most of James's disappointed persona continue to live on. But just living is not necessarily a triumph, and "insight" can (and often does) make matters even worse.[15]

Both Chekhov and James understood, each in his own way, the inevitably tragicomic nature of unfulfillment, of thwarted potential, of needless waste. Each was too much of an ironist to permit for very long the expression of mere lament; the elegiac was not to be laid bare but only to be suggested. What might have been could too often obscure what is; and the terrible waste of a life might well come from too much preoccupation with waste itself. Indecisiveness, the lure of perfection, and the long wait did not always result in wisdom, nor did they ensure the ripe harvest. Instead we might have the empty canvas, the "too late" syndrome, the sold orchard, the stuffed seagull, the absent Moscow. The worlds of Chekhov and James have more in common than may first appear, for in both worlds the endless and often convoluted activity turns out to be much ado about nothing. But the price of self-consciousness is self-cancellation. When Hamlet tries to become Don Quixote, tragicomedy is inevitable.[16]

5 The Past as Parent: Ibsen, Kafka, Faulkner

Many things would be explained if we could know our real geneal-ogy.

—Flaubert, letter to George Sand, 1866

That the past confers its sins upon the present and indeed threatens the future is a characteristic "discovery" of the nineteenth century. To begin with the concept of time itself is an essential element in any culture's view of its pastness, and as J. H. Buckley has demonstrated, the nineteenth-century notion of time (in England especially) under-went several critical shifts.[1] This was true as well on the Continent, and in much the same patterns. One can identify a kind of historical guilt, an obsession with and abuse of history which set the stage for a number of attitudinal changes that spilled over into the first two or three decades of the twentieth century, and to which I have already alluded in earlier chapters. There was nothing extraordinary in the idea that human beings might by example, if not by heredity, pass on to their progeny a kind of bad seed: that we are known by the com-pany we keep is an old adage. Yet usually such problems were avoid-able: choose your friends and companions with prudent vigilance, and you will more than likely diminish or even eliminate your prob-lems. Such is the advice in, say, *David Copperfield*. The idea that one could be an innocent victim seemed a little barbaric, something like the old curses in folklore or Fate in Greek tragedy. Yet it is precisely this kind of curse, passed on from father to son, and, on a parallel level, from past to present, which, in different ways, the three authors dealt with in this chapter reintroduced with a vengeance.[2]

Although their examples were often individual and biological, the determinism which underlies each—and each is different—seems linked to a more macroscopic vision of culture, time, and history. Zeitgeist remains an apt combination of words: Time-spirit, the spirit *of* the time and the spirit *in* time. Somehow personal history and cultural history become not merely intertwined but sometimes entangled in the nineteenth century, and out of such entanglements emerged an overdetermined inseparability. If Providence had failed, it had failed not only in a cosmic sense. The annointing finger was missing, as it is often found to be missing from an individual's life, especially in the plays of Ibsen: a wasted ego trapped in the ruins of its own devastation, deluding itself about heights, transcendences, and second chances of which none is even remotely available. Or when available, such climbings into the mists or to the tops of towers indicate not transfiguration but certain death.

The so-called unlived life, as much as if it were the lived life, occupies the same time (and space). Its unlivedness is after all nothing but a subjective interpretation, a consciousness, a judgment rendered by the individual's survey of personal experience. What is absent from the life, however brief, can never be wholly articulated, especially when the judge has a full life-span to evaluate. In Ibsen's plays people are often voided of love, commitments, pity, faith in other humans, humility; but these are abstractions with little habitation and less name. So the focus is less on what has been missed—less on absence—and more on the presence of absence: more on the rage of the self that misses (whatever it may miss) than on elegiac regret. Whereas Chekhov's characters tend to lament the lost past, Ibsen's tend to rage more against the untenable present. The Ibsenean elegy is more a sense of outrage and disbelief than a feeling that life had never been seized at all. Ibsen's characters believe they have lost something once possessed; Chekhov's bitterly complain that they have never had anything in the first place, or if they have had it it was merely illusion anyway.

The guilt that often accompanies a sense of the past is a general feeling of distance from something both sacred and dreaded, a state of high anxiety and ambivalence about what might be seen as a wreck of values now lost and somehow a world superior to anything available. Far from elegiac, this feeling about the past is often suffused with hostility, reproach, and eventually an ironic good riddance which transforms guilt into pure hatred and total disavowal. The past becomes an evil present that has designs to murder its offspring, that is, the present, and so conquer the vacated space, the future. Schiller's insistence that every "human being has his paradise, his golden age, which he remembers with enthusiasm to the degree that he possesses something of the poetical in his nature" needs to be amended: some human beings seem to have no golden age to remember, only one never had at all. Deprivation, therefore, not grieving, is their mood and motive for mourning and melancholia. Herbert Lindenberger, who quotes the above from Schiller, adds: "Through the connection Schiller is establishing between communal and individual memory, he is able to accommodate solitary retrospective experience within the realm of pastoral." The tension which Lindenberger considers so vital for the achievement of genuine pastoral is present only when there is an active element, a dynamic; this was Schiller's ideal. Like Dr. Johnson, Schiller had little use for a merely bucolic poetry that leads—or tries to lead us—back to a lost Arcadia. Instead, as Lindenberger correctly stresses, Schiller insists that we are to be moved " 'forward to Elysium.' " Further, argues Lindenberger, it is the "precariousness, the tensions, the historical dislocations which give idyllic moments their intensity—and also their momentariness . . . because calmness seems to sit best with us when it is hard earned."[3] As the century progresses, that calmness almost totally disappears. Instead of moving from an irrecoverable Arcadia to a new Elysium, we are being led along a road that becomes more than a detour—"un saison en enfer." The past is held responsible as much for our collective as for our individual miseries. We neither mourn it nor wait upon future salvation: we ache, either for what never was or for what we think has been unfairly taken from us by fate or by our own mistakes. Even while we resent and blame the past, we seem also to stand accused by it for not having lived up to its expectations. Here again we view history as a parent and apply to it our personal dynamic: the struggle to please, the feelings of having failed, the ambivalence of respect and resentment. Such feelings, among others, inform much of the work of Ibsen, Kafka, and Faulkner.

I
Ibsen: Climbing Up the Abyss

Ibsen dealt energetically with all the multitude of problems that create the lived—and the unlived—life; I will seek out a few examples. In play after play, from *Brand* to *When We Dead Awaken*, Ibsen kept before us the central question of life's "meaning," which so many of his characters brood about even in the midst of living that meaning itself. They brood about their dispossessed lives, about the irrecoverable past, the sins inherited or acquired, which torture their driven existence, often to disaster. In various ways, and with various strategies, Ibsen's characters are forced to face the truth—and the lies that hide the truth—that either negates their lives or, when realized, here and there, as in *Little Eyolf*, might offer the way toward salvation. By truth Ibsen did not mean literal truth (was he not the poet who also argued the validity of the *Lebenslüge?*), but psychological truth. So in *The Wild Duck* the "Truth" is destructive for everyone; the destroyer, however, had he recognized this psychological truth about Truth, would have been saved from the awful destruction he sets into motion. In the main, life is meaningful for Ibsen through a transcendence of egotistical love, purely personal love, narcissism, to some form of sharing love that feeds not *off* people but *to* them. When the bereft parents in *Little Eyolf* decide to love each other by means of learning to love the poor waifs in their neighborhood, whom they have always ignored, the way for hope remains open. Or when Rosmer and Rebecca West give themselves to each other in a double suicide, redemption may be possible, though Ibsen leaves sufficient doubt for us to wonder whether that path was not in its own way an act of narcissism. In most of his plays, however, Ibsen was more clearly pessimistic; the lure of salvation is held out only to be negated by subsequent actions. Even the discovery of psychological truth will not help Brand, or Hedda Gabler, or Mrs. Alving. And in the last plays—*John Gabriel Borkman, The Master Builder, When We Dead Awaken*—Ibsen's vision is indeed grim, relentless, unforgiving.

Throughout Ibsen's plays "too late" reverberates, usually with the solemnity and finality of tragic intimations. In addition, Ibsen seems intent not only to offer us the sins of the fathers visited upon the children but also actual child-murder, either quite directly, if unknowingly, or by more indirect and sometimes highly symbolic means. "Children" can also be inanimate objects, the manuscript, say, in *Hedda Gabler*, an unfinished book in *Little Eyolf*, a work of art in *When We Dead Awaken*. Children, real or inanimate, come in the way and, in some cases, having executed a sacrifice are in turn themselves sacrificed. The child of Brand and Agnes, little Eyolf, Hedda Gabler's unborn child, Hedwig Ekdal, Oswald Alving, Solness's children—all are in some sense victims of paternal neglect.[4] *Brand* (1866) chronicles the price a man must pay for placing a suprahuman exclusivity on his human love. Brand's unbending nature, as the driven man enslaved to a created God who will not compromise, effectively causes the death of his child and, eventually, his wife as well. His relentless pursuit of his ideal constrains him to a climate which the young child cannot survive: but one duty is deemed higher than another, priest rises above father and husband. Every shred of memory connected to the child must be divested, not even a relic may be kept. Agnes, his wife, dies of grief; and Brand permits his dying mother to leave this world without ablution. His famous "All or Nothing" constitutes a saintliness that begs for sinners, and his misguided belief in the efficacy of Will blinds him to humble human needs. By the end of the play, as he is about to be buried by an avalanche, Brand is a man who has wasted his prodigious energies in pursuit of a life that has left him no moment in which to live. He is a man deprived of everything, an Abraham or a Job without insight and without second chances; even his ideal, which originally prompted his stern self-sacrificing acts (which sacrificed others in the process), has come to nought as he dies realizing his misplaced trust in a mistaken understanding of God.

In the remaining plays Ibsen is less absolute in his treatment of wasted lives, but certainly no less clear in his intentions. Peer Gynt (1867) is Brand's other self, a rake who wastes a life pursuing not abstract ideals but personal self-aggrandizing goals. In that play, too, the hero is bereft of everything when the time of his life is about to run out, and his repeated pleadings with the Button-Moulder for more time are not merely a plea for a stay of execution but a request for another chance. Peer cannot believe he should leave the world so empty-handed:

> There's one who remembered, and one who forgot; there's one who squandered, and one who saved. Oh, Destiny. . . . There's no turning back! Oh, Sorrow! *Here* was my Empire set![5] (Act V)

In *The Master Builder* Solness, the great builder, is also a murderer of the young. Not only does he fear the young Ragnar Bovick as a direct threat to his mastery, but he also destroyed his wife, Aline, and indirectly their two young children; everyone is a displacement threat:

> The change is coming. I can sense it. And I feel that it's coming closer. Someone or other will set up the cry: Step back for *me*! And all the others will storm in after, shaking their fists and shouting: Make room—make room—make room![6] (Act I)

For Solness the irony is that his achievements—and they seem considerable—are negated by his pathological fear of being supplanted: the lived life becomes unraveled in the throes of constant anxiety, and so becomes unlived in the process, for there is no solace. He can eventually rise only to fall to his death. The bizarre Hilda comes to validate his megalomania: "Nobody but you should have a right to build." He "willed" the fire that destroyed his literal and figurative home; after that he has been a haunted and homeless man.

The fate of the master builder is, of course, ironic, for he, builder of homes, now has none of his own: another homeless "Faust." True, he is now finishing a new house with three nurseries that will never be inhabited by children, but the futility of this gesture becomes clear to him:

> Human beings don't know how to use these homes of theirs. Not for being happy in. And I couldn't have found use for a home like that either—if I'd had one (*With a quiet, bitter laugh.*) So that's the sum total, so far, as back as I can see. Nothing really built. And nothing sacrificed for the chance to build either. Nothing, nothing—it all comes to nothing.

Solness has been twice dispossessed: once by the fire (which ironically set him on his way as a builder), depriving him of wife and children (his wife, Aline, never recovers from the shock the fire set in motion), not only house but home; and once again when he comes to see his life as having been wasted, as having come to nothing, voided of meaning either for himself or for others. His often-professed fear and dread of youth is really a fear and dread of its recurrence in the guise of his own promise: the hoofbeats he hears behind him are not merely the generations that will displace him—though they are that indeed as well—but the haunting memories of possiblities in his own youth now, as he perceives them, unfulfilled, come to "nothing." While articulating his anxieties about the future, Solness is also revealing the dreaded repetition of the past. His hatred of Ragnar and his cruel behavior toward this young aspiring builder are explicable only if we see Ragnar as a putative son who threatens, in Solness's mind, to displace the father. By refusing his approval he effectively sentences him to oblivion. Having destroyed Ragnar's real father, Solness has taken on himself, however unconsciously, the role of surrogate, but it is that of the punishing father.

But in *Little Eyolf* (as in *The Lady from the Sea*) Ibsen gives his characters a second chance. Sentimentally Dickensian, the play is artistically inferior, but its desperate attempt to snatch a form of redemption from almost certain disaster prefigures perhaps the darkness of the last three plays. The plot of *Little Eyolf* is complicated by a latent incestuousness between the husband and the woman he discovers to be his half-sister. Taken only as the story of the couple and their son, the narrative is straightforward. Almers and Rita, while in an embrace of passion, have left their baby son on a table from which he somehow slips and as a result of the fall becomes permanently lame. With his bright mind and his little crutch, the boy becomes an unconscious accuser, and for Rita an insuperable obstacle to her husband whose guilty attention is now absorbed in two objectives: to educate his son and to finish his book on *Human Possibility*. When he decides to make Eyolf his "whole life's work," Rita pleads for part of his attention by declaring that such total immersion in the child will also totally deny her. Her husband accuses her of selfishness; Eyolf deserves nothing less:

> RITA: But if Eyolf had never been born? Then what?
> ALMERS (*evasively*): Well, that's different. Then I'd only have you to think of.
> RITA (*her voice low and tremulous*): Then I could wish I'd never borne him.
>
> (Act I)

And that terrible thought, here made manifest, sets the tone of the remainder of the play's action. Again neglected, little Eyolf drowns, and now the parents are steeped in guilt, recrimination, counter-accusations. Both realize that neither had ever been able to win their son's heart as had the half-sister of Almers, Asta: "And now," says Almers, "it's too late! Too late!" (Act II). He is now willing to share his book with Rita, and she offers to help him. "To do my work, you mean?" "No," she replies, "To live your life." She pleads, "Oh, let's just live our lives out together, as long as we can!" But Almers is unconvinced:

> Live our lives out, yes. But with nothing to fill them. Waste and emptiness altogether, everywhere I look. (Act III)

Only when both recognize that "Human Possibility" begins in reality—in the shanty town beneath them, in the children that need to be saved, and that they must learn to love—only then do they find a basis for going on with life, a second chance to live.

In the next two plays—Ibsen's last—the view is uncompromising: there are no second chances; lives are worn out by life in a waste of hatred and emptiness; and meaning is all but annihilated. *John Gabriel Borkman* is a bitter tableau of gnawing and haunting obsession. Borkman, the financier whose ruined empire has reduced him to isolation and to pacing on his second-story-room floor, is a man who has traded all his energy and genius for the fruits of living rather than its process. No less than Arnold Rubek, the renowned sculptor of *When We Dead Awaken,* Borkman is a dead man—has been for years. He will not, and cannot, acknowledge this, but we know it from his first appearance, even when he is off-stage and heard only as the pacing and unseen man upstairs. A victim of his megalomania, he has left three people to fend as they can: a wife he never loved, a sister-in-law whom he cashed in (though he did love her) like so much capital, and a son whom he finally loses to life; or an attempt at least to live it.

John Gabriel Borkman was originally imprisoned for business crimes; released eight years before the play opens, he has spent his time in yet another prison, the empty room upstairs, where he dreams in vain for his return as a great Titan of banking. Below his room the world of wife, jilted sister-in-law, and son passes by; into his room he permits only an old partner who comes to share his talk of a future which does not exist. In a certain macabre sense Borkman's existence is a repeated phenomenon. Three times he has not lived but been a bystander: when he rose to power and lost human contact, in prison, and in his room. Each episode is more deeply corrosive, each more depriving, for him and especially for his wife and her "desolated life," who also awaits in her fantasy life an "avenger" in the person of her son, Erhart, to come and right all her wrongs. Mrs. Borkman's son, however, has been partly raised by her sister; he is something of a stranger to his mother, and her dreams for his future have as little substance as those of her husband upstairs. Her sister, Ella, knows this: "It's only something you dream about. Because if you didn't have that to cling to, you're afraid you'd give away to total despair." So for eight years two people have lived imprisoned on different levels in a doomed house. The situation has something of the ancient tragic in its rigor, its threat: "Hear that, Ella! Listen! Back and forth—back and forth, the wolf pacing."

Only the old faithful clerk occasionally comes to visit; and only after dark, when on occasion his daughter plays the piano for the prisoner—plays the *Danse Macabre* for him. On these visits Foldal brings a tragedy he has written in his youth, which he appears from time to time to read to John Gabriel Borkman, who believes "unshakably" that it is "good." But mainly Foldal is the good retainer, the Fool who listens to the ravings of his King: how "they" will demand he descend from his exile and take charge of the bank again—an eventuality the timid Foldal ventures to think is "an awfully remote possibility." Borkman demands belief: "If you don't believe my fate will change—" Against "all reason" Foldal asks? And poor Foldal cannot play the Fool to this King any longer: "There's no precedent" for the miracle Borkman has waited for these eight years. Furious at Foldal's lack of belief, Borkman banishes him forever, accusing him of lying to him as well:

> Haven't you sat here, lying hope and faith and trust into me?

Foldal's defense is disarming:

> Those weren't lies as long as you believed in my talent. As long as you believed in me, I believed in you.

And Borkman's response is honest:

> Then we've practiced mutual deception on each other. And perhaps deceived ourselves—both of us.
>
> (Act II)

Foldal feels that such deception was part of friendship, but he now has doubts—"The dreadful doubt—that I've botched my whole life up for the sake of a fantasy." So ironically he confessed that he came to Borkman for support just as Borkman had looked to him for the same help. Two men have indeed deceived each other—each for a different reason toward a different purpose.

When Ella, Borkman's sister-in-law, enters, Borkman receives yet another confession and accusation, for Ella, who has not seen Borkman for years, now laments: "A lifetime wasted." Borkman objects; his life is not "wasted," his hopes not yet dashed. But Ellen accuses him of being a "murderer," of killing her capacity to love—and live—by trading her for a man he needed to fulfill his ambitions, making for Ella what she describes as "this sterile, empty desert within me—and around me, too," full of "desolation" and "emptiness" (Act II).

John Gabriel Borkman, too, recognizes that he has spent his life in futile hopes:

> I've holed myself away up there and wasted eight priceless years of my life! The very day I was released, I should have moved out into reality—iron-hard, dreamless reality! . . . (Act III)

However, this does not imply defeat; he merely resets the machinery of more delusion, that he will begin "from the bottom again. It's only by his present and his future that a man can expiate the past." Erhart, the son, for whose soul the two sisters have fought so hard, will not remain trapped. Neither sister shall win, for Erhart wants freedom: "I want my chance to live. . . . I want to live my own life." He will not work, but just "live! live! live! . . . It's happiness I want! I'm young! I want to live, live, live!" (Act III). In the end he will leave them all to try and do just that: to live. Borkman, viewing one last time the "kingdom" he had lost "when I died," confesses his love to Ella and dies, and the two sisters remain now with "a dead man and two shadows . . . " (Act IV).

For all its weaknesses as a play, *When We Dead Awaken* was a fitting epilogue (Ibsen's term) to his plays, for once again the motif is that of wasted lives, false sacrifices, unbridled egotism, all of which have governed his previous plays, beginning with *Brand.* Nowhere are the sins of the past more metaphorically presented; indeed in its structure and often in its imagery the play returns to some of the elements we connect with the verse plays rather than those in prose. (The play also bears a resemblance to Chekhov's *The Sea Gull,* at least in the picture of the artist who "uses" people merely to further his art.) Once again Ibsen begins with a declining relationship; a marriage is on the verge of collapse, and in the ensuing acts we discover how and why.

Rubek, the great sculptor, has created a masterpiece, "Resurrection Day," which has brought him success and worldwide fame. Married to a younger woman, who seeks life, he is obviously failing her and driving her to seek solace elsewhere. That solace she eventually finds in the vital, uncouth, nonintellectual hunter, Ultheim, a very much less subtle version of a Lawrentian gamekeeper. Rubek's model for "Resurrection Day" is a once-young and beautiful model who sacrificed her life for what Rubek considered an "episode" in his artistic career. When she leaves him, she is forced to dance and expose her body not to artists but to gaping crowds in cabarets; eventually she goes mad, and when we meet her, accompanied by a nun, she hovers between two worlds: still mad but lucid enough to remember the past. Irene considers the masterpiece, "The Resurrection," "our child," and once more we hear how its father had, over time, murdered it. First he added to it; then he altered the model's position and prominence, even her joyful face. The masterpiece came to resemble an image of his own egotism—and his doubts. Rubek pleads: "let's stop talking about the past"; but they cannot: he has had many children, she says, but has "Murdered them. . . . Just as soon as they came into the

world. . . . One after another." Rubek does not yet understand her.
"For many years I was dead," Irene says; ". . . now I'm halfway beginning to rise from the dead." She had given him her "young, living
soul." And this has "left [her] empty inside" (Act I).

Having met Irene again stirs in Rubek a reassessment of his past life
and his present, and it leads also to a confession: Rubek would substitute "life" for all "the talk about the artist's high calling and the artist's
mission, and so on . . . ," which now strikes him as "empty and hollow. . . ." But the "life" Rubek envisions is still too ethereal for his
wife: she requires the vulgarity of the bear-hunter. This, as it turns
out, suits Rubek, who has grown "tired and bored and worn out" and
seeks a different vitality than earthiness. He persuades himself that he
has discovered new life, new meaning, in a "transfigured" Irene, who
protests she is not transfigured but "risen" from her madness, and
that not completely. Repentant, he admits that her departure was like
a "laying waste to [his] life." In desperation he seeks deliverance:

> You have the key [he tells Irene]! You alone have it! (*Beseeching
> her.*) Help me—so I can try to live my life over again!
> IRENE (impassively, as before). Empty dreams. Aimless—
> dead dreams. *Our* life together can never be resurrected
> . . . .
> RUBEK: Oh, Irene—that might have been our life—and we
> lost it, you and I.
> IRENE: We'll see what we've lost only when—(*Breaking off.*)
> RUBEK (*with an inquiring look*): When—?
> IRENE: When we dead awaken.
> RUBEK (*shakes his head sorrowfully*): Yes, and what, really, do we
> see then?
> IRENE: *We see that we've never lived.* (italics mine)
>
> (Act II)

"Too late, Too late," Irene says to Rubek's desperate attempt to bring
her back to life. "The desire to live," she laments, "has died in me"
(Act III). So, at the end of the play, they disappear in the "peaks of
promise," up in the mountain mist, to certain death, as they pass by
the bear-hunter and the wife, Maja, on the way down to the rough-
hewn world of reality. The ending of this play is no romantic delusion
but, as in *The Master Builder, Rosmersholm,* and *Hedda Gabler,* a realization that the past cannot be recovered, that the present is untenable,
and that only a form of transcendence lies in the future. Ibsen did not

preach this as a "philosophy"; he simply created plays in which characters must inevitably come to such conclusions.

Ibsen's characters are obsessively haunted by a past they often wish to change, to relive, to extirpate, but before which they are powerless. The past, Ibsen suggests, cannot be altered; it may often—as it does— make the present unlivable, and it may even point to a future which is transcendent, though sometimes such a future is merely death and emptiness, as in, say, *Ghosts* or *John Gabriel Borkman.* Many of Ibsen's characters are classic narcissists for whom

> . . . life is characterized by the progressive difficulty of maintaining the hope of recapturing a sense of narcissistic perfection. . . . The illusion of starting again with another mate is a common reparative fantasy. With such a person, they feel . . . they can achieve the greatness that has eluded them. They look outside themselves . . . rather than introspectively consider their inner lives as the source of their difficulties.[7]

The unrelieved plaints of so many characters constitute an echo in the plays. They not only wish to alter or justify or forget the past: they wish also to have a second chance to live through its time, a time inevitably gone and in no earthly way recoverable. Surely one of the most symbolic scenes in all of Ibsen is when Peer Gynt returns home to see his past auctioned off, especially the "invisible cloak [he] wore the night when he flew off with Ingrid!" Nor is there anywhere in Ibsen greater clarity and poignancy than when Peer encounters all the undone deeds of a wasted life—the Thread Ball, the Withered Leaves, and especially the Sighing in the Air:

> We are songs,
> You should have sung us . . .

And the Dewdrops:

> We are the tears
> that were never shed;

Or, finally, the Broken Straws:

> We are deeds,
> You should have performed us;

The Button-Moulder's arrest warrant reads: " 'Collect Peer Gynt; he has utterly failed in his purpose in life . . .' " Few of Ibsen's characters escape such judgment.

II
Kafka: Descensus Averni

Perhaps with the exception of Yeats's *Purgatory*, Kafka's "The Judgment" is the most terrifying father-murdering-son story in all of literature (only Abraham's potential sacrifice of Isaac, had it been carried out, might have surpassed it, and one wonders whether Kafka knew this?); it has, like most of Kafka, eluded readers, especially when they have sought to find a key with which to possess the story's total meaning. No such key exists; Kafka simply did not provide us with texts that can be possessed. To "deconstruct" them may be useful, but even here the hazards are foreboding as well as forbidding. Perhaps for that reason alone one can feel less uneasiness in approaching a story that has already been subjected to so many ingenious readings.[8]

Of course most of Kafka's work, itself unfinished, is nothing but a long analysis of the unlived life—or, in Kafka's case, perhaps the nearly *unlivable* life. Like the author himself, Kafka's characters find themselves placed in repeated confrontations with life, impeding them at every step from attaining even minimal goals. Joseph K., K., Gregor Samsa, and Georg Bendemann, the young man of "The Judgment," all are overpowered by the authority of the father. All fathers, all authority, necessarily represent the past, since anything that supersedes us also lays claim to a prior existence. Just as the father begets his progeny, only to rule it, so distant authority bends us with its laws and humbles us with its power. Georg Bendemann is, therefore, a prisoner of his own history—his past—and "The Judgment" may be seen as a historical parable in which the past, seemingly buried and benign, suddenly asserts its authority with true vengeance, delivering, just as in ancient tragedy, its fatal curse. The "sin" Georg commits is that of trying to divide and separate out past, present, and future: to succeed his father in business and to marry; to bury the past and to begin a future. "The child is father to the man"—or is he?

Such a reading seems no more "right" or "wrong" than others; the only point being made is that, paradoxically perhaps, Kafka's work is rather ahistorical, at least with respect to identifying his fictions with real events, past or present. However, almost all his work touches on the problems of the past, present, and future in a paradigmatic way, individualized rather than allegorized. And in this respect "The Judgment" seems the most useful of all his works for the present study.

Like several other of his major works, "The Judgment" is a family story. Implicit in the family is the struggle between generations, which also translates itself, in encompassing ways, as a struggle between past and present. As always the archetypal contest, best exemplified in the authority figure of the father, sets father and son against each other. As the son feels it is time to supersede the father by taking over his roles, he may also wish to declare his ascendancy by preparing the way for a reversal of roles: he shall marry, beget progeny, himself become father, not only to his own children to come but to his father as well. That cycle we can all recognize; intrinsically it is compounded of inevitability and repetition, and constitutes a normal sequence. Kafka, however, manages to radicalize the process, to reify the archetypal pattern, indeed ultimately to subvert it. What would happen—Kafka seems to speculate—if the father does not accept the son's supervening him; what if the father breaks the cycle and, as father and past, retaliates, warning the son (present) that he will not surrender to a future which takes no account of him? What happens in that event is precisely the course of the story that Kafka worked out in "The Judgment."

Georg Bendemann's mother has been dead for two years; since that time Georg has necessarily taken on the father's responsibilities in the family business. The two men live at home, but there they scarcely see each other. As the story begins Georg is writing a letter to his bachelor friend in Russia at last telling him of his engagement and his plans to marry. It is this letter and its news which Georg, on what is surely a rare occasion, brings to his father on a Sunday afternoon. From this ensues the remainder of the story.

The bachelor friend, self-exiled in Russia, has forfeited the future; he had become a "permanent bachelor," and nothing can succeed him. He is son but can never become father (precisely what will make its terrible impression on Georg's consciousness). The friend's exile in Siberia (spatially empty and distant, as readers have noted), is a dead past: it is clear that the friend has chosen this life, has "lost touch with affairs at home," has increasingly consented to more and more "remoteness."[9] Georg reasons correctly that so alienated a man cannot be happy, cannot feel at home, and a home is for Kafka an important trope, for it embodies a past/present/future dynamic. Hence the friend (the past) remains in his pastness, "humiliated . . . homeless and friendless." Since his mother's death Georg "and his aged father had kept house together," though we learn that their contact at home is nearly nonexistent. We learn, too, that his father "had prevented him from taking any initiative of his own during his mother's life-time," when the present still ruled as an intact unit, parentage still being joint. On the mother's death, the father had "kept himself more in the background," has seemingly begun to slip into the past, like the friend to whom he says (it is no wonder) he feels allied. Now Georg has hesitated telling these two representatives of the past his plans for the future: in short, his engagement. When he expresses this hesitation to his fiancée, she pointedly retorts: " 'If you've got friends like that, Georg, you should never have got engaged,' " a remark into which much has been read. On the most fundamental level it seems fairly clear that it is the fiancée's understandable challenge: if you have doubts about joining me for a future because you fear the past, you should not have made your commitment.

Finally Georg has summoned up the courage not only to make that commitment but also to confront the two people who represent pastness with his decision. So he writes the letter telling his friend of his engagement and then brings it to his father's room, which "for months" he had not visited, for "there was indeed no call for him to go there," seeing his father during the workday in the warehouse (a division which also clearly demarcates their estranged life). Territori-ally speaking, home has already become a place of father-burial. As Georg tells his father that he has written his friend of the impending marriage, he also emphasizes how his father understood how difficult this friend was. To approach the father through the friend seems tactically logical but also underlies Georg's need for circumlocution. Almost pleading with his father that he of all people understood this difficult friend, Georg in effect tries first to neutralize the friend before assuaging the father, who is, after all, not in Siberia (though in a sense he, too, has been exiled) but before his very eyes. The "toothless" father—Kafka makes a point of showing how old the fa-ther *looks*—demands the "whole truth" from his son. " 'Have you really got a friend in St. Petersburg?' " he demands, to which at first Georg replies cunningly: never mind the friend; the father is impor-tant. How does the father feel in this closed-up room? Georg will offer him *his* bed (because he will be vacating it to occupy, metaphorically at least, the father's). Kneeling by the father's side, he hears him say that there is no friend, and the ambiguity here (as has been suggested) is that, as he will later say, the friend is not Georg's but his, the father's.

Georg begins to shed his father of the vestiges of identity—dirty underwear, for example. He lifts him like a child, guilty at having so neglected him, and "without more ado he resolved quite firmly to take his father . . . into his *future establishment*" (italics mine). If we have been attentive, we know that this thought is fatal to Georg's survival, for the past cannot—will not—be taken into the future in the posture of some toothless, impotent relic. This the father knows as he prepares to teach Georg a lesson that will cost Georg his life. As he is being carried into the other room, he plays with Georg's watch chain so much so that Georg "could not put him down on the bed straight away, so firmly did he cling to [it]." As a past about to rise up in all its powerful strength—and the past exercises that strength as Kafka knew—the father reminds the son that he cannot escape time, that the continuum is unbreakable, and that the hubris of trying to break it is accountable with one's own life. In the ensuing scene the father traps Georg by goading him into the admission that he is "well covered up" in the new bed, buried and contained. With a fury this very much alive past divests himself of any weakness and leaps up as if out of his grave with a nightmarish " 'No!' " The friend in Russia is a " 'son after my own heart,' " he says, for obviously the friend is not a disrespectful rebel going around burying the past. Indeed he (the father) and the friend have been in league, for Georg had been "playing him false"; only a selfish desire to get married and bury all others and leave them behind motivates the son: so runs the accusation. In the spatial "vastness of Russia" Georg can see his friend "so well [he] touched his heart as never before." In the distance Georg recognizes the permanent bachelor, the good son, and is empathetic; in front of him looms the "nightmare vision" of his father. At this juncture Georg must realize that the past cannot be exiled to Russia either, no more than it can be mummified in his own bed. " 'I've been representing [your friend] here on the spot' "; " 'I've formed a splendid alliance with [him] . . . ,' " the father says tauntingly and reproachfully.

The father's accusations are bitter and constitute an exhaustive catalogue of protests against encroachment: "And my son went about the world exulting, concluding deals that I had prepared . . . ," that is, fulfilling in the present what the past had prepared, and this without giving credit due. Georg cannot resist making a clown of his father, belittling him, thinking murderous thoughts: "what if he fell and smashed himself to pieces! These words went hissing through his brain." But the past will not be reduced and cannot be expunged so easily, in spite of its anachronistic presence, the father throwing at him an "old newspaper, with a name that was already quite unknown to Georg." We are reminded of Henry James's "The Jolly Corner," when Georg says: "So you've been lying in wait for me," for in truth our past does just that, and unless we can exorcise it there is no letting go and it will haunt us into nightmare. Being told he was both an "innocent child" and a "devilish human being" allows Georg to see the cycle of life in perspective. The sentence of death by *drowning* is appropriate enough, for the river into which Georg lets himself fall is a traditional symbol of time so that the punishment is being swallowed up by a relentless stream of time which allows no divisions of past, present, future. Georg's exorcism comes too late: " 'Dear parents, I did always love you' "; the father, the past, has conquered, has shown power, wrath, and the ability to pass judgment on our life—or death.[10]

If we accept this reading, what does it mean? Is Kafka so deterministic that he does not permit us the opportunity to escape from our past? In the touching and revealing *Letter to his Father* (never delivered to its intended reader), Kafka made it clear how important he felt was the necessity for all humans to cut their ties and create a forward motion into the future under the auspices of freedom:

> Marrying, founding a family, accepting all the children that come, supporting them in this insecure world and perhaps even guiding them a little, is, I am convinced, the utmost a human being can succeed in doing at all.[11]

We have read enough of Kafka's difficulties in achieving this: the fear of the father, the repeated attachments to women which became detachments, twice engaged and twice disengaged to the same woman. All these personal difficulties also bear down on his works so preoccupied with the burden—or, as I have called it, the sins—of the past. For Kafka the past was unforgiving; to avenge itself against the threat of time which effectively creates it, the past would struggle mightily. Its ability to reassert itself even when it seems weak and nearly dead, and indeed its strength to execute a death sentence, is the judgment of "The Judgment." Of course it makes no sense to say that the future can be stayed, for it cannot; but the sacrifice of Georg's life is one exacted, from time to time, by the past to assert its power as a force not to be dispensed with easily or with impunity. It demands recognition and will never itself concede defeat. Its surcease is final only when it has been appropriated and intermingled with the future, and that can happen only (speaking anthropomorphically) when the past dies in that process of appropriation. Kafka's dread of his father may well have been the psychic wound so many have recognized, but his fear of the power of the past and its authority and vengeance was not without good cause. As history was for Joyce the past was for Kafka too a nightmare from which he tried to awaken; and once, when he achieved that, he found himself to be a giant insect.

The elegiac element in Kafka's story is, of course, embedded in the motif of forced return to childhood helplessness. Even Georg's exclamation, coinciding with his suicidal descent, is that of a child asking for forgiveness and love, asserting its rightness and innocence after punishment has been meted out. Faulkner's Quentin in *The Sound and the Fury* and his very similar suicide suggests a parallel case, only Quentin's death is clearly more self-motivated. But, like Georg, Quentin could neither defeat time nor the past, and while his father was a cynic who discouraged any thoughts of suicide, the contributing urgency, surely, of Quentin's death is his inability to measure *up to* (rather than measure) his father's manliness, a strength of cynicism which, despite his alcoholism, made old Compson a formidable figure. So Kafka's elegy, like Faulkner's, but even more pointedly, is an ironic lament of one who returns to the past not wistfully but is banished to it by force for disobedience to the father. It is an ironic reversal of the Fall: Georg is willing to go into the world of risks on his own, but premature departure pushes him not only back but beyond, to the ultimate innocence, a death which, in its watery grave, has all the import of a birth and a resurrection, and with bitter irony he is being condemned to death in order to try life over again. His attempt to live life is effectively subverted; and the future planned becomes the future unlived.

Kafka's own life was wasted by tuberculosis, that waste being literal; his duties as an insurance attorney were performed with rigor and success, but we know from the letters and diaries that he considered that life a waste as well. Indeed, only the art of writing made him feel alive, if uneasy. Yet tragically everything we know informs us that in the end even writing failed him: the uncompleted novels, the brief pieces, the tormented way he analyzed the demands of his craft, the final order to Max Brod to destroy his work. Truly Kafka was a connoisseur of waste.[12]

III
Faulkner: Immaculate Perception

" '*Et ego in arcadia,* I have forgotten the latin for hay.' Father said. 'There, there,' he said, 'I was just joking.' " This scrap of remembered utterance emerges from the mind of the idiot, Benjy, whose simultaneous jumble of past and present memories launches *The Sound and the Fury*. Faulkner's novel, more than most that have been considered here, is an elegy that celebrates the passing of a way of life. It is self-evident that Faulkner's aim in the Yoknapatawpha novels was to trace the declension of the South from the antebellum era to the postwar years, charting in the process the decline of the South by chronicling the fortune of several families. And so "*The Sound and the Fury* records the fall of a house and the death of a society."[13] Yet within every novel individuals emerge whose fate, however much it may be part of a larger scheme, seems also to be sprung by more immediate events; these are characters whose Sybil leaves may be read not merely within the decline of a culture but, microcosmically, within the progressive decline of a single family. Such is the case in *The Sound and the Fury*.

Quentin Compson's suicide, like Georg Bendemann's, is consummated by a drop from a bridge into a river; it is—also like Georg's—a sacrifice to the destructive urgings of the father, though in Quentin's case this is a more indirectly rendered, and indirectly perceived, process. Quentin's father, an alcoholic misanthrope and master of the cynical conundrum, does not literally condemn his son to death by water; yet the effect of father upon son—as the son perceives it—is nothing less than a death sentence. When Quentin adds up everything "Father said" and gave, he can come to only one conclusion: his own death. Quentin's story is focused upon the one day of his death, "June Second 1910," which forms the second part of the novel immediately following Benjy's chaotic account.

Quentin's story begins with the memory of his father's gift of a watch: ". . . I give you the mausoleum of all hope and desire; it's rather excruciatingly apt that you will use it to gain the reducto absurdum of all human experience. . . . I give it to you not that you may remember time, but that you might forget it. . . ." The section concludes (just before the final paragraph) with another memory of a conversation with Quentin's father:

> . . . someday in very disgust [a man] risks everything on a single blind turn of a card no man ever does that under the first fury of despair or remorse of bereavement he does it only when he has realised that even the despair or remorse or bereavement is not particularly important to the dark diceman. . . .

Quentin never does realize this; he risks everything and commits the ultimate gesture of despair or remorse or bereavement": he gives himself to the dark diceman. Whether Quentin's act is occasioned by guilt over his incestuous longings for his sister or whether it is out of fear (however unjustified) of having both failed and offended his father is debatable, but only insofar as we measure degree. Both reasons cause him to wish to leave this life, and certainly shame and fear in the face of the father dominate the whole section. Ironically Quentin cannot, as his father advised, "forget" time: he can indeed only remember it. At the beginning of his last day of life he deliberately smashes his watch; this act is not merely committed to kill time but to offer up time's gifts—life itself, which he no longer feels worthy of inheriting. Time continues to be an obsessive preoccupation for the remainder of Quentin's last day of life; the only reason he must ask for and seek out the time is that he has mutilated his own instrument in an act both self-destructive and propitiatory: "*Father I have committed . . .* " Just before he buys the flatirons that will weigh down his body in the water, he recalls, "Father said clocks slay time. . . . only when the clock stops does time come to life." Truly Quentin must retain such faith, a conviction that *his* time, in whatever realm, will begin only when "the clock stops," when he is dead to clock time. Such faith may be a further stimulus to self-destruction and destruction of his father's gift of time, the gift of wrong time, the gift of life.

The father's cynical posture vis-à-vis life and his instructive conundrum that the gift was given to "forget" time both combine in Quentin's disintegrating mind as the father's death sentence. If clocks "slay time," they slay life; if the gift was given in order to forget not to remember, its inherent and explicit symbolic value for Quentin is clear enough: die. It is in some sense the same message conveyed to Georg Bendemann when his father clung tenaciously to Georg's watch-chain. Quentin understands and acts; "I tapped the crystal [of the watch] on the corner of the dresser and caught the fragments of glass in my hand and put them into the ashtray and twisted the hands off and put them into the ashtray. . . . The watch ticked on." If Quentin needed reinforcement in his resolve, this is certainly it: the hands of the watch merely show the designation of time; time itself cannot be destroyed (or forgotten) in *this* life. Throughout his disordered and nevertheless planned day, Quentin continues to hear the dismembered watch like a heartbeat: "time is your misfortune Father said." Quentin's suicide is self-consciously sacrificial and transcendent: "Father said that . . . Christ was not crucified: he was worn away by a minute clicking of little wheels." That Quentin conceives of his death as a possible resurrection is repeatedly implied: "and when He said Rise only the flat irons," a statement ambiguous only to the reader perhaps, not to Quentin.[14]

Quentin repeatedly refers to his shadow, which he sometimes loses, then recovers, and once destroys, "tramping my shadow into the dust," the death preceding the death. He cannot really make himself

whole after discovering his unbearable sense of loss when his sister
loses her virginity to a stranger who intrudes into his Arcadian life.
The father tries but fails to dissuade him from his utter despondency;
he cannot hear the words as they are meant:

> Purity is a negative state and therefore contrary to nature. It's
> nature is hurting you not Caddy and I said That's just words
> and he said So is virginity and I said you don't know. You can't
> know and he said Yes. On the instant when we come to realise
> that tragedy is second-hand.

When Quentin proposed a double suicide to Caddy, she had agreed
("all right can you do yours by yourself"), but he could not then carry
it out. The object of his homicidal impulse is, after all, himself. She
even offered herself to him, but he could not bring himself to that
either—not out of shame but out of a desire to keep intact his own
visionary image of purity.

In his essay on *The Sound and the Fury,* Jean-Paul Sartre writes that
for Faulkner "the past is never lost, it is an obsession. . . . For Faulkner, time must be forgotten." The two statements only appear to be
contradictory: the past is an obsession, and yet time also needs to be
forgotten. Indeed it is Faulkner's decapitation of time (Sartre's metaphor) that leaves the past intact to haunt his characters. Obviously the
continuing validation of time running on would make for the eventual, and normal, separation from the past simply by means of distanc-
ing. "If the future has reality, time withdraws us from the past and
brings us nearer to the future; but if you do away with the future, time
is no longer that which separates, that which cuts the present off from
itself."[15] Sartre finds this an absurdity, and he chastises Faulkner for
perpetuating the illusion of a futureless existence that he blames on
Faulkner's "despair"—a metaphysic that was for Sartre unacceptable,
for it forfeited growth.[16] Sartre's reasoning may be sound, but his
diagnosis appears to be wrong. We now realize that Faulkner was not
a tendentious writer, yet he makes clear, especially in *The Sound and the
Fury,* that he means to offer us neither despair nor sentimental hope:
for Faulkner the process of dissolution and decline is tested against
the ability to survive. Only the Negroes survive, not because they are
hopeful—they are, if anything, "tragic"—but because they maintain
continuity; they do not abandon time, nor do they pay it any special
heed or homage, for living through time is a way of *becoming* that
renders unnecessary the contemplation of *being*.

Such self-analysis is what finally fashions Quentin's demise. His refusal of a future is a refusal to grow beyond that point at which his paradise and innocence have been compromised. Unable to deny the pain of loss he experiences when his sister becomes sexually involved with an outsider to his life, he can salvage the past only by rejoining it in death. Now he understands only too well his father's dictum: "I give [this watch] to you not that you may remember time, but that you might forget it," for the destruction of the watch is, in addition to all I have said already, also an admission of defeat in the face of time. Quentin cannot—nor wants to—forget, but he knows that so long as he lives by time, time will eventually force him to forget, force him into a future he cannot survive. In one sense, then, Quentin murders the future; but in a far more important sense he falls a victim to the past. Father had also said: "Only when the clock stops does time come to life"; and a translation from Quentin's perspective might well be: "Only when you stop time present will you regain time past," since for Quentin "life" is neither growth nor survival but *retrieval*. His consummation with the flowing river is indeed, in his mind, not only a resurrection but the retrieval of loss, the repossession of that of which he has been dispossessed.

That *The Sound and the Fury,* as so much of Faulkner's major fiction, is preoccupied with loss, individual and cultural-collective, need not be argued: it is self-evident. The sins of the fathers are indeed visited upon the children; the burdens of the past break most of those who attempt to carry those burdens into an inhospitable future. Hence the disintegration or annihilation of whole families seems to be a logical structural metaphor to carry out a design that accentuates the futility of willed continuity. It may be an exaggeration to say, as a critic recently has, that Faulkner implies that "If only the clock of history were stopped, time would come to life again and men could once more inhabit an innocent world."[17] The issue owns no such clarity: there is, in Quentin's mind, forward time and backward time, and his memories on the last day of his life, like all memories, are of the past; his attempts to make some contacts with the present remind us of his ambiguous relationship with "the clock of history." Quentin's conception of history, though it is buttressed with certain images of the southern chivalric code, is basically one of personal *history*. And his vision of innocence is not confined to Edenic tableaux of a strifeless existence but to temporal indifference, to the inseparability of self to others. This leaves him vulnerable to temporal intrusion and to the invasive disturbance of an "other," whether it is Caddy's suitor or husband-to-be. An acceptance to Caddy's wedding (he makes an altar of the invitation on his dresser—an altar to the dead) would be tantamount to an acceptance of his separability. That is clearly not possible. What haunts Quentin, therefore, is not the past but the possibility of a future; the past does take its vengeance on him, as it did—in one form or another—on the inhabitants in the worlds of Ibsen and Kafka. Yet Faulkner's version of this vengeance is ironically narrated since it is seen by Quentin as salvation. His being accused of kidnapping the little girl in the bakery (he calls her "sister") is a final attempt to find some fragment of the past in the present, and from this point of view the charge of kidnapping is entirely accurate. Being arrested merely underlies the futility of the act; the arrest puts the full imprimatur of time on his day: it serves as a shadow of the arrested time itself, and it seals his fate as a victim. Father was right; Quentin's living in time must be killed so that Quentin resurrected *from* time may live. (Again this is not so different a perception than that of Kafka's Bendemann.)

In a critique of Sartre's analysis of *The Sound and the Fury*, Cleanth Brooks has correctly stressed Faulkner's implicit sense of continuity: "Man's very freedom is bound up with his sense of having some kind of future. Unless he can look ahead to the future, he is not free." Quentin's foreclosure of his future is not, however, so interpreted by him; his freedom, he reckons, lies in his choice to seek a way of preventing the future from devouring the past (growing beyond his pain into self-sufficient manhood would constitute his future, and it is what father really counselled) or preventing the past from devouring the present (his state of desolation now beyond endurance). Death is beyond compromise: it is allowing present and future to have their way, leaving the dimension of the past, the only one in which Quentin can find his peace. Paradoxically, his unlived life becomes the means of his only hope for fulfillment, though such fulfillment, of course, must be finite and can by definition have no sense of futurity: "Quentin's obsession with the past is . . . a repudiation of the future." Brooks understates the problem when he observes that "Quentin was apparently closer to his father and the influence of his father on him was obviously very powerful."[18] The reality is that for Quentin the father and the gift of the watch are Time personified; the father's disdain for mechanical time only reinforces the sense of inexorable time the father comes to represent: inexorable time, like the image of Father Time and his scythe, is also Death. So the very ridicule the father heaps upon clock-time makes clear to Quentin the virtual command of the fateful advice: forget time. For such forgetting there is only one solution, and Quentin chooses it, obedient not only to the past but to himself; indeed, like Georg Bendemann: "I said Mother and Father."[19]

The drowning suicides of Georg Bendemann and Quentin Compson act out a nightmarish conversion (or perversion?) of the Narcissus myth. Bendemann's *amour-propre* is ambiguous. Certainly the father makes it clear that as father he sees his son as "devilish" in his self-absorption—his narcissism. So much does the father feel betrayed by an ungrateful son that he passes a death sentence. It is as if that sentence commands in gesture something like a verbal equivalent. "I sentence you now to death by water!" has a subtext: You have been gazing at yourself at my expense, my neglect; gaze no more, drown yourself and thereby make real the communion of yourself and your image in an embrace of death. Kafka's Narcissus drowns exclaiming that hopeless cry of love for his "dear parents," a cry of guilt and despair. Bendemann does *not* jump: he lets himself fall; it is a passive act. Kafka's own fear and guilt of self-actualization (especially his dread of marriage) was not only his ambivalence of sharing his tortured craft of writing with anyone else. In addition, Kafka invests Georg with powerful feelings that all love and attention, whether directed toward fiancée or friend in Russia, amount to a self-love he cannot sustain.

In the case of Quentin Compson the father is no less important, but for young Quentin the precipitous figure (and the "event" as well) centers on his sister, Caddy. Certainly no "healthy" young man can be so obsessed with a sister, and it does not take much reflection to see that his incestuous longing is really a relationship that begins, and ends, with himself. His preparations for his watery grave are made before the mirror in his room at Harvard. He has written suicide notes, remembers to get a "fresh handkerchief," to brush his teeth, and take his hat. He prepares so meticulously for the river it appears as if he were keeping a rendezvous with his lover. And in a sense that is absolutely the case, for Quentin articulates his gesture toward the river in Cambridge because he was unable to articulate anything near that other river, where he almost committed incest, where he was almost ready to participate in a double suicide, for sister Caddy seemed inseparable from himself. Loaded with flatirons, Quentin drops from the bridge, like Bendemann, with obsessive thoughts about "Mother and Father."

6 "Et in Arcadia Ego": Joyce, Mann, Woolf

The Modern hero moves from the heroic deed to the heroism of con-
sciousness, a heroism often available only in defeat.
      —Irving Howe, The Idea of the Modern

In his justly famous essay, "Et in Arcadia Ego: Poussin and the Elegiac Tradition," Erwin Panofsky traces the literary and iconographic history of this phrase and, in the process, provides some helpful guidelines for analyzing a certain mode of modern pastoral, or elegiac, fiction. Panofsky's argument is intricate, and not all of it is relevant to present purposes. Its main points may be summarized as follows. First he establishes that Arcadia itself represents the so-called " 'soft' golden age primitivism," a place where there is "plenty, innocence and happiness," life without pain and, presumably, without death. Various poets and, as it turns out, various painters have depicted Arcadia, and their points of view were not always consistent with one another. Virgil, it appears, is the forerunner of a particular form of elegiac sentiment which seemed to find a culmination in the English graveyard school of poetry in the mid- to late eighteenth century: "Virgil does not exclude frustrated love and death; but he deprives them . . . of their factuality. He projects tragedy either into the future or, preferably, into the past, and he thereby transforms mythical truth into elegiac sentiment." So was born the modern concept of Arcadia, distant in time and space. Painting of Arcadia began with the picturing of tombstones and death heads, and the implication to some seemed clear enough: Death, too, was in Arcady—a "present happiness [was] menaced by death." Panofsky then proceeds to develop his argument by demonstrating that the modern mistranslation of the Latin phrase as "I, too, lived in Arcady" was not the product simply of ignorance but of changing interpretations of Arcadia and Death's intrusion into its supposedly inviolate territory. For this purpose he concentrates on two paintings by Nicholas Poussin (the second of which hangs in the Louvre). In the first painting shepherds are seen approaching a tomb, a skull on top of the motto inscribed on the sarcophagus—indeed directly on top of the word "Arcadia." The shepherds seem to be more intent on the inscription, surprised by the death's head. The painting is moralistic: it warns against taking life for granted; the speaker of the motto is Death itself, saying, in effect, "Even in Arcady, I, Death, hold sway." Five years later Poussin painted his second picture. Here the scene is quite different. Gone is the death's head, and with it the surprise and anxiety of the shepherds and shepherdesses. Instead they "are immersed in mellow meditation on a beautiful past." In addition, they are preoccupied less with the tomb than with the person buried in it. We have moved from "thinly veiled moralism to undisguised elegiac sentiment." That elegiac sentiment is the herald of a wholly new perspective; it supersedes attitudes toward death (indeed toward life as well), on the uses of the past, on the "concrete" versus the "universal." The Louvre painting appears to imply, Panofsky argues, that the occupant of the tomb has lived in Arcady and is now dead: all things are mutable, even Arcadians. Now "the whole phrase [is] projected into the past: what had been a menace has become a remembrance." Remembrance is the trigger of elegiac sentiment; it eventually spawns regret, *ressentiment,* frustration, revolt, despair—in fact many of the manifestations of the elegiac offered in the present study. What Panofsky explores is the change in taste, how quiescent melancholy becomes something very different. Panofsky himself indicates how Poussin's melancholy "could lead to reflections of almost *opposite* nature, depressing and melancholy on the one hand, comforting and assuaging on the other. . . ."[1]

In the discussion that follows, Panofsky's analysis of "Et in Arcadia Ego" is featured in different orders of meaning: Joyce, Woolf, and Mann each deals with the implications of the phrase, and both paintings, both meanings; shock and acceptance or moral elegy and exemplum are negotiated, though never in any mutually exclusive way. Death intrudes in all three works; the responses will vary. But the elegiac tone is a sign of regret for an irrecoverable past and an anxiety about an unknowable future, neither of which can sufficiently fill the present long enough to sustain a fully meaningful life.

I
Joyce: Memory and Desire

Pastoral elegy, in any definition, must carry the suggestion of nature as solace, however ironic the juxtaposition might be. And since Joyce was a supreme ironist, we must expect that his most elegiac story in *Dubliners,* "The Dead," will make use of nature in a contrapuntal way that expresses both its irony and poignancy. Indeed, in one sense, "The Dead" explores the disappearance of nature as a consoling force, nature as an obliterating snowfall which both annihilates the structured world of Gabriel Conway and provides him with the release from the pain which the realities of that world would have caused him. As so often with Joyce, we move simultaneously along parallel paths; "symbol" never intrudes, never superimposes itself on reality but, as it should, ideally, symbol really is reality merely perceived from a different point of view.

"The Dead" is, of course, very much a story of recall and memory, of regret for a passion spent, never duplicated, and hence leaving an emptiness in both husband and wife of which one must assume they will henceforth be very conscious. Gabriel Conway and his wife, Gretta, arrive at the Christmas ball in Gabriel's aunts' house on a snowy night in good spirits, a settled couple. Galoshes and all they come, Gabriel to perform his duty, to offer the annual toast to the Misses Markam, and Gretta to perform hers—to admire her husband's way with words. But before the evening is out they will be changed because of a memory she has of a young boy of seventeen who, she says, died for her.

The story begins with Gabriel's inside comfort, housed and warm and domiciled; it makes him think instead of the indifferent white of nature on the other side of the window:

> Gabriel's warm trembling fingers tapped the cold pane of the window. How cool it must be outside! How pleasant it would be to walk out alone, first along by the river and then through the park! The snow would by lying on the branches of the trees. . . . How much more pleasant it would be there than at the supper-table![2]

Such reveries are pointedly aimed at dissociation from the protectiveness which he seems so ably to supply as much as to enjoy. Clearly Gabriel is of two minds, of two desires, and one pulls him away from the other. When he delivers his toast, he is momentarily suspended between the predictably dull aunts and the future of uncertain terrain: "Therefore, I will not linger on the past."

But Gabriel does not yet know that he is fated to linger on the past, even if obliquely, through the sensibility of his wife. At the conclusion of the evening, waiting for her, he glimpses her on the staircase listening to the song which he later discovers was sung to her by a desperately ill young boy in love with her, long ago, in the buried past. That air, "The lass of Aughrin," is like a tolling bell for Gretta. On the way back to the hotel Gabriel feels a sudden and inexplicable desire and tenderness for Gretta (he knows nothing yet of the meaning of this song), seeing and feeling in her being something aroused, he knows not what:

> Like the tender fire of stars moments of their life together, that no one knew of or would ever know of, broke upon and illumined his memory. He longed to recall to her those moments, to make her forget the years of their dull existence together and remember only their moments of ecstasy. For the years, he felt, had not quenched his soul or hers.

But his tenderness and desire find no response in an abstracted woman whose thoughts are in the past. Neither rage nor desire finds a sympathetic mark. When she kisses him tenderly, he is overjoyed, but when he seeks out her secret and hears her response, he is crushed. Young Michael Furey of the gasworks had truly a passion and had died for her, and Gabriel is suddenly made to compare himself to a young, sick boy whose memory has so moved his wife: "A shameful consciousness of his own person assailed him." He sees himself as "ludicrous," a "pennyboy" for his aunts, "nervous," a sentimental orator, in fact a rather "pitiable fatuous fellow" now full of shame. Gretta's elegiac memory has unwittingly turned Gabriel into a reverse reflection of the past, into the dullness of the present which cannot match. When she articulates her story with all its attendant pathos and grief, Gretta can fall asleep. But Gabriel is annihilated:

> So she had had that romance in her life: a man had died for her sake. It hardly pained him now to think how poor a part he, her husband, had played in her life. . . . His curious eyes rested long upon her face . . . and, as he thought of what she must have been then, in . . . her first girlish beauty, a strange, friendly pity for her entered his soul. He did not like to say even to himself that her face was no longer beautiful, but he

knew that it was no longer the face for which Michael Furey had braved death.

It would be easy to call these thoughts just revenge, but the matter is more complicated. True, Gabriel forces his wife back into the present, heals his hurt by allowing himself the luxury of bringing Gretta into *his* time, no matter how much her feelings had sojourned in the past. That way he can see a mutual truth, join with her in a common elegy for years gone by: the air has become a dirge for both their lives. He thinks of how soon Aunt Julia will die; his fears are prompted by generosity. True, he admits, "he had never felt like that himself towards any woman, but he knew that such a feeling must be love." What he had felt earlier that evening then was desire, lust, but not what Michael Furey had felt, surely, not that kind of consuming love. Nor could he ever feel it. That time had long since passed, if ever it was there at all. Now the snow he watches brings him to a sense of inner and outer obliteration into that "region where dwell the vast hosts of the dead." Indeed, his own "identity was fading out into a grey impalpable world: the solid world itself, which these dead had one time reared and lived in, was dissolving and dwindling." Gabriel is separated from the phenomenal world which itself is disappearing in the rapidly falling snow. Such annihilation is here called a "swoon," a kind of death, a descent, like the snow itself, into the spatial universe. It is like a dissolution, however temporary, which forces him to acknowledge something beyond self-pitying regret, namely, that even he is a part of Gretta's memory of Michael Furey, part of "all the living and the dead," part of the past and the present. Desire had fathered regret; the past insinuated itself into and destroyed the present. Yet whatever life he had not lived—nor would in the future—the consciousness of what he had missed, and was missing, however painful, was itself perhaps partial redemption.

II
Mann: The Way Up Is the Way Down

There are three reasons why *The Magic Mountain* has been included in this study. First, the circumstances of the sanatorium itself lend themselves with ease to the idea of narcissism. Second, although there appears to be a tendency to read the novel as a progressive journey toward its hero's enlightenment, it will be argued here that this enlightenment is very dubious: for what Hans Castorp "learns" up in his hermetic, snowbound enclosure is either forgotten as a faded dream or is in no way useful or applicable "down there"—down, that is, in the real world. And third, the method Mann uses to make these points is clearly to make everything circular, that is, to make the circle his leitmotif. Of course, this does not mean that Castorp ends up exactly where he began; but it is relatively easy to demonstrate that Castorp's massive learning projects, impressive when we watch them in the rarified air of the "Zauberberg," is in the end caught in a spiral of devolution. A simple Schubert *Lied* is not quite on par with the disputations between Settembrini and Naphta to which the reader has been listener for hundreds of pages nor to the encyclopedic book learning that drove Castorp to probe the very inner depths of life and death. In addition, the nature of circularity appears to signal a kind of futility. Like the end of one of his precious phonograph records, Hans Castorp's long and earnest investment comes to a scratchy halt. All complexities are unraveled simply by the stark necessities of reality: war and survival. Castorp has moved from dodging verbal darts to avoiding lead bullets, from the hermetic to the all-too-close proximity to life far more ominously shadowed by death than it ever was on the magic mountain.

Whether or not Hans Castorp survives the war in which we last catch a glimpse of him at the end of *The Magic Mountain*—and his creator gives him a poor chance at best—does not, of course, constitute the basis for including him as one who does (or does not) belong as an exemplar of the unlived life.[3] His ultimate survival is irrelevant, both to that question and to the novel itself. Once Mann bids adieu to his hero, the issue of his "future" is settled, so it is therefore only the life we see that counts. However "ironic" the novel may be, and few have argued that it is not, there is a good case to be made for Castorp's education, for seeing the novel essentially as a *Bildungsroman*, a notion that Mann encouraged, not only in the novel but comments about it. Even were one to agree with the view that the novel is a parody of the traditional *Bildungsroman* (another aspect of its irony), it is difficult to see the hero emerge from his seven-year experience untouched by what has occurred on this bewitched mountain. Yet what precisely comprises this educational experience, and of what use it is in the end—these questions remain legitimate issues.

Whatever insights Hans Castorp earns (and it is not argued here that he earns none) are unfortunately turned moot at the end of the novel, and for two reasons. First when the spell is broken and he descends from the mountain, the insights earned up there on the mountain are not easily (if at all) negotiable to the flatland. Paradoxically, Castorp's insights, whatever they be, can serve him only where he no longer can remain: among the sick he would perhaps be more healthy; but among the healthy he would gradually need to become again much like them in order to survive. It is made very clear throughout the novel that the two worlds of mountain and flatland are distinct, discrete but separate, measured by a distance which, when traversed in either direction, truly changes the traveler. Hence the assumption that Hans Castorp can simply carry down his education along with his luggage is naive. Second, there is the war itself and Castorp's participation in it. It is not the innocence of death which may negate his education gained on the mountain but the innocence of flatland life. A great part of what Castorp sees, as Mann himself insisted, is embodied in the famous epiphany, the dream-vision in the section titled "Snow," where he learns that only humans are given the privilege of mastering dialectics, or preserving through all the turmoil of events a kind of "negative capability." Yet the historic moment of 1914, which forces him to choose sides, negates the very core of that insight. Hans Castorp's life is likely to be wasted by that choice, however unavoidable it may have been, just as millions on millions of such lives were wasted in the Great War. (It is an interesting gloss on language that since the Vietnam War the word "wasted" has become synonymous with killing or being killed.) Once Castorp leaves the mountain—as he must given what he has "learned"—his life has become a waste; below waits the great abyss, the conflagration, depriving him at one blow not merely of a future but of a past as well, whether or not he physically survives the carnage. That is one of the ultimate ironies of Mann's novel.

It is death above all that encircles the book from beginning to end, in all its masks; to call the novel "A Study in Death" would not be inappropriate. Yet for all the emphasis on death, Mann separates out, rather clearly and systematically, what precisely about death he wishes to explore and in what order. Furthermore, the novel, in addition to supplying us with a good deal of humor—gallows and other—and irony, is not without its antithesis to death. In fact, as readers have noticed, antithesis may be the structural as well as the thematic device that binds the work, holds its massive details in some semblance of balance. East and West, Naphta and Settembrini, Mountain and Flatland, Health and Disease—and Death and Life: these are some of the dialectical counterparts which are engaged over two lengthy volumes. Yet another, less obvious antithesis is the important, and sometimes explicit, antithesis between a certain idyllic world, encased within the hermetic universe of the mountain, and the intrusion of its antithesis—call it death, the Fall, the path East of Eden.

The magic mountain itself, however whimsically at times it may be depicted, is an idyllic world, somewhat of a distorted microcosm of that idyllic world of which Hans Castorp dreams in "Snow." More than idyllic, it is also elegiac, suffused though it is with disease and death, suffering and mutability. Patients on the mountain lounge in blissful repose, clearly in an Arcadian world shaped in the image of tubercular visitants whose disease, as Mann well knew, permitted them to swing from moods of elation to moods of depression, from quiet, peaceful acceptance to all-out resistance. It would make no sense simply to say that death is in this Arcadia, since in this Arcadia everyone knows that fact only too well. But the mere presence of death, however much it is avoided by patients, is not what matters. The idyllic and pastoral world of the sanatorium is protected from all outside intrusions by a silent conspiracy of the dwellers themselves, and it is this evasion which Castorp finds so difficult to understand and to adjust to during the initial seven months into his stay.

For the Hans Castorp who arrives on the magic mountain, death is not an unpleasant, new, or surprising experience. Had he not, indeed, experienced it so early, was not death one of his primal *Urerlebnisse*? And as we recall Poussin's two paintings of Arcadia, we can be very sure that the young Castorp would have identified with the second, the one depicting a quiet and dignified acceptance of death, free of terror, grief, or surprise. Yet in this respect especially, Castorp has much to learn, and his primary education is essentially an extended seminar on the meaning of death: it occupies nearly half the book. Initially he is introduced to death in such a bizarre way that he can only chuckle. The roads in winter are so clogged with snow, he is told by his cousin, that the dead are bundled up and sent down the mountain slopes by bob-sled. Castorp cannot resist the humor of that story, but he also rebukes his cousin in the midst of a "violent, irrepressible laugh": "On bob-sleds! And you can tell it me just like that, in cold blood! You've certainly got pretty cynical. . . ."[4] When he arrives in his room and is informed that it needed to be fumigated because someone had "died here day before yesterday," Castorp thinks it is "ripping," but again underneath such offhandedness lies protest. For Castorp death has not been a matter of laughter but of reverence, silence, hushed respect. On the very next page he hears the gentleman rider's awful cough, a "perfectly ghastly sound," which does not even seem "human" and further disconcerts him. With so much talk of death and such inhuman sounds, no wonder he tells Dr. Krokowski that he, Castorp, was "thank God, perfectly healthy."

The early pages of *The Magic Mountain* introduce us very formally to the hero's experience of and perspective on death and dying; that Castorp will learn at close range more about death than he knew is clear, but the tenacity with which he holds on to his early impressions is telltale. Only as his own idyllic view of death, with tuberoses arrayed against the stink of death, is invaded by more than a fly on the corpse of his grandfather, an external fact, will he begin to perceive death differently. That does not occur until he becomes truly aware of his own mortality, and this will take time, something of which Hans Castorp has a generous amount.

Mann describes in great detail a scene early on when Castorp strains his body unused to these heights. He ventures on a walk and encounters a mountain stream, "picturesque" footbridges, a scene blue with "bell-like blossoms" growing everywhere; fir trees lining the view to either side, a "remote and lovely spot" with the sound of "rushing waters" and "solitude," a "rushing waterfall" (there will be another one much later in Hans Castorp's experience) and the "idyllic sound of its monotonous . . . prattle." This Arcadian landscape, which Castorp regards from a bench, is rudely interrupted by blood: a nosebleed, a mere trifle, though, of course, both a warning and a physical counterpart to his spiritual reverie. (Can one imagine, say, Wordsworth distracting us with a *nosebleed* in the opening lines of "Tintern Abbey"?) From such a physical reminder Castorp sinks into a total "annihilation of time and space," a dream of Privislav Hippe, the young boy of his youth who so much resembles the mysterious Madame Chauchat. What he dreams of will be repeated later (the borrowing of a pencil), but the dream intercepts, and interrupts, the contemplation of the beautiful country scene and the distressing nosebleed. (Later, in "Snow," blood will again interrupt an idyllic vision.) When he comes out of it, he has learned his first lesson: "Taking walks up here is very beautiful—but appears to have its difficult side." In its very triviality, the scene prepares the way, allows us to concentrate on Castorp's continually changing views of death and on his understanding of the dialectic which death enforces. In this Arcadia there is always Death.

Specifically, for the present context, there are several major events: his taking up the cause of the moribund; the dream-vision of "Snow"; the visit to the waterfall with Mynheer Peeperkorn; and Peeperkorn's death scene, which dovetails into the remainder of the novel. Each of these events reveals more than merely a major shift in perspective on death: they all underscore Castorp's significant discovery that life is not the only antithesis to death (or vice versa); that evil equalizes good; that energy equalizes enervation; that action equalizes inaction; that what is gained is equalized by what is lost. Man may be, as the author pronounces, "lord of counter-positions"; but the price for this is itself a circularity which, while it may attempt to resemble the positive aspects suggested in Nietzsche's "eternal recurrence," really ends up being more akin to the pessimistic whirlwind of Will promulgated by Nietzsche's former mentor and later *bête noir,* Schopenhauer.

So far, events suggest the following: the recognition that as human beings we stand between ever-recurring dialectic results in a standstill. Had the war or some other event not exercised its power to extricate Castorp by forcing him to make a choice, he might have stayed yet another seven years—or forever; and forever he would have been the victim of those later emotions which lassitude engenders: indecision, ennui, irritability, languor, isolation. To say that Castorp "wasted" seven years of his life is, on one level, absurd since he "learned" so much; but on another level, the "waste" is indisputable: a metaphysical insight which paralyzes and throws one into a vortex of repetition is the worst kind of waste, and no one more than Castorp is its total victim. In *The Magic Mountain* Schopenhauer defeats Nietzsche, and from that point of view the novel is in large measure profoundly pessimistic. Not until Beckett's *Waiting for Godot* is the subject of *waiting* treated so lavishly and so devastatingly.

"Phlegmatic . . . and energetic": so at one point Settembrini, the emotional rationalist, identifies the dialectic. For all the fun Mann pokes at the "organ grinder" with his checkered, tattered trousers, Settembrini is not to be ignored, for he alone understands the dilemma: he has himself been its prisoner. Settembrini sees in Castorp's reverential obeissance toward death not merely a tendency to make negation respectable, but a danger of forgetting the élan vital, life, action, change. Castorp's flip and easy bandying with the concepts of Time, as if it matters little whether one speaks of a day, a week, a month, or years, always infuriates Settembrini because Time is so precious in his value system: Time contains the enabling moments of commitment; Timelessness (which is "Asiatic") denies and annihilates them. " 'This barbaric lavishness with time is in the Asiatic style. . . . We Europeans . . . have as little time as our great and finely articulated continent has space. . . . *Carpe diem!* " *Carpe diem,* not *ubi sunt:* there is *no time* for that. Settembrini pits the finite, the classical, the contained, against the infinite, the romantic, the loose: and, as for Goethe, the former is health, the latter disease. " 'Severed from life,' " Settembrini warns, " '[death] becomes a spectre, a distortion, and worse. For death, as an independent power, is a lustful power, whose vicious attraction is strong indeed; to feel drawn to it, to feel sympathy with it, is without any doubt at all the most ghastly aberration to which the spirit of man is prone.' " And most upsetting and puzzling to young Castorp: " 'Disease and despair,' Settembrini said, 'are often only forms of depravity.' " That Mann meant this to be taken seriously is all too clear from his authorial intrusion some pages later when he reminds us that his hero lacked "any reasonably satisfying explanation of the meaning and purpose of man's life."

When, during the famous X-ray scene, Castorp is able to see his own fluoroscoped hand, "he looked into his own grave," and "for the first time in his life he understood that he would die."

Hans Castorp at the Movies and at the Cemetery

"Totentanz" ("The Dance of Death") is a very rich section, for its two major episodes, Castorp's visits to the movies and to the cemetery with a young moribund girl, Karen, conceal as much as reveal much of the meaning of the novel. The gentleman rider, whose cough so much startled and distressed Castorp, has died. Castorp now resolves to be truly "human," to spend some time with the "severe cases," the moribundi, and he freely admits this will do as much good for him as them. He at least would ease his own conscience, would give death its due, take it "seriously" and render it "respect." Half a year into his stay, Castorp has become, for the moment, very sober. Armed with flowers, and with his reluctant accomplice, cousin Joachim, the two embark on their visits to the hopelessly ill.

One of their patients is a dying nineteen-year-old girl, Karen Karstedt, frail, bony, clearly not long for life. Still ambulatory, they take her to concerts, bobsled races, and one day to the cinema at the Bioscope Theater. Mann's description of the silent movies (there are several, some of them newsreels), accompanied by music, takes on highly symbolic values. Life—"chopped into small sections"—"flitted across the screen," an arrival and departure of images, a jerky movement, a "phantasmagoria of the past" limited to small space and yet capable of arousing strong feelings. The playlet is of "love and death," an Oriental ruler, a harem of naked bodies, a scene of lust, cruelty, and a glimpse of an executioner. So in the space of a piece of canvas, time passed before their eyes. When it was all over, the audience was quiet, the images they had just seen having somehow repelled them.

Indeed they move with embarrassed gestures, they fidget, accustoming their eyes to the bright light, "wishing themselves back in the darkness"; they have become self-conscious. The ruling despot has died under the executioner's knife; the world comes to life: presidents, viceroys, rajahs, crown princes. Faraway places came into view: cock fights in Borneo or savages and elephants, Siam and Japan, Russia and Palestine. To each of these spatially distant parts, temporally linked on the screen, they were witness: "Space was annihilated; the clock put back, the then and there played on by music. . . ." A closeup of a woman with swelling breasts and "full of animal life" threatens the audience; they seem discomfited by this vicarious invasion of their senses—and fascinated. The vision on the screen, however, was not aware of its viewers, as they were of it: it "was not of the present but of the past," and when *Finis* appeared on the screen, they knew that "the cycle would presently unroll itself again."

So the cinema was an internal repository, recycling (as later in the novel the phonograph record will) the same images, repetitively. The mechanisms which capture, hold, and can represent, repetitiously, a temporal moment hitherto lost and usable once only captivated Mann. They helped him to underscore the more obvious cyclic patterns of time in *The Magic Mountain:* the days, weeks, months, years, which seem somehow to run into one another without temporal demarcations, without a sense of formal motion. The eventual monotony and danger, as well as the elusiveness, of the circle are gradually impressed upon the reader at the same time that Mann allows increasing dialectical tension to develop. These chafing opposites, however, rarely result in any synthesized resolution, so that even dialectics become repetitious and circular.

After the cinema scene, the comrades in illness—Castorp, Joachim, and the dying Karen—visit the local cemetery, the one surely where, as all three understand, Karen herself will soon be buried. The opposition of life and death is an obvious contrast to the mechanical time-machine of the cinema, which repeats time with a relentless symmetry. But, one realizes, the major point of the scene is not merely the obvious life-death antithesis but the death-in-life figuration which, like Poussin's second painting, shows these "Arcadians" accepting death's inevitability, seeking out the grave and the tombstones, not stumbling upon them by chance. First there had been visits to the bobsleds with their downward-hurling speed—crashing thrusts sucking their way in prearranged ice roads; then to the circular mimetic time-machine; finally to the cemetery, "up the narrow path"—down/circular/up: Hell, Purgatory, Paradiso. Or, if not exactly Paradiso, an approximation of it, an O altitudo! On the way up they encounter a beautiful view, and they take it in, contemplatively, and proceed through the gates. "No soul was to be seen or heard, the quiet remoteness and peace of the spot seemed deep and unbroken *in more than one sense*" (italics added). (The German for cemetery, *Friedhof*, literally means "court of peace.") Mann describes sentimental monuments and stone angels standing in the snow. But his purpose is never more direct or more serious. The "little stone angel" holds his finger over his lips, and "[it] might have passed for the genius of the place—the genius of a silence . . . [which it] guarded [and which] was far from being empty of content or character." Had they hats, the gentlemen, this would be the place to remove them, but, alas, they were bareheaded. The irony is gentler but the meaning earnest. Reverence, yes, but surely beyond—if but a step—the contest over his grandfather's bier between tuberoses and the insistent fly. For this was a cemetery of the young: the average lifespan of the dead was "not much more than twenty years" (about what the cemeteries would be like after the Great War). As they pause to read the "mournful inscription" on a gravestone, Castorp "stood relaxed"; the cousin was "very self-controlled"; even the deathly ill Karen was "smiling a strained little smile." It is, for all its peace, a strained scene, and the inscription they read (we are not told its words) might well be in the spirit of "Et Ego in Arcadia"—in *both* its meanings.

From this somber scene we move to its antithesis, Walpurgisnacht, during which circularity of quite another sort will occupy Hans Castorp—the blindfolded "fool's" drawing of pigs. Several times Settembrini has cautioned Castorp about the waste of a continued sojourn on the mountain, urging him to return to the flatland. But such advice has no effect, for it collides with a combination of a woman and a touch of disease. On Walpurgisnacht, Castorp will quarrel with his mentor Settembrini (under the influence not only of Madame Chauchat but of drink), and he will succumb to hopeless "love." Castorp joins the celebrants in their diversion of trying to draw, with closed eyes, the shapes of a pig, and circles become distorted and jagged, the drawings lacking all coherence; pigs, such as they are, emerge dismembered, "eyes were outside the head, the legs inside the paunch," and so forth. The evening has reached a state of *dis*integration.

By the time we begin the second volume, with its unanswerable question, "What is Time?", we have ourselves, as readers, been spread thin. "The ocean of time, rolling onwards in monotonous rhythm," carries us forward. "The year was running out," seasons melt into seasons, virtually unnoticed. Circles and cycles. The newly philosophically-minded Castorp is instructing his practical-minded cousin on the nature of circles, about the cyclic movements of the seasons; they cannot be taken for granted, for their rhythms have a more profound meaning: "You feel you're being fooled, led about in a circle, with your eye fixed on something that turns out to be a moving point. A moving point in a circle. For the circle consists of nothing but such transitional points without any extent whatever; the curvature is incommensurable, there is no duration of motion, and eternity turns out to be not 'straight ahead' but 'merry-go-round!' " "Tragic joy," Castorp explains, "triumphant sadness—that was what made our ancestors leap and exult around the leaping flames. They did so as an act of homage to the madness of the circle, to an eternity without duration, in which everything recurs—in sheer despair, if you like." Having delivered himself on the despair of the circle, Castorp is now ready to encounter the master dialectician, Naphta, on the very next page. The conversations between the two antagonists, Settembrini and Naphta, will eventually also turn into circles. But momentarily the two antagonists provide the illusion of dispelling the despair about the circle. When the chief physician, Hofrat Behrens, pronounces him fit—"you may go"—, Hans Castorp refuses to leave. He has been sucked into the vortex of timelessness; it is a fate more serious than tuberculosis, and, of course, there is the hope of once more seeing a certain woman. From now on this is the disease he suffers from, the sloth of eternal repetition, and there are nearly six years left: "The wheel revolved"—and it will do so many times more.

The circularity so dominant in the section "Snow" is, as I suggested, intercepted by a dialectic, but again the dialectic dissolves, this time into the recesses of the dreamer's memory. In the second year of his stay, Castorp, now better acclimatized than when he was felled by a nosebleed, makes forays into the surrounding mountainside, and skis into the white stillness, which so much reminds him of the expanse of a sandy beach of his childhood. This solitariness gives him a false sense of freedom, and so his boldness exceeds his prudence, and he is suddenly surprised by and trapped in an unexpected snowstorm. Attempting to reverse course and head for home, he predictably goes in circles, returning to the very spot from which, with great effort, he had resolved to make his way back home: "You went in a circle, gave yourself endless trouble under the delusion that you were accomplishing something, and all the time you were simply describing some great silly arc that would turn back to where it had its beginning, like the riddling year itself. You wandered about, without getting home," a sentence that has multiple reverberations. In a semidelirious state, with some port in him to boot, Castorp has his (or his creator's) dream about the simultaneity of Good and Evil, Life and Death, Peace and Violence, Innocence and Corruption. In a way this dual vision is like viewing *both* Poussin paintings, side by side, simultaneously. Or perhaps even more apt, the first scene, which beholds the second scene, encompasses the meaning in both paintings: the horror and terror of death and putrefaction beheld silently and in the knowledge of its perennial existence.

Mann himself pronounced this scene as definitively holding the key to his novel, and in some ironic way it probably does. The first part of the dream—the sunny landscape—is a pure eclogue, an idyll, an Arcadian scene. If it is, as well, elegiac, it is so only in contrast to the scene which it opposes, the scene of horror, mourning not so much for any loss but for its necessity, its inevitability. With near ecstasy Castorp gazes at the beautiful people, adult and children, goats on rocks, youths tilling the land, the beloved sea. It is a beauty which is nearly painful; it resembles Aschenbach's final vision in *Death in Venice*. The two gray witches offering their blood sacrifice in the unholy Temple complete the "bliss" with "terror" which he now realizes we as humans must bear witness to simultaneously: "he has dreamed of man's state, of his courteous and enlightened social state; behind which, in the temple, the horrible blood-sacrifice was consummated." Like Conrad's Kurtz, he has seen "the horror," and the italicized sentence (the only one in the novel) appears to seal his understanding: "*For the sake of goodness and love, man shall let death have no sovereignty over his thoughts.*"

To paraphrase Mann, to live is to be partaking of the process of dying, so we must countenance terror and violence in the midst of serenity and peace. We humans, Mann says, are doomed to coexistence, we are indeed lords of counter-positions; the very process of life is countermanded by opposites. Love, not Reason, shall rule us; and death, as John Donne wrote, shall have no dominion over life. Nevertheless, death is not relegated to oblivion; it is not to be evaded by reverence or sanctity; it is not to be resisted with empty rhetoric, such as mark some of Settembrini's tirades. The allegorical division in Castorp's dream appears to suggest some kind of cleavage between bliss and horror, and perhaps the device of the dream-vision is misleading; yet Mann clearly meant to portray the two scenes as part of a unity, the "silent recognition" of the "terror" being an acceptance that in no way invalidates the bliss and joy of life. But Castorp's confident "Now I have it fast" soon turns to "What he had dreamed was already fading from his mind," not merely because such is the nature of dreams but because the conscious balance of the two visions is impossible to the waking consciousness. What we dream, however, can alter us even if we do not recall the dream itself. Castorp's behavior does not markedly change after his dream-vision because effects are slow to gestate and reveal themselves only gradually and later on—when he is truly ready. In time we can see clearly that, however unspoken, the dream-vision has made him *think* differently. The positioning of "Snow" is situated well past the middle of the novel but not the middle of his stay. He will remain five long years beyond that dream-vision, and even in the timelessness of the magic mountain, that is a long time.

When Hans Castorp stands yet once again at a deathbed (one more such vigil awaits him), tuberoses and fly have been superseded; reverence and the hush of solemnity have been replaced with a genuine sense of loss, with tears not for death but for the dead—for the dead Joachim, his good brave cousin who tried so courageously to defy death and has lost. Castorp is still "reverently watching" his cousin die, but there is a personal involvement in the death that had been missing in all the others to which Castorp had so far been called upon to witness. Joachim's death closes the sixth and penultimate chapter of the novel. We stand now on the threshold of the final, the seventh chapter, beginning as did the previous chapter with a disquisition on Time and the difficulties of narrating Time itself, narrating what Man calls a "time-romance." Now clearly a "seven-sleeper," Castorp is fully immersed in the sea-sand-and-Snow configuration, which evokes vast empty space, "wastes" to which he has now committed himself with little hope of extrication—indeed with little wish for it, "strengthened in his vicious time-economy, his baleful traffic with eternity. . . ."

So Mynheer Peeperkorn's recognition of the futility of resistance, leading eventually to suicide, is something Castorp can now much better understand than when he first arrived and saw Herr Albion playing recklessly with a pistol. But before that fated event, Castorp and Peeperkorn become close blood brothers united by their common love for Clavdia Chauchat. One May morning they plan an excursion to a waterfall, a scene with so much irony and humor it is often read as a parody not only of Peeperkorn but also of all he embodies: the irrational, the mysterious, the incomprehensible. That, however, may be only a diversionary tactic; Mann's real purpose in the waterfall scene lies elsewhere.

They gather by a waterfall—surely Mann was also thinking of Faust's confrontation with that challenging phenomenon of nature—in a wood which we are told quite explicitly is not routine but "picturesque, exotic, even uncanny. . . . A complete, a bizarre transformation, a bewitched and morbid scene. For the trees were sick of this rank growth, it threatened to choke them to death. . . ." The sound of the waterfall is "infernal," cascading down the rocks; the sound is not that of an idyllic landscape but of "hissing, thundering, roaring, bawling, whispering, crushing, crackling, droning, chiming . . . enough to drive one senseless." Although the visitors wish to spread out their picnic lunch out of hearing of this infernal rumble, their host sternly insists that they remain in close proximity to this watery din. Poor Settembrini despairs of engaging in any "human interchange of ideas," and he is right; what they are witness to is a visual pantomime; Peeperkorn's words may be lipread only, for human articulation is easily subdued by nature's. Muteness, however, does not equal noncommunication. The image of Peeperkorn holding forth—which Mann freely associates with "the ritual of impropriety of the heathen priest"—suggests the conversion of human impotence to the potency of mimicking nature itself. Gesture reigns supreme here; gesture informs this scene with its predictive suggestions of what is soon to occur: if and when the human struggle is over, resistance and rebellion are childish. Instead, Peeperkorn's mute speech seems to convey, we must join the phenomena to which we are ultimately destined rather than fear or evade what is not fearful nor avoidable. No wonder that on this night Hans Castorp sleeps "light and fitful by portents of which his soul knew naught," for very soon he will stand by Peeperkorn's deathbed, where the mute speech was transformed into the mute act, a suicide not to evade death but to acknowledge its obviously superior power, a joining with the Will by self-objectification. (Schopenhauer opposed suicide, but Peeperkorn's is, in every way, so ritualistic and so designed with purpose, he might have approved its logic if not its execution.)

Castorp becomes a semipermanent resident, waiting—well, waiting for what? "Everything appeared to have gone permanently and increasingly awry, as though a demonic power . . . had suddenly taken control. . . ." Down in the flatland, clear signs of an upcoming upheaval reach and penetrate the hermetic mountain, but Castorp continues to play patience—and, eventually, those records whose sole guardianship he has appropriated to himself. Now, as at the Bioscope Theater, Castorp once more beholds the magic of the stored memory, which by mere human manipulation can repeat itself indefinitely. Of course, he is now far more self-conscious even in *un*consciousness:

> He saw in his sleep the disk circling about the peg, with a
> swiftness that made it almost invisible and quite soundless. Its
> motion was not only circular, but also a peculiar, sidling undu-
> lation, which communicated itself to the arm that bore the
> needle, and gave this too an elastic oscillation, almost like
> breathing . . .

The very next morning he hears the baritone singing "Blick' ich
umher in diesem edlen Kreise"—"I glance around me in this noble
circle." Around the perhaps not so noble circle of the suspect séance
table the ghost of Joachim materializes, the vertical ghost accenting
the spherically arranged creatures who have disturbed his eternal rest
as phonograph records whirl out their crazy spin: "The record had
run off. . . . But no one stopped the machine. The needle went on
scratching in the silence, as the disk whirred round" like ceaseless
time. Only Castorp can "stop" the machine—until the next turn.

The second demon Castorp encounters is Irascibility ("Gereitzheit":
here Lowe-Porter's "Hysterica passio" is not helpful), to which he finds
himself as susceptible as the rest. It is also the spirit of "descent," the
circular way in which Naphta falls dead after shooting himself in the
head, staggering, tottering, beginning yet another circle, "a few steps
backward . . . [executing] a right turn with his whole body. . . ." When
the war at last breaks out down there, and the shot at Sarajevo reverberates up here, the enchantment is at last broken. Castorp realizes his
liberation has not come about through existential choice but through a
choice made by existence outside himself, "the operation of exterior
powers" which now took control over everyone. Earlier, while listening
to such masterpieces as *Carmen* and *Aida, Tristan and Isolde* and *Faust,* or
such precious pieces as *L'Apres Midi d'un Faune,* Castorp has also been
stirred by a simple *Lied,* Schubert's "Der Lindenbaum," lyrics by
Bürger, a simple song—or was it? It is this song which we last hear from
his lips as he dodges bullets and shells on the battlefield, receding like a
cinematographic shot into the distance. During that earlier time, when
he had indulged his incorrigibly romantic spirit in that *Lied,* Mann had
made him face up to its lure: "What was the world behind the song,
which the motions of his conscience made to seem a world of forbidden
love? It was death." So it was, in many ways. *The Magic Mountain* is not
about death; it is, among other things, a magisterial elegy in prose on the
death of a whole civilization. Begun before the war, interrupted by it,
completed after it, this novel embodies the deep and devastating shock
of the death of a world Mann himself loved and cherished and was
never really reconciled to losing. The simple song expressed it all,

expressed, that is, one sensibility of love and death with which Hans Castorp held fast to the bitter end: Schubert's *Lied* was "the fruit of life, conceived of death, pregnant of dissolution. . . . Ah, it was worth dying for, the enchanted *lied*!" Die for it perhaps he will, like a hero who "died for the new, the new word of love and the future. . . ." But that we shall not be given to know. To the end Castorp remains more *spiritual* than he might wish, true to form, or reverting to form if one wishes; he was aware of "spiritual backsliding" which Settembrini had warned him was a "disease." But there was no hope, for Castorp could simply not help himself: he loved the "nostalgic lay, the sphere of feeling to which it belonged," a sphere of feeling that in the end superseded words, dialectics, and intellect.

From that perspective Castorp's seven years were certainly for naught, for no amount of lessons could rid him of his basic nature—his national nature perhaps since Settembrini's nationalism or Naphta's taste for silk were similarly ingrained, not susceptible to rational assessment, totally in contradiction to verbal professions, respectively, of peaceful universalism and Christian Marxism. What Castorp learns in seven years is undone by a simple *Lied;* for however much he has learned—and it is considerable baggage he has accumulated—the great irony is, as was stated at the start, that he cannot use it down below in the flatland world, where it simply ceases to have any efficacious application. So he must join his countrymen, seize upon the archetypal *Lied* to cheer himself up in the midst of impending death. Castorp's unlived life is trapped between the past (his heritage) and the future, and he can negotiate between them only on the precarious fields of battle, where his chances of prevailing are slim.

The emphasis here has been to focus on the particular way in which the magic mountain becomes for Hans Castorp his version of, say, Chekhov's cherry orchard, for in certain respects, though it may not immediately seem so, Mann's novel is very Chekhovian. The slow dripping motion of time, the often monotonous pace, the sometimes tragicomic or even perverse characters and situations, the serious and the wistful in conflict with the pragmatic, the real, the emphasis on illness, death, and characterological paralysis, the dubious efficacy of language—all these, for all their distinctive Mannesque character, find some ancestry in Chekhov. Most of all the question of what Hans Castorp can do with all his experiential wisdom once he leaves his hermetic habitat, once he is *dis*enchanted, has been raised; and it is suggested that he can indeed do very little with it.

In "The Making of *The Magic Mountain*," Mann admitted that Howard Nemerov had hit the nail on the head when he called Castorp a

"Questor Hero," "forever searching for the Grail . . . wisdom, consecration, the philosopher's stone. . . ." In short, Mann suggests he is writing a version of *Bildungsroman:* "If he does not find the Grail, yet he divines it in his deathly dream, before he is snatched downwards from his heights into the European catastrophe." Well, perhaps; perhaps not. That is to say it is possible to conceive of Mann's novel as a truly enchanted tale in which, once the dreamer awakens, once the illusion is destroyed, once the enchantment is disenchanted, the ordinary returns to the ordinary.

Such a reading places Mann's novel among distinguished company: Shakespeare's *Winter's Tale,* Calderón's *Life is a Dream,* Kleist's *Prince of Homburg.* And the essential form of the novel encourages such a reading. Hans Castorp's seven years, for all their intellectual and spiritual stimulation, are negated by his descent to the flatland and its war. That is the nature of his dilemma: on the magic mountain he cannot remain ordinary; in the flatland he cannot remain the inquiring philosopher who luxuriates in "stock-taking." In the beginning, as Goethe decided, was not the Word but the Deed. For seven years Castorp lives in virtual isolation, but this can hardly be called a life lacking in growth and some kinds of fulfillment; on the contrary, Mann thinks of it as a time of enhancement, a time of *Steigerung.* All well and good were that time packageable for return to the flatland. Since this is not so, the seven years quickly become a dim memory, an enchanted somnambulism. What Castorp embraces in his commitment to war is what Settembrini called "back-sliding," though once a decision to depart has been forced, there can be no turning back for either man. The song he sings is also a dirge, its elegiac qualities clear enough in its words, but they also raise the personal elegy to more universalized levels, for the *Lied* in its way is Hans Castorp's elegy for the lost years on the magic mountain itself. After all, the Müller lyrics recall with considerable sadness a time of peace, an idyllic moment out of time, remembered now in the midst of the deep of night darkness, cold wind:

Ich musst auch heute wandern	Today I had to wander past it
Vorbei in tiefer Nacht,	in the deep of night; and in
Da hab ich noch im Dunkel	the darkness I closed my eyes.
Die Augen zugemacht,	And its branches rustled as if
Und seine Zweige rauschten,	They were speaking to me: Come
Als rief sie mir zu:	here to me, companion, here

Komm her zu mir Geselle,   you will find your peace.
Hier findest du deine Ruh!   (Translation mine)

I committed myself early on to designating this novel as Schopen-hauerian; Mann's essay on Schopenhauer (1938) gives us more clues than Schopenhauer himself. In Schopenhauer, the only possibility for happiness is the "repose" from the blind urges of the Will. But this, says Mann, is precisely what is denied to us so long as we persist in feeling desire. Now Castorp feels plenty of desires on the magic mountain, erotic and heuristic, the former of which Schopenhauer felt to be especially destructive. But Castorp also desires repose, and to a certain extent during the course of seven years he progressively achieves it. There are various routes of escape from the Will: the ascetic state, the aesthetic state, a disinterestedness (Kantian in origin). And even the intellectual (knowledge), the pursuit of which much preoccupies Cas-torp, was an antidote: "How could a denial of the will come out of life, which was after all through and through a will to life?" From one perspective, then, the sealed world of the magic mountain contains a number of escape routes from the Will, just as the descent to the flatland reimmerses the hero into the maelstrom once more—with a vengeance. The Great War, in that sense, is merely an overarching objectification of the Will. Mann himself links his novel to Schopen-hauer in his essay: "Whoever is interested in life, I said in *The Magic Mountain,* is particularly interested in death."[5] The great paradox of Mann's novel is that, for all its death and dying, the mountain offers an Arcadian idyllic existence, timeless, even spaceless, in which one may learn to accept the fly and the tuberoses, indeed to transcend both and be granted the ability to hold in balance life and death, as Hans Castorp eventually does. All that ends when descent places him into quite another threat to life, not the normal processes of illness which from birth on we are all heir to—to live is to be perpetually dying—but the externally imposed cataclysm of death which with ran-dom violence threatens and destroys. The flatland and its conflagra-tion *are* the Will whirling Hans Castorp with unthinkable intensity. The magic mountain had served as a brief sanctuary of which Castorp learned to take full advantage. That was the true lesson, the real *Bildung* of the mountain; its temporariness is dictated as much by the inherent nature of enchantment as if it were something like the air itself—thin "up there" when compared with "below." To an extent, though the irony of *The Magic Mountain* has long been recognized, one might be even bolder and propose that the novel formulates a

kind of cosmic joke, placing its hero between lassitude and an unnatural life and commitment and unnatural death.

No pun intended, *The Magic Mountain* is a book about "conspicuous
consumption." Tuberculosis is the ideal disease to objectify Mann's
points: the reclining patients, lying idly in their lounge chairs, are of
necessity self-absorbed. Every action revolves around them, from eating and leisure time to examinations and the various orders to take
their temperature or collect their sputum. So in one sense all patients
are narcissists, mourning their bad health, while at the same time, in
many instances, luxuriating in that very illness. It is as I have already
noted a fortuitous, and hardly accidental, decision for Mann to choose
an illness that has such highs and lows. For even the chief medical
director, Hofrat Behrens, an early victim, alternates between severe
melancholy and jolly participation with his patients. Of course, tuberculosis was a killing disease, and many die in the course of the novel.
Yet it is among the survivors that we most note their total absorption,
not merely in their health and its progress but in that of others. Such
care for others is seldom a gesture of genuine concern; rather patients
wish to find cases (better or worse than theirs) with which to make
comparison.

In his or her own way, the major characters become narcissists with
no exceptions, except that each acts out that narcissism in a different
way. Settembrini and Naphta are opposites, deliberately created as
such; but their self-absorption is equally intense. In some fashion
Castorp becomes the most narcissistic figure in the novel, and in his
defense he must. For a number of reasons Castorp does not wish to
get well, even when the doctors declare him cured and ready to leave.
Love has come in the way, love has managed to turn an ordinary self-
involved young man (who takes almost ecstatic pleasure in his cigar-
smoking) into a melancholic who uses illness as a means of preserva-
tive self-reflection—"stock-taking." Madame Chauchat explains that
illness gives her freedom; cousin Joachim Ziemssen, for different reasons, does the same, projecting onto his role as a disciplined soldier his
curative objectives. Naphta, the Marxist Jesuit, lives among silk and
riches, indulges in language itself by becoming a chronic disputant
lovingly embracing his words as they flow ceaselessly from his mouth.
Mynheer Peeperkorn is an embodiment of narcissism, even in the way
he commits suicide, and his challenge of language against nature in
the waterfall scene is a magnificent representation of this melancholic
"personality": he firmly believes he can outdo the waterfall, or, to put
it differently, he really feels it hardly matters as long as he controls the
event—which he does.

Eventually the seven-year tenant on the mountain slowly emerges as a loner by choice, something that began after his confrontation with death and nothingness. Castorp, too, is melancholy, sinking into the trance of "dangerous" music. Clearly the whole community at Davos is populated with narcissists for whom the greatest challenge is their health, hour to hour, day to day, year to year. That some do not die and "survive" to remain even beyond Hans's departure is testimony to the power of illness. For to those on the mountain, the flatland is a distant microcosm, whereas they believe, by and large, that they inhabit the macrocosm. And in a sense they do, even as it changes its mask back and forth between a genuine island of paradisiac pretensions, a haven and a kind of Heaven, to Circe's island, where men are turned to pigs.

III
Woolf: The Narrow Bed

Mrs. Dalloway has often been read as an affirmative novel. By her own admission, Virginia Woolf initially intended that the novel's heroine, Clarissa Dalloway, die at the conclusion, either by her own hand or presumably of a weak heart. Then Woolf decided to create Clarissa's "double," Septimus Smith, the shell-shocked schizophrenic who, in effect, does the deed for Clarissa, for it is he, not Clarissa, who dies. This appears to have created a neat structural symmetry consistent with a psychological need for the author as well as the character to survive. In her final assessment of the young man's death, Clarissa Dalloway appears to be placated, after her initial shock, by the propitiatory and vicarious occurrence of this death. Such a reading of the novel (and it has been admittedly stated in oversimplified terms) does not seem amiss; and intentional fallacy not withstanding, it has the seal of approval from the author. However, on closer look it is an unsatisfactory reading; it clearly leads to false assumptions, and it deprives the novel of some of the unresolved ambiguities which characterize Woolf's fiction, especially *Mrs. Dalloway*.

Mrs. Dalloway is foremost about middle-age crisis, as we speak of it today: "The novel, like so much of Virginia Woolf's fiction, is elegiac."[6] Essentially *Mrs. Dalloway* anatomizes the fear of death and of growing old, and its major characters are throughout regretting their lives, second-guessing their choices made when they were young. Above all, it is a novel about cheering oneself up, especially with respect to Mrs. Dalloway herself, her former lover, Peter Walsh, her husband, Richard, and in the closing pages Sally Seton, the once-vibrant poet, now a mother of five sturdy sons. This attempt, in one way or another, of these people to validate and justify their choices, even in the midst of doubt and regret, forms the major ambiguity of the novel's texture. To a certain extent it does depend how convincing these self-reassurances are for the reader, but it will be argued here that sufficient doubt is explicit in the text so as to make it reasonably clear that at novel's end, though surely they "make the best of it," as they themselves might put it, the human company of this book is neither happy nor reconciled to life, nor to death, though in one case, Clarissa Daloway's, there is at least an attempt to understand death sufficiently to allow her to continue to live. And this is why, probably, Woolf did not kill her off herself. In much of Woolf's fiction, especially in *To the Lighthouse* and *Mrs. Dalloway,* there is an undercurrent of something exceeding bitterness, perhaps something close to hatred. Yet in both novels that hate looks for—and receives—compensations: in *To the Lighthouse* it is artistic vision and maternal loving in a merger of two characters, Lily Briscoe and Mrs. Ramsay; in *Mrs. Dalloway* it is the sort of stoic confrontation with death that may indeed look toward Beckett: "I can't go on, I'll go on."

Clarissa Dalloway and Peter Walsh were in love, and had each followed his or her passion, they would have married. It is as senseless for us, as in a sense for them, to speculate how such a union might have worked out for either or for both, though each engages in such speculation throughout. What we know is that Clarissa Dalloway is not happy despite her social status, a healthy daughter, and a solicitous husband who, however, is unable to say to her: "I love you." She has banished herself to a "narrow" bed in the attic where she maintains, as she herself puts it, her perpetual virginity: "It was all over for her. The sheet was stretched and the bed narrow. She had gone up into the tower alone. . . . The door had shut. . . . I am alone for ever. . . ."[7] As for Peter Walsh, the man she might have but did not marry, he has returned from India, divorced and in love with a married woman of twenty-five (Mrs. Dalloway is fifty-one; Peter Walsh, fifty-two). His visit to Mrs. Dalloway, whom it seems he has not seen for at least five years, shatters him, and he spends the remainder of the novel observing and judging his past and his present and, like Mrs. Dalloway, none too eagerly contemplating the future. Much of the time on the June day and night which occupies the timespan of the novel is spent warding off old age, death, and, most important, the memories of his love for Mrs. Dalloway. As he tells a mutual friend at the evening party which closes the novel, he has "No sons, no daughters, no wife," and "He had not found life simple. . . . His relations with Clarissa had not been simple. It had spoilt his life. . . . One could not be in love twice. . . ." For, he might well have added, he has never fallen out of love with Clarissa Dalloway.

Septimus Smith's story is fused with the main story almost like a Shakespearean subplot, and it serves a contrapuntal function in the novel's thematic pattern. Of this later; meanwhile Clarissa and Peter spread across the pages, and to get a sense of the development and subtlety of their interaction, alone and together, it is necessary to spend some time tracing their contact chronologically.

London, of all great cities, is undoubtedly the most interpenetrated with green parks and other pastoral manifestations. By design or not, London offers an almost divided image between city and country, and Woolf took advantage of this fortuitous landscape. It is perfectly natural, then, that while walking through London the book's characters should be walking past or through parks. Still Woolf's emphasis on such idyllic scenes is worth special attention, for such scenes on this sunny day call up that fateful summer at Bourton which Clarissa recalls on the first page of the novel—that summer when she and Peter Walsh decided to take different paths, apparently to their mutual regret, for their separation has taken out of each an irrecoverable piece of life, has left an emptiness neither can replace. Also that summer at Bourton was full of idyll, full of walks, trees, sunshine—and, yes, flowers, which object we are told in the opening sentence she is on her way to purchase. That this idyll was insinuated with ominous clouds of strife, jealousy, anger, tears, rejection, and grief makes it no less a memory that causes both Clarissa and Peter poignant joy and poignant pain to recall. It may be impossible to measure precisely how much of *Mrs. Dalloway* is devoted to memories, but in the first one hundred pages (about the first third of the novel) about one half occupies the joint reminiscences of their Bourton days of youth, love, disappointment, and dissolution.

Clarissa will buy her flowers (and receive them); Richard will bring them, in place of words. Flowers: Peter will dream of them; Sally Seton will tear them from the earth. To each according to his or her being. Roses, especially, appear, and the rose, a common enough flower in an English novel, nevertheless has its thorns, is multifoliate, and forever stands as mute commentator about and communicator with love. So to begin with, Mrs. Dalloway will buy the flowers herself.

She has been ill and clearly looks older, gray ("white"), and the journey through the streets of London is by way of a recuperative, restrictive outing. She is buoyant: "What a plunge!" to take this upon herself. And at once the air reminds her of Bourton, when she was eighteen, and of a contemplative look at Bourton's flowers disturbed by Peter Walsh's ironic and unromantic " 'Musing among the vegetables?' " Peter is remembered: his eyes, his boyish grumpiness, his smile, his penknife—leitmotifs for his appearance in the novel, either in person or in Clarissa's thoughts. The first ring of many which Big Ben sounds immediately provides us with the pattern of time as the characters perceive it: "First a warning, musical; then the hour, irrevocable." Clarissa loves the tumult of the London streets: " 'I love walking in London. . . . Really it's better than walking in the country,' " and indeed June had "drawn out every leaf on the trees": it almost might be Bourton at that. Peter was no nature lover, however; he was a man concerned with "the state of the world," and musing in St. James's Park "she had been right . . . not to marry him," for there was too much sharing, too much surrender of self. He in turn had taken his revenge, called her "Cold, heartless, a prude," but what had *he* achieved all these years? Nothing, really: "he had never done a thing they talked of: his whole life had been a failure." But already Mrs. Dalloway feels detached from her surroundings, as if "far out to sea and alone"—the way Virginia Woolf herself would die. Disturbing thoughts invade her tranquillity: "she always had the feeling that it was very, very, dangerous to live even one day." The thought that she had once "thrown a shilling into the Serpentine" arrives as a harbinger of death, for on hearing that Septimus Smith has thrown himself from a window she will recall again, at the very close of the novel, that "she had once thrown a shilling into the Serpentine," never anything more. This throwing of the coin insistently brings to mind loss, loss of life itself, a feeling that she must "cease completely," that the world she beholds must do without her presence. For the first time she reads the refrain from *Cymbeline:* "Fear no more the heat o' the sun / Nor the furious winter's rages." And self-conscious of her looks, her separateness, she offers a plaint: "Oh if she could have had her life over again!"

The next time she thinks of the lines ("fear no more . . .") she is shaken by what seems a momentary desertion: her husband has gone to lunch with Lady Bruton without her. Abandonment causes her to shiver, and Clarissa knows that she feared time itself, and read it on Lady Bruton's face "as if it had been a dial cut in impassive stone, the dwindling of life; how year by year her share was sliced, how little the margin that remained. . . ." The image of a *stone* dial being *sliced* down dramatizes Clarissa Dalloway's dread. We are told how thin she is already; and while there is evidence of inner strength, her fragility is communicated. Indeed, her fear of time and death, of the price you pay when time has run out, is accentuated by her equally terrified state of separateness, one which, as many have remarked, she both covets and fears. That she now feels herself already in a metaphorical shroud is made amply clear by her choice of image and metaphor: "There was an emptiness about the heart of life; an attic room. . . . Narrower and narrower would her bed be. . . . So the room was an attic; the bed narrow . . . she could not dispel a virginity preserved through childbirth which clung to her like a sheet." It is immediately thereafter that she recalls the occasionally fulfilling quiver she would feel with another woman, a passage so orgiastic in tone it is almost a surprise to read it in Woolf, for it evades nothing. There is the memory of the moment of ecstasy and bliss, the kiss on the lips from Sally Seton: "the most exquisite moment of her whole life. . . ." Home from her journey to buy flowers, which began so happily and has ended with such troubled thoughts and feelings, she experiences a "sudden spasm" as if, at fifty-one, "the icy claws" had seized her. Whereupon enter Peter Walsh, unannounced, indeed unexpected, as if he came like a realized object materializing before her eyes after the deep thoughts she had given him all that morning.

Peter Walsh is perhaps a more important presence in the book than some have been willing to see, not because he is interesting in his own right but because he has such a profound impact on Clarissa Dalloway, not only on her past but also on her present. Clearly she does not expect his arrival on this day of her party, and as with Sally Seton's arrival later that night, also unexpected, even unsolicited, Woolf was not concerned with probability. Peter Walsh's presence and Bourton's were so heavy a burden on Clarissa's mind that when she returns from her flower shopping his arrival becomes as logical as if she had summoned him by means of a medium.

What he first notices, after years of absence, is her age, her having grown older. Clarissa finds him aged as well, but still "enchanting," wondering: "why did I make up my mind—not to marry him? she wondered, that awful summer?" (Both Clarissa and Peter will resort to the word "awful" to describe their memories of that long past time at Bourton.) After the start of their unexpected (yet expected) encounter, they parry, each thinking much the same about the other. " 'This is what I made of [life]. This!' " Clarissa offers: "And what had she made of it? What indeed? sitting there sewing. . . ." Tears fill her eyes; such elegiac emotions frighten Peter:

"Yes," said Peter. "Yes, yes, yes," he said, as if she drew up to
the surface something which positively hurt him as it rose.
Stop! Stop! he wanted to cry. For he was not old; his life was not
over; not by any means. He was only just past fifty.

And he was in love with a woman of twenty-five. Playing with his
horn-handle penknife seems all that is left at such moments, but even
that will not help on this occasion, for in confronting his love for a
young woman, Peter Walsh is pierced by its absurdity, reading her
derisive thoughts, "at his age, how silly!" Like a child, "he burst into
tears," and his shameless weeping unburdens torrents of feelings:
regret and failure, impotence and ridiculousness, anger and self-pity.
Such spontaneous weeping rouses Clarissa—for the only time in the
novel—to genuine feelings of touch: she takes his hand, she kisses
him, they are cheek to cheek. So here they are, these two aging lovers
who, for all their rational justifying as to why they did not remain
together, quite obviously feel, for the moment, that perhaps they
ought to have done so after all. Only half-ironically, Clarissa, behold-
ing suddenly herself as spectator to this melodrama, thinks, "If I had
married him, this gaiety would have been mine all day!" With
wounded masculinity, as his metaphor makes clear, Peter Walsh as-
sesses the scene in male sexual language: "Effort ceases. Time flaps
on the mast. There we stop; there we stand. Rigid, the skeleton of
habit alone upholds the human frame. Where there is nothing . . .
feeling hollowed out, utterly empty within. Clarissa refused me. . . ."
This flagging of masculine spirit, which has just experienced the
mothering comfort of Clarissa's femininity, past the time where it
evokes any physical pleasure but rather the memories of not having
had them, signifies as well a relationship between the two which has
not, despite the years, been entirely severed. We must not neglect
Septimus Smith (nor will we), but the fact that he was named a "double" to Clarissa by Woolf herself has tended to draw away the more
human seesaw relationship Clarissa has with Peter Walsh. Smith's
"double" function may be vicarious sacrifice, as has been often suggested, but Smith's life in the world is wooden, immobile, and insofar
as affecting Clarissa important only as the fact of death which invades
her moment of triumph: her party. It is from beginning to end not
Smith, whom she never knows nor meets, but Peter Walsh who touches her (as she him), and it is perhaps far more Peter Walsh's
aliveness than Septimus Smith's death which releases her from fearing no more, for he has with his presence rekindled, however pain-

fully, feelings long dormant, if not dead. He has made her feel things which Richard Dalloway, for instance, could not. His presence during that June evening has brought to life the regret of his long absence, and regretting, as Virginia Woolf well knew, is better than having nothing to regret. Peter Walsh has yet to realize this, for at this point the pain of the past too much intrudes upon the absurdity of *his* present, as he asks what in the world he is really doing pursuing a young married woman with children off there in India, seeing lawyers, he the man who almost married this silver-haired woman. He is immobilized and panicky:

> . . . She had been ill. . . . It was her heart . . . and the sudden loudness of the final stroke tolled for death that surprised in the midst of life. . . . No! No! he cried. She is not dead! I am not old, he cried . . . as if there rolled down to him, vigorous, unending, his future.

And so cheering himself up with repetition, "He was not old, or set, or dried," "He had not felt so young for years," he follows a young woman in the streets, fantasizing sexual conflict, fancying himself desirable, available. It was, after all, Clarissa's heart, not his, that had been ailing; broken, perhaps *his* heart had mended long ago, had it not? For such delusionary self-deception he will pay a price, the nightmare on the bench at Regent's Park, as, among infants and nursemaids, he sits down and falls asleep. The nightmare is of "that summer" at Bourton. The dream-vision of the "Solitary Traveller" is richly textured and arches over toward Clarissa more successfully than any of Septimus Smith's incoherent and apparitional visions. Peter Walsh is a sentimentalist, but only in dream does Woolf permit him lyric prose, "the visions which proffer great cornucopias full of fruit to the solitary traveller or, murmur in his ear like sirens lolloping away on the green sea waves, or are dashed in his face like bunches of roses. . . ." He sits beside what is described like one of the Fates, the "grey nurse" who moves "her hands . . . like one of those spectral presences which rise in twilight. . . ."

Peter Walsh sees himself truly now ("he is elderly, past fifty") not pursuing, in his dream, a young woman in the streets of London but a forest creature resembling more an abstraction of the eternally feminine luring him, beckoning him, drawing him to extinction. Like a figure in life about to be fixated into a realm beyond life (perhaps art), frozen and sucked up:

> So, he thinks, may I never go back to the lamplight; to the
> sitting-room; never finish my book; never knock out my
> pipe . . . rather let me walk straight on to this great figure, who
> will, with a toss of her head, mount me on her streamers and let
> me blow to nothingness with the rest.

In his dreams Peter Walsh is a Prufrock, "formulated, sprawling on a
pin," wondering if the lady to whom he dare not broach the "overwhelming question" will in the end, "settling a pillow on her head," say:
"That is not what I meant at all. That is not it, at all." Beyond the wood is
yet another vision, "an elderly woman who seems . . . to seek, over a
desert, a lost son": she comes to the door shading her eyes, raising her
hands, a white apron blowing in the wind. Is it Death? Is it Time? Is it
Clarissa's messenger of the past? He arrives at a village. Women stand
around and knit; men dig (graves?) in their gardens. It is evening; it is
"ominous." Again all seems "still"—"as if some august fate, known to
them . . . were about to sweep them into complete annihilation." At last
inside a house; a landlady; "an adorable emblem which only the recol-
lection of cold human contacts forbids us to embrace," and, taking up
the marmalade, shutting the cupboard, she pronounces, in effect, the
end: " 'There is nothing more to-night, sir?' " But he is a *solitary* traveler: "to whom does . . . [he] make reply?" if he is annihilated? With
suddenness he awakens next to the "elderly nurse" and the "sleeping
baby"—surely death and birth, youth and old age—and cries out,
" 'The death of the soul,' " saying out loud, " 'Lord, Lord!' " as he
recognizes he has been dreaming of Bourton, of "that summer," when
he was "so passionately in love with Clarissa." So Peter Walsh has his
visions of the past amidst the premonitions of the future—stretches of
waste "which ceaselessly float up, pace beside, put their faces in front
of, the actual thing; often overpowering the solitary traveller and taking away from him the sense of the earth, the wish to return," in short,
the vision of death itself. The "lost son," witness to the "death of the
soul," finds anguishing solace only in reiteration of the past and in the
reality of the present. He will, after all, be at Clarissa's party. The
"extreme suddenness" which accompanies his awakening saves him
from annihilation. What lingers is idyllic Bourton, sheep, flowers,
woods—and the intrusive prudery and coldness of Clarissa, the inflicted pain of rejection; quarrels, followed by "twenty minutes of perfect happiness" at the lake.

The final scene is recalled with so vivid an affect that the imagery
cunningly defines in every aspect the delineation of a tarnished bliss,
wasted passion: "The fountain was in the middle of a little shrubbery,

far from the house, with shrubs and trees all round it. There she
came, even before the time, and they stood with the fountain between
them, the spout (it was broken) dribbling water incessantly." She is like
"iron"; he weeps. " 'It's no use . . . this is the end"—melodrama, but it
remained true. Using the same word Clarissa had, Peter Walsh recalls:
"It was awful, he cried, awful, awful!" Recalling her recent tenderness
is balm for old wounds: "Here he was at the crossing"; and at the
crossing he hears the old woman's song ("love which has lasted a
million years, she sang") of a lover dead for centuries, of "death's
enormous sickle," all this near the "green and flowery" tube station
opposite Regent's Park. Singing of "some primeval May," rouses Peter
Walsh to make his offering of a "coin." Clarissa had flung *her* coin into
the Serpentine; Peter Walsh has moved to reward the ancient lay sung
by a mythy-minded woman who recalled love. The difference defines
them, for Peter is forever the romantic; behind all that grumpiness
and his irritating habits there was, indeed, "the lost son." Nor is Peter
Walsh unmindful of the need to seize the day, no less than Clarissa. At
times the attempt to make Peter the practical-minded contrast to the
sensitive Clarissa fails because it underestimates the depths of the
feelings that Woolf herself has bestowed on him, however infantile
and underdeveloped they have remained. Peter Walsh seizes the present precisely for the same reason as Clarissa does: to stave off the
painful past and the lurking future that lead to old age and death.
"Life itself, every moment of it, every drop of it, here, this instant,
now, in the sun, in Regent's Park, was enough. Too much indeed."
And quickly the self-reassurance: "It was impossible that he should
ever suffer again as Clarissa had made him suffer." Yes: "She had
influenced him more than any person he had ever known." With that
thought he surveys thirty years of friendship with "absences and inter-
ruptions." Always it seemed Clarissa had somehow surfaced for him:
whether on board ship or in the Himalayas, unsolicited, unwished, she
came anyway with her prim and critical self; or "ravishing, romantic,"
and mostly the memories were of Bourton, of the country: "One scene
after another at Bourton. . . ." Clarissa had sent him a letter—an impulsive and for Peter a disquieting gesture: But what had prompted
her pleasure? Clearly,

> She had felt a great deal; had for a moment, when she kissed
> his hand, regretted, envied him even, remembered possibly . . .
> how they would change the world if she married him perhaps;
> whereas, it was this; it was middle age; it was mediocrity; then
> forced herself with her indomitable vitality to put all that aside,

there being in her a thread of life which for toughness, endurance, power to overcome obstacles, and carry her triumphantly through he had never known the like of.

They had both in a way survived. Her toughness costs her; he imagines her in tears writing her letter. But he, too, is convinced their marriage would not have been successful. But Clarissa had "sapped something in him permanently," and she would not let go. Yes, he would, after all was said and done, accept her invitation; he would come to her "offering," her party, and offer himself! On his way to the party, to which he walks, he passes other kinds of parties—parties of "young people," parties he and Clarissa Dalloway would never have. He quite loses himself in this vibrant tumult. The awakening comes when he reaches the Dalloway house; for solace he can but revert to the blade of his pocketknife, literally to steel himself. For a long time, at Clarissa's party, he will stand and sulk in a corner.

So both Clarissa and Peter arrive at the party thoroughly impressed by their respective memories of a past which holds only possibilities, not realizations. "Life," Clarissa muses, "was that—humiliation, renunciation." Clarissa, however, is determined that her "offering" be a success, and it is manifest that these parties have taken the place of achieved triumphs not to be found elsewhere in her life. All these lonely and discrete persons—what a "waste" not to bring them together, to join and connect them, to assemble them: it was in some sense a vicarious act of connection for Clarissa, not quite a re-creation of Bourton, but in some respects like it, a momentary victory over isolation, out from under her narrow bed in the attic. Into this Arcadian world arrive the Bradshaws "shockingly come late," nearly says Mrs. Bradshaw, not come at all. The reason soon becomes clear, as Sir William informs Mr. Dalloway that a young man who had been in the war, a patient, has committed suicide: "Oh! thought Clarissa, in the middle of my party, here's death, she thought." Possessed of a horror of death, she is offended by this intrusion: "What business had the Bradshaws to talk of death at her party? A young man had killed himself. And they talked of it at her party—the Bradshaws, talked of death." This reaction recalls Poussin's first painting: shock, surprise, disquiet. Clarissa has not yet accepted the sudden appearance of death; more than appearance, more like a confrontation. Even Clarissa's imaging of this death is frightened and frightening: "He had thrown himself from a window. Up had flashed the ground; through him, blundering, bruising, with the rusty spikes. . . . And the Bradshaws talked of it at her party!" Clarissa's thoughts on death, and on *this* death, then take the shape of a progressive threefold development: (1) from existential understanding to (2) survivor guilt to (3) reconciliation.

First comes existential understanding that death was both "defiance" and a way of "communicating," people trying somehow to penetrate an elusive "centre . . . mystically," and recognizing that to these mysteries "there was an embrace in death." Second comes the responsibility in life, the guilt of survival. Initially there is, what Yeats called, the "crime of death and birth," in Clarissa's thoughts, "the terror, the overwhelming incapacity . . . this life to be lived to the end . . . an awful fear." And in some way Clarissa feels that Septimus Smith's death was "her disaster—her disgrace . . . her punishment. . . ." She had been guilty of scheming, of pilfering, of self-indulgence—in short, of surviving. Finally she reaches the plateau of reconciliation, for true, the young man had committed suicide, yet "she did not pity him," she will cease to fear the heat of the sun, for she *must* survive, she must go back to her party, her one-night Arcadia. After all, "She felt somehow very like him—the young man. . . . He made her feel the beauty . . . the fun. But she must go back. She must assemble." She must shore up the fragments of her ruins, for what else is there to do? In a sense Septimus Smith's suicide exorcises the life missed and validates the one that still remains to be lived. These last thoughts are prompted by observing the old woman across the street going to bed, putting out the light, accepting, in her old age, another night and the inevitability of another day. Indeed, "what an extraordinary night!" But this last passage is difficult. What beauty and fun did Septimus Smith's suicide make Clarissa Dalloway feel? What is the nature of this second and far more accommodating encounter with death, calling to mind Poussin's second painting?

Of course one must not take literally Clarissa's feeling "glad" at another person's death or thinking it illumined for her "fun." What she means is somewhat clarified by her saying it as the clock strikes, yet one last time in this clock-ridden book, and "the leaden circles dissolve," liberating her "from the little room" just as Sally Seton has clearly not reached such understanding, telling Peter Walsh, at that very moment, that perhaps life was a prison: "Are we not all prisoners? She had read a wonderful play about a man who scratched on the wall of his cell, and she had felt that was true of life—one scratched on the wall." Clarissa, for this one moment, is a released prisoner. Septimus Smith's death had freed her by now making survival a necessary (and respectable) concomitant of continued "offerings." She had not gotten out of life what she had wanted, clearly; she had much to regret; much had been irretrievably lost. More than a coin had, after all, been tossed into the Serpentine. But death now came as a visiting consolation, not his death alone but the fact of death, for it commanded in a certain way that one await its coming, like the old woman across the street, with a kind of silent dignity and elegant expectation.

There is much of Chekhov in Virginia Woolf, much certainly in *Mrs. Dalloway*. Woolf best expressed her appreciation of Chekhov in an essay she called "The Russian Point of View." Responsive to the notion that Russian literature is suffused with a "deep sadness," she admits that, initially, it is not "simplicity" but "bewilderment" that Chekhov creates. Especially the inconclusiveness of his endings arouses her curiosity and, ultimately, her admiration. When we reach the end of a Chekhov story, we are apt to say, "But is it the end?" There is the feeling of having "overrun our signals. . . . These stories are inconclusive, we say," working on the premise of a prejudiced preoccupation of what proper endings ought to be. In time we do appreciate that Chekhov always wrote with "intention, in order to complete his meaning." What becomes apparent is not the completion of the story but its meaning. Like herself, Chekhov seemed to Virginia Woolf to be "enormously" interested in the mind, "a most subtle and delicate analyst of human relations."

So once we become accustomed to such subtleties as those in Chekhov (and other Russian writers), the so-called "conclusions of fiction fade into thin air," the "tidying up"—marriages, deaths, and so on—seem to be somewhat superficial. "Nothing is solved, we feel; nothing is rightly held together. . . ." And what once seemed "casual, inconclusive, and occupied with trifles" now shows itself to be the result of "an exquisitely original and fastidious taste," expanding our "horizon" and impressing upon us the depths of consciousness.[8] That such an appreciation of the "Russian point of view," especially Chekhov's, anticipates both an apologia for her own work as much as a felt affinity with the Russians is clear. Woolf was to be criticized for her own inconclusiveness and narrowness, for trifling with life; her defense came in part by means of such essays as "The Russian Point of View," "Mr. Bennett and Mrs. Brown," and others, but most of all she offered her novels where she sought out those expanded boundaries by means of a certain inconclusiveness and a minor canvas, by creating depths of awareness and intensity of feeling rather than, say, the grand passions or the meticulous realism she saw, respectively, in Dostoevsky and Tolstoy.

The outcome of *Mrs. Dalloway*, then, is by no means as clear as it might seem. Whatever Woolf may have intended by shifting her original plan, Clarissa's death, and instead creating her "double," sufficient evidence remains to keep us from exaggerating Clarissa Dalloway's triumph over death, time, life, age, illness, and frailty. Clarissa survives, true; so do Peter Walsh, Richard Dalloway, and Sally Seton. The brush with death, at first so dulling, becomes an opportunity for Clarissa to understand her own need to continue her "offerings" (parties are only one such manifestation). In the next novel, *To the Lighthouse*, people die in bracketed sentences, and Mrs. Ramsay simply disappears, almost like the Fool in *Lear*. Unlike Clarissa, Mrs. Ramsay is given no opportunity to dialogue with the problems of death at all. Clarissa is still privileged to get that chance, for her survival is really necessary to the novel's motif, which is not death but the inexorable approach to it by way of a life that has been at the very least unsatisfactory. The case for Peter and Clarissa has been made: two middle-aged people groping with the painful memories of a past, neither recovered from mutually inflicted wounds, each brought to tears by their encounter, each still full to the brim with longings, regrets, doubts, guilt—the "Chekhovian" spirit. To relegate the larger metaphysical issues about time, life, death to a background rather than foreground is in no way to diminish the novel. Quite the contrary; though it may elicit controversy, the minimalization of metaphysical issues makes *Mrs. Dalloway* Virginia Woolf's most human novel, meaning by "human" precisely the "Russian" inconclusiveness she so admired in the novels of Turgenev, Dostoevsky, and Tolstoy, each of whom, when he ventured too far afield, strayed into distracting territory. Woolf had a weakness for trying to achieve parallelism and clinching unities which do not always succeed.

In *To the Lighthouse*, equal if not superior in achievement to *Mrs. Dalloway*, Lily Briscoe's painting is concluded just as the boat, ten years later, reaches the lighthouse, and the symmetry in that novel is far more organically achieved than in *Mrs. Dalloway*. Yet even there the climactic moment may lie more in Lily Briscoe's reveries, or in the touching reconciliation, however brief, between father and son, than in the self-conscious epiphany of the last page. Woolf may indeed have been in conflict within her own critical creed between her inclination to leave matters in the "Russian manner" or to attempt symmetrical closure. In *Mrs. Dalloway* this strain is documented in her Preface, where she outlines her changes of course. Septimus Smith, interesting as he is, convenient as his death may be, was probably an artistic mistake. It does not—one is glad—destroy the book, but it may hang upon it an abstraction which the rest of the novel somehow denies. Nothing better, and more honestly, describes some of the uncertainty of the novel's ending than Peter Walsh's exclamation in response to Sally Seton's "One must say simply what one felt": " 'But I don't know . . . what I feel.' "

No one in this novel has achieved what he or she has sought. Certainly neither Clarissa nor Peter, nor the hated Miss Kilman, nor Septimus Smith; not even Sally Seton, mother of five strong boys, with her poetry now spilling out as party gossip and trivialized conundrums about life with a capital *L*. Richard Dalloway, M.P., has not even made it to the Cabinet. His brief encounter with Clarissa in the novel, his inability to articulate feeling, pronounces only failure. Only Clarissa's daughter, Elizabeth, is not yet swallowed by a future. Other than that, *Mrs. Dalloway* is a novel about the past and what inevitably awaits us ahead. The present is merely a brief interval, then, which is precariously poised and gingerly traversed. It is an irony that a novel so much concerned with a wistful elegiac sigh about a lost past and a fearful and often terror-struck panic about the future should have earned its reputation as being concerned with the intensity of the present.

One must not misunderstand. The use of time in the novel is a genuine achievement. While the insistent tolling of Big Ben may be overdone, the fact remains that the characters are—and must be— most acutely aware of time, not at all as some sort of philosophical abstraction but as a measure of placing their lives in some sequence. Hence the happy idea of seizing a single day, which may appear to be derivative of *Ulysses,* has quite different aims from Joyce's. For Woolf the day provides a microcosmic springboard for excursions into the past. Bourton and that "awful summer" are, as illustrated, not simply memories: they occupy, to enrich the metaphor, a spatial expanse to support a temporal tolling of "real time." Clarissa Dalloway and Peter Walsh contemplate their lives, and both seek a way to survive into a future they realize is getting shorter for each. The resurrection of memory, the powerful presence of a past, only intensifies feelings of loss and dispossession. Yet paradoxically, the very intensity of those feelings makes for their salvation, their recognition that they will carry on, that even in the midst of temporary Arcadias the permanence of death does indeed announce itself, intrudes, and liberates. What makes that bearable is not escape or transcendence but the very aliveness of strong feelings, however painful, which, it is made clear, surface in both Clarissa and Peter as reminders that each had at least once had the capacity to be deeply moved. Peter Walsh's final thoughts define this sharply in the last line of the novel's final page: "What is this terror? what is this ecstasy?"

Part III

Survivors: The Missing Future

Introduction

. . . understanding is made possible primarily by the future . . .
—*Heidegger,* Being and Time

The individual has withdrawn into his inner being: externally one discerns nothing of him anymore.
—*Nietzsche,* On the Advantage and Disadvantage of History

Christopher Lasch has devoted a chapter to "The Survival Mentality" in *The Minimal Self,* and in it he recounts and analyzes what has become both an "in" idea and a neologism: "survival(ist)." As he points out, our current generation appears obsessed with crisis and, in turn, ways of "surviving" such crises. Since everything from birth to death is a minefield, we have been deluged by manuals and other instrumentalities that promise us, reassuringly, a series of coping strategies for survival. There is survival from the ridiculous to the sublime, from how to survive final examinations to how to survive a nuclear holocaust. It has, he observes correctly, resulted in a "trivialization of [the concept of] crisis."[1]

The idea of survival in this section is of a different kind and therefore needs to be separated from the popular notions current today. By "survivor" I mean to invoke some stoical sense of existential survival: Beckett's "I can't go on, I'll go on." Life is never simple; and crisis, Freud might say, is the rule, not the exception. (The phrase "crisis intervention" suggests some interesting notions we now hold about what constitutes "crisis.") If life is indeed a continuous crisis (obviously with changing levels of intensity), then a continuous use of palliatives will turn us into addicts. To "survive" in the sense used here is to incorporate the pain and incorporate its absence, which is not painlessness but a failure to recognize that what seeks to be incorporated is indeed the pain of existence. (That is Ivan Ilyich's final "insight.")

So Hemingway's Frederic Henry in *A Farewell to Arms* incorporates his pain while Flaubert's Frédéric Moreau fails to realize how painful his life has been. As we shall see, it was Hemingway's intention to make that point incontestably clear, and it was probably this, more than anything else, that made ending the novel so problematic for him. Of course, both protagonists are able to survive, but perhaps Hemingway's argument is simpler than it seems. To survive with pain (rather than denying it) is "existentially" speaking "authentic," while the other kind of survival is just that: going on with no sense of what has really been lost. Beckett's humanity knows pain all too well, and it survives by waiting it out until death (which in Beckett occurs rarely) intervenes in some unspecified future. Death in Beckett is rare because he wants us to focus on the process of survival, that being often nothing short of endless repetition and waiting. There may be gradual disintegration, but there is no specific "end" to pain; indeed even a cursory reading of Beckett shows us that the perpetuity of pain *is* the point. On one paradoxical situation survivors of all kinds are generally agreed: although they appear to be surviving for a future, a future is precisely what they do *not* have.

The phrase "existential survival" has a pretentious ring about it, and it needs to be properly anchored. Perhaps the best place to drop anchor is in Heidegger's conception of Being, although, of course, we cannot exhaust such a connection here, only allude to it. What Heidegger provides us with is *Dasein*, existence or Being, and within that complex conception the notion of survival can be measured and understood more clearly.

Heidegger's *Dasein*, which George Steiner translates literally as "being there," makes its appearance in *Being and Time* (*Sein und Zeit*), published in 1927. In "The Ideology of Modernism," Georg Lukács attacks Heidegger's specific notion that humans are merely the end product of a process Heidegger calls "*Geworfenheit ins Dasein*"—what appears to be a rather grim view that we are "thrown into" existence with no particular origins and no particular teleological purpose.[2] Hence our only way of surviving is to define ourselves "authentically." Lukács's distaste for Heidegger's Nazi sympathies feeds into his dismissal of such an antisocial and seemingly hopeless metaphysic. (In fact, Lukács and Heidegger, as Lucien Goldmann has shown, have in common some essential base.)[3] But beyond political animosity lies a valid critique of one aspect of modern literature: characters who have neither a past nor a future—in short, characters "thrown into" existence in the fictions they inhabit. They lack "perspective," that is, placement into socio-historical contexts. Such a lack promotes and encourages an "absence of meaning" and "reduces art to naturalistic description"; it presents a fictional world of "total impotence" (Kafka), and by depriving characters of any chance of development (and hence, hope, insight, and change), it effectively posits as irrevocable "the disintegration of the world of man." Such concerns clearly show Lukács's Socialist Utopian bias in favor of the hopeful and optimistic vision for a future (a relic of the 1930s, when that view was adopted by so many apolitical "Marxists" in the arts). Nevertheless, the division between the hermetic character without a seeming context, without past or future, and the rooted human being with an anterior source and a posterior meaning is useful. Lukács really identifies the *survivors* in modern literature, that is, those who make their separate peace with history and survive not only out of some narcissistic urge to indulge in the moment's pleasure, but with a gesture that informs a wholly *neutral* and frighteningly *dis*passionate view of life. To survive—in these instances—is merely to exist until time has run its course; to exist without much complaint, without regret, without hope.

However, Heidegger also introduced the concept of "authenticity" of Self and Being. "The attempt to achieve authenticity is expressed by 'resoluteness.' " And as Lukács surely knew, "This is the term which Sartre translates as *engagement,* and which has passed into Anglo-Saxon cultural and political speech as 'commitment.' "[4] What in fact happens in much of the literature Lukács attacks is this: pastness and futurity are compacted into a very brief presence/absence, often a single day. *Ulysses, Mrs. Dalloway,* "The Judgment," "The Dead," Pirandello's major plays—all are ostensibly time-bound by a single day, but of course that single day releases torrents of the past and, by implication, the future, too. *The Sound and the Fury* is divided into four days (three days in one year and one in another, eighteen years earlier) but delivers a family saga of full novel length. *The Metamorphosis* and *Death in Venice* are novellas, but their actual story-time is brief, as is that of each of Henry James's last three completed sizable novels. This is not to suggest that prior to the twentieth century, or close to it, there were no works of fiction (classical plays were another matter altogether) that did not confine themselves to brief time spans. For example, *Werther* (1774) covers less than two years, and *Le Rouge et le Noir* (1830) covers little more than that and is almost three times as long as Goethe's novella. Yet it is not difficult to generalize and support the statement that modern fiction tends either to be about an undetermined but briefly *felt* time span in contrast to the leisurely novels of the

eighteenth and nineteenth centuries wherein authors took special delight in developing a cumulative opus, often depicting two or three
generations—*Familienromane, Bildungsromane,* Romances. Therefore,
the shortening of the narrative time span in modern fiction is a complex issue; it is inserted here in a limited way only, with particular
relevance to the questions about past, present, and future that have
been and will be raised.

In the case of an almost unbearable present, the reason for a com-
pact narrative time span is to minimize memory and to eliminate the
future as any sort of realm in which we seek to be. Coleridge writes
that it is necessary "to make Life as continuous as possible, by linking
on the Present to the Past. . . ." Indeed, the "Present is a phantom
known only by it's pining, if it do not breathe the vital air of the
Future," and the future is the "Image of the Past projected on the mist
of the Unknown," glorified and beatified.[5] Yet the present must always be the fixed point of the compass, the attended, and attentive,
center; its often painful and nearly unbearably intense grief is self-
reflexive. Memory only intensifies the suffering, and projection into
futurity presents not "goals" or eventual surcease to suffering but an
empty and barren time where the only certainty is repetition, as Beckett demonstrates in *Waiting for Godot.* So to survive is literally to be—to
sustain oneself into an uncharted time dissociated from "history" and
eventually from any normative conception of self, at least in relation
to movement. While clearly on the move (as long as one is alive), the
survivor remains static: there is no development; there is only the next
moment, and the next, in some seemingly unceasing rhythm without
closure. There is accommodation to renunciation, not even the
illusion—if that is what it was—of the "light" vouchsafed to Ivan
Ilyich.

The long death scenes of nineteenth-century fiction are stimulated
by more than the obvious convention of realistically representing a
death overseen by an extended family in predictably ritualistic detail,
Dickens and Dostoevsky holding such scenes still, as it were, like a
tableau vivant. No doubt the reading public of serialized novels awaited
these scenes with high expectancy and must have found them cathartic
and even healing. Even Thomas Mann inserted them into his novels,
especially *Buddenbrooks* and *The Magic Mountain.* However, in mid- to
late nineteenth-century and early twentieth-century fiction, we can also
discern, often quite systematically, curtailed or omitted long death
scenes, and some writers devoted themselves more to the process of
dying itself. Often the actual death is an intended anticlimax: Georg
Bendemann's sudden leap into the river or Quentin Compson's, too;

Heathcliff's almost hidden death, which has no witness; Bazarov's rapid demise; Septimus Smith's jump from the window; the bracketed sentence in which Virginia Woolf dispatches several of her main characters in *To the Lighthouse*—these raise some interesting issues. Certainly we are no less fascinated with death than our predecessors, but it appears that modern writers are more intent on giving their characters the more difficult task: living over dying. The reader is deliberately spared death scenes, not out of consideration but quite the contrary: living deaths are never cathartic, and much of modern literature, by witholding finality, deliberately witholds relief. As I have noted, Chekhov's dying scientist in "A Dreary Story" is not given the three-day "passion" of Tolstoy's Ivan Ilyich, and it can therefore be argued that, as a consequence, it is the more painful, less redemptive of the two stories. In work after work—the apotheosis is perhaps Beckett's trilogy—we observe the unrelenting process of suffering without relief. Death is denied rather than achieved, for the solution of death is after all, in one sense, far too simple. Hesse's hero in *Steppenwolf*, eager for death, is condemned to live; so is Camus's hero in *The Fall*. One aspect of Modernism is surely that it brings us the complex to ponder without providing its solutions. Joyce is a prime example in that the "endings" to his two major novels, *Ulysses* and *Finnegans Wake*, are exemplary models. The latter work "ends" with the word that circles us back to the first word of the book, and the former concludes with an unpunctuated "yes," spoken by Molly Bloom in her end*less* soliloquy. Whether in fact that "yes" fails to accomplish "The End"—the phrase novelists used to delight in reaching as much as their readers—remains debatable, but if there is a sense of no ending, it is surely deliberate.

Frank Kermode, in *The Sense of an Ending*, believes that there are "paradigmatic expectations" in the reader which the modern and contemporary novelist delights in destroying. The suspended nonending of so much of modern fiction therefore projects the travail of living, not dying. We exist to survive such travail, wounded perhaps, deprived, even dismembered in body or mind or both (Beckett), even metamorphosed into alien forms. Kermode's speculation that the apocalyptic ending hangs over so much of modern thought and fiction would confirm one reason why the moderns felt no obligation to project a literal ending of plot or character. Since the Apocalypse is the universal "end," individualized endings would be no more than incidental observations. Further Kermode suggests that modern fictions have "moved away from the simplicity of the paradigm; they have become " 'open.' " So we are all deprived of what Kermode, paraphrasing Kenneth Burke, calls "cathartic discharges." All of this conspires to create "transi-

tion" (the name, incidentally, of the avant-garde journal in which Joyce
published parts of *Finnegans Wake*): "Since we move from transition to
transition, we may suppose that we exist in no intelligible relation to the
past, and no predictable relation to the future"—a statement remarkably close to those made by Lukács.[6]

Uncertainty of the future and devaluation of the past have many
roots, only one of which—an important one—we have come to associate
with the decadence of *fin de siècle,* especially in England and France.
While Nietzsche railed against the epigoni syndrome, the feeling of
exhaustion, of entropy, grew more and more powerful and created
self-induced prisons for countless characters in fiction and drama who
felt there was, quite literally, no exit. The "intellect," wrote Pater in his
essay "Winckelmann" (1867) "demands completeness, centrality." This
essay was written and published a year before the notorious "Conclusion" to *The Renaissance* (first published in book form in 1873). In that
"Conclusion" Pater (wittingly or unwittingly) lays the groundwork for a
compacted present. For Pater what Kermode called "transition to transition" was "moment to moment":

> . . . the whole scope of observation is dwarfed into the narrow
> chamber of the individual mind. Experience . . . is ringed
> round for each one of us by that thick wall of personality. . . .
> Every one of those impressions is the impression of the individ-
> ual *in his isolation,* each mind keeping as a solitary prisoner its
> own dream of a world. (Italics added)

This is one avenue toward compactness of time, in which moments
pass one after another, where a "single moment" is so difficult to hold
still but must be held in order to make its duration intense enough to
be felt to its limits. Pater defined art as moments which give us "the
highest quality" of themselves and "simply for those moments' sake."[7]
We used to call this "art for art's sake," but this phrase describes Pater
very superficially. What Pater anticipated is Heidegger's "thrownness
into Being," our individual existence within a flux, our *Dasein,* giving
us at best a small chance of surviving "moment to moment."

Habermas recognizes the continuing crisis of the present in somewhat changed terms: "these forward gropings, this anticipation of an
undefined future and the cult of the new, mean in fact the exaltation
of the present." In turn, what he calls the "new time-consciousness"
(Wyndham Lewis saw its problems in 1927 in *Time and Western Man*)
makes difficult demands: it "does more than express the experience
of mobility in society, acceleration in history, of discontinuity in every-

day life. . . . [It] discloses the longing for an undefiled, an immaculate and stable present."[8]

What precisely may be inferred from the "immaculate and stable present" may be problematic, but inevitably one conclusion we may infer is that it implies a discarded past and an absent future. Under the guise of a potentially optimistic vision of an existentially "authentic" present, there lurks the dread of terminal Being. Beckett's limbless moribundi are metaphors for a shrinking consciousness. Gone is memory (the past), gone is expectation (the future), but ever here is the dying being (the present). In this respect Lukács's fears about one aspect of Modernism are difficult to ignore, nor is he alone in having expressed them.

The so-called autonomous self is no doubt largely the consequence of a loss of "belief in a collective destiny," as Irving Howe wrote in *The Idea of the Modern*. What autonomy of self exacts as a price for its autonomy has been variously and copiously explored in analyses of Modernism, and some of these problems were raised in the Introduction.

7 Negation of the Future: Survivors in Flaubert and Hemingway

> *How can we be concerned with the past*
> *And not with the future? or with the future*
> *And not with the past?*
> —*T. S. Eliot,* The Family Reunion

> *Disillusion can become itself an illusion*
> *If we rest in it.*
> —*T. S. Eliot,* The Cocktail Party

Arcadia received its life by refusing to be caught in the whirlwind of time. Spatially removed, its claim to isolation from mutability made it especially, and self-consciously, ahistorical. However, the historizing habit in the nineteenth century often became an intense attempt to locate, to give everything habitation and a name—a fact neither new nor unexplored. Yet it is the clash between vague Arcadian longings and the historicizing self-consciousness which produces in the nineteenth century and in the early decades of the twentieth a new phenomenon which Balzac, who might be its first exponent, called *Les Illusions Perdues* (*Lost Illusions*), an impressively long novel published in 1843. Again the theme of the young hero who is quickly disillusioned and corrupted, usually by moving from the country to the temptations of the city, is so pervasive that few novels over a period spanning almost a century do not fall into that general category. So we must refine still further and seek and separate out those fictions in particular that chronicle not only disillusion but the survival of disillusion; that feature heroes (they are mostly male) whose lives are

wasted twice: once in pursuit of the ideals they cannot attain (illusion) and once again in the state of survival (delusion). That the fate
of these survivors is sheer survival need only be suggested; we need
have no chronicle of their survival past the last page of the novel, for
what concerns us here is their negation of the future, not their
future itself. Death has been, as we have seen, a liberating force,
either to the character to whom it occurs or because the character, in
observing it, is chastened. Chekhov's characters are in some sense
survivors; so are some of Ibsen's. But we deal in this chapter with a
very special form of survival, a survival that contains a certain inner
death and impotence, and one that is constrained rather than stirred
by resentment. The survivors we speak of are no longer deceived by
life, and in full possession of their *dis*illusion they acknowledge the
failure of experience, the incapacity to harvest wisdom, the capri-
ciousness of life, and despite all that the necessity, somehow, to survive into a negated future with only the memories of a bitter past to
sustain them. Such a framework constitutes a central episode in the
history of modernism.

As suggested in the Introduction to Part III, Lukács sees literary
modernism as divided between the "dynamic and developmental" and
the "static and sensational," Mann versus Joyce, or as he put it in one
of his chapter headings, "Kafka or Thomas Mann?" The "developmental" obviously allows the dialectic to produce infinite movement,
and rather than precluding the future, it virtually ordains it. Lukács's
human individual is the "*zoon politikon*, a social animal," and the "Sein
an sich," or " 'ontological being' " is not divisible from environment.
This is both Hegelian and Marxist, but the implications go beyond
strictly ideological boundaries. In modernism Lukács sees the Hegelian *Entfremdung* (alienation) at its limits, and glorified. He even
distinguishes between what he calls the "basic solitariness of man" and
"individual solitariness" (yet another form of narcissism), that which is
subjective, "the product of inner necessity, as with Tolstoy's Ivan
Ilyitsch or Flaubert's Frédéric Moreau in the *Education Sentimentale*."
In the latter instances the solitariness, Lukács argues, the general
dynamic of society, "goes on as before": that is, the individual isolation
is not institutionalized, and we see such characters as merely being
"certain human types" who impress on themselves their own exile.
Since I will shortly speak specifically of *L'Education Sentimentale*, we
should keep this in mind; though Lukács's distinction may not entirely
work, it is helpful nevertheless in a comparison of Flaubert's book
with Hemingway's *A Farewell to Arms* and in assessing the mutations
the "solitary" has undergone between 1869 and 1929.

In invoking Heidegger's *Geworfenheit ins Dasein* (throwness-into-being) Lukács does so—as I have indicated—*dis*approvingly, accusing such a postulate as cancelling "*potentiality*" (development, future). Characters so thrown into being exist as total isolatos, void of contact with the world, not shaped by nor shaping it either. By surrendering to total subjectivity writers like Joyce negate "outward reality" (Joyce was a poor example), and Beckett (a far better case) creates only "dissolution of personality," and thus we have embraced the "eternal incognito" with the attendant sojourn in states of neurosis, illness being, of course, an ineffectual and static protest against society. Such attitudinal postures Lukács considers escapist; they glorify perversity and end in nihilism—and, by implication, in solipcism as well. With his Marxist perspective Lukács sees the historical process in Hegelian terms: the dialectic ensures that "the future is the present." It is the present which is pivotal, then, and its links to past and future ensure change, amelioration, optimism.[1]

Lukács's perspective, however, is constrained by his doctrinal agenda and useful only in a limited way: it offers an accurate diagnosis. Judgment is another matter altogether, and here he succumbs to a naive and reductive paradigm that all too simply divides the "good" moderns from the "bad," those connected to roots for the sake of an optimistic vision of the future versus those who separate out of both past and future, thus rejecting social(istic) hope. Nevertheless, his observations focus on linkages that aid us in seeing how Flaubert and Hemingway lead clearly to Beckett. Quite aside from the evidence that Hemingway was consciously absorbed in Flaubert's *L'Education Sentimentale* when he was writing *A Farewell to Arms*, the line of development is self-evident. Flaubert's Frédéric Moreau is almost a new type in fiction: the Static Self. This is not to suggest that Frédéric "learns" nothing, nor that he stays precisely the same throughout the novel. In any literal sense that would be absurd. But *what* he learns is debatable and *how* he changes is as well. Such a word as "growth" is too rich for Frédéric Moreau (as also for Frederic Henry); for "growth" implies genuine development and a broadening of mind and spirit to new insight about Self and Other. Both characters, different as they are in significant ways, share a kind of emotional atrophy, and that certainly portends Beckett's dramatis personae: there is a lack of connectedness between any present self and a former self. We know precious little about Frédéric Moreau's "past" (except that, on the whole, it was rather unpleasant); about Frederic Henry we know virtually nothing. He is a character waiting, as it were, for Beckett to come along.

Although Hemingway was foremost among the modern exponents

of a certain form of negativism, he learned much it seems from his "true Penelope," Flaubert, and it was Flaubert, indeed, who, in *L'Education Sentimentale,* perhaps wrote the prototype for the kind of anti-*Bildungsroman* I have been describing, the static novel in which development is neither toward "wisdom" nor resolution. (The apotheosis of this "genre" was, of course, Flaubert's unfinished *Bouvard et Pécuchet,* a novel of wasted lives written with a cosmic grin.) Therefore, to discuss *A Farewell to Arms* and *L'Education Sentimentale* together creates a kind of bridge between the nineteenth- and the twentieth-century versions of a certain form of paralysis, yielding a clearly discernible line of development that reveals significant changes and adaptations. Hemingway by no means merely wrote a modern *L'Education;* he transformed that novel to suit his own needs, and he brought its meaning to ultimate ends, to the threshold of contemporary nihilism: Beckett and after.[2]

Hemingway was fond of applying baseball analogies to French writers; of Flaubert he said that he "always threw them perfectly straight, hard, high and inside." Flaubert does not appear to occupy a special place in the several "lists" Hemingway drew up from time to time, although when asked whom he considered to be his "literary forbears—those you have learned most from," he named Flaubert second among thirty writers, painters, and composers. In *Green Hills of Africa* he speaks admiringly of Flaubert's "discipline," and he remarks of Flaubert's bust in the Luxembourg Gardens as one "*that we believed in, loved without criticism, heavy now in stone as an idol should be.*" In 1948, when he filled out a roster of "heroes" for Lillian Ross (which included an RAF officer and Napoleon's "rear guard commander in the retreat from Moscow"), the names of Flaubert and Thurber "rounded out" the list. *L'Education Sentimentale* is mentioned by its French title in an *Esquire* essay; and Hemingway borrowed the novel in English from Sylvia Beach's Shakespeare and Company on October 12, 1925, and returned it on October 27, the same year. About two and a half years later he began writing *A Farewell to Arms.*[3]

I
Frédéric Moreau and Frederic Henry:
Possessed by Self and Dispossessed of Other

On a single sheet of paper, now in the Kennedy Library, Hemingway wrote down a large number of possible titles for *A Farewell to Arms.*

Some appear in groupings, and one such grouping, in Hemingway's hand, is the following:

> Education of the Flesh
> The Carnal Education
> The Sentimental Education of Frederick Henry
> The Sentimental Education

Hemingway claimed that he chose his titles after he had completed a book. Since this sheet bears no date, the procedure cannot be verified in the case of *A Farewell to Arms*. Clearly, however, Flaubert's novel was on his mind, enough to propose three possible titles that link his novel with Flaubert's (the fourth entry *is* the English title of Flaubert's novel, perhaps merely a reminder to himself).

In addition to this list of titles, there are other particulars that connect the two novels, one of which is the Christian name of the respective heroes: Frédéric Moreau and Frederic Henry.[4] One should not be put off by Hemingway's exchange with George Plimpton about the naming of characters:

> INTERVIEWER: "How do you name your characters?"
> HEMINGWAY: "The best I can."

The eventual naming of Hemingway's hero was not arbitrary. An undated item in the Kennedy Library (240), consisting of two chapters, is an early version of *A Farewell to Arms*. Written in the third person, these chapters deal with the wounded lieutenant's arrival in the hospital in Milan. The wording is in many places verbatim with Chapter XIII of the present novel, but there are two striking differences: first, the lieutenant is not in love with any nurse but fantasizes that perhaps he will have one to fall in love with; second, the name of the wounded soldier is *E*mmett *H*ancook, a thin disguise for *E*rnest *H*emingway. The hero's name had obviously not yet been chosen.

Both *L'Education Sentimentale* and *A Farewell to Arms* feature heroes who survive. Whether their experiences teach them anything about life, whether they are the wiser for having experienced, remains a lively point for debate. Frederic Henry is a much younger man at the end of his experiences than Frédéric Moreau, whom Flaubert brings—with some dispatch at the end—into middle age. Frédéric Moreau has been called a Nobody, an antihero, a failure, an egotist, a narcissist, all of which designations have been applied to Frederic Henry and his progeny. As Harry Levin reminds us, "None of the sad young men of contemporary fiction, the anti-heroes of our time, is exempted from paying his respects to his predecessors. . . ."[5]

The two young men have in common a number of experiences. Both encounter the bordello before they feel love. In Frédéric's case the experience is an abortive adolescent event, followed some years later by his infatuation, his idealized passion, for Madame Arnoux (also unconsummated). For Frederic Henry the experience is most real, a bordello-in-wartime furlough, followed in turn by his gradual, and consummated, love for Nurse Catherine Barkley. In the first as well as the second *L'Education Sentimentale* Flaubert analyzes the claustrophobic atmosphere developed by two people in love who ultimately exhaust themselves on each other, sexually and spiritually. (The "first" *L'Education Sentimentale,* completed in 1845, was published posthumously. Except for the theme of claustrophobic love, it bears little resemblance to the mature work. The hero's name is Henry.) Hemingway treats a similar situation in *A Farewell to Arms,* although he manages it more obliquely, leaving the reader to work out much of it himself—according to his own theory of writing—especially, as we shall see, with respect to the ending.

Each book has for its backdrop a situation of turmoil which acts upon the heroes and to which they react. For a brief time they participate in the Revolution of 1848 and World War I. Although Hemingway's Frederic is much more caught up in the war than Frédéric is in the Revolution, both face the dilemma of uncommitted commitment and extrication from it. Each eventually makes a "separate peace" with events; both escape with a woman to spend some idyllic time out of reach of cosmic upheaval—Frédéric and Rosanette at Fontainebleau; Frederic and Catherine in Switzerland. Both beget children who die (in Frederic's case the child's death causes the death of the mother as well). From a certain point of view each hero fails to achieve his goals, initially goals of involvement and later goals of detachment. At one point during their idyllic sojourn with their women, both men read newspaper accounts of the friends and events they have abandoned and feel guilt and emptiness. In the final pages of each novel both heroes seem to acknowledge a sense of waste, of their own lives—even of life itself.

Of all Hemingway's novels, *A Farewell to Arms* has remained a puzzle for critics, and Frederic Henry a troublesome hero. The same may certainly be said of *L'Education Sentimentale* and Frédéric Moreau. For how we read the endings may well determine the meanings we attach, in each instance, to the novels as a whole. Hemingway's struggles with the endings are now available in his own hand, and we need no longer trust only his word when he told Plimpton that he rewrote the last page of *A Farewell to Arms* thirty-nine times. Flaubert's problems surfaced mostly after publication, and his various defenses are mobilized in the correspondence.

How we view Frédéric and Frederic is crucial, and there is no consensus of opinion on either character except that, generally, descriptions of both have been negative. Both emerge from an unsatisfactory family and home life; indeed Hemingway's hero seems so detached we scarcely get more than allusions to his past. Neither man is physically described, Hemingway's writing in the first person making such description difficult. Both books were victims of critical outrage, not primarily for violation of language (there was some of that) so much as for their pessimism, their failure to uplift the reader's spiritual barometer. Perhaps most important, both men are survivors of an education (assuming one allows there is an "education") in some sense "sentimental" and, therefore, at best temporary. Their survival is at best attenuated. What precisely Flaubert meant by *"sentimentale"* is still debated, and Hemingway avoided in his final choice of title any suggestion of emulating Flaubert. Still, Flaubert suggests that in part at least *"sentimentale"* means the process of continual hope successively interrupted and undercut by events seemingly beyond control.

It is obvious that Hemingway's Frederic begins with a certain grim cynicism and develops, as the story moves ahead, a measure of caring through his love; Frédéric, on the other hand, experiences precisely the reverse: he begins as a young man imbued with the romantic ideals and hopes of innocence, and he ends by becoming cynical, harsh, for some readers even cruel. Experience strips him of illusions. The essential difference is that Hemingway's Frederic (unlike Flaubert's Frédéric) experiences a circular sequence of feelings: cynicism, illusion, confirmation of illusion—or disillusion. When we first meet Frederic Henry, he is unsure, a pleasure seeker without any special moral awareness. As he falls in love with Catherine, "truly" as Hemingway might say, he experiences the paradox of a deep personal commitment to her, accompanied, eventually, by a disengagement from the rest of the world. After her death he seems drained and returns to some form of cynicism, although whether that word is appropriate depends on how we read the ending.

The *L'Education Sentimentale* of 1869 is a difficult work, not because very little happens (though that makes for some problems), but because Flaubert's vivisection of a pointless life is both painful and absurd. If "absurd" conjures up the more recent literary connotations, this is not damaging to the argument: writers like Ionesco or Pinter are legitimate heirs to Flaubert. The often-referred-to wish which Flaubert expressed, to write a novel about "nothing," suggests some of the difficulties one faces in reading *L'Education Sentimentale*. Flaubert wanted to write a work in which form superseded any specific subject matter, thereby creating a "nothing"; however, such a "nothing" would not take the place of content or meaning. There was no solipsism in Flaubert's intention: "What I should like to write, is a book about nothing . . . dependent on nothing external, which would be held together by the internal strength of its style . . . [a book] in which the subject would be almost invisible. . . ."[6] (Compare what Hemingway told Plimpton: "I always try to write on the principle of the iceberg. There is seven-eights of it under water for every part that shows.") Within this temporal and psychic stasis, however, Flaubert never permits the reader to forget time, or, to put it more specifically, the aging of the characters, although readers have commented that such aging is scarcely ever noted, and when it is there is surprise, even shock. All movement in Flaubert's novel is in the end stationary: this is part of its "nothing."

It is equally true that movement in *A Farewell to Arms* is virtually always embodied in the namimg of seasons rather than the occasion of specific actions. In *Hemingway's First War*, Michael Reynolds has plotted narrative time. The first seven pages cover almost two years: summer 1915 to spring 1917 (p. 263); the remainder of the novel traverses approximately a year. But even that year passes seasonally, and only the logical sequence of Catherine's pregnancy reminds us of "real" time. It has been suggested that *A Farewell to Arms* is "dominated by linear imagery," and that this dominance of "linear-geometric imagery . . . seems related to Frederic's attempt . . . to slow down and order the passage of time and flux of circumstances, to 'control' Time and instability with *thought*. . . ." Such a method appears to "impose design on memory," and, by accepting the linkage of "Time and sorrow," to cast the book into a "temporal realm of geometric form."[7] Hemingway's interest in Cézanne and the Cubists is not coincidental: he often attempted to achieve similar effects in his prose, abstract and linear, and the justly famous opening paragraphs of *A Farewell to Arms* are, as Hemingway acknowledged about his work in general, Cézanne's landscape translated into prose. "Cézanne is my painter," he told Lillian Ross, "I learned how to make a landscape from Mr. Paul Cézanne."

Flaubert's stasis is achieved by cumulative details which fail to accumulate. For instance there has been some argument whether Frédéric Moreau, who does indeed age, grows old physically without any redemptive feature to his "sentimental" education; whether it is possible to age without in some sense growing up, not merely old. Yet only in the penultimate scene, when Frédéric has a long-delayed encounter with Madame Arnoux, the ideal he has so long pursued, is there a possibility of some ambiguity. Is Frédéric's behavior cruel or gallant? Is he preserving an ideal after all, as Victor Brombert suggests, or is he finally aware of that ideal's mortality when Madame Arnoux loosens her hair and it falls gray over her shoulders?[8] However that question is resolved, Flaubert was not satisfied with ending his novel at this quite logical juncture; he added what has come to be known as the "Epilogue." Here Frédéric and his friend of his youth, both now middle-aged, review their past. Both reminisce and extol their adolescent visit to the brothel, which had ended in failure, and critics have pointed (whether favorably or unfavorably) to the banality of such an ending. For Frédéric this was the happiest of times and his friend, Deslauriers, agrees that may well have been the best time of their lives they can recall. Earlier in the conversation they have acknowledged their failure: What is the reason for the failure of their pursuits? Frédéric's pursuit of love, his friend's for power? Perhaps, Frédéric suggests, he had not walked a straight-enough line ('le défaut de ligne droite"), and the friend agrees, adding that in his case it may well have been the opposite, too much rigidity ("excès de rectitude") too much "logique," just as Frédéric had too much "sentiment."

The conjunction of "logique" and "sentiment" constitutes a form of dialectic for the novel, the combination offering a clue as to what Flaubert meant by "sentiment" and "sentimentale." Deslauriers is a foil to Frédéric: from the beginning he is portrayed as a cynical hustler, whose forays into the world are marked by calculation and indifference to loyalty. That he fails in the end is testimony not to his timidity but to his inefficiency, to the inefficacy of calculation, to the superiority of others. The excess of "logique" he offers as a reason for his failure we associate more with success; but this is a "logique" similar to the sort which sent Julien Sorel to the guillotine. When Flaubert said he was writing "l'histoire morale des hommes de ma génération," was he not saying what Lermontov said when he promised us the "hero of our time" or what Camus meant when he said that Meursault in *L'Etranger* was the only Christ we deserved? In defense of *L'Education Sentimentale* advocates insist that Flaubert's mission was, indeed, to write a critical history of a generation that failed, but he seems surely to have been less interested in the historical phenomenon and more in the human. The final irony, after all, is Frédéric's very earnest commitment to *live* and the little he has to show for such an effort at the end.

Hence the circularity of the final paragraphs suggests the meaninglessness of Frédéric's "education," proof that "at the end of the novel [Frédéric] is not more 'educated' than he was at the beginning." His "life has not been an education at all." Worse still, Flaubert considered "sighing over one's lost illusions . . . also a bourgeois trait":[9] Frédéric fails twice. This awareness that bemoaning one's fate amounts not merely to an admission of failure but to an expression of vulnerable sentimentality provided Hemingway with a host of problems with his Frederic and the ending of *A Farewell to Arms*. He was determined, it seems, to have an ending, and a hero who reflects it, which does not betray any sentimentality or self-pity. Frederic Henry would neither sigh over his fate nor acknowledge personal failure: life was the villain—or so it seems. A closer look suggests a vaguely guilt-ridden sense of melancholy. The "mourning," if it can be called that, comes at the end.

The initial impressions of Frederic Henry are not those of a very prepossessing young man. He goes on furlough to brothels rather than to the cold Abruzzi, to which the priest had invited him; he begins his affair by taking advantage of a psychically wounded and vulnerable woman; he "gets her in trouble" despite repeated warnings from Nurse Ferguson that he take care not to; he shoots a soldier for deserting yet deserts himself; he runs, if not out of fear, worse still, out of prudence; he is flippant and superior toward the more conventional attitudes which regard brandy drinking and fornication in a hospital bed bad form and bad treatment for the patient; and when he loses Catherine he seems unable to grieve, not because he lacked love but because when life is gone he sees no way of relating to a dead body, and memories simply do not work.

These represent a mere fraction of the charges that have been leveled against Frederic Henry,[10] yet critics have countered each weakness with a strength, each fault with a virtue. A fictional character who elicits such contradictory responses is either the product of an incompetent writer or of one who recognized such contradictions and deliberately left us to ponder them. Hemingway belongs to the latter; and Frederic Henry resembles Turgenev's Bazarov, to whom readers have had equally contradictory reactions (and whom Hemingway knew all about): a man neither lovable nor villainous. There is one significant difference, and Hemingway must have realized it: Bazarov dies; Frederic Henry survives. Some readers cannot forgive that, for survival generates not merely a shared guilt, but a realization that survival is necessarily an affirmation of narcissism accompanied by a corresponding loss of responsive feelings for others. Experience neither educates nor consoles; it wounds and hardens.

Frederic Henry fails to harness his experiences; he is a passive bystander registering its effects as if he were truly split in two, one half observing the other. For all his bravado against those he dislikes, one would be hard-pressed to find him reacting with active passion, whether to love or war, to pain or death. He is almost frighteningly the observer, the somnambulist who stalks the story in contrast to the excitable Rinaldi, the sometimes hysterical Catherine, the upset-to-tears Nurse Ferguson, the animated priest, the cursing and joking soldiers under his command. Even the doctor who delivers Catherine's dead child is more able to articulate grief than the father who lost it. This does not mean Frederic is a man without feelings, only one whose ability to express them—whether happy or sad—is inhibited, not by a stiff upper lip, not by some "code" of Hemingwayesque bravery (it is Catherine who is appropriately called "brave"), but by a paralysis that emanates deep from within the self. Frederic Henry suffers from what any good family doctor could diagnose as severe depression, or on a more general level, a classic case of melancholia.

Frederic's depression, his sadness, is a given state from the first pages of the novel. The war, the retreat, the desertion, the flight to Switzerland, Catherine's death—none of these seems to develop Frederic's inherent melancholy: together they merely confirm it. All pleasures appear to him temporary; and his love for Catherine (though quite genuine) does not compensate for his overall affective impotence, his implicit narcissism, which, at the end of the novel, turns into "rage" and *ressentiment*.

Hemingway did not wish his readers to establish reasons and causes for Frederic's state, but rather to observe how such a mind, passive and yet receptive, functions under the strain of experiences that would break most human beings. For Frederic his melancholia is his defense: it sustains him and permits him to survive, not merely physically, of course, but in that state of disconnectedness—with people, time, and things. His famous attack against abstract words and expressions ("glory, honor, courage," "in vain") and his honest admission that only numbers, dates, and names of certain villages now conveyed meaning are symptomatic of his despair. He has been disconnected from language; correlation is with concrete things, but limited. Appropriate as his disgust with hollow words may be, his inability to reconstruct what has been deconstructed becomes immobilizing. Even the connection to things has become fragile. Frederic's losses, his dispossessions, only confirm what he seems predisposed to expect, or even what he sometimes appears to predict as inevitable. Hence deprivation is a return to a normal state; temporary happiness is expected to be temporary.

What, then, about the accusation that such states of feeling are salvageable only by total self-indulgence? Hemingway's style, we are told, often deceives us: characters are not what they seem; there is understatement; toughness is a veneer for sentiment (even sentimentality). Although there is some truth in all this, in *A Farewell to Arms* Hemingway succeeded in creating a tension between impulse and articulation, between implied sentimentality and successful suppression of it. The result is a bitter harvest of feelings, the forlorn and the sad, which create in Frederic Henry a sense of distance from the reader, not quite enough to put him entirely out of reach of our sympathy, but sufficient to prevent us from really sharing his hardships.

More important, however, in illustrating Hemingway's problem—the suppression of the inclination toward sentiment—is the ending, or the endings. The ending we have has been praised and blamed for the same reason: it is either praised as a marvelous piece of understated prose; or it is condemned as the ultimately bleak *nada* that aptly concludes a book, hollow, empty, unfeeling. After Catherine has died Frederic forces himself into the hospital room despite the protests of the nurses. He closes the door and turns out the light, but "it wasn't any good. It was like saying good-bye to a statue. After a while I went out and left the hospital and walked back to the hotel in the rain."

Hemingway was not far off the mark when he told Plimpton that he rewrote the ending of *A Farewell to Arms* thirty-nine times. The manuscripts of the alternative endings comprise a packet of some thirty-eight pages, but some of the alterations between one ending and another are so slight that an accurate count is difficult. Here is one version:[11]

> Finally I slept; I suppose because I was so tired. When I woke the sun was coming in the open window and I smelled the spring morning after the rain and saw the sun on the trees in the courtyard and that moment everything was the way it had been, then I saw the electric light still on in the daylight by the head of the bed and I knew that I was alone from then on x that was all gone now and it would not be that way any more.

Such an ending seems unfeeling, insensitive, perhaps even callous. How could a man sleep after such loss (we acknowledge he must, but do we want to read about it)? And, once awake, how could he be so gratefully conscious of all the life-giving smells and sights: the sight of the sun in the trees, the smell of an after-rain spring morning? Only the electric light from the night before, still burning as vigil, shocks him into the realization of the present state of loss, the inescapable feeling of aloneness. By the time we read to the end of the paragraph we may have accused Frederic Henry of too much to leave room for forgiveness. Not a mere economy of words and feelings was involved in getting the ending right, then, but a placement of Frederic Henry on the edge of our judgment. In the ending that Hemingway finally let stand, all that is suggested in the other alternatives is conceivable. Frederic Henry is not one to commit suicide; and the structure of the narrative reassures us that the story is told from the perspective of survival: it is a story that has already happened. So we know that he has slept, smelled, seen the sun, though we also feel his loss and his isolation. How he copes with this is, Hemingway decided, inappropriate to describe. As a survivor Frederic Henry *has* coped, and he has taken little else from his experience save the certainty of mortality, hardly a matter that needs amplification.

That problem of coping with life after loss lies very close to the surface of *A Farewell to Arms,* as it also does—though in different terms—at the end of *L'Education Sentimentale.* That is: the ability to cope acceptingly with life, whether through religious faith or simply faith in life, may indeed be a matter of wisdom, and if it is, Frederic Henry is wanting. But what if such matters are not wisdom but luck? What if faith is a matter of the genes, of "being born that way"? (from unpublished MS page numbered #324). What if one is, alas, not "built" for faith, just as one may not be built tall or broad-shouldered? It is a pressing question, although Hemingway was wise to have omitted the explicit exposition of the problem, for he everywhere implies it. Something in Frederic Henry precludes him from transforming experience into wisdom—perhaps because he was not "lucky" enough to be born that way. In any case, experience and aging do not necessarily bring wisdom as reward. That, Hemingway suggests, is the real *Lebenslüge* of the nineteenth century, that people, like civilizations, progress toward wisdom, that aging rewards us with self-knowledge, insight. In rejecting this notion—even in questioning it—Hemingway has broken the spell of the *Bildungsroman* tradition as few had done before, with the exception, of course, of Flaubert.

All the discarded titles in the Flaubert grouping contain the word "education," and Hemingway seems to have found it impossible to convey how (if at all) Frederic Henry underwent an "education." To imitate Flaubert would have been false, since it should by now be clear that Hemingway set out to write quite a different novel. True, Frédéric Moreau is also one of life's survivors, but he is never subjected to the personal pain and loss inflicted on his later namesake. The "sentimental" in Hemingway's book has little to do with romantic illusions, but a great deal to do with how to protect oneself from them. "No," protests Rinaldi, "we never get anything. We are born with all we have and we never learn. We never get anything new. We all start complete." Though at this point he speaks as the "snake of reason," a phrase he applies to himself, there is evidence that by the end of the novel he has converted Frederic to his view. Beyond Flaubert, then, Hemingway took the next step: the creation of a protagonist who is aware of the dangers of a sentimental education, but who cannot resist instincts of the flesh or spirit and who becomes for a time an unwilling participant in a process he had every intention of avoiding. The clash between the desire to avoid entanglements and the inevitable failure to do so—that and the ultimate survival of these entanglements—form the elements of such "education" as there may be in *A Farewell to Arms*. What you learn is mostly (perhaps wholly) what you already know: death is the only certainty. Some die sooner; others are destined to survive and try not to remember.

In the "Paris Letters" Pound wrote in 1922 for *The Dial* he made an effort, in Poundese, to defend Flaubert, whom he called in *Hugh Selwyn Mauberley* his "true Penelope." In particular, Pound appreciated *L'Education Sentimentale*, asserting that Flaubert did not leave merely "two masterpieces—*Bovary* and the *Trois Contes*" but also "two masterworks . . . *L'Education* and the *Bouvard et Pécuchet*." (He does not explain the distinction—if there is one—between "masterpiece" and "masterwork".) Although *L'Education Sentimentale* was "burdened with data," he justified this, for the book was not merely a "sonnet of the chief character," but of a "period"—the life of an epoch. Furthermore, the crowded canvas was carefully designed. Flaubert, contends Pound, was perhaps the first novelist to conceive of a paragraph of prose in the terms of "economy" and "perfection" we had always associated with lyric poets.

Most important for Pound was Flaubert's expert treatment of the "inevitable and quotidian," which exceeded even Dostoevsky's. In creating a kind of "everyman," Flaubert had successfully deployed a sense of the inevitable: "nothing that any character will *do* will alter his case; the whole thing is there and *stays* as long as human limitations are human limitations." In Flaubert's world "there is no answer . . . there is *no* easy way out. . . . the impasse is a biological impasse." (One recalls Catherine's remark that "You always feel trapped biologically.") That is the "biological impasse" Flaubert and Hemingway both recognized. The sense of nonmovement to which many of Flaubert's readers, including Proust, gave their attention is also something Pound noted. "Human capacity, perseverance, endurance," he observed, all produce merely a "continuing static" and the condition of a given situation "will continue to be an impasse." *Impasse*, then, is perhaps the best word to describe the world of *A Farewell to Arms*, for the impasse of human relationships is the microcosm for the impasse of the war which seems to go on without end, a war fought on mountains where advance and retreat create a choreography of temporary patterns, neither decisive victories nor defeats. In the war, as in the lives it rules, "there is no answer."

Flaubert and Hemingway wrote out of very different cultural milieus, and the former is as incontrovertibly French as the latter is American. Yet there is little doubt that among the young Americans in Paris in the 1920s it was Hemingway who responded most easily to Flaubert's perspective of modern life. In the "Paris Letters" of 1922, Pound lay down a challenge which may not have been directed at his newest pupil but which that pupil seems to have accepted:

> Joyce, growing steadily out of Flaubert, parallels *Trois Contes,* and *L'Education* without passing his predecessor; in *Ulysses* he has gone further. The American writer, if he be serious, must recognize that our indigenous product has only got as far as Maupassant in the short story, and as far as H. James in the novel. It remains to be seen whether anyone will undertake to catch up with the gigantic *sottisier*.[12]

Pound's rating system of writers bears an uncanny resemblance to Hemingway's later habit of using such metaphors as the boxing ring and speaking of "beating" other writers, or fighting them to a draw. It is certainly possible he had read Pound's piece or heard him speak in its manner. The evidence, internal and external, suggests, as we have seen, that when Hemingway undertook to write *A Farewell to Arms* he had read and absorbed a good deal of Flaubert. Certainly Hemingway's debts to Flaubert in such matters as style, use of detail, spatial structure, unheroic heroes, contempt for false morality, irony, and a host of other broad areas are everywhere in strong evidence and merit a special attention no one has yet attempted.

Literary history is a series of mutations, adaptation, and changes of form and matter, With respect to these two novels one example suffices. In *L'Education Sentimentale* there is no consummation between Frédéric and his idealized love, Marie Arnoux: they merely grow older. And since the novel begins with an eighteen-year-old youth enraptured by a woman considerably older, at the time of their final meeting he is middle-aged and she is a gray-haired matron. The scene of their last encounter remains one of the most startling in fiction. Yet Hemingway was no longer content with such an ending. Catherine dies—suddenly, irrationally, young, leaving a lover equally young to survive this loss. Flaubert's ironic and slow portrait of disintegration, which gathers in a welter of detail and becomes an essential aspect of the novel's style, emerges in Hemingway as a sudden, traumatic, final dispossession. The theme of paralysis has perhaps lost nothing of its magnitude in this mutation, but the suddenness and the literal loss of life on which Hemingway insists signal a new and different kind of despair. Whereas Flaubert's ending shrugs, Hemingway's shudders. We have come a long way, in substance and in style. Flaubert's twenty-seven years have been appropriately and ruthlessly compressed by Hemingway into scarcely more than a year.

There is in much of modern literature almost a conscious "negation of history," a posture which Lukács describes:

> First, the hero is strictly confined within the limits of his own experience. There is not for him . . . any pre-existent reality beyond his own self, acting upon him or being acted upon by him. Secondly, the hero himself is without personal history. He is "thrown-into-the world": meaninglessly, unfathomably. He does not develop through contact with the world; he neither forms nor is formed by it. . . . The narrator, the examining subject, is in motion; the examined reality is static.

This condition fits Frederic Henry even more than it does Frédéric Moreau, since the latter at least has many illusions that he is, within a historical framework, effecting—and affected by—the actions of the world. For Lukács the principal consequence of such solitariness is the negation of human potential. There are "abstract" and "concrete" potentialities, but only "in the interaction of character and environment can the concrete potentiality of a particular individual be singled out"—such a character must live in a "palpable, identifiable world." No one would suggest that Frederic Henry's world is unreal or unidentifiable, but its reality serves as background. Nor is Hemingway interested in exploring his hero's psyche. What is left is a sense of compression: the character, unable to respond to the historical world, and unwilling to think through his internal history, remains not so much aloof as undefined. There is no contradiction between the sense of immediate time, which Frederic Henry measures carefully, and the lack of a larger perspective. Indeed there may almost be an inverse relationship (not only in Frederic Henry but in other modern isolatos): the more the hero is attached to immediacy, the less he is able, or willing, to contemplate anything beyond immediacy.

Paradoxically, despite the historical contexts both sought to create, neither Flaubert nor Hemingway was able (or wanted) to place his hero into the flow of history; neither envisioned a genuine past or a potential future beyond fantasizing about trivia in Flaubert and the abrupt severance of all relationships in Hemingway. Moreover, Flaubert resisted closure: no great genius, no great book, he once wrote, has any final conclusions, as humanity itself is in constant motion. Humanity, like history, is like an endless dream (perhaps a nightmare), each an "éternel problème." Hemingway would not have disagreed. In an almost hermetic world, there can be no "education" in any sense for Frédéric Moreau or Frederic Henry: no movement, no development. In principle, and speaking metaphorically, one must concede that Flaubert and Hemingway almost succeeded in writing novels about "nothing."

It is precisely the triviality of what the two friends in L'Education Sentimentale remember—the youthful bordello misadventure—which so clearly illuminates how Flaubert assaulted elegy itself with irony. For this episode aside, his two protagonists cannot select a single purposeful moment invested with that sense of loss required by the genuine elegiac tone; they can bring forth nothing on which their imagination can seize as worthy of recovery. The final visit by Madame Arnoux to the now-aging Frédéric has effectively undercut his possibly elegiac memory for an unattained ideal: it represents perhaps Flaubert's most triumphant display of "romantic irony." Once she exposes the reality of time—her white hair is after all only its objectification—there is nothing left for Frédéric: nothing to mourn, nothing to hope to retrieve. Shudders of revulsion do not make for elegy. Frédéric has always been a narcissist for whom consummation would clearly undermine the illusion that has fed his self-absorption.

If it is argued that it is after all their *youth* that these two middle-aged men recall, and that this is perfectly normal, the irony merely increases, for the memory underscores not a true reminiscence, such as, say, Proust's, but an echo of incompleteness, the unconsummated, the fragment of expectation, not fulfillment. Experience has done nothing for them but to negate itself. They do not *recall* their youth, they reenact it by means of their elated memory of *failure*. It is as if nothing has intervened. Like Bouvard and Pécuchet (though admittedly on a different plane), Frédéric and Deslauriers are essentially children, and in the end their "memory" may in a certain sense not even be eligible to be so classified. In *L'Education Sentimentale,* the unlived life is to a large extent unrecognized by those who have traversed its empty space.[13]

Lukács makes two points that effectively define the limits to which the motif of the unlived life has been brought: the confinement of the hero to his own experience and a lack of connection between hero and experiential world. The "static" reality around which the character moves robs the relationship between subject and object of a reciprocal dynamic and renders it null and void. The "ontological solitariness" of which he speaks (with an assist from Heidegger) becomes quite different from the isolation that had beset some of the personages discussed in earlier chapters. For now the very personal history which previously had seemed so essential is eliminated, creating characters whose identity is encapsulated solely in some sort of quintessential ego. Lukács calls this "negation of history," and, of course, it is. Yet it is also a negation of the future, and it is one of several ways in which the human condition is pinned down on some present moment, cut off from origins as well as from continuity. Hemingway's insistence that not only the mother but the child must die is a prelude to those many abstract characters of contemporary fictions who do not even have a child to die, who are instead so sterile, so disconnected, that the question of continuity is not even at issue.

This has spilled over into popular-culture fiction. A recent commentator notes: "In much of contemporary North American fiction, the self-possessed characters have no history; rootless and disconnected, they are atomistic individuals calculating their self-interest . . . conceived and raised to adulthood in a vacuum." Even the dynamics of parent-children relationships are gone (cited are novels like Mann's *Buddenbrooks* [1901], Lawrence's *Sons and Lovers* [1912]); even the fiction of the 1960s and 1970s retained rebellion as a sign of conflict, and conflict as a sign of connecting. But "In the 80's, connecting links between generations are loosening and the family is replaced by the self-possessed individual."[14] The beginnings of this unraveling of connection began in the last century, in the fiction of—among others—Flaubert and, in the 1920s, in Hemingway's "orphans."

8 Modern Progeny: Beckett and the Unlivability of the Lived Life

I often wonder what it would be like if we were to start our life over again. . . . In that case . . . every one of us would . . . do his utmost not to repeat himself.
—*Quoted from Chekhov's* The Three Sisters *in the epigraph to* Biography: A Game *by Max Frisch*

Poulet describes Proust's retrieval of time as a kind of descent at the end of which Proust finds "fragments of his former life . . . a starlighted nothingness." Furthermore, Proust has "no more hope in the future, and he no longer enjoys the present." Such a condition is "perennial desire" lacking future hope and "faith in the present," a combination that consigns one to eternal rummaging in the past. Hence, in such a scheme, the past tyrannizes, for it "is *the already lived* [life] that saves *the living;* otherwise it would fall into the insignificance of oblivion even before being *lived.*" Such passages look uncannily toward Beckett, who was obviously sensitized to Proust, about whom he wrote an interesting monograph.[1]

On one level *A la recherche du temps perdu* is a massive elegy, a social and family chronicle composed, like an epic, after the event and concluding at the very last apocalyptic moment of collapse. Its major thematic strain—of retrieval or recovery—clearly signals its starting point: *loss.* And while it was tempting to deal with Proust's version of elegiac fiction here, the dimension of the work was sufficiently intimidating. Instead, Beckett's monograph seemed to serve not as a substitute but as a revealing gateway into Beckett, who incorporated Proust and then went beyond him. After all, in Proust there *is* clear memory, even though it may be argued that in the end Proust's (or Marcel's) recovery of the past is finally no more sustaining than Swann's final conquest of Odette—a waste of Swann's life, one recalls, for a woman who was not even his "type." Still, in Proust's elegiac paradigm there is at least the search itself: frantic, monomaniacal, and, in the clearest sense, narcissistic. The prowler of the past gathers "fragments" of memory to rehabilitate, to reconstruct an isolated and severed observer in order to achieve some form of unified consciousness. Failing that, the process itself at least has served as the activity toward recovery, using that word in all of its several meanings.

In his *Proust* Beckett sees a man who, on his way to the Guermantes, "feels that everything is lost, that life is a succession of losses . . . because nothing survives" except memories, "the disturbed images of voluntary memory . . . dislocation and adjustments . . . enduring boredom . . . a life so protracted in the past and so meaningless in the future . . . that his death would be a termination but not a conclusion." After spending almost all of his postadolescent youth in solitude, Proust reemerges to enter a world that is as evacuated of joy as he is himself, a world "that has long since ceased to interest him." Validated by Schopenhauer, Proust, Beckett believes, creates a "will-less stasis" in music, the " 'amabilis insania' . . . 'hölder Wahnsinn.' " The link to Schopenhauer is crucial, for he deeply affected Proust's configuration of any personal survival, what Schopenhauer called the *principium individuationis*. For, Beckett says, Proust "thinks how absurd our dream of a Paradise with retention of personality, since our life is a succession of Paradises successively denied, that the only true Paradise is the Paradise that has been lost. . . ."[2] Of course, Proust's "Paradise Lost" is not Milton's, not the Fall from Eden; though it is a "fall" nevertheless, a fall from childhood innocence to adult rage, from passionate need to passionless pursuit, from distorted dream to aborted reality. And that, for Beckett, opens the gate as it were for his own versions of the elegiac, beyond Proust's "contemplative stasis" to something like the stasis of purposeless *waiting*.

I

Beckett's fiction is still far behind in recognition and discussion afforded it than the more famous plays.[3] But it serves us well as a concluding text, for by the time we reach Beckett's trilogy (*Molloy, Malone Dies*, and *The Unnamable*), we have perhaps reached a terminal point in charting the unlived life. For in Beckett it is not the *unlived* but the *unlivable life* that he asks us to ponder. The distinction is not trivial. Those who suffer the regret of the unlived life are aware, at least to some extent, of the source of their pain, namely, what is called to mind, the possible moment of life missed or "too late" to recover. However, those who find life unlivable—at least in Beckett—have scarcely a memory of the past;[4] their dilemma, simply put, is existence, having been born into a world they must endure as they await, mostly helpless, a slow dying, a consummation so devoutly wished that sometimes suicide becomes a serious alternative (as it does in *Godot* and several other plays).

Despite all the humor, and all the resignation, Beckett's three novels, whatever else they may say to us, communicate an unredeemed despair: life is simply not livable. Not only that, but more to the point, life is not *worth* living: there *are* no missed opportunities, no "too late" laments, little wistful pining for second chances. And as Camus's Clamence says in *La Chute,* perhaps "Fortunately!" for second chances, Camus implies, would merely put us back on the same track that brought us to where we are. In short, life's opportunities offer only grief and, in the end, death. Life is a lifelong vigil for death, in itself hardly an original discovery but, in Beckett's fiction especially, an analyzed condition. The trilogy might easily be called: *Waiting for Death.*[5] Each of the three protagonists in the novels waits to die, and their collective memories of the lives lived—what little of such memories remain—are seldom elegiac, nor do they offer temporary solace. Their pain is not over what has been lost but over what has already been, and still must be, endured. Even the outrage against death, which pervades so many of the works discussed here, is in Beckett muted. If there is frustration or irritability, it is caused by the slowness of the process of dying and by the deprivations and indignities that dying imposes on us before it finally lets us go—if indeed it even comes to that. That is why suicide, though never committed, is contemplated in much of Beckett's work. Even waste, which is so powerful a metaphor in all three novels— in *The Unnamable* the narrator is a limbless torso—no longer carries with it the earlier burden of loss for which retention was at least a possibility. In Beckett incontinence is not merely a physical symptom; his preoccupation with waste becomes physical as well as philosophical: the trilogy is full of descriptions of urination and defecation. Spiritual waste has been distilled into biological waste: the metaphysical turns increasingly into the scatological.

Dispossession is treated like putrefaction, an inevitable process of mental and physical decay—dismemberment, attrition, diminution that precede the awaited cessation of suffering. Beckett's characters do not act out their despair like Ivan Ilych or Gregor Samsa; there is no plaint laying bare a sense of being victimized by mortals or immortals, no sense that life is unfair: there is revulsion, irritation, pathos, sardonic humor, and a posture that admits acknowledgment, even acceptance, of futility, rather than a series of mobilized defensive strategies to defeat it.

One must be careful in reading Beckett's work to recognize how easily one can be trapped into one sentiment sometimes immediately contradicted by its opposite: "I can't go on, I'll go on." Still the divided selves of his fictions do follow certain patterns, and these can be monitored, traced, positioned. *Molloy* begins with an admission by its protagonist: "I haven't much will left. . . . The truth is I don't know much. . . . I sleep in [my mother's bed]. . . . I have taken her place. . . . All I need now is a son"—that is, continuity, which, of course, is denied.[6] This evacuation of will and memory characterizes Molloy, Malone, and the Unnamable, each progressively worse off than his predecessor, so that the creature of the last novel has not only been dispossessed of a name but of his limbs. The self left is not merely mutilated and anonymous; it is in a literal sense stripped bare. Beckett literalizes what Conrad had groped for through metaphor more than half a century earlier in *Heart of Darkness:* a disembodied voice, a hollow man.

Molloy does remember his name, but why and how he got into a bedridden position remain a mystery to him. He is unable to remember the name of his town; his present state is truly a "throwness-into-being," rootless, without history, without future. "I have ceased to live. . . . To decompose is to live too, I know, I know, don't torment me . . ."(25). Under the circumstances he must question the whole concept of freedom, "For I no longer know what I am doing, nor why . . ." (45). Yet "there were times," he admits, when "I forgot not only who I was, but that I was, forgot to be" (49). Such conscious loss of consciousness makes his vigil the nightmare it is. For Molloy suicide does not become the solution; his fate is to lie in bed and endure, not heroically, nor with the hope of catching some redemptive flicker through all the darkness, but simply because there is nothing else to do. Fiction is systematically stripped of its most hallowed device: the moment, however brief and ambiguous, when something is *understood.* "Perhaps it is already too late" (87); with a past forgotten, the future is "unspeakable" (80). Using his crutches, Molloy crawls like a reptile, "Flat on [his] belly, using [his] crutches like grapnels . . ." (89), just as the metamorphosed Gregor Samsa had crawled in his room. But Molloy is far more truncated from the coordinates that bring us a sense not merely of place but of identity, something Gregor Samsa, with painful awareness, retains to the very

end. Now and again scenes of Molloy's life appear to him; but neither
he—nor we—can piece these fragments together into any pattern.

The second section of *Molloy,* also narrated in the first person, is
about Moran, the man sent on the mission to find Molloy, for reasons
not clear. Moran's search is quest, but it is shrouded in incompleteness, like some Audenesque mystery:

> ... Moran making ready to go without knowing where he was
> going, having consulted neither map nor timetable, considered
> neither itinerary nor halts, heedless of the weather outlook,
> with only the vaguest notion of the outfit he would need, the
> time the expedition was likely to take, the money he would
> require and even the very nature of the work to be done. ...
> (124)

So a virtually memoryless invalid is the quarry of a quest by a hunter
seemingly ignorant of why he is on the hunt, or of how and where he
should proceed.[7] Moran sets out on his journey with his rebellious
son, tracking the side roads and being as inconspicuous as possible to
avoid detection. Beckett's motive is not clear, but a parody of the quest
motif cannot be far from his mind: it seems almost too obvious not to
be one aim of this strange pursuit. "What was I looking for exactly? It
is hard to say" (136), for he seems to be unaware of what to do with
Molloy if he finds him. Steadily growing weaker, Moran moves on (he
even kills a man when threatened), but the search has no external
structure: he "kept losing his way" in unfamiliar country. Shortly
before the novel ends, his own futurity—his son—abandons him.
Steadily growing weaker, he ceases to eat, and it is not until his superi-
ors find him that he is "saved"—in fact, sent home to die. Both Molloy
and Moran are unmediated personifications of waste. Moran has
spent a whole winter searching; in the spring he is ordered home,
never having fulfilled a mission that was at best uncertain, at worst
suicidal. For both Molloy and Moran life is neither to be grieved nor
missed, nor to be sought and retained. Life is something they experience on a level of unconsciousness so keen that even to say they
experience it is questionable.

"Coma is for the living," says Malone in *Malone Dies* (194); what, then,
is for the dying? Occasional consciousness, passive awareness, "a mini-
mum of memory," which is "indispensable, if one is to live really" (207).
"Whence that child I might have been," he asks (208), not, one notes,
"whence that child I once was." And, of course, by extension: whence
that man that might have become? Like Hans Castorp, but in a very

different dimension, Malone has lost track of time: day, week, month, all demarcations have ceased to have meaning, and with such loss the loss also of past, present, and future. For Malone all conditions are cancelled: "I shall go on doing as I have always done, not knowing what it is I do, nor who I am, nor where I am, nor if I am" (226). Malone's life, insofar as we can call it that, is a steadily deaccelerating existence; as he himself observes, the less sustenance he takes, the less waste he surrenders. The opening sentence of *Malone Dies* is disarmingly simple: "I shall soon be quite dead at last in spite of all" (179). A memoir writer, a diarist, Malone must write: it is the one activity that can accompany the wait for death. Writing is part of what he calls the "reckoning"; for Malone it has not been "too late" but "too soon":

> All my life long I have put off this reckoning, saying, too soon, too soon. Well it is still too soon. All my life long I have dreamt of the moment when, edified at last, in so far as one can be before all is lost, I might draw the line and make the tot. (181)

This grace, too, will be denied. For Dostoevsky's Underground Man, that archetype of emotional isolatos, consciousness was the cause of all his suffering, but consciousness, he says, he would never willingly give up. For Malone "the loss of consciousness . . . was never any great loss" (183); nor was he "much given to nostalgia" (186). Wherein the difference? For one thing, the Underground Man values his spiteful battle against life; it sustains him. Beckett's characters (especially in the trilogy) are indifferent to such challenges. For them the struggle is neither won nor lost but, to all intents and purposes, nonexistent, illusory. To lose consciousness, therefore, is merely to lose what was never nurtured or, if possessed, valued. Pain does not flow from one's awareness of it but from its pesty persistence, a distinction Ivan Ilyich had to understand and to choose between, realizing in the end that awareness alone defined the terms of encounter applicable to easing the pain itself. For Malone "*nothing is more real than nothing*" (192). As he says, "This is awful" (191). The closest he comes to expressing personal elegy is to say, "Perhaps I have lived after all, without knowing . . ." (195). Life, like the pencils he now keeps losing, is lost, the pencils that record (or try to) not so much a life but its expiration: the waiting. Crutches and stick are lost like pencils, and is not the pencil itself a crutch, a stick? Malone is stranded in his bed: "the best way to pass unnoticed is to lie down flat and not move" (235). "I am lost. Not a word" (263).

Strangely enough, the most poignant chords of regret are spoken by the most dismembered character of the trilogy, the torso of The Unnamable, a being stripped of "all those things that stick out," including penis and nose: "I was not always sad, I wasted my time," he tells us, "abjured my rights, suffered for nothing, forgot my lesson" (306). No need for him to think in order to despair (Keats). Again, only a "voice" is left, "this meaningless voice which prevents [one] from being nothing and nowhere . . ." (370). Yet, despite all this evacuation of meaning, the Unnamable finds solace in regret, indeed discovers it alone as the potential of overcoming the dread and emptiness of indeterminate waiting:

> Regretting, that's what helps you on, that's what gets you on towards the end of the world, regretting what is, regretting what was, it's not the same thing, yes, it's the same, you don't know, what's happening, what's happened, perhaps it's the same . . . the same regrets, that's what transports you, towards the end of regretting. (371)

Life is a seamless encounter with indistinguishable time, past and present held together by chronic regretting: "some people are born lucky, born of a wet dream and dead before morning" (379–80).

The Unnamable's monologue is directed toward no audience ("no one left"): it is reflexive narration, "It's . . . I who am talking to me about me" (394). So to self-denial: "it's not I . . . not I . . . if only it could be about him . . . I'd deny him, with pleasure . . ." (402). He has lost the ego's last weapon, to distinguish self from any other, even to remain able to split the self that one is from the self that one would like to be. "Yes," he concludes, "my life, since we must call it so . . ."; yet "I don't know if I, ever lived . . ." (396). The trap is critical, even for this time of waiting, for to wonder if one has ever lived, in Beckett's sense, goes far beyond the Jamesian or Chekhovian wonder: it is after all to wonder whether life itself exists. It is not merely memory and awareness that have been lost; the abandoned voice, from the disembodied torso, seeks to verify its very existence in a former self that *was* namable. Existence precedes the ability to ponder its meaning or, as the case may be, its meaninglessness (this is more than "essence"). Beckett's characters—as almost most readers agree—doubt that existence itself. And what precedes existence? That may indeed be the question raised in all three novels, one to which any firm answer will be always elusive, for if existence itself remains in doubt, what precedes it, however named, is also in doubt: infinite regression. Hence we are bound to begin in the same uncertainty with which we end. Perhaps this is what Heidegger meant by his use of the word "falling," which one critic has interpreted as referring to our "inescapable tendency to conceal the truth about ourselves and the world." The anxieties of the protagonists of the fictions I have discussed in previous chapters are always identifiable. Beckett's *angst* is not fixed, nor easy to seize; it does not even "float." Again, as Heidegger conceived it, it resembles what he defines as anxiety that "is not anxiety about some thing or other, but about 'nothing': about our openness, emptiness, no-thingness."[8]

Such a stark self-consciousness of absence (or in Beckett's terms, "silence") is a function of memory—or its perversions. The Unnamable's aloneness ("I am of course alone. Alone. That is soon said" [292]) is comforting only to the point of reassuring him of the only existence he can be certain about, his own, but its effect is also to short-circuit memory of attachment. "Past happiness in any case has clean gone from my memory, assuming it was ever there" (293). He is unable to situate beginnings, something to "relate to his abode," and being thrust into a state of being with no ancestral events occasions a different terror of isolation, one which forces him to seek the origins of disjointed nightmares, "forbears . . . houses where lamps are lit at night . . . where do they come to me from?" (294).

This emotional amnesia is accompanied by physical paralysis, eyes that "can no longer close as they once could" (301), and an apparently contradictory condition in which one is "not heading anywhere," or feeling anything, but is nevertheless seized "greatly" by "fear" (302). In this abiding "mortal inertia," the Unnamable has ceased to ask direct questions; he is an echo of Eliot's Prufrock, that prototype of "mortal inertia" and mortal amnesia: "Respite, then, once in a way, if one can call that respite, when one waits to know one's fate, saying, Perhaps it's not that at all . . ." (370).

Without teleology and ontology, Beckett's character has become an unattached and literal lump of matter. Disintegration is so complete that his plight, it is implied, is to sojourn in a Dantesque hell, "unable to go forward or back, not knowing where you came from, or where you are, or where you're going. . . . And there is nothing for it but wait for the end." Yet no one can be certain what—or even if—the end *is:* "not being able to die, live, be born" (370), a deliberate declension of reverse chronology: future, present, past. To the end his own identity escapes certainty ("I knew I had memories"); self-awareness is fragmentary, so much so that self-identification becomes impossible: "But it's not I, it's not I, where am I, what am I doing, all this time . . ." (399), a cry of anguish repeated three pages later.

If there is to be death, the Unnamable will die "a stranger in the midst of strangers, a stranger in my own midst" (396), being, like Byron's Harold, a century and a half earlier, a "ruin" himself. Beckett's use of silence has often been noted by his critics—both as a device (especially the pauses in the plays) and as a word.[9] "Silence" appears a dozen times in the last three pages of the last novel of this trilogy, as if the word itself finally wrenches the work to a close, to silence. Its very insistence, of course, asserts itself as its opposite, too: the Unnamable's silence is a frozen shriek, like Munch's scream, the dread that simply cannot be articulated except by silence, the immobilized body failing to carry out the stimuli of the immobilized mind, which, disoriented even about its own existence, can only complete itself in the ultimate contradiction of knowledge ("it will be I") and ignorance ("I don't know, I'll never know"), of emotional closure ("I can't go on"), and ineluctable tropism ("I'll go on")—the two phrases that conclude the trilogy.

II

"Nothing to be done" are the familiar words that begin *Waiting for Godot*,[10] and they have, at least, two meanings. First, these words tell us that Beckett's characters live in place and time beyond or outside routine expectations. In some sense the whole play is like the brief scene Lear is given on the heath: it is wrenching, full of rage and sorrow, and it borrows from the rest of *Lear* its clown or fool, his wise buffoonery, and the deep sense of hope undermined—more sinned against than sinning. However, at the same time that the opening words suggest the end of "doing" and promise us a play of no action, they, of course, also imply the sense of futility that pervades. There is indeed nothing more that can (or will) be done, nothing more one can *do*, that is, to alter the *status quo*. It has been almost universally observed that from start to finish the play is unmoving (and unmoved): there is the interlude with Pozzo and Lucky; there is the Boy announcing the regrets that Godot will not be coming "today"; there is the curious growth of a few leaves in Act II on a tree bare in Act I, though Beckett pointedly says that it is "*Next day, same time. Same place.*"

"There's no lack of void," Estragon replies to Vladimir to the question, "And where were we yesterday evening according to you?" (Act II). The reply echoes Milton's Satan and Marlowe's Mephisto,

> Hell hath no limit, nor is circumscribed
> In one self place, for where we are is hell
> And where hell is must we ever be . . .

The void is where we are. Estragon says: "I'm in hell!" Vladimir and Estragon, separated in the night from each other, are joyous in their reunion; they have been so used to each other that separation, even for a night, is painful. Vladimir is astonished to discover, however, that despite his having missed Estragon he had also been "happy." Hurt and shocked, Estragon incredulously asks: "Happy?" Well, Vladimir concedes, "perhaps it's not quite the right word." What about now? Estragon prods. The reply sums up the triple bind of *waiting*—for a Godot or for no one:

> Now? . . . (*Joyous.*) There *you* are again . . . (*Indifferent.*) There *we* are again . . . (*Gloomy.*) There *I* am again. (Italics mine) (Act II)

You, we, I: this declension surely signifies Vladimir's dawning realization which, put into more reflective terms, would read: Other, Community, Self. For Beckett such a declension defines priorities: we begin with dependence on Other, whether parent, sibling, or friend; we move on to a period of relationship where Other may even include Other*s,* where the communal instinct is satisfied. Yet, like all three "I's" of the trilogy, we leave this world alone. So Vladimir ends with "I" rather than beginning with it, though begin with it he did, with birth itself. Beckett's three ages of mankind are correspondingly accompanied by joy, indifference, and gloom. Each emotion has its moment in the process of waiting, but the overriding one remains gloom, not because the play is inherently sad (it is), but because its sadness lies in the dilemma of wanting joy and even indifference while recognizing that it is now time for the gloom of solitary "I" that goes forth into the death-watch alone. Romantic "gloom" and solitariness were often a celebration of the melancholic rebellion through which the Self asserted its independence from Other and Community. Beckett recognizes this as posturing, and is closer to the mark in his realization that, stripped of Other and Community, the "I" is reduced only to game-playing, to waiting for a finality.

"All my lousy life I've crawled about in the mud!" cries Estragon, "And you talk to me about scenery!" (Act II). He's never been anywhere but here, he insists, a metaphorical admission by the less philosophic-minded of the two that the gloom is his alone, too: "I've puked my puke of a life away here, I tell you! Here!" (Act II). This

despairing insistence that his life has never been other than this present state of misery and destitution reaffirms the *sense* that both express, namely that, though there are a few remote memories of another time, this existence is the only existence. Vladimir knows there is
"nothing to be done":

> We wait. We are bored. (*He throws up his hand.*) No, don't pro-
> test, we are bored to death, there's no denying it. Good. A
> diversion comes along and what do we do? We let it go to waste.
> Come, let's get to work! (*He advances towards the heap, stops in his
> stride.*) In an instant all will vanish and we'll be alone once more,
> in the midst of nothingness! (Act II)

And how and when have they got where they are? This question of time
missed and time wasted, or time never had, hovers over the play until,
in Act II, the now very changed Pozzo cries out, "*suddenly furious*":

> Have you not done tormenting me with your accursed time! It's
> abominable! When! When! One day, is that enough for you,
> one day he went dumb, one day I went blind, one day we'll go
> deaf [note again the declension—this time, *he, I,* and *we*], one
> day we were born, one day we shall die, the same day, the same
> second, is that not enough for you? . . . (Act II)

In his earlier appearance, it is Pozzo who "consults his watch" and
Vladimir who says, "Time has stopped." Lucky's soliloquy repeats two
phrases: "reasons unknown" and "left unfinished," and both point to
the center of life itself. We are forever where and when we are for
reasons unknown: life, no matter when it ceases, is always unfinished.
"What's a year now?"[11] asks Krapp in *Krapp's Last Tape;* time no
longer measures the present, only the past. Listening to himself on
tape is, like Hans Castorp's engagement with his phonograph records,
or his singing of Schubert's "Lindenbaum," an ancestral link of uncertain nature. Recapitulation, memory, is painful:

> Be again, be again. (*Pause.*) All that old misery. (Pause.) Once
> wasn't enough for you. (*Pause.*) Lie down across her.

A dramatic rendition of some elements in Chekhov's "Boring Story,"
Krapp's Last Tape makes a significantly different point, namely, that
even recovery of a lost love is of no use as solace against the solitariness of the "I" whose "voice over" controls, manipulates, and domi-

nates that memory. That Beckett, despite his emphasis on silence, should choose to deploy a taped voice rather than, say, a diary of written words, is no accident. Words once etched into a tape can echo back later in time and can be separated from the present more harshly than the written word—and more precisely, at will. The play begins with rejection: "Just been listening to that stupid bastard I took myself for thirty years ago. . . ." The tape recorder is a mechanism that can be moved forward and backward; it can be made to skip and replay, select out and focus. Its immediacy is mitigated by total control over its behavior, so that in a sense it can be made more remote, more neutralized than a diary, where the alternatives would be to turn pages or literally to tear them out without chance of retrieval. The core of something like *The Diary of a Superfluous Man,* with all its self-pity and elegiac excesses, is not so different from the tape recorder; but Beckett's ingenious idea of using the tape recorder turns the horizontal trajectory of narrative in Turgenev into a jagged narrational journey on a verbal and structural roller coaster that twists and turns back on itself. This ability to stop and start and retrace at will enables him to make Krapp's most elegiac statement into a verbal replication of the tape-recording process: forward; backward? No, forward:

> Perhaps my best years are gone. When there was a chance of happiness. But I wouldn't want them back. . . . No, I wouldn't want them back.

III

As a topos the unlived life is, of course, inexhaustible. The elegiac response to it is but one of several that might have formed the locus of this study, but Beckett—the true "progeny" of the topos in our time—seems appropriate precisely because he seems to be on the edge of elegy, shading from the elegiac to something that parodies it. Gaev's apostrophe to the bookcase in *The Cherry Orchard* already prefigures this delicate shift: The scene is absurd, parodic, comic, and infinitely poignant. The most wrenching speech in *Godot* (although others might choose differently) is Vladimir's exhortation to life and action, neither of which can any longer be engaged. Hence the speech is not only futile but, however unintentional, also mock-elegiac, close to parody with its deliberate reminder of Hamlet's dilemma, a speech serving, for this study at least, as a *summa* of the subject beyond which lie some of the arid plains of contemporary fiction that move beyond parody to avoidance, beyond dispossession to the inability even to conceive of anything of which to be dispossessed, beyond loss to the inability to identify or name it. Here, then, is Vladimir's apostrophe to life and action (it reads hauntingly in places like Trofimov's speech, "All Russia is our garden") and the single-word responses by Estragon and Pozzo:

> Let us not waste our time in idle discourse! (*Pause. Vehemently.*) Let us do something, while we have the chance! It is not every day that we are needed. Not indeed that we personally are needed. Others would meet the case equally well, if not better. To all mankind they were addressed, those cries of help still ringing in our ears! But at this place, at this moment of time, all mankind is us, whether we like it or not. Let us make the most of it, before it is too late! Let us represent worthily for once the foul brood to which a cruel fate consigned us! What do you say? (*Estragon says nothing.*) It is true that when with folded arms we weigh the pros and cons we are no less a credit to our species. The tiger bounds to the help of his congeners without the least reflexion, or else he slinks away into the depths of the thicket. But that is not the question. What are we doing here, *that* is the question. And we are blessed in this, that we happen to know the answer. Yes, in this immense confusion one thing alone is clear. We are waiting for Godot to come—
> ESTRAGON: Ah!
> POZZO: Help!

Once we are arrived at *Endgame,* performed only three years after *Godot,* we have reached the curse on progeny that Yeats foreshadowed in *Purgatory:*

> HAMM: Accursed progenitor!
> . . . .
> HAMM: Scoundrel! Why did you engender me.
> . . . .
> HAMM: It's the end, Clov, we've come to the end.[12]

When progeny—that is, future—is cursed, the present is unlivable and the past is neither mourned nor missed but forgotten.

IV

This has not been a study of "death," although all elegy implies, of course, that some kind of death has taken place, whether of a person, an age, or—as is the case here—of the missed life. Still, depictions of death and dying in many manifestations are not unrelated to a good number of the elegiac fictions I have been discussing. In Beckett's trilogy, however, as well as in most of his plays, the border between life and death is often blurred. What makes, say, Chekhov, Tolstoy, or even Kafka so poignant is the sharp and clearly defined line that has been drawn up between life and death; and when we cross from one to the other, especially in those works where actual death occurs, the structure of the work shudders. Nevertheless, even when the elegiac ends with a death, it preoccupies itself almost wholly with life, however "elegiacally" it does that. As is evident in the works I have discussed so far, their subject may at times be death in its various forms, but their object is so situated as to be facing life and backing up against death. Put another way, our elegiac fictions have not been confrontations with death (not even in Chekhov or Tolstoy) but with life, a life found often to be wanting to be sure, but only in contrast—as I said at the beginning—with what might have been.

Beckett almost reverses this pattern. His characters (certainly the protagonists in the trilogy) do confront death. It is not the classic combative confrontation, not the moral lesson of the fall from the wheel of fortune, or the sudden vision of the reaper who waits for Everyman, the sights and smells of *memento mori*. Instead death is already an intruder in life; it reigns over the bedridden who have no rear view that remains in any sense intact enough to be called a past. As the present is unremittingly vacant, the future is merely an extension of it. Most important, there is no struggle, only the endless waiting itself. And it is surely a telling fact that in Beckett's work no major protagonist actually dies, which is not to say we are not certain that they *are* dying and *will* die. Nor is "death-in-life" meant to summon up details of an arid life (though that is suggested in some of the plays, especially in *Krapp's Last Tape*.). Whatever life is recalled is too fragmented to make coherent memories, and the implicit challenge to the reader is to see whether life is really separable from death, whether memory of past can ever be a bulwark against the waiting that so overarches Beckett's works. Waiting is not even perceived as a process or an activity, nor is it a bridge between memory and extinction; waiting is, quite simply, death itself, holding little if any dread, or the promise of release, let alone the chance of redemptive vision. Existence is as truncated as the physical body representing it. In the trilogy time has broken itself down into nonlinear refractions, and there can no longer be in any of its several senses any meaningful reflection. Conceived horizontally, the "last tape" in Beckett is really no different from the first.

Conclusion: From Solitude to Alienation—and Beyond

Whence came this dissaffection? I searched and found the answer: it came from my amour-propre . . . *[which] still rebelled against reason.*

—*Jean-Jacques Rousseau, Eighth Walk,*
Reveries of the Solitary Walker

We had the experience but missed the meaning.
—*T. S. Eliot, "The Dry Salvages"*

In Mann's *The Magic Mountain* the lovable if somewhat out-of-date Italian humanist, Settembrini, son of the Enlightenment, is a member of a league whose chief project is to compile an encyclopedic *Sociological Pathology*, "a lexicon of all the masterpieces having human suffering for their central theme." Sometimes one wishes such a lexicon would exist, for this study of the unlived life has touched on several surrounding "pathologies." At times there has been a temptation to stray. Quite aside from narcissism, mourning, melancholia, and strategies for survival—all of which were touched upon—how could one ignore the issues of alienation, loneliness, solitude (all related but discrete), misanthropy, *angst*, sickness "unto death," and so much else? Indeed *A History of Human Discontent* would be an admirable project for some group of compilers (no one individual could achieve it); but then to create such a lexicon would leave us in the same dilemma as we face with the Encyclopedists: as Yeats said, we cannot "know" truth, only "embody" it. Yet I cannot close this study without a fleeting glance at the concept of Solitude, for surely it is a state in which we find modernity defined, especially as solitude turns to alienation from life itself.

I

In view of the seemingly limitless freedom generated by the French and Industrial revolutions, it was inevitable that a deep sense of disappointment was ready to replace the initial euphoria. No doubt there were critical shiftings in all areas: in class structure, in variety of opportunities, in the solidification of an ever-growing group that garnered power and wealth. Every rudimentary textbook will give us chapter and verse, and one needs no help from any formal Marxist analysis to recognize these "deep structures" that revolutionized the way we live and think about our living. All our authors touch on the subject of these changes; some make it central to some of their work: Turgenev, Chekhov, Ibsen, Kafka, Mann. It is also logical that, displaced from high hopes and great expectations, the individual strikes out against society, and, often failing to achieve much in that direction, recoils upon the self. That is why it was suggested early on that narcissism is both a key and a link to our special isolation of the elegiac response to loss of self. The curious convergence of energy and discontent—or the energy *of* discontent—was the subject of chapter 1, and in Beckett it turns finally into a distilled discontent the other side of melancholy or self-loathing. In Beckett the game is lost while the players remain in suspended animation, reduced to incoherence and even imbecility often in the midst of uttering, like Shakespeare's Fool, fragments of great wisdom.

With respect to its view of the value of self, European culture experienced almost convulsive changes. So long as theology had held out mystical or ascetic ideals that promised divine fulfillment, it was unworthy and worthless to value the earthly self. On the other hand, denial of self did not come naturally: a reading of Augustine gives us some feeling for the cost of renunciation for the believer. If it did not turn to God, the self had few options: turn against the world; turn against oneself; at times both. This became one source of "narcissistic rage": self-laceration without a God had no comforts. Solitariness necessarily becomes narcissistic when it is no longer in the service of a higher power, and increasingly the passive and melancholic state of late eighteenth- and early nineteenth-century solitude becomes transformed into aggressive and self-destructive hate. The original solitary seeking quietude becomes a foraging guerrilla who snipes at his surroundings, courting wounds and then nursing them. More and more frequently, fictional protagonists take up a combative posture (which sometimes turns into posturing).

That was not the way matters began, for solitude and self-reflection were sought as a balm, states to savor and restore the soul. Rousseau's solitary walks were intended as a kind of stock-taking: "reverie" is a positive activity. Even so, Rousseau's reveries sometimes led him to nightmares, to the edge of the abyss, despair, and self-pity. In the Seventh Walk, Rousseau admits that he "became solitary or . . . an unsociable misanthropist, because I prefer the harshest solitude to the society of malicious men which thrives only on treachery and hate."[1] The Swiss physician Johann Georg Zimmermann spent his life writing on solitude (*Über die Einsamkeit*), and in 1784–86 published a multivolume treatise on the subject with a long subtitle: *On Solitude, or the Effects of Occasional Retirement on the Mind, the Heart, General Society, in Exile, in Old Age, and on the Death Bed*—a description that covers the present subject from Byron to Beckett. Zimmermann, who succumbed to persecution mania and died insane, devoted his treatise to a discussion of the advantages and disadvantages of solitude, and in range and detail his work resembles Burton's *Anatomy*. It takes a strong spirit, he concludes, to endure the "various fatigues of continued solitude," else one is likely "soon [to] become melancholy and miserable." Specifically we are warned against the dangers of moroseness and turning against society. Tranquillity is to be cultivated to counter, not to escape from, "an excess of social pleasures." Indeed, if such isolation proves to be harmful rather than healing, we had best return at once to social intercourse. Like a good man of the Enlightenment, Zimmermann preaches restraint from excess, especially from "irrational" solitude, when it "frequently overclouds the reason, contracts the understanding, vitiates the manners, inflames the passions, corrupts the imagination, sours the temper, and debases the whole character. . . ."[2] Though this sounds quaint and simple to modern ears, the doctor's perceptions were on target. We use a different vocabulary, such as *"ressentiment,"* and "narcissism," but the language conveys much the same meaning. By the late eighteenth century the dangers of solitude showed up everywhere in European literature. Excessive solitude led to an "unhealthy" severance from society, and so the modern concept of "alienation" was born and still thrives.[3]

The most significant change in the perception of "alienation" is from the state of seeking it out (as "solitude") to becoming its victim. Byron's heroes, for instance, were, more often than not, self-styled exiles: they chose alienation, which they considered more a separation

from the "herd" than contemplative separation. Despite the occasional melancholic laments, the Byronic hero (and his heirs) is not
overly concerned about the "negative" effects (or affects) of solitude.
The slow but clear shift from controlling alienation to being controlled by it defines, to some extent, a major problem of modernism.
Intellectuals or artistic heroes in Rilke, Hesse, Mann, Proust, Gide,
who begin to experience some ambivalence toward the solitude that
isolates (i.e., alienation) represent a transition to the future unheroic
victims of, say, Sartre, Camus, Beckett, who are sometimes both desen-
sitized to the performance of defiance and yet not quite prepared to
abandon their isolation for the false idols of what they consider meaningless, inauthentic, hypocritical. Yet the shift in orientation from
benign solitude to hostile alienation is no mere change of words, and it
has developed in that direction for nearly two centuries. Whether a
"post-modernism" as of now exists is still debated, and how the post-
moderns deal with "alienation" is beyond our scope, but here we have
brought the classic modern story to an end-point with Beckett, for he
represents the clearest boundary in the analysis of elegiac response to
loss of self from Romantic Ancestry to Modern Progeny.[4]

II

Alienation defines our unhappiness. Not only are we unhappy with
the world, on which we heap our scorn, but also with ourselves: frustrated, angry, resentful, disappointed, despairing. We are a breed
apart indeed, and unlike any other animal in the kingdom we have a
sense of what we think happiness might be and an equally strong
sense of what it is like not to have attained it. In short, a good deal of
recorded history seems preoccupied with an assessment of states not
achieved or achievable, with regret and loss, with a doomed perspective of the present looking piningly at the past and with terror at the
future.

Dr. Johnson, tutored by the ancients and the Bible, and with an
enlightened sense of resigned sadness, attempted to tell us that, in a
sense, mourning and wanting (wishing) are fruitless states of waste and
lassitude. He knew this distemper well, and suffered from it all his life.
Some sixty years later, in the next century, Schopenhauer counseled a
similar course of acceptance, calling it sheer folly to pursue individual
goals in a will-determined world of illusory phenomena. In the following century, our own, Freud agreed with both Dr. Johnson and Schopenhauer, appealing to our sense of sanity to accept the inevitable

uncertainty that scientists like Heisenberg and philosophers like Wittgenstein developed into "principles." We are prisoners of our past, Freud insisted, and only our recognition of that state can free us. The Existentialists were to refine Freud, preaching *engagement* but conceding that, after all, authenticity of self was more achievable than grand visions of self-aggrandizement. Anguish itself was liberating.

The literature of the nineteenth century displayed an especially impatient posture, both with the world and with ourselves. It was then that we began to express our sorrow in personal terms. Much of the excessive Romantic self-pity, rebelliousness, and suicidal gloom may summarily be subsumed under the expression of the elegiac cry of personal loss. Such private expressions of grief, beginning as far back as Rousseau's *Confessions* and Goethe's *Werther,* became a leitmotiv in the nineteenth and well into the twentieth century.

The simple question needs to be asked: *Why* did these expressions of personal grief, regret, and wistful elegiac mourning over one's lost moments—indeed one's life, one's self—emerge at all? Surely feelings of personal disappointment have always been felt; what then made them so pervasive, so much the stuff of art itself, so orthodox in expressiveness that after certain Romantic exaggerations had been subdued, their articulation became not merely a subject matter accepted but expected?

Early on in the century Wordsworth had noticed—and with a mixture of regret and opportunism—that the reassurance of nature was insufficient, that the "sole self," as Keats called it, was the beginning and end of our lives. Nature could console, but it was also a spatial counterpoint to the temporal anxieties of our ever-moving lives; and the high tension engendered by time's forward thrust also progressed from the familiar trope to personal anguish, that is, from a convention to a confession, the exposure of self.[5]

Time was wasting not merely the cosmos, it was devouring our lives. One response to potential loss was a new version of *carpe diem* that historians have called "aestheticism"; quite another was the confrontation with waste that became, in time, in its very starkness, its deliberate unsentimentalism, a poignant and personal expression of deprivation. Disillusion with earlier urges toward the infinite became expressions of closure—even enclosure: the finite was eventually seen not as the natural prescribed course of our lives but as punishment meted out arbitrarily and cruelly. Those who escaped into realms of beauty or other transcendent states effected temporary escapes, no less painful in the end. For the rest the encounter between a striving individual and an indifferent clock could produce nothing short of helplessness.

In turn helplessness paralyzed lives and, in the fictions I have examined here, turned them into vigils, into processes of *waiting* (whether James's John Marcher or Beckett's Vladimir and Estragon), into existences governed by the acute self-consciousness of inactivity and uselessness, superfluity and disillusion. In a recent study of "elegiac romance," Kenneth A. Brufree stresses the "unavoidable fact of modern life—the experience of catastrophic loss and rapid cultural change, and the need to come to terms with loss and change in order to survive."[6]

Elegiac fictions are often related to, but not the same as, pastoral fictions.[7] In the pastoral novel, critics like Michael Squires still find the "intense nostalgia for a Golden-Age past, for what is distant in time and space . . . the lost unity of human and natural worlds."[8] Dialectically, pastoral fiction, like pastoral poetry, continues the debate between the merits of city versus country, "complexity and simplicity," accompanied by the effort to create an "idyllic contentment" and opposition to modern encroachment on such an ideal.[9] The personae of elegiac fictions have no such illusions; any intense nostalgia on global levels is either absent or ironic. One critic sees in Henry James, especially in the earlier fiction, the stress of reality that causes James to create a "recurrent motif in his dramatizing the basic human need to deny death or an insufferable actuality." To accompany this motif James invokes the "Arcadian image," not literal but implied: the transcendent scene invaded by an "intruding horror" of reality—of death in Arcadia. A good many of James's characters, therefore, deny death and appear to be striving obsessively to "gather ideals into a perfect harmony,"[10] and such a view in no way contradicts their elegiac posture: to recognize that no such harmony was possible and to lament the virtual impotence in the face of attempts to achieve it.

In his discussion of elegy, Peter V. Marinelli has accurately defined "nostalgia" as an emotion of those who must be "conscious of having experienced a loss." It is precisely this that differentiates pastoral from elegy: the first remains hopeful of fixing in its sights, by means of the "backward glance," an existing palliative—a past to oppose the present, a memory to assuage pain; the second knows that the "backward glance" is foreshortened to one's personal lifeline, and there no Arcadia exists, except perhaps in excerpts of memory. Even these are fraught with the kind of painful longing as are those fleeting images, for instance, in T. S. Eliot's "visions" of gardens and roses and the sea. The pastoral vision seeks an "escape from the overwhelming present in a sanctified past or in some indistinct future."[11] On the other hand, the personalized elegiac experience I have dealt with assumes that neither past nor future is anything but the immediate evidence of what has already been wasted or what will continue to waste or, at the very least, preclude "escape." The pastoral envisions liberation, however temporary; the elegiac (in the sense we have used it here) sees only imprisonment.

In her study of the classical pastoral elegy from Theocritus to Milton, Ellen Z. Lambert points to the essential "optimism" which is "always beneath the surface of Arcadian melancholy," and reminds us of the elegist's "power to transcend death . . . to deny it." These are important points. It is, she maintains, sorrow itself that gives rise to the "music" of elegy; indeed she makes a distinction between the classic concept of elegy and personalized elegy without stating it as such: "One way of dealing with loss is to confront it head-on. The opposite way is to allow oneself to become so absorbed in the gestures of grief that the loss itself becomes unreal to us."[12] Death is also made part of the natural cycles of life in the conventional pastoral elegy, placed into "nature's world . . . of decay and regeneration"[13] and thus stripped of that quality of unfairness and intrusion that so characterizes the texts I have analyzed. Therefore, the distinction between the pastoral and the elegiac fictions that have been the focus here needs to be clear. The traditional elegy nurtures its sadness as part of a universally accepted structure in which what giveth and taketh is acknowledged and validated; the modern elegy confronts loss and death—eventually—"head-on," and that collision brings no sweet sorrow, no gentle melancholy, but rather a harsh and often devastating encounter with emptiness itself. The difference is articulated by Wallace Stevens's "The Snowman," who,

> . . . nothing himself, beholds
> Nothing that is not there and the nothing that is.

Much of modern literature, even when comic (or more often ironic), is a lament for the disinherited past when it embraces as well as when it reviles the future.[14]

In an interesting chapter, "Romantic Losses," Jean-Pierre Mileur perhaps goes too far in his interpretation of Freud: "Freud's conclusion [in "Mourning and Melancholia"] that the disposition in melancholia originates in a narcissistic object-choice . . . [suggests] that literature is being accused for the loss of the poet's narcissistic ego-ideal—a dream of greatness. . . ." This appears to be a misunderstanding of Freud's intentions in "Mourning and Melancholia." Freud indeed asserts that melancholia "originates" in "narcissistic object-choice," yet one concludes that primarily such object-choice is one's self. From that it follows that the melancholic ends up mourning for the "lost" self even as that self may be diminished of its potential "greatness." That was suggested in the introduction to Part III; it is not, therefore, "literature" that Freud accuses of letting down the creator (this is a deconstructionist paradigm) but quite the opposite. It is *in* literature that the artist displaces personal loss of self-esteem and creates, in his or her own stead, those personae I have surveyed: narcissists, mourners and melancholics, survivors—all of whom in the process of being created restore to their author the ego-ideal that was in danger of being lost or not being achieved in the first place. This does not always work, and too many examples stand as sad testimony, from Novalis to Nerval, to Kleist, Kafka, and Virginia Woolf. No simple displacement/ replacement theory can explain why the creative act fails, even when it is rather explicitly mobilized to survive the creator's own, sometimes pathological, melancholy. The artist's self-denigration is, of course, a peculiarly modern by-product of the change in the artist's function as we move from patronage to independent anonymity. That begins to happen in the mid-eighteenth century and accelerates, so that by the twentieth century, the artist-victim, the antisocial and alienated rebel, divorced from the common cultural life, becomes a cliché figure: "we moderns are permanently alienated from the nurturing sources of creative genius."[15] Or, of course, the equation can be reversed, and while the meaning would not change, the emphasis might be closer to fact; that is, the "creative genius" has become alienated from the source of what sustains the artist: what Yeats summed up with typical immodesty as "past, passing, and to come."

III

Erich Fromm states flatly that *"Destructiveness is the outcome of unlived life."*[16] Published over forty years ago, this does not sound novel today, but applied to the fictions surveyed here, the general outline of Fromm's conclusion remains valid. For "destructiveness" resembles to a large degree Nietzsche's (and later Scheler's) *"ressentiment."* The more destructiveness in the individual, the more life has been "curtailed." Organic life, meant to expand, will, when thwarted, drive energy inward to effect a kind of implosive self-destructiveness. Where does such destructiveness originate? It is, says Fromm, "rooted in the unbearableness of individual powerlessness and isolation."[17] The desire to escape from unbearable feelings so induced creates and enhances destructiveness. And the "conditions of isolation and powerlessness" create both "anxiety" and the "thwarting of life," or repression. Fromm was perhaps the first of the "potentialists," and he believes that our self-realization, once thwarted, recoils and causes its baser opposites to mobilize. Unlived life is, of course, for Fromm another way of describing unrealized "potentialities"—"sensuous, emotional, and intellectual."[18] Fromm recognizes that the price of surrendering one's individuality is the loss of selfhood; one may appease one's anxieties but at a substantial cost. On the other hand lies the danger of overindividuation, which incurs "growing isolation . . . insecurity . . . doubt [about] the meaning of one's life . . . a growing feeling of one's own powerlessness and insignificance. . . ." So for Fromm the solution is, as it was for Lukács, social integration, something like the "primary ties" we presumably experienced communally in the Middle Ages. Others have held such nostalgic views, from the Romantics through Yeats, and although there may be a kind of truth in the solace of communal salvation, there is also the possibility that, as we have come to realize, communal individuation can subdue as much as liberate. Fromm's diagnosis, and even his prognosis, seem correct; his course of treatment may be questionable. The dictum that "once paradise is lost, man cannot return to it"[19] is a salutary reminder that elegiac plaint serves no palpable purpose. Yet "spontaneous activity" and "solidarity" do not always ameliorate the sense of loss that accompanies thwarted life. We have seen that such a recognition of waste can give rise to more than destructiveness or *ressentiment:* it can, for example, be the occasion for making peace with oneself, albeit at the expense of carrying on struggles one once held essential (Tolstoy, Brontë, Kafka, among others). Perhaps Fromm's notion might be amended to stipulate that the "outcome of unlived life" is the activity of destructiveness, *or* quite its opposite: the passivity of waiting, either in some state of peaceful inertia or painful paralysis. So at any rate it appears to apply to Beckett and beyond.

In the initial stages of expressing the condition of the unlived life, there was still hope—the hope that the experience of having missed life could at least serve as liberating or illuminating. In Kafka (and beyond him) such revelations are charged with irony; Kafka's stories seem to end in grimaces that convey both shame and unredeemable defeat. There is surely no Arcadia in them, nor is there an Elysium. And the present collapses on itself to crush the individual, to reduce him to minimality.

Günter Grass's Oskar in *The Tin Drum* preempts such harsh domination by anticipating the crush of life and willing a dwarfish state, an act of circumventing—or trying to—the humiliation of first growing and *then* being reduced. This maneuver too, as readers of *The Tin Drum* know, does not really succeed. Nevertheless, even in Grass there remains a personalized cry of dislocation, an echo of a life that might have been, a madness that is well aware of the sanity to which it cannot aspire because sanity betrays. Stunted growth is perhaps the ultimate metaphor of the unlived life: the incessant drummer beats out the dirge of life denied—even if it is self-denied. The adult mind forever joined to the child's body is the *reductio ad absurdum* of the unlived life, for in the figure of arrested childhood through retardation also lies the sum total of human pain and regret. Nothing, it would seem, can surpass this impasse.

IV

Is it any wonder that Dickens experienced difficulties with the ending of *Great Expectations*?[20] Great expectations were still deeply embedded, even in mid-century, from the original Romantic myth-makers. And was it not more than a piece of shrewd compromising to have provided two endings, the so-called happy and the unhappy ones? I have tried to show that from the beginnings of Romanticism great expectations (Novalis's *Erwartung*) were systematically thwarted, lacking fulfillment (*Erfüllung*). And the tracing of this motif might well have included some observations on Dickens's novel, except that perhaps its hero is permitted—even in the unhappy ending—more fulfillment than we have found in the works chosen here. Nevertheless, Dickens's dilemma was clear enough: if the hero is to be chastened by life, and if he is to learn that even great expectations result in something less than the equivalent rewards, how, then, does one conclude such a parabolic novel? Pip's life is no waste (except in his unfulfilled love with Estella in the "unhappy" ending), and it is certainly not in our sense an unlived life. Still, in spite of its successes, it falls far short of what was imagined. Dickens was clearly at war with his own expectations of himself as a novelist and with the expectations of his own age, which continued to demand, on the whole, a perpetuation of the magic of fulfillment while at the same time developing an increasingly skeptical perspective on the validity of such a course.

Demythification of expectations came later in England than on the Continent; it was perhaps not until Hardy that what had traditionally been called "pessimism" truly took hold, and it continued through much of James and virtually all of Conrad. It was this "pessimism" that so frustrated Lawrence whenever he confronted his contemporaries, though his own novels are markedly ambiguous in their endings, the fulfillment seldom realized, only hinted at as a possibility. Enough has been said about Joyce's "yes" that concludes *Ulysses,* but no reader of that novel can fail to see that it, too, has its share of elegiac undertones and overtones. Indeed is it not the very sense of loss that Molly Bloom affirms with her "yes"?

Freud's overdeterministic conclusions about the human condition are rooted in his conviction that all joy (as much as all dread) is buried in the shell of childhood, and that to be "cured" (a word he might not use) of our neurotic illnesses we must break that shell and, however temporarily, recover the living past before putting it to rest. Memory, what once was and what we once thought might have been (but could never be), remains the trigger that psychoanalytic treatment seeks to pull in the patient's psyche. Anti-Freudians have called this a joyless and hopeless posture in which life is seen at best as an accommodation to loss and frustrated "expectations," but Freud would (and did) respond by calling such protestations proof of his dim view of reality. Whatever else Conrad meant by having Kurtz cry "The horror! The horror!" in *Heart of Darkness,* one can be certain that he meant Kurtz's cry to indicate the moment of discovering futility and waste, even for one who had sojourned in the deepest abysses and returned from its unnamable excesses. The motif of the unlived life is in part at least an anticipation of Freud's codified overdetermined conclusions which, as early as 1818, Schopenhauer (who exercised an influence over Freud) laid down in *The World as Will and Representation,* and that, at the end of the century, Nietzsche attempted so valiantly, but unsuccessfully, to challenge. The "life force" and the "death wish" may eventually have met on a field of battle (the date of such combat is arguable and not decisively important), but the outcome remained uncertain at best. Some, like T. S. Eliot, courted seduction by divine forces; others, like Yeats, sought reconciliation in the cycles that were bound always to recur; and still others, like Kafka and Beckett, found no place to drop anchor. What remained was only the waiting, a secular version of the medieval *contemptus mundi* without, of course, the reward beyond it. *Fin de partie.*

So at least we have come to "endgame" with modernism. Already there are signs that post-modernism is producing a revisionist perspective on the overdetermined and nihilistic grimness of the classic modern dilemma expressed in the canon examined here. A book just published contains several essays that offer a far more "optimistic" view on the condition of "loss" than the one we have seen expressed. One essay is entitled "Science and the Fragile Self: The Rise of Narcissism and the Decline of God." Its author offers no solution to the dilemma posed by his title, but he does express a hope: "it does seem to me that an un-flinching examination of the conflict between our wishes and our limita-tions is possible." In "A Philosophical Critique of the Concept of Narcis-sism: The Significance of the Awareness Movement," the author at-tacks the "moralistic" analysis of modern culture as "narcissistic": "The term 'narcissism' is reactionary. Its use denigrates the current social change, and opposes the greater social change which experiential intri-cacies now implies—and may bring about." And in an essay titled "Psy-chopathology in an Age of Nihilism," the editor, calling nihilism a "cancer of the spirit," sets out to search for an "ontological" meaning to redress human suffering and invest it with worth by insisting that expe-riencing our suffering makes suffering itself meaningful. This is, of course, not entirely a new idea, yet it is plainly set against the merely despairing articulation of the suffering self. "If the modern Self is not well, the body of history will carry its illness." That is, "social disorder" parallels (and in a sense is a causal factor) of the self's suffering. Put simply: the fault of our condition lies in the "social disorder," not the self; and this shift of responsibility is not only a repudiation of Freud but of much of what followed in the classical view of the afflicted self as portrayed in the "elegiac fictions" that have been my subject. "Nihilism" is interpreted in this essay as "essentially . . . self-destruction," and in the tradition of Nietzsche and Heidegger, the author of the essay prom-ises to construct an "ontology" that can overcome (perhaps) the evident linkage between social and self.[21] After all, Nietzsche's *cri de coeur* was for life, against death; for health, against disease; for self-determination, against victimage. In effect, the argument runs, if we suffer, if we sustain loss, if self is subject to so much threat and subjuga-tion, let us at least become aware of how to understand the process and its beingness, its ontology. With such understanding perhaps there may be after all some final release in which our full consciousness plays a central and controlling role? To respond affirmatively is simplistic; to dissent is perhaps too grim. At best it remains a question.

Notes

Preface

1. Published by Harvard University Press, 1972.

2. *Narcissism and the Text: Studies in Literature and the Psychology of Self,* ed. Lynne Layton and Barbara Ann Shapiro (New York and London: New York University Press, 1986), 31.

3. Recently an entire issue of *magazine littéraire* (July–August 1987) was devoted to "Littérature et Melancholie," a subject that drew many contributions, including one called "Les abîmes de l'âme, une entretien avec Julia Kristeva," by Dominique A. Grisoni. Julia Kristeva has just published *Soleil Noir, Dépression et Mélancolie* (Paris: Gallimard, 1987).

Introduction

1. Sigmund Freud, "Mourning and Melancholia," *Standard Edition of the Complete Psychological Works of Sigmund Freud,* trans. James Strachey, vol. 14 (London: The Hogarth Press, 1957), 246. This distinction will be more closely examined in the Introduction to Part I: "Mourners and Melancholics."

2. Alastair Fowler, *Kinds of Literature: An Introduction to the Theory of Genres and Modes* (Cambridge: Mass.: Harvard University Press, 1982), 136–37, 210. Although Fowler acknowledges the emergence of the elegiac novel, he does little to illustrate it or to suggest its dominance and importance.

3. Freud, "Mourning and Melancholia," 247.

4. For an excellent discussion of nineteenth-century enclosures, see Victor Brombert, *The Romantic Prison: The French Tradition* (Princeton: Princeton University Press, 1978). Brombert moves from the Romantic concept of prison as providing "inner freedom" to Sartre's very un-Romantic view of prison as entrapment. (It was tempting to include Goncharov's *Oblomov* in this discussion, for is this bedridden hero not a quintessential type, forever making his enclosures? But the novel raises too many other controversies.)

5. Allied to elegy is pastoral, on which much has been written. Among the more stimulating studies that include nineteenth- and twentieth-century

works are the following: William Empson, *Some Versions of Pastoral* (Norfolk, Conn.: New Directions, 1950); Harold E. Toliver, *Pastoral: Forms and Attitudes* (Berkeley: University of California Press, 1971); Michael Squires, *The Pastoral Novel: Studies in George Eliot, Thomas Hardy, and D. H. Lawrence* (Charlottesville: University of Virginia Press, 1974); Renato Poggioli, *The Oaten Flute: Essays on Pastoral Poetry and the Pastoral Novel* (Cambridge, Mass.: Harvard University Press, 1975). See also Conclusion, note 2. Fowler writes: "With modern genres, boundaries are . . . indistinct and shifting, overlapping and allowing intricate mixture" (*Kinds of Literature*, 39). See, for example, Ralph Freedman, *The Lyrical Novel* (Princeton: Princeton University Press, 1963).

Of the many studies on the Golden Age motif, see Harry Levin, *The Myth of the Golden Age in the Renaissance* (Bloomington: Indiana University Press, 1969), and Russell Fraser, *The Dark Ages and the Age of Gold* (Princeton: Princeton University Press, 1973).

6. Frost's famous "The Road Not Taken," many commentaries to the contrary, seems to be a parody on the subject the title announces. Frost appears to suggest that we can never really know what the "other" road might have been. But he acknowledges the powerful effect such speculation has on choices we *have* made.

7. The Renaissance poet conflated microscopic and macrocosmic loss. Renaissance scholars pointed out long ago that in Donne's "The Untimely Death of Elizabeth Drury," the death mirrors not only the death of Elizabeth I but the whole world:

'Tis all in pieces, all coherence gone . . .

8. Friedrich von Schiller, *Naive and Sentimental Poetry*, trans. Julius A. Elias (New York: Frederick Ungar, 1960, 125). Subsequent references are incorporated in the text in parentheses. For one of the most lucid discussions of Schiller's conception of the idyll (and of the implications of much of the whole of Schiller's essay), see Herbert Lindenberger, "The Idyllic Moment: On Pastoral and Romanticism," *College English*, 34, 3 (December 1972), 335–51. For a comprehensive appreciation of the general meaning of Schiller's theory of modern poetry, see Georg Lukács, "Schiller's Theory of Modern Literature," in *Goethe and His Age*, trans. Robert Anchor (London: The Merlin Press, 1978). See also Lore Metzger, *One Foot in Eden: Modes of Pastoral in Romantic Poetry* (Chapel Hill and London: University of North Carolina Press, 1986), 10–42, for an extended discussion of how Schiller's theoretical ideas are applicable as a "heuristic tool for looking at pastoral poetry beyond generic rules and beyond the battle of ancients and moderns" (42). The book concerns itself with the English Romantics.

9. Joel Whitebook, "Saving the Subject: Modernity and the Problems of the Autonomous Individual," *Telos*, 50 (Winter 1981–82), 93–102. Also relevant is a general study of "modern" fiction, Frederick Garber, *The Autonomy of the Self from Richardson to Huysmans* (Princeton: Princeton University Press, 1982).

10. Jeff Livesay, "Habermas, Narcissism, and Status," *Telos*, no. 64 (Summer 1985), 79.

11. Whitebook, 79–82, 97.

12. Among the many volumes on each of the aforementioned, I cite here only a selective number which over the years I have found most helpful. Other references will be found to individual chapters: Frederick J. Hoffman, *The Mortal No: Death and the Modern Imagination* (Princeton: Princeton University Press, 1964); Robert M. Adams, *Nil: Episodes in the literary conquest of void in the nineteenth century* (New York: Oxford University Press, 1966); Reinhard Kuhn, *The Demon of Noontides: Ennui in Western Literature* (Princeton: Princeton University Press, 1976); Ihab Hassan, *The Dismemberment of Orpheus: Toward a Postmodern Literature* (New York: Oxford University Press, 1971); Marie Jaanus Kurrick, *Literature and Negation* (New York: Columbia University Press, 1979); Ellen B. Chances, *Conformity's Children* (Columbus: Slavica Publishers, 1978); Jesse V. Clardy and Betty S. Clardy, *The Superfluous Man in Russian Letters* (Washington, D.C.: University Press of America, 1980). See also Harry Slochower, "Suicides in Literature: Their Ego Function," *American Imago*, 32 (1975), 389–416. One of the most pithy and illuminating treatments of Romanticism is Rudolph Binion's "Notes on Romanticism," *The Journal of Psychohistory*, 11, 1 (Summer 1983), 43–64.

13. The Romantics began very early to recognize that if Arcady was irrecoverable, Elysium must be posited at least as a goal. There is everywhere in Romantic literature a manifest or latent conflict between the ache of hopeless backward-glancing and the tentative joys of forward-looking, between pastness and futurity, between the cyclic and the linear. When Yeats left as the opening line to his *Collected Poetry* "The woods of Arcady are dead," he realized the burden that the rest of his work took on in accommodating to that fact. As for the various forms of madness in nineteenth-century literature, no *definitive* study yet exists.

14. *Complete Essays of Schopenhauer*, trans. T. Bailey Saunders (New York: Willey Book Company, 1942), "On the Wisdom of Life: Aphorisms," 73.

15. Hayden White, *Metahistory: The Historical Imagination in Nineteenth-Century Europe* (Baltimore and London: The Johns Hopkins University Press, 1973), 237–42.

16. Arthur Schopenhauer, *The Will to Live: Selected Writings of Arthur Schopenhauer*, ed. Richard Taylor (New York: Frederick Ungar, 1967), 199–200.

17. *Complete Essays of Schopenhauer*, "On the Sufferings of the World," 2–4; "The Vanity of Existence," 19; "The Ages of Life," 114.

18. Friedrich Nietzsche, *On the Advantage and Disadvantage of History for Life*, trans. Peter Preuss (Indianapolis and Cambridge: Hackett, 1980), 28, 32, 44.

19. White, 347.

20. Ibid., 116.

21. Max Scheler, *Ressentiment* (published in German as *Über Ressentiment und Moralisches Werturteil*), ed. Lewis A. Coser (New York: Schocken Books, 1961), 45–46.

22. *The Letters of Gustave Flaubert, 1830–1857*, selected, edited, and translated by Francis Steegmuller (Cambridge, Mass.: Harvard University Press, 1979), 213.

23. Matthew Arnold in particular was fond of both the German *Zeitgeist* and the English Time-spirit, and indeed these terms formed one of the cornerstones of his commentaries on art, culture, and history. See Joseph Carrol, *The Cultural Theory of Matthew Arnold* (Berkeley: University of California Press, 1982).

24. Poggioli, *The Oaten Flute*, 145.

25. Abbie Findlay Potts, *The Elegiac Mode: Poetic Form in Wordsworth and Other Elegists* (Ithaca: Cornell University Press, 1967), 235.

26. Georges Poulet, *Studies in Human Time*, trans. Elliott Coleman (Baltimore: The Johns Hopkins University Press, 1956), 26–28. See my "Absence and Presence in Yeats's Poetry," *Yeats Annual*, I (London: Macmillan, 1982), 48–67. On time in general and specifically on past, present, and future, see Stephen Kern, *The Culture of Time and Space, 1880–1918* (Cambridge, Mass.: Harvard University Press, 1983), chapters 1–4. For some original insights on history and time, see Rudolph Binion, *After Christianity: Christian Survivals in Post-Christian Culture* (Durango, Colo.: Logbridge-Rhodes, 1986). I wish to thank my colleague for sharing some of his thoughts with me.

Introduction: Part I

1. *The Standard Edition of The Complete Psychological Works of Sigmund Freud*, 69–102. Freud's essay is seminal, but also, most of the time, quite technical. Some of its postulates have been under revisionist scrutiny from the beginning. It should be remembered, however, that Freud called the essay "An Introduction."

2. Heinz Kohut, "Thoughts on Narcissism and Narcissistic Rage," in *The Psychoanalytical Study of the Child*, vol. 27 (New York: Quadrangle Books, 1972), 380–82. This essay, in expanded form, is published in Kohut's *The Search for the Self: Selected Writings of Heinz Kohut: 1950–1978*, vol. 2, ed. Paul H. Ornstein (New York: International Universities Press, 1978), 615–58. One of the prime examples of Kohutian "narcissistic rage" is Dostoevsky's Underground Man and his "narcissistic injury." Since I have written on this work elsewhere, I have chosen to omit it here. (See *The Unknown Distance*, chapter 4.)

3. *Narcissism and the Text*, 1.

4. Kohut, "Thoughts on Narcissism and Narcissistic Rage," 395–96.

5. Léon Wurmser, *The Mask of Shame* (Baltimore and London: The Johns Hopkins University Press, 1981), 18, 48.

6. Reuben Fine, *Narcissism: The Self, and Society* (New York: Columbia University Press, 1986), 17, 23.

7. Wurmser, 48.

8. See Herbert Marcuse, *Eros and Civilization: A Philosophical Inquiry into Freud* (New York: Random House, 1955), chapter 8: "The Image of Orpheus and Narcissus." Marcuse's analysis is superficial and somewhat naive. Paul Zweig's work, on a similar track, is more solid (see note 14).

9. Alexander Lowen, *Narcissism: Denial of the True Self* (London: Colliers

Macmillan, 1983), ix, x, 25, 93. Lowen's view of narcissism is especially harsh. Even a cursory reading in the literature on narcissism reveals a sharp division between those who still view it as a potential for self-actualization and those who view it as a neurosis or psychosis, destructive to self and to others.

10. Arnold Rothstein, *The Narcissistic Pursuit of Perfection,* second revised edition (New York: International Universities Press, 1984), 67.

11. Ibid., 90.

12. See Heinz Kohut, *"Death in Venice* by Thomas Mann: A Study About the Disintegration of Artistic Sublimation," in *The Search for the Self,* vol. 1, 107–30. Kohut's analysis is excessively inferential, tied as it is to strict psycho-analytical assumptions.

13. See J. Brooks Bouson, "The Repressed Grandiosity of Gregor Samsa: A Kohutian Reading of Kafka's *Metamorphosis,"* in *Narcissism and the Text,* 192–212. Given its self-imposed constraints, the essay is both eminently readable and instructive.

14. Paul Zweig, *The Heresy of Self-Love: A Study in Subversive Individualism* (New York and London: Basic Books, 1968), 250–51, 257, 268.

15. Christopher Lasch, *The Culture of Narcissism: American Life in an Age of Diminishing Expectations* (New York: W. W. Norton, 1979). In addition, several studies of a general nature are of interest. Louise Vinge, *The Narcissus Theme in Western Literature up to the Early 19th Century,* trans. Robert Dewsnap, Lisbeth Gromlund, Nigel Reeves, and Ingrid Soderberg-Reeves (Gleerups: Lund, 1967); Hans-Jürgen Fuchs, *Entfremdung und Narzissmus: Semantische Unter-suchungen zur Geschichte der 'Selbstbezogenheit' als Vorgeschichte von französischen 'amour-propre'* (Stuttgart: Metzler, 1977). Both volumes are disappointing: the first reads like a dissertation which needs pruning and focus. Although there are benefits to be derived from the history of the Narcissus theme, the encyclo-pedic approach makes the reading tedious; the second work never fulfills its promise, especially with respect to the word *Entfremdung.* However, there are some very interesting sections dealing with *amour de soi* and *amour-propre,* especially the importance of Rousseau and the shift toward a "positive" view of self-love.

16. For a summary of recent approaches to the self with commentary by Kohut, see *Advances in Self Psychology,* ed. Arnold Goldberg (New York: Inter-national Universities Press, 1980); another volume, heavily Kohutian, is Rich-ard D. Chessick, *Psychology of the Self and the Treatment of Narcissism* (Northvale, N.J., and London: Jason Aronson Inc., 1985).

17. Tobin Siebers, *The Mirror of Medusa* (Berkeley: University of California Press, 1983), 73.

18. Freud, "On Narcissism: An Introduction," 90.

Chapter 1

1. The Romantics avoided closure. Often, as in, say, the case of Coleridge, grandiose projects never completed defeated them; sometimes the incomple-

tion was a kind of replication of the ruin, a kind of synecdochic cast of mind which had the effect of making the part stand for a whole that was clearly out of reach. See a very extended discussion in Thomas McFarland, *Romanticism and the Forms of Ruin: Wordsworth, Coleridge, and the Modality of Fragmentation* (Princeton: Princeton University Press, 1981), and Marjorie Levinson, *The Romantic Fragment Poem: A Critique of Form* (Chapel Hill and London: The University of North Carolina Press, 1986). In England there was, of course, a very strong feeling of melancholia and elegiac plaint in the so-called grave-yard poets, but the mood we examine here was very different, though certainly not unrelated. Gray's famous lament that tombstones cover many a "mute inglorious Milton" may be a conventional device, but it prepares the way for the more personalized sense of the missed life. See also a much older but still useful study, Eleanor M. Sickels, *The Gloomy Egoist: Moods and Themes of Melancholy From Gray to Keats* (New York: Columbia University Press, 1932), especially chapter 3, "Sic Transit Gloria Mundi."

2. Poulet, *Studies in Human Time*, 26, 29, 32.

3. I have relied on the translation by Walter Arndt, *Norton Critical Edition of Faust* (New York: W. W. Norton, 1976). In one instance (in italics), I have made my own translation because the relevant point seemed better served.

4. The quotations are from "Hamlet and Don Quixote," trans. Moshe Spiegel, *Chicago Review*, 17 (1965), 92–104. For special emphasis, see Eva Kagan-Kans, *Hamlet and Don Quixote* (The Hague: Mouton, 1975).

5. On Goethe and Rousseau, see Ernest Cassirer, *Rousseau, Kant and Goethe*, trans. James Gutman, Oskar Kristeller, and John H. Mandall, Jr. (New York: Harper Torchbooks, 1963). The translation from Rousseau is from *Reveries of the Solitary Walker*, trans. Peter France (New York: Penguin Books, 1979), 88.

6. I have relied on the Nabokov translation, *Eugene Onegin*, 4 vols. Bollingen Series LXII, Pantheon Books (New York: Bollingen Foundation, 1964).

7. Although Byron was an obvious link to Pushkin, recent Pushkin criticism seems by and large to ignore *Childe Harold's Pilgrimage*. There are scant references to the poem in A. D. P. Briggs, *Alexander Pushkin: A Critical Study* (Totowa, N.J.: Barnes and Noble, 1983), or in John Bayley, *Pushkin: A Comparative Commentary* (Cambridge: Cambridge University Press, 1971). J. Douglas Clayton writes that "Pushkin considered Byron's heroes the personification of the poet himself," *Ice and Flame: Aleksander Pushkin's Eugene Onegin* (Toronto: University of Toronto Press, 1985), 201–2, notes to chapter 4. See also Sona Stephan Hoisington, *"Eugene Onegin:* An Inverted Byronic Poem," *Comparative Literature*, 27, 2 (Spring 1975), 136–52. But again the essay makes connections to Byron's "oriental tales" (e.g., *The Corsair* or *The Captive of the Caucasus*) rather than to *Childe Harold's Pilgrimage*. The general conclusion is that Byron was a "satirist" while Pushkin was a "parodist," and that in *Eugene Onegin* Pushkin was essentially "debunking the Byronic hero." I prefer to regard any such "debunking" as the function of a deliberate confrontation of

the hero *as reader* with what he reads—critically, as Onegin's annotations clearly indicate.

8. Albert Cook, "Pushkin: The Balance of Irony," in *Thresholds: Studies in Romantic Experience* (Madison: University of Wisconsin Press, 1985), 125–238. The quotation is from p. 138.

Chapter 2

1. Even by mid-Victorian standards, Heathcliff, who dies at thirty-nine, was still young.

2. Introduction, *A Hero of Our Time*, trans. Paul Foote (New York: Penguin Books, 1966), 10. I have, however, used the Nabokov translation: *A Hero of Our Times*, trans. Vladimir Nabokov (New York: Doubleday, Anchor, 1958). See Lermontov's poem "No, I am not Byron; I am Different" (1832), juvenilia perhaps, but consistent with later attitudes.

3. The view of Pechorin as a thoroughly unrepentant cad, "indifferent to people," "leaping into the void of immorality," "insatiable," is simplistic. See Jesse V. Clardy and Betty S. Clardy, *The Superfluous Man in Russian Letters* (Washington, D.C.: University Press of America, 1980), 9–11.

4. *Hegel on Tragedy*, ed. Anne and Henry Paolucci (Garden City: Doubleday, 1962), 309–11.

5. The best Marxist account of *Wuthering Heights* is by Arnold Kettle, *An Introduction to the English Novel*, 2 vols. (London: Hillary House, 1951), vol. 1, chapter 5.

6. There is an interesting suggestion by Ronald B. Hatch, "Heathcliff's 'Queer End' and Schopenhauer's Denial of the Will," that Heathcliff's death is an involuntary realization of the Schopenhauerian will, against which it is futile to struggle. This view, while suggestive, deprives Heathcliff of the strength of a personal and final decision. It is true that Heathcliff does not set out to starve himself, but his pattern of breakdown is hardly involuntary. For nearly two decades he has wanted to join the dead Cathy; now he can find no reasonable cause for further delay. (See *Canadian Review of Comparative Literature*, vol. 1, 47–64.)

7. In accordance with her thesis, Chances sees Bazarov as a loser, an outsider whose fate is meted out because he fails to conform: "The issue . . . is not only sons versus fathers, but rebellion versus submission" (*Conformity's Children*, 81). However, like Heathcliff, Bazarov himself questions the meaning and direction of his "rebellion."

8. I have used the *Norton Critical Edition of Fathers and Sons*, trans. Ralph Matlaw (New York: W. W. Norton, 1966). For an insightful essay on Turgenev and nature, see Kenneth N. Brostrom, "The Heritage of Romantic Depictions of Nature in Turgenev," *American Contributions to the Ninth International Congress of Slavists*, Kiev, September 1983, in *Literature, Poetics, History*, vol. 2, ed. Paul Debreczeny (Columbus: Slavica Publications), 1983, 81–95. In

the same volume, see also John Mersereau, Jr., "Don Quixote—Bazarov—Hamlet," 345–55.

9. This point is explored at length by David Lowe in his *Fathers and Sons* (Ann Arbor: Ardis, 1983), chapter 1: "Structural Patterns: Parallels and Contrasts."

10. See Dorothy Van Ghent, *The English Novel: Form and Fiction* (New York: Harper & Row, 1953), 153–70. Van Ghent focuses on the image (and metaphor) of the window.

11. I have used the *Riverside Edition of Wuthering Heights*, ed., V. S. Prichett (Boston: Houghton Mifflin, 1956).

12. Freud, "Mourning and Melancholia," 246, 251.

Chapter 3

1. Kenneth N. Brostrom writes that for Turgenev "a spiritualized vision of nature retained affective power," but there was also "the vitality of its antipode, Romantic *Weltschmerz*—ironic pessimism and despair which could find no relief in the momentary ecstacies of transcendence," "The Heritage of Romantic Depiction of Nature in Turgenev," *American Contributions to the Ninth International Congress of Slavists*, 81–82.

2. I have used *Five Short Novels*, trans. Franklin Reeve (New York: Bantam Books, 1961).

3. Of particular help have been the following: Logan Speirs, *Tolstoy and Chekhov* (Cambridge: Cambridge University Press, 1971), chapter 19; and Beverly Hahn, *Chekhov: A Study of the Major Stories and Plays* (Cambridge: Cambridge University Press, 1972), part IV.

4. I have used *The Oxford Chekhov*, trans. Ronald Hingley (London: Oxford University Press, 1970), 5. See Appendix II, p. 231, quoted from a letter to A. N. Plesheyev, 30 September 1889.

5. I have used *The Death of Ivan Ilyich and Other Stories*, trans. Aylmer Maude, ed. David Magarshack (New York: New American Library, 1960).

6. See Hahn, 64–66.

7. See Johannes Urzidil, *There Goes Kafka*, trans. Harold A. Basilius (Detroit: Wayne State University Press, 1968). Urzidil recalls how, in Kafka's mind, Karl Brand's *A Young Man's Legacy* (published posthumously) came to be associated with "The Death of Ivan Ilyich." According to Urzidil, Kafka must have known Tolstoy's story when he wrote *The Metamorphosis* (1912). Kafka's tale shows "the influence of Tolstoy's shocking depiction of the gradual, inevitable, and incomprehensible death of a human being. . . . And thus the reference to the life and death of Ivan Ilyich in combination with the life and death of Brand may well have been concatenated with the life and death of Gregor Samsa. . . ." (93–94). Also by the same author, "Memoirs, Meetings with Franz Kafka." This essay suggests what the later piece elaborates: "The hint that Tolstoy's 'Death of Ivan Ilyitch' closes the ring between the life and

death of Karl Brand and the life and death of Gregor Samsa in 'The Metamorphosis.' " In *The Menorah Journal,* 40 (Spring 1952), 115.

8. Philip Rahv, "The Death of Ivan Ilyich and Joseph K.," *Literature and the Sixth Sense* (Boston: Houghton Mifflin, 1969), 40, 45.

9. Stanley Corngold, *The Commentators' Despair: The Interpretation of Kafka's Metamorphosis* (Port Washington, N.Y.: Kennikat Press, 1973).

10. I have used *The Metamorphosis,* trans. Stanley Corngold (New York: Bantam Books, 1972).

11. Nearly all Mann criticism has been occupied with the motif of death in Mann's work. Two early studies, still valuable, are: Hans Kasdorff, *Der Todesgedanke im Werke Tomas Manns* (Leipzig: Hermann Eichblatt, 1932); Lydia Baer, *The Concept and Function of Death in the Works of Thomas Mann* (Philadelphia, 1932). Even though Baer's essay could not take account of post-1932 works, her statement on *Death in Venice* still stands up: "Of all Thomas Mann's characters Gustav Aschenbach is most ripe for death" (34).

12. See my discussion of *Buddenbrooks* in *The Unknown Distance: From Conscience to Consciousness, Goethe to Camus* (Cambridge, Mass.: Harvard University Press, 1972), chapter 5.

13. I have used the translation of Kenneth Burke (New York: The Modern Library, 1970).

14. See Thomas Mann, *A Sketch of My Life,* trans. H. T. Lowe-Porter (New York: Alfred A. Knopf, 1960): ". . . nothing is invented in *Death in Venice . . .* [everything was] all there . . ." (46).

15. See Richard Winston, *Thomas Mann: The Making of an Artist* (New York: Alfred A. Knopf, 1981), 268–69. The man identified himself as Count Moes.

Introduction: Part II

1. Robert Burton, *The Anatomy of Melancholy,* ed. Floyd Dell and Paul Jordan-Smith (New York: Farrar & Rinehart, 1927), 274. See also Lawrence Rabb, *The Elizabethan Malady: A Study of Melancholia in English Literature from 1580–1642* (East Lansing: Michigan State University Press, 1951), especially chapters 4 and 5. For an overview of melancholy beginning with the ancients, see Raymond Klibansky, Erwin Panofsky, and Fritz Saxl, *Saturn and Melancholy: Studies in the History of Natural Philosophy, Religion, and Art* (London: Thomas Nelson & Sons, 1964). The authors distinguish melancholics: "Thus, alongside the tragic melancholic like Hamlet, there stood from the beginning the comic 'fashionable melancholic' . . ." (235). See also Bridgett Gellert Lyons, *Voices of Melancholy in Renaissance England* (New York: Barnes & Noble, 1971), especially "Melancholy Types in Satire and Comedy," 23–44. Two recent studies of a general nature are relevant: Stanley W. Jackson, *Melancholia and Depression: From Hippocratic Times to Modern Times* (New Haven: Yale University Press, 1986), and Gregory Rochlin, *Griefs and Discontents: The Forces of Change* (Boston: Little, Brown, 1965). Jackson's book is an exhaustive history of melancholia and depression, as the title indicates, and it is written in a

style accessible to the nonmedical expert. Its narrative is strictly neutral and the volume serves as a splendid history of the subject. Rochlin's volume is broader and deals with a variety of problems suggested in its title. There are some very interesting remarks on both mourning and melancholia and narcissism, which, of course, play an important role in this study.

2. Jackson, *Melancholia and Depression*, 322ff.

3. Freud, "Mourning and Melancholia," 250. Further references are incorporated into the text in parentheses.

4. For a series of essays that touches on the subject, see *Memory and Desire, Aging—Literature—Psychoanalysis*, eds. Kathleen Woodward and Murray M. Schwartz (Bloomington: Indiana University Press, 1986).

5. Nietzsche, *On the Advantage and Disadvantage of History for Life*, 28. (See note 16 of Introduction.)

6. Rochlin, *Griefs and Discontents*, 128–29.

Chapter 4

1. See Karl S. Guthke, *Modern Tragicomedy: An Inquiry into the Nature of the Genre* (New York: Random House, 1966).

2. For the plays I have used *Chekhov: Four Plays*, trans. David Magarchack (New York: Hill and Wang, 1969). Among the numerous studies of the plays I found the following of help: David Magershack, *Chekhov the Dramatist* (London: Methuen, 1980); Robert Brustein's chapter on Chekhov in *The Theatre in Revolt: An Approach to the Modern Drama* (Boston: Little, Brown, 1962); the various comments on Chekhov throughout Bert O. State's *Irony and Drama: A Poetics* (Ithaca: Cornell University Press, 1971); Beverly Hahn, *Chekhov* (see chapter 3, note 3); and, most recently, Richard Peace, *Chekhov: A Study of the Four Major Plays* (New Haven: Yale University Press, 1983). In his discussion of *Uncle Vanya* Peace correctly points out the significance of Astrov's passionate concern with the waste to which Russia's forests are being exposed; he might have made a still-stronger case for how Chekhov parallels this waste of nature with the waste of human nature. See also *Chekhov's Great Plays: A Critical Anthology*, ed. Jean-Pierre Barricelli (New York and London: New York University Press, 1981).

3. For "The Diary of a Man of Fifty" I have used *Fourteen Stories by Henry James*, selected by David Garnett (London: Rupert Hart-Davis, 1948). For the remaining texts I have used *The New York Edition* (New York: Charles Scribner's Sons, 1908).

4. This story was first published in 1871 in *The Atlantic Monthly*. James twice revised it (1875 and 1884), but he "rewrote" it for inclusion in the New York Edition. See headnote to the original text in *The Tales of Henry James*, vol. 2, ed. Madbool Aziz (Oxford: The Clarendon Press, 1978), 42. The final version is verbally much more heavily slanted toward the "too late" motif.

5. *The Notebooks of Henry James*, ed. F. O. Mathiessen and Kenneth B. Murdock (New York: George Braziller, 1955), 183–84. See also John Bowlby,

Attachment and Loss, 3 vols., *Attachment* (1), *Separation* (2), *Loss* (3) (New York: Basic Books, 1969–80).

6. Walter Pater, *The Renaissance: Studies in Art and Poetry*, ed. Donald L. Hill (Berkeley: University of California Press, 1980), 189.

7. For an interesting discussion of Strether's speech, see "Freedom in *The Ambassadors*," in Charles Shug's *The Romantic Genesis of the Modern Novel* (Pittsburgh: University of Pittsburgh Press, 1979), 87–99.

8. See the editors' headnote to "Project of Novel by Henry James," *Notebooks*, 371.

9. Ibid., 227.

10. Ibid., 375.

11. Ibid., 227.

12. One wonders whether T. S. Eliot was thinking of James when, in "The Dry Salvages," he wrote:

> . . . the train starts, and the passengers are settled . . .
> Fare forward, travellers! not escaping from the past
> Into different lives, or into any future;
> You are not the same people who left that station
> Or who will arrive at any terminus,
> While the narrowing rails slide together
> Behind you; . . .

13. James, *Notebooks*, 375.

14. William R. MacNaughton, *Henry James: The Later Novels* (Boston: Twayne Publishers, 1987), 79. Two other recent books are: Alan W. Bellringer, *The Ambassadors* (London: George Allen & Unwin, 1984), and Courtney Johnson, Jr., *Henry James and the Evolution of Consciousness: A Study of "The Ambassadors,"* especially pp. 95–98 on the "revolution" of Strether's "consciousness." Johnson's argument elevates Strether's consciousness to a state of "transcendence" and "transformation," and he rejects the term "renunciation" to describe Strether's final judgments (108ff). In this argument Strether is transformed into something almost Buddhistic ("transcendental consciousness," 109), a kind of "witnessing" which is a quasi-religious experience (115). In addition, Strether has found "free will," and his existential choices of abstention are the happy exercise of that newly acquired power. Such an argument, subtly put, is nevertheless (I believe) far too sanguine about Strether's losses—whether prior to his "transformation" or beyond it.

15. Joyce A. Rowe, *Equivocal Endings in Classic American Novels: The Scarlet Letter; Adventures of Huckleberry Finn; The Ambassadors; The Great Gatsby* (Cambridge: Cambridge University Press, 1988), 75–99.

16. Chekhov and James are in some respects remarkably alike, if not in scope then in their conceptions of the tragicomic potentials of human life. Both were keen observers of human absurdity, vanity, egotism. And yet both had a generous understanding of authentic courage and authentic despair. H. Peter Stowell has linked these two writers with respect to style: *Literary Impressionism: James and Chekhov* (Athens: University of Georgia Press, 1980).

Chapter 5

1. Jerome Hamilton Buckley, *The Triumph of Time: A Study of the Victorian Concepts of Time, History, Progress, and Decadence* (Cambridge, Mass.: The Belknap Press, 1966).

2. The idea of a generational curse, biologically and culturally determined, was of course a major motif in nineteenth-century fiction, especially in the numerous *Familienromane* from Zola to Mann and Proust.

3. Herbert Lindenberger, "The Idyllic Moment: On Pastoral and Romanticism," *College English*, 34, 3 (December 1972), 347, 351.

4. See James E. Kerans, "Kindermord and Will in 'Little Eyolf,' " *in Modern Drama: Essays in Criticism*, ed. Travis Bogard and William I. Oliver (New York: Oxford University Press, 1965), 192–218.

5. All quotations from *Peer Gynt* are from the edition translated by Peter Watts (New York: Penguin Books, 1966).

6. All quotations from Ibsen's prose plays are from *Ibsen: The Complete Major Prose Plays*, trans. Rolf Fjelde (New York: Farrar, Straus, Giroux, 1965). For an interesting analysis of *The Master Builder*, see Bettina Knapp, *Archetype, Architecture, and the Writer* (Bloomington: Indiana University Press, 1986), 1–12.

7. Rothstein, *The Narcissistic Pursuit of Perfection*, 301.

8. See *The Problem of "The Judgment": Eleven Approaches to Kafka's Story*, ed. Angel Flores (New York: Gordian Press, 1977).

9. The quotations from "The Judgment" are from the new translation by Malcolm Palsey in *The Problem of "The Judgment."*

10. One recalls Shakespeare's *Henry IV, Part II*, the scene when Hal, believing his father dead, prematurely takes the crown and muses about its transference of power. When the still-very-much-alive king-father confronts his son, Hal protests, "I never thought to hear you speak again. . . ." To which the king replies,

> Thy wish was father, Henry, to that thought.
> I stay too long by thee, I weary thee.
> Dost thou so hunger for mine empty chair
> That thou wilt needs invest thee with mine honours
> Before the hour is ripe? . . .
>
> .   .   .   .
> . . . thou wilt have me die . . .
> Thou hidest a thousand daggers with thy thoughts,
> Which thou hast whetted on thy stony heart,
> To stab at half an hour of my life.

11. Franz Kafka, *Brief an dem Vater/Letter to His Father*, trans. Ernest Kaiser and Eithne Wilkins (New York: Schocken Books, 1953), 99.

12. For a Lacanian account of Kafka's confrontation with writing, see Charles Bernheimer, *Flaubert and Kafka: Studies in Psychopoetic Structure* (New Haven and London: Yale University Press, 1982).

13. Irving Howe, *William Faulkner: A Critical Study,* 2d edition (New York: Random House, 1962), 46.

14. It has been suggested that Georg Bendemann sees his death in a similar way, though the text is less explicit in Kafka's story: "On the stairs, down which he sped . . . he collided with the charwoman . . . 'Jesus!' she cried."

15. Jean-Paul Sartre, "On *The Sound and the Fury:* Time in the Work of Faulkner," in *Aspects of Time,* ed. C. A. Patrides (Manchester and Toronto: University of Toronto Press, 1976), 206, 208.

16. See Lukács's critique of modernism in *Realism in Our Time.*

17. John Pikoulis, *The Art of William Faulkner* (Totowa, N.J.: Barnes and Noble, 1982), 29.

18. Cleanth Brooks, *William Faulkner: The Yoknapatawpha County* (New Haven and London: Yale University Press, 1963), 329, 336.

19. Compare with the ending of "The Judgment": "Still holding on, with a weakening grip, he . . . called out softly: 'Dear parents, I did always love you', and let himself drop."

Chapter 6

1. Erwin Panofsky, "*Et in Arcadia Ego:* Poussin and the Elegiac Tradition," in *Meaning in the Visual Arts* (Garden City, N.Y.: Doubleday, Anchor, 1955), 295–320.

2. All quotations from "The Dead" are from James Joyce, *Dubliners* (New York: Viking Press, 1967).

3. The best single work on *The Magic Mountain* remains Herman J. Weigand's *Thomas Mann's Novel "Der Zauberberg"* (Chapel Hill: University of North Carolina Press, 1964). In addition, the following have been helpful: Frank Donald Hirschbach, *The Arrow and the Lyre: A Study of the Role of Love in the Works of Thomas Mann* (The Hague: Martinus Nijhoff, 1955), 53–84; T. J. Reed, *Thomas Mann: The Uses of Tradition* (Oxford: The Clarendon Press, 1974); Reinhard Kuhn, *The Demon of Noontide,* 346–55; Erich Heller, *The Ironic German: A Study of Thomas Mann* (London: Secker and Warburg, 1958), 169–214; Eckhard Heftrich, *Zaubermusik* (Frankfurt-am-Main: Vittorio Klostermann, 1975); Susan Smith Wolfe, "Thomas Mann's *Der Zauberberg:* The 'Snow Spiral,' " *Seminar,* 3 (November 1977), 270–77. On Mann and time, see Fritz Kaufmann, "Thomas Mann in the Degradation and Rehabilitation of Time," in *Aspects of Time,* 172–78.

Critics have noted the prevalence of the number 7 in the novel (seven years' stay by the hero, seven tables in the dining room, Castorp's room number 34—3 plus 4—and so forth). My colleague Richard Lansing suggests, in a recent essay, the importance of numerology in the Middle Ages and the Renaissance. Numbers, he contends, "could symbolize the concept of falling short," and "the number eight came to symbolize eternity, because 8 goes one beyond 7, the traditional number of time and existence" (Richard Lansing, "Ariosto's *Orlando Furioso* and the Homeric Model," *Comparative Literature*

Studies, 24, 4 [1987], 315.) This makes sense in an ironic way, for Mann teases us into believing Castorp's mountain experience to be somehow "transcending," yet—whether or not he was conscious of all the implications of it—clearly he means 7 to remind us, among other things, that Castorp's sojourn is indeed one that "falls short" and remains, despite appearances, below "eternity" or "human immortality" but is very much steeped in "time" and in "existence."

    4. All quotations from *The Magic Mountain* are taken from H. T. Lowe-Porter's translation (New York: Alfred A. Knopf, 1964).

    5. Thomas Mann, "Schopenhauer," in *Essays by Thomas Mann,* trans. H. T. Lowe-Porter (New York: Vintage Books, 1957), 272–83.

    6. James Naremore, *The World Without a Self: Virginia Woolf and the Novel* (New Haven: Yale University Press), 110.

    7. All quotations from *Mrs. Dalloway* are from the Harvest Book edition (New York: Harcourt, Brace & World, 1953). The critical literature on Virginia Woolf, especially of late, has become voluminous. In addition to Naremore's study (see note 6), the following have been helpful: James Hawthorn, *Virginia Woolf's Mrs. Dalloway: A Study in Alienation* (Sussex University Press, 1975); Michael Rosenthal, *Virginia Woolf* (New York: Columbia University Press, 1979); Beverly Ann Schlack, *Continuing Presences: Virginia Woolf's Use of Literary Allusion* (University Park and London: The Pennsylvania State University Press, 1979); Roger Moss, "*Jacob's Room* and the Eighteenth Century: From Elegy to Essay," *Critical Quarterly,* 23, 3 (Autumn 1981), 39–54; Howard Harper, *Between Language and Silence: The Novels of Virginia Woolf* (Baton Rouge: Louisiana State University Press, 1982); Lucio P. Ruotolo, *The Interrupted Moment: A View of Virginia Woolf's Novels* (Stanford: Stanford University Press, 1986), chapter 5, 95–117; and a tease of an essay, Edward Mendelson, "The Death of Mrs. Dalloway: Two Readings," in *Textual Analysis: Some Readers Reading,* ed. Mary Ann Caws (New York: Modern Language Association, 1986), 272–80. Mark Spilka's *Virginia Woolf's Quarrel with Grieving* (Lincoln: University of Nebraska Press, 1980) is excellent not only on *Mrs. Dalloway* (47–74) but on Woolf and the psychogenic origins of all her work. In his chapter "Mrs. Dalloway's Absent Grief" Spilka essentially delineates an elegiac view of the novel, but it differs from my own in that its focus is especially on biographical correspondences to the work, an approach that yields insightful readings.

    8. Virginia Woolf, *Collected Essays,* vol. 1 (London: The Hogarth Press, 1966), 238–53.

Introduction: Part III

    1. Christopher Lasch, *The Minimal Self, Psychic Survival in Troubled Times* (New York and London: W. W. Norton, 1984), 62. (Lasch concedes that aspects of the "minimal self" are synonymous with his earlier view of narcissism.)

    2. Lukács, *Realism in Our Time,* trans. John and Necke Mander (London: Merling Press, 1963), 17–46.

3. Lucien Goldmann, *Lukács and Heidegger: Towards a New Philosophy,* trans. William G. Bollbower (London: Routledge & Kegan Paul, 1977). Both Lukács and Heidegger, Goldmann observes, come out of the ". . . Hegelian tradition, the rejection of the transcendental subject, the conception of man as inseparable from the world which he is part of, the definition of his place in the universe as historicity" (7).

4. George Steiner, *Martin Heidegger* (New York: The Viking Press, 1978), 108.

5. *Collected Letters of Samuel Taylor Coleridge,* ed. Earl Leslie Griggs, vol. 5 (Oxford: The Clarendon Press, 1971), 266. (The quotation is from a letter to Charles Aders [1823] which is quoted from by Steiner in *Martin Heidegger* [see note 4 above]).

6. Frank Kermode, *The Sense of an Ending: Studies in the Theory of Fiction* (London: Oxford University Press, 1967), 6, 102. See also Alic A. Kuzniar, *Delayed Endings: Nonclosure in Novalis and Hölderlin* (Athens and London: University of Georgia Press, 1987).

7. Walter Pater, *The Renaissance: Studies in Art and Poetry,* ed. Donald L. Hill (Berkeley: University of California Press, 1980), 182, 187–88, 190.

8. Jürgen Habermas, "Modernity versus Post-Modernity," *new german critique,* 22 (Winter 1981), 5.

Chapter 7

1. Georg Lukács, *Realism in Our Time,* 17–46, "The Ideology of Modernism." All quotations from Lukács in this chapter are from this section of the book.

2. Hemingway has been accused of "nihilism," or worse, but his grimness notwithstanding, he is still far from, say, a Beckett. His characters are often beaten; they despair of being dealt a fair hand in life. Yet they are essentially distraught because they fall short of great expectations, not because they believe that expectations in themselves are always useless. See Hugh Kenner, *Flaubert, Joyce and Beckett: The Stoic Comedians* (Boston: Beacon Press, 1962).

3. Lillian Ross, "How Do You Like It Now Gentleman?" in *Hemingway: A Collection of Critical Essays,* ed. Robert P. Weeks (Englewood Cliffs, N.J., 1962), 23; George Plimpton, "Ernest Hemingway," in *Hemingway and His Critics,* ed. Carlos Baker (New York: Charles Scribner's Sons, 1935), 27, 71; Carlos Baker, *Ernest Hemingway: A Life Story* (New York: Charles Scribner's Sons, 1969), 465; Ernest Hemingway, "Monologue to the Maestro," *Esquire* (October 1935), 174A; Richard Lyman, "Hemingway's Library Cards at Shakespeare and Company," *Fitzgerald-Hemingway Annual* (1975), 195.

4. For some rather ingenious suggestions and comments on Frederic Henry's name, see Michael S. Reynolds, *Hemingway's First War: The Making of "A Farewell to Arms"* (Princeton: Princeton University Press, 1976), 158–59. Reynolds links Hemingway to Stendhal, suggesting that Stendhal's Christian *nom de plume* was Frédéric (he was also, of course, *Henri* Beyle), and he offers

some other possibilities, none from Flaubert. Reynolds makes extensive use of the materials in the Kennedy Library. (See also Robert O. Stephens, "Hemingway and Stendhal: The Matrix of *A Farewell to Arms*," *PMLA*, 88 [March 1983], 271–80.)

5. Harry Levin, *The Gates of Horn: A Study of Five French Novelists* (New York: Oxford University Press, 1963), 63.

6. *The Letters of Gustave Flaubert, 1830–1857*, selected, edited, and translated by Francis Steegmuller (Cambridge, Mass.: Harvard University Press, 1980), 154. The original reads: ". . . ce que je voudrais faire, c'est un livre sur rien . . . sans attache extérieure, qui se tiendrait de lui-même par la force interne de son style . . . [un livre] où le sujet serait presque invisible. . . ." See Flaubert, *Oeuvres Complètes, Correspondence*, II (Paris: Louis Conard, 1910), 345.

7. William Adair, "Time and Structure in *A Farewell to Arms*," *South Dakota Review*, 13 (1975), 169–71.

8. See Victor Brombert, *The Novels of Flaubert: A Study of Themes and Techniques* (Princeton: Princeton University Press, 1966), 125–85, for a redemptive reading, especially of the penultimate chapter. Without saying so, R. J. Sherrington takes the opposite view of this scene, *Three Novels of Flaubert: A Study of Techniques* (Oxford: The Clarendon Press, 1970).

9. Sherrington, 329 and note.

10. Scott Donaldson embodies most of the negative interpretations of Frederic Henry in a section titled "Frederic Henry, Selfish Lover," in *By Force of Will: The Life and Art of Ernest Hemingway* (New York: The Viking Press, 1977), 151–62.

11. Since my original work on the Hemingway manuscripts, many have now researched them. Notable are two essays by Bernard Oldsey. The first, "The Sense of Ending in *A Farewell to Arms*," *Modern Fiction Studies* 23 (Winter 1977–78), 491–510, makes extensive use of the manuscript versions of the endings in the Kennedy Library, classifying them: "The Religious Ending," "The Live-Baby Ending," etc. Oldsey's reading of *the* ending is more flexibly optimistic than mine, but the essay is a revealing and tactful analysis of how an author struggled to finish his story. The second essay, "The Genesis of *A Farewell to Arms*," *Studies in American Fiction*, 5, 2 (Autumn 1977), 175–85, alludes to the title sheet and the two early chapters written in the third person.

12. Pound, "Paris Letters," *The Dial*, 72 (April 1922), 404, and *The Dial*, 73 (September 1922), 333, 336–37. For a different kind of impasse in *A Farewell to Arms*, see Robert Murray Davis, " 'If You Did Not Go Forward': Process and Stasis in *A Farewell to Arms*," *Studies in the Novel*, 2 (Fall 1970), 305–11. Pound and Hemingway quickly became close friends in 1922, soon after Hemingway's arrival in Paris. In 1921, to mark the centenary of Flaubert's birth, an *Edition du Centenaire* was published which Pound praised, both for its availability and inexpensiveness. In *A Moveable Feast* (New York: Charles Scribner's Sons, 1964) Hemingway reports that Pound advised him: "Keep to the French. . . . You've plenty to learn there." See Harold M. Hurwitz, "Heming-

way's Tutor, Ezra Pound," in Ernest Hemingway, *Five Decades of Criticism* (East Lansing: Michigan State University Press, 1974), 8–21. For more on Flaubert's impact upon Anglo-American literature, see Richard Sieburth, *Instigations: Pound and Remy de Gourmont* (Cambridge, Mass.: Harvard University Press, 1978).

13. For a fresh view, see Lynne Layton, "Narcissism and History: Flaubert's *Sentimental Education*," in *Narcissism and the Text*, 170–89. Layton makes several points of importance. She diagnoses Frédéric's problem as symptomatic of the "romanticism/cynicism antinomy" which is at "the heart" of the novel. This antinomy is characteristic of the "narcissistic personality"; and, following Kohut, she sees Frédéric's "narcissistic injury" as leading him not only to disillusionment but to "rage" (170–71, 178). In addition, she suggests (very provocatively) that the Revolution of 1848 is central to the novel, and that "narcissism pervades [Frédéric's] politics as well as love . . ." (182). The whole impasse of the novel shows an overall sense of "powerlessness" (185), and at the end Frédéric and Deslauriers are "both defenseless against feelings of worthlessness" (188).

14. Elinor Lenz, "The Generation Gap: From Persephone to Portnoy," *The New York Times Book Review* (August 30, 1987), 1, 36–37.

Chapter 8

1. Poulet, *Studies in Human Time*, 303–5.

2. Samuel Beckett, *Proust* (New York: Grove Press, 1957), 49–50, 50–51, 70, 14.

3. Beckett's fiction is discussed in passing in many books. For a selective list of works giving special treatment of the novels dealt with here, see John Fletcher, *The Novels of Samuel Beckett* (London: Chatto and Windus, 1964). Also: Dieter Wellershof, "Failure of and Attempt at De-Mytholigization: Samuel Beckett's Novels," and A. J. Leventhal, "The Beckett Hero," both in *Samuel Beckett: A Collection of Critical Views,* ed. Martin Esslin (Englewood Cliffs, N.J.: Prentice Hall, 1965); A. Alvarez, *Samuel Beckett* (New York: The Viking Press, 1973), 25–74; H. Porter Abbott, "The Harpooned Notebook: *Malone Dies* and the Convention of Intercalated Narrative," in Samuel Beckett, *Humanistic Perspectives,* ed. Morris Beja, S. E. Gontarski, and Pierre Astier (Columbus: Ohio State University Press, 1983), 71–90. In addition, the following two studies discuss the trilogy from philosophical perspectives: David H. Hesla, *The Shape of Chaos: An Interpretation of the Art of Samuel Beckett* (Minneapolis: University of Minnesota Press, 1971), chapter 4, "Which I is I?" 86–128; and Lance St. John Butler, *Samuel Beckett and the Meaning of Being: A Study in Ontological Parable* (New York: St. Martin's Press, 1984). The latter offers an analysis of Beckett that parallels him to Hegel's *Phenomenology of Mind*, Heidegger's *Being and Time*, and Sartre's *Being and Nothingness*. Its argument is, more often than not, both insightful and ingenious. It is also too often forced. In addition: G. C. Barnard, *Samuel Beckett: A New Approach, A Study of the Novels and Plays* (New York: Dodd,

Mead, 1970); Eugene Webb, *Samuel Beckett: A Study of His Novels* (Seattle: University of Washington Press, 1972); Eric P. Levy, *Beckett and the Voice of Species: A Study of the Prose Fiction* (Totowa, N.J.: Barnes and Noble, 1980), especially 54–71. See also *Critical Essays on Samuel Beckett*, ed. Patrick A. McCarthy (Boston: G. K. Hall, 1986), especially the essays on the trilogy, 55–91; Susan D. Brienza, *Samuel Beckett's New Worlds: Style in Metafiction* (Norman and London: University of Oklahoma Press, 1987); Gabriele Schwab, "The Intermediate Area Between Life and Death: On Samuel Beckett's *The Unnamable,*" in *Memory and Desire: Aging—Literature—Psychoanalysis,* ed. Kathleen Woodward and Murray M. Schwartz (Bloomington: Indiana State University Press, 1986), 205–17.

4. It may be argued that in several of Beckett's works, including the trilogy, the characters' memories are not actual reproductions of a real past but, rather, a series of disconnected flashback images (cinematographic in technique) that penetrate the surface of the present. Many of these "memories" are lyrical, even elegiac, though their content is vague: *Nell* (elegiac): "Ah yesterday!" (*Endgame*).

5. "Waiting seems an appropriate metaphor for [Heidegger's] Dasein's comportment towards Being. Waiting is a condition which does not necessarily affect one's daily projects but which underlies all of them." *Samuel Beckett and the Meaning of Being,* 176. See also Ruby Cohn, "Waiting is All," *Modern Drama,* 3 (September 1960), 162–67, and Romona Cormier and J. L. Pallister, *Waiting for Death: The Philosophical Significance of Beckett's "En Attendant Godot"* (University: University of Alabama Press, 1979).

6. For citations from the trilogy I have used the Grove Press one-volume edition: *Molloy, Malone Dies, The Unnamable: Three Novels by Samuel Beckett* (New York: Grove Press, 1955). The quotation is from page 7. Page numbers for subsequent citations are incorporated in the text.

7. Some have argued that Moran and Molloy are two sides of the same person, that Moran's pursuit is of himself or his self. See Hesla, *The Shape of Chaos,* 111ff. Hesla sees the trilogy as circular, the last lines of *The Unnamable* (the third book) leading back to the first line of the first, *Molloy.*

8. Michael E. Zimmerman, *The Development of Heidegger's Concept of Authenticity* (Athens: Ohio University Press, 1981), 43, 64.

9. See Leslie Kane, *The Language of Silence: On the Unspoken and the Unspeakable in Modern Drama* (Rutherford, N.J.: Fairleigh Dickinson Press), 105–31; this study deals with Beckett's plays. Also Allen Thiher's provocative "Wittgenstein, Heidegger, the Unnamable, and Some Thoughts on the Status of Voice in Fiction," in *Beckett: Humanistic Perspectives,* 80–90; Ihab Hassan, *The Literature of Silence: Henry Miller and Samuel Beckett* (New York: Alfred A. Knopf, 1967); and Hélène L. Baldwin, *Samuel Beckett's Real Silence* (University Park: The Pennsylvania State University Press, 1981), especially chapters 1, 3–5.

10. Probably more has been written on *Godot,* in English and French, than on any other Beckett work. Ruby Cohn's *Casebook on "Waiting for Godot"* (New York: Grove Press, 1965) remains—despite its date—a useful compilation. For an interesting perspective, see Sidney Homan, *Beckett's Theaters: Interpreta-*

tions for Performance (Lewisburg: Bucknell University Press, 1984), 31–57. I have used the Grove Press edition. See also Judith A. Roof, "A Blink in the Mirror: From Oedipus to Narcissus and Back in the Drama of Samuel Beckett," in *Myth and Ritual in the Plays of Samuel Beckett,* ed. Katherine H. Burkman (London and Toronto: Associated University Presses, 1987), 151–63.

11. I have used the Grove Press edition.

12. I have used the Grove Press edition.

Conclusion

1. Rousseau, *Reveries of the Solitary Walker,* 112.

2. John George Zimmerman [*sic*], *Solitude or the Effect of Occasional Retirement,* trans. from the German (London, Glasgow, and Dublin: Thomas Tegg, R. Griffin, and Co., and B. Cummings, 1827), 383, 394.

3. According to the OED, alienation as "Mental alienation: Withdrawal, loss, or derangement of mental faculties, insanity" was first used in *The Monk of Eversham* in 1869, though under the heading of "estrangement, or state of estrangement in feelings or affection," it lists, not surprisingly, Burton's *Anatomy of Melancholy. The Complete Oxford English Dictionary,* vol. 1 (Oxford: Oxford University Press, 1971), 55.

4. See Jay MacPherson, *The Spirit of Solitude: Conventions and Continuities in Late Romance* (New Haven: Yale University Press, 1982). This is an often-interesting but strangely fragmented book. Of special interest to my study are "Elegy and the Elegiac," 37–58, and "Narcissus: Echo: Siren," 75–96. MacPherson makes reference to Zimmermann's *Solitude* (see note 2 above), 56–58.

5. Again the commentary on the self—from sociopsychological to literary perspectives, is voluminous. For a rather rudimentary, if useful, volume, see Charles I. Glicksberg, *The Self in Modern Literature* (University Park: The Pennsylvania University Press, 1963), especially "The Self without God," 3–11. In the last decade or so, discussion of self has often leaned on Kohut or some form of existential self. Post-existentialists have tended to treat the self, by way of deconstructing it, as an ephemeral and elusive entity with little, if any, objective existence. In addition, see Hans Jürgen-Schultz, ed., *Einsamkeit* (Stuttgart and Berlin: Krenz, 1980). The essays range from the loneliness of the death of a husband or wife to its use as a literary theme. It is dedicated to Erich Fromm. Also of interest is *Man Alone: Alienation in Modern Society,* eds. Eric and Mary Josephson (New York: Dell, 1952). Most of the essays reflect an anticipation of the turbulent Sixties and early Seventies yet to come. The subject of solitude is vast and its literature ranges widely from the perspectives of social psychology to literary theme.

6. Kenneth A. Brufree, *Elegiac Romance: Cultural Change and Loss of the Hero in Modern Fiction* (Ithaca: Cornell University Press, 1983), 15.

7. A recent general study of pastoral is Andrew F. Ettin, *Literature and the Pastoral* (New Haven and London: Yale University Press, 1984). For an excel-

lent bibliography, see David Raphael Thuente, "Pastoral Narratives: A Review of Criticism"; this annotated review is supplemented by an extensive bibliography, in *Genre*, 14, 2 (1981), 247–67.

8. Michael Squires, *The Pastoral Novel: Studies in George Eliot, Thomas Hardy, and D. H. Lawrence* (Charlottesville: University of Virginia Press, 1974), 13.

9. Ibid., 213.

10. Howard Pearce, "Henry James's Pastoral Fallacy," *PMLA*, 90 (1975), 845–46.

11. Peter Marinelli, *Pastoral* (London: Methuen, 1971), 9–10.

12. Ellen Zetzel Lambert, *Placing Sorrow: A Study of the Pastoral Elegy Convention from Theocritus to Milton* (Chapel Hill: University of North Carolina Press, 1976), 95, 97–98. For a recent study on Romantic pastoral, making good use of Schiller, see Lore Metzger, *One Foot in Eden: Modes of Pastoral in Romantic Poetry* (Chapel Hill and London: University of North Carolina Press, 1986). Recently published is Anthony Storr, *Solitude: A Return to the Self* (New York: The Free Press, 1988).

13. Ibid., xxv.

14. For an excellent recent account of the provenance of modern irony, see Lilian R. Furst, *Fiction of Romantic Irony* (Cambridge, Mass.: Harvard University Press, 1984).

15. Jean-Pierre Mileur, *Literary Revisionism and the Burden of Modernity* (Berkeley: University of California Press, 1985), 192–268. The quotations are from pp. 195 and 1.

16. Erich Fromm, *The Fear of Freedom* (Routledge & Kegan Paul, 1942), 156.

17. Ibid., 154.

18. Ibid., 156.

19. Ibid., 29.

20. Of course, "great expectations" in Dickens's milieu were viewed primarily in monetary terms. But Dickens's title is not unself-consciously multilayered.

21. *Pathologies of the Modern Self: Postmodern Studies on Narcissism, Schizophrenia, and Depression,* ed. David Michael Levin (New York and London: New York University Press, 1987). See Jeffrey Satinover, "Science and the Fragile Self: The Rise of Narcissism, the Decline of God," 84–113. The specific quotation is from p. 110; Eugene T. Gendlin, "A Philosophical Critique of the Concept of Narcissism: The Significance of the Awareness Movement," 251–304. The specific quotation is from p. 304; David Michael Levin, "Psychopathology in the Epoch of Nihilism," 21–83. The specific quotations are from pp. 23–25. See also in the same volume, Jennifer Radden, "Melancholy and Melancholia," 231–50. See also Stanley Corngold, *The Fate of the Self: German Writers and French Theory* (New York: Columbia University Press, 1986), especially the Introduction, chapters 3, 4, and 7, and the Postscript.

Index